The Tenacity of Unreasonable Beliefs

SOLOMON
SCHIMMEL

The Tenacity of Unreasonable Beliefs

Fundamentalism and the Fear of Truth

OXFORD
UNIVERSITY PRESS

2008

OXFORD
UNIVERSITY PRESS

Oxford University Press, Inc., publishes works that further
Oxford University's objective of excellence
in research, scholarship, and education.

Oxford   New York
Auckland   Cape Town   Dar es Salaam   Hong Kong   Karachi
Kuala Lumpur   Madrid   Melbourne   Mexico City   Nairobi
New Delhi   Shanghai   Taipei   Toronto

With offices in

Argentina   Austria   Brazil   Chile   Czech Republic   France Greece
Guatemala   Hungary   Italy   Japan   Poland   Portugal   Singapore
South Korea   Switzerland   Thailand   Turkey   Ukraine   Vietnam

Copyright © 2008 by Oxford University Press, Inc.

Published by Oxford University Press, Inc.
198 Madison Avenue, New York, New York 10016

www.oup.com

Oxford is a registered trademark of Oxford University Press.

Library of Congress Cataloging-in-Publication Data
Schimmel, Solomon.
The tenacity of unreasonable beliefs : fundamentalism and the fear of truth / Solomon Schimmel.
   p. cm.
Includes bibliographical references and index.
ISBN 978-0-19-518826-4
1. Religious fundamentalism—Psychology. 2. Psychology, Religious. 3. Faith and reason. I. Title.
BL238.S32 2008
200.9'04—dc22   2007051125

Among the publishers and/or copyright holders who have generously given permission to use
extensive quotations from copyrighted works are the following:
ArtScroll / Mesorah Publications, Ltd., for material from Nosson Scherman, *Chumash: The Stone Edition*, 1993.
Oxford University Press for material from Bernard Susser and Charles Liebman, *Choosing Survival:
Strategies for a Jewish Future*, 1999; and E. E. Evans-Pritchard, *Witchcraft, Oracles and Magic
Among the Azande*, 1976.
Wm. B. Eerdmans Publishing Company for material from George M. Marsden,
Understanding Fundamentalism and Evangelicalism, 1991.
Zondervan Publishing Company for material from Wayne A. Grudem, *Bible Doctrine:
The Essential Teachings of the Christian Faith*, 1999.

9 8 7 6 5 4 3 2 1

Printed in the United States of America
on acid-free paper

ACKNOWLEDGMENTS

I N THE COURSE OF writing *The Tenacity of Unreasonable Beliefs* I have benefited from the advice, support, and in many instances the trenchant criticism of numerous individuals. Their input constantly accompanied me, as what began as a paper delivered at the American Academy of Religion in 1996 gradually evolved into this full-fledged book. Given that scores of people have been involved in small or large part in discussions about sections of the book, I cannot thank all by name. However I will mention a few to whom I am especially grateful, and ask forgiveness from those whom I have not mentioned but who feel that they deserve to be acknowledged in print.

David Berger, Julie Bowen, Eli Clark, Theo Dagi, Dov Greenspan, Barry Mesch, Baruch Schwartz, David Shatz, and Daniel Statman corresponded with me at length in response to reading sections of early drafts of the manuscript or to questions or requests I had made of them. I deeply appreciate the efforts they expended to seriously reflect in writing upon what I had to say, to point out errors and flaws, to make constructive suggestions, or to write for me reflections on their own religious experiences. I would have liked to have included in the book my full correspondence with them, but editorial considerations have prevented me from doing so. Some of this correspondence, and that with others as well, will, with permission, be made available on the Internet companion site to this book, on the blog *The Tenacity of Unreasonable Beliefs* (http://tenacityofunreasonablebeliefs.blogspot.com). I have tried to take into account their comments as I was writing and revising the manuscript over several years.

I would like to thank the three outside reviewers for Oxford University Press who read the original book proposal and excerpts from an early version of the manuscript. They made excellent suggestions that induced me to transform what was originally intended to be a book that focused narrowly on Orthodox Judaism into one that addresses aspects of Christianity, Islam, and religious philosophy as well.

Jeremy Brown, Erica Brown, Harvey Bock, and David Gordis read and constructively commented on selections from drafts of early versions of the manuscript. To Jeremy I owe a special thanks for his enthusiasm and for helping me organize some of the numerous materials that I had collected in the early stages of writing the book.

Richard Dimond's gracious hospitality to me in his home in Southwest Harbor, Maine, provided me with several weeks of tranquility to work on the manuscript without distractions.

For many years I have had the pleasure of participating in a Shabbat afternoon Talmud study group where from time to time I have discussed this book with Harvey Bock, Jeremy Brown, Gene Fax, Phil Fishman, Michael Hammer, Allan Lehmann, Danny Lehmann, Barry Mesch, Jerrold Samet, Richard Shore, and Richard Israel *alav hashalom.*

The assistance and support of the Hebrew College library has, as always, been essential for my work and has been provided with grace and goodwill.

My gratitude goes to Cynthia Read, my editor at Oxford University Press, for her interest and her encouragement, and her constructive criticisms and suggestions. As I wrote about Cynthia in another book, I admire her willingness to give me the freedom to say what I want to say even when she might not be comfortable with it, or might even be offended by it. I don't know how much longer she will tolerate me, but I hope that her patience has not yet worn thin.

My wife, Judith, and my children, David, Atara, and Noam, have each contributed in their way to this book, not least of all by bearing the brunt of my deep attachment to and ambivalence toward Orthodox Judaism for many years as manifested in words, thoughts, and deeds.

Having thanked so many individuals for their input, I must emphasize that none of them are responsible for the deficiencies or errors in the book. These are exclusively my responsibility, as are the values and attitudes expressed in it and its tenor.

I am well aware that while articulating and discussing the ideas in this book on various venues on the Internet, at academic conferences, and now in final written form, I have offended and I will offend many people. I will be disappointed if *The Tenacity of Unreasonable Beliefs: Fundamentalism and the Fear of Truth* does not provoke and anger religious fundamentalists because in addition to being, hopefully, a work of serious scholarship and analysis, it is also a polemic against Jewish, Christian, and Muslim scriptural fundamentalism. I hope that its sometimes provocative and polemical tone will not prevent readers from thoughtfully reflecting upon its substance and taking it to heart.

CONTENTS

The Tenacity of Unreasonable Beliefs

<table>
<tr><td>CHAPTER ONE</td><td># Why This Book?
Autobiographical Reflections</td></tr>
</table>

THIS BOOK ORIGINATED in my attempt to understand *why* modern Orthodox Jews believe that the Pentateuch (*Torah* or *Humash* in Hebrew) was revealed in its entirety by God to Moses at Mt. Sinai or during a sojourn of forty years in the wilderness in the late second millennium BCE, in the face of overwhelming evidence and logical arguments against such a proposition. I also wanted to understand *how* these modern, well-educated, Orthodox Jews deal with the facts and arguments that challenge this central religious belief of Orthodoxy. These two questions fascinate me as a psychologist interested in the workings of the mind, and in the relationship between beliefs and emotions. Another reason for exploring this topic was my sense that this belief, and what it implies, has, at times, adverse ethical and psychological consequences, both for the believers themselves and for others who are affected by the believers.

I will use the acronym TMS, which stands for Torah to Moses at Sinai (or Torah to Moses *from* Sinai) as shorthand for this doctrine or dogma of Orthodoxy. The alternate view, accepted by virtually all academic scholars of the Bible, I will refer to as MSPM, an acronym for the *multiple-source post-Mosaic* hypothesis of the authorship and origins of the Pentateuch.

As I delved into the psychology of religious belief, especially of "scriptural fundamentalism," I expanded my interest to include ultra-Orthodox (*haredi* in Hebrew) Jews, who do not identify themselves as "modern Orthodox." This group, of which there are many subgroups, affirms TMS with a certainty and passion that leaves no room for even an iota of doubt about its historical truth.

It also became apparent to me that fundamentalist Christians who believe in the divine authorship, inerrancy, and infallibility of the Bible, and Muslims who believe in the divine authorship, inerrancy, and infallibility of the Koran, have much in common with Orthodox Jewish believers in TMS. I therefore examine Christian and Muslim "scriptural fundamentalists" as well, while retaining my original focus on Orthodox Judaism.

These Jewish, Christian, and Muslim "scriptural fundamentalist beliefs," and derivatives of them, are very implausible in light of current knowledge about the origins and contents of the Pentateuch and the rest of the Hebrew Bible, the Christian Bible (i.e., the "Old" and the New Testaments), and the Koran. This knowledge comes from modern academic study of the Bible and the Koran, and from other scholarly and scientific disciplines as well.

I use the terms *fundamentalist* and *fundamentalism* in a very narrow sense. By *scriptural fundamentalist* I refer to a person who believes, and affirms with certainty, that God has literally authored and revealed a "sacred scripture" that is inerrant and infallible, and that this "sacred scripture" is absolutely authoritative for all of humankind. This is what Orthodox Jews believe about the Pentateuch, many Christians believe about the entire Bible, and almost all devout Muslims believe about the Koran. "Scriptural fundamental*ism*" refers to the religious ideology that espouses such a view.

Any ancient fixed text that is used as an ongoing guide to belief and to a way of life needs to be interpreted. Substantial sections of the Bible and of the Koran lend themselves to more than one understanding. That is one reason why there are numerous commentaries on each of these scriptures. The commentators often disagree on the meaning of a word or passage. They will also differ on the purpose, message, or context of a passage.

Scriptural fundamentalists, and especially their religious leaders, interpret their sacred texts all the time, although they often deny that they are doing anything more than explicating what the text "clearly" and "unambiguously" says and means. Some scriptural fundamentalists tend to be "literalists" in their reading of their scripture, but this isn't always and necessarily the case.

Orthodox Judaism teaches that along with the Pentateuch that was delivered to Moses at Sinai, God gave Moses an oral tradition as well. When there is an accepted oral tradition about a passage in the Torah, it is the oral tradition and not the passage's "literal" sense that determines its "true" meaning. Orthodox Jews are not only "scriptural fundamentalists," but "oral tradition" or "rabbinic" fundamentalists as well. They consider the biblical text, as interpreted by rabbinic tradition, to be God's teachings and will, and authoritative. They also tolerate in their system multiple traditions about what is the oral tradition, so there is a substantial degree of flexibility in how a biblical passage is understood. However, there are limits to this flexibility. Every Orthodox Jew agrees that in the Torah, God has prescribed a death penalty for violation of the Sabbath and for adultery, although the rabbis might have differed in their precise definition of what constitutes a violation of the Sabbath or an act of adultery. Moreover, there are many Pentateuchal passages about which there is no oral tradition. Orthodox Jews will usually understand these literally, except when a metaphorical or poetic sense of a passage is a more plausible reading. In all cases, Orthodoxy claims that it is in possession of the actual words that God has authored and revealed, in the Torah, and as such knows, for the most part, what God wills for Jews and for all of humankind.[1]

My examination of Orthodox Judaism will undoubtedly offend many Orthodox Jews. In fact, in 1996 I posted several questions to a few electronic discussion groups of Orthodox Jews, inquiring about their beliefs, and presented a paper on this topic at the annual conference of the American Academy of Religion (AAR), titled "The Tenacity of Unreasonable Beliefs in Modern Orthodox Jews: A Psychological Analysis." My questions, the discussion that ensued, and my paper generated considerable hostility and controversy. This book includes much of that material, so it already has a provocative track record.

One thing that some people found offensive was my attempt to delve into psychological reasons for their beliefs, and in this book I expand upon this attempt. I think it only fair, therefore, in a spirit of reciprocity, that at the outset I explain something of my own personal "psychology of loss of belief." Moreover, in addition to the motives of intellectual curiosity and concern about the moral implications of "biblical fundamentalism," as reasons for exploring the topic of the "tenacity of unreasonable beliefs," my personal history has also played a role in the writing of this book.

Several months before the 1996 AAR session I had presented an early version of my paper to my colleagues at Hebrew College, at a faculty colloquium. That version did not address in detail the issue of whether there are any negative moral, ethical, or intellectual consequences of allegiance to the doctrine of TMS. One of my colleagues,[2] in response to my presentation, said to me, "Sol, what's your agenda?" He was probing, in other words, why I was bothering to address the issue—was it simply "intellectual curiosity" about an interesting psychological phenomenon—an attempt to better understand what some have referred to as the "compartmentalization" of experience that is part of the consciousness of the modern Orthodox? This question induced me to reflect more honestly about why indeed I was so interested in this question, and whether I indeed had an "agenda" of which I myself was not fully aware. Upon reflection I acknowledged that I really would not be particularly intrigued with the "psychology of belief" per se if, for example, I knew that a Martian had a certain "unreasonable belief" that in no way impacted upon me. Who cares what the Martian believes, as long as it doesn't affect me or those who are important to me?

The more I have studied the phenomenon, the more I have become "intellectually" interested in it, as I have come to appreciate its complexity, psychologically and philosophically. However, an even stronger recent motive for studying the psychology of belief in other religions, especially in Islam, has been 9/11 and the threat of Islamic fundamentalism to me and all that is dear to me. The better we understand the psychology of belief and of believers, especially of fundamentalist believers who advocate violence and terror, the better we might be able to "defundamentalize" them, in other words, wean fundamentalists from their dangerous beliefs.

However, at the time, I wasn't particularly interested in examining why Christians, Muslims, Hindus, Buddhists, or other "believers" "tenaciously" cling to what to me are highly implausible beliefs. Others, such as psychologists interested in "cognitive dissonance," or philosophers interested in epistemology, might want to understand the Martian, but curiosity about the psychological phenomenon, though intriguing to me, was not the only, or perhaps the primary motive, for my exploring this issue. I realized that there was something deeper that troubled me and spurred me on. The more I thought about this, the more I came to realize that in addition to intellectual curiosity, I was motivated by several additional factors.

I was justifying to myself, in a psychological sense, and to "others" (such as Orthodox family members), in an intellectual sense, my "heresy" vis à vis Orthodoxy. I was also expressing my latent resentment toward those teachers and rabbis, and the culture and ideology that they represented, whom I felt, in retrospect, had either been dishonest, disparaging, or demeaning in the way in which they had responded to the religious doubts and questions that I had raised during my adolescence and early adulthood years. I desired to critique those individuals (alive or dead) and the ideologies that formed their worldviews, which impugned—and continue to impugn—whether explicitly or implicitly, my (and many others') character, intelligence, and motives when I challenged the Orthodox ideological fold and rejected its doctrines and its claims to authority.

I did not feel such resentment toward my parents, who though pained by my non-Orthodox beliefs as an adult—and in the case of my mother, frequently critical of me for them—did not "reject" me. Moreover, growing up in a modern Orthodox home and environment, I was taught to love and did deeply love the Orthodox way of life, rather than fear divine punishment if I failed to follow it, although I definitely was to feel guilty if I violated *halakha* as my parents, especially my mother, understood it. The fear of divine punishment, and even greater obsessiveness with halakhic performance, were more pronounced in some of the "right wing" yeshivot that I attended.

Many "rebels" against Orthodoxy are also rebelling against parents who were punitive and unloving in their transmission of Orthodox tradition, especially its rules and regulations. I once had a lengthy conversation with an activist in an anti-haredi organization. He spoke of his deep resentment toward his right-wing, domineering, Orthodox father, with whom his childhood relationship was troubled and unhappy. I pointed out to him that his polemic and crusade against the haredi world is really a way of "getting even" with, or continuing his long-standing battle with, his deceased father. He acknowledged that there was a psychological truth in what I had noted.[3]

My feeling is that there were some significant negative moral, ethical, and intellectual consequences that derived from or were deeply connected with the belief of Orthodoxy in the revelation of the Torah by God to Moses at Sinai, which I point out later in the book. This applied to modern and ultra-Orthodox culture alike, although not necessarily in identical ways. Proponents of Orthodox belief systems and culture need to acknowledge these negative consequences and do something about them.[4]

I would also like to provide individuals in Orthodox communities—especially but not only haredi ones, who are intellectually and/or emotionally frustrated and stifled in them, and who feel condemned to silent acquiescence to their unhappy situation—with some moral, intellectual, and psychological support by giving them a better understanding of their communities and some material that might help them break out of their confines.[5] And I would also like to try to persuade fundamentalists to give up their beliefs and adopt more rational ones.

––––––

I begin then with a brief accounting of my journey from Orthodox believer to *apikorus* (heretic), at least as viewed from an Orthodox perspective. From childhood through my early 20s I was Orthodox in practice and belief, and consciously aspired, from my teenage years, to be devout. In my early 20s, while still a yeshiva student in Jerusalem, I realized that I was no longer able to believe in the basic theological tenets of Orthodox Judaism.

My religious doubts had actually begun quite early, perhaps when I was thirteen or so, and I will try to reconstruct some of them. I am aware that these are merely fragments of memories. They leave out much of what "really happened" and most of what was unconscious, but it is the best that I can do.

I found it difficult to accept the idea that the Jews were chosen by God for a special relationship. Then, when I became aware of modern biblical scholarship, my belief in Torah to Moses at Sinai was challenged. I was also troubled by what troubled Job—that the righteous suffer and the wicked prosper. I was also influenced by James Joyce's *A Portrait of the Artist as a Young Man* and Thomas Hardy's *Jude the Obscure,* novels of coming of age and loss of Christian faith that described much of my own feelings and experiences. Throw into this incubating cauldron of doubt the theory of evolution and an encounter with Hume on miracles,[6] and other philosophers studied in college, and I had more than enough to make me wonder whether what I was being taught to believe in and socialized to practice at home and at yeshiva was indeed true and binding. These doubts and the existential crisis that they engendered were powerful and ongoing, if waxing and waning, experiences for a good number of years. Yet I spent much energy trying to defend Orthodoxy for myself against these doubts, or in denial of the conflict. I vacillated between faith and skepticism.

In my senior year in college I decided that if Orthodox Judaism was to be the way of life for me, then I had to embrace it more fully. I decided to go to Israel to study in an advanced level yeshiva and immerse myself fully in learning Torah and Talmud—give Orthodox Judaism, as understood and inculcated in the world of the yeshiva, a chance, so to speak, to prove itself. Eager to learn, I flew to Israel a few hours after I took my last final exam, not being interested in graduation ceremonies. College was something I attended to satisfy my parents (although I did enjoy my studies very much).

The yeshiva experience in Israel didn't buttress my faith. On the contrary, I was so disillusioned by the unethical behavior of some of the leaders of the particular yeshiva in which I was studying that it only added another reason to question Orthodoxy. If this is what Torah learning can produce, it can't be divine revelation.

However, even as my struggle between faith and doubt continued, I maintained my Orthodox ritual observances, as I found many attractive aspects to Orthodox values and lifestyle. I also was not aware that there were thoughtful non-Orthodox models for Jewish living and commitment, whether religious or secular. I did not know that serious and knowledgeable Jewish thinkers had tried to respond to the questions that gnawed at me while they remained strongly identifying, though not Orthodox, Jews.

My religious doubts, which had incubated from early adolescence, at times surfacing but more often repressed, finally erupted with full force one day when I was around 23 years old. I don't remember the exact day, but the experience was profound. I was standing on a street corner in the Geula neighborhood of Jerusalem and I had a sudden Eureka-like insight. In a flash, the traditional viewpoint and all of the apologetic defenses of it that I had constructed over the years appeared untenable and indefensible on rational grounds. The alternatives, existentially bleak as they appeared to be (and maybe are), were so much more convincing. The experience was emotionally wrenching, because it removed the meaning structure of my life.

The nineteenth-century French philosopher Jouffroy describes the emotional impact of his loss of faith in Catholicism at a particular moment, which reminds me of my feelings:

> This moment was a frightful one; and when toward morning I threw myself exhausted on my bed, I seemed to feel my earlier life, so smiling and so full, go out like a fire, and before me another life opened, sombre and unpeopled, where in future I must live alone, alone with my fatal thought which had exiled me thither, and which I was tempted to curse. The days which followed this discovery were the saddest of my life.[7]

My eureka moment also engendered the very strange experience of a shattering of my self-definition and sense of self. I had always known myself (and had been known) as the sincerely religious *yeshiva bochur* (young yeshiva student). But who was I now? Shlomo (my Hebrew name) the *apikoros* (heretic)? I hardly knew such a Shlomo. Was he me? Was I him? How should I now behave—the way I was used to behaving, in other words, ritually observant, praying, wearing the *yeshiveshe* garb (e.g., a suit and black hat)? How do I relate to my family, to my dearest friends, to the people of the *yeshiveshe* world to whose homes I was invited for *Shabbat,* who assumed that I was of *shlomey emuney yisrael* (the community of the faithful)—one of "theirs"? These were kind, warm people. Do I tell them who I now am and what I really believe? Do I act upon my conviction that whether or not there is a God, he did not reveal this Torah and that hence the entire *halakhic* structure that is built upon that premise no longer has any authority for me (and from my new perspective, for them either)?[8]

My experience of loss of faith was similar, too, to that described by Alan Mintz in his book *Banished from Their Father's Table,* referring to the nineteenth-century yeshiva students who lost their faith in the traditional religion in which they had been raised:

It was not so much that the world of faith had been purposefully rejected but that at a certain point its plausibility had simply collapsed. The world that had once been thick with symbols and texts, sacred times and covenanted obligations, providential signs and redemptive promises was, suddenly, not there. What had been lost, moreover, even if it was no longer tenable, was also no longer replaceable...This intellectual and metaphysical negation was deepened by the loneliness that resulted from the break with family and community.[9]

In retrospect, my personal experiences seem almost trivial. The "loss of faith" experience of the *yeshiva bochur* (yeshiva student) had been almost a rite of passage for thousands in Europe and later in the United States. There was nothing novel in my doubts or in my experiences. However, just as sophomores are not aware that their "profound" insights and experiences are often reinventions of the wheel, I was unaware of the pervasiveness in Jewish society of my grappling with Orthodoxy and rejecting of its tenets. I had not been too familiar with the literature of the nineteenth-century Jewish Enlightenment or of modern Jewish philosophy, which are replete with discussions of the theme of grappling with and eventual rejection of Orthodox Judaism.

During the past 250 years, hundreds of thousands of Jews who were socialized in traditional or Orthodox homes and cultures experienced challenges to their religious beliefs and practices. Some resisted and warded off these challenges; others reformulated their beliefs so as to feel that they were compatible with modernity—especially the neo- or modern Orthodox, Conservative, and Reform Jews, as well as other non-Orthodox Jews, who defined themselves as religious. Some Jews "succumbed" to the challenges of modernity, professing agnosticism, atheism, or secular humanistic Judaism. Numerous individuals raised as devout Christians or Muslims underwent analogous experiences. My story is for the most part but a variation on a recurring theme experienced by myriad others.

However, even if in historical perspective the loss of faith of religious adolescents or young adults is a common phenomenon, to me my experiences were far from trivial.

During the period of my doubts, and after my eureka experience, I feared the emotional and social consequences of rejecting the faith and tradition into which I had invested so much of my emotional and intellectual energies. I was afraid of hurting my family and of their reactions if I were to declare my skepticism, let alone act upon it.

"Coming out" wasn't immediate, and from an external, behavioral perspective has been far from total. I didn't reveal my changed self to my family for a while, and when I did it was with some sensitivity. It deeply hurt some family members and bothered others. It affected the quality of our relationships, creating emotional distance and tensions. Some of these might have been based upon real changes in how they related to me and how I related to them; others were probably based upon my projections of what I imagined they thought and felt about me, which might not have always been accurate.[10]

So where am I now? I do not believe the TMS view of Pentateuchal authorship and origin. I find the view of post-Mosaic authorship of the Pentateuch, as the final product of a redaction of multiple sources authored over many centuries, to be much more plausible. Whether or not there is a God cannot be proven. Science doesn't need God to explain how things work. There is no evidence of a moral order in the universe, or of any divine theodicy of ultimate justice. Ecclesiastes' view is plausible—at death we return to dust and nothing of our essence lives on after us (although our children and the long-term effects of what we have done in our lives, do).

I am unsure of whether I can consider myself to be religious or spiritual, even though I still practice many traditional rituals. Can skepticism, agnosticism, or even atheism be compatible with spirituality? Yet at times I yearn for the spiritual and religious experiences that I had in my youth. *Shirey neshama* (soul songs and songs of yearning) evoke deep religious emotions in me. One example is *Yedid Nefesh*:

Beloved of the soul . . . draw your servant to Your will . . .

My soul pines for your love. Please, O God, heal her now by showing her the pleasantness of Your radiance. Then she will be strengthened and healed, and gladness will be hers . . .

It is so very long that I have yearned intensely, speedily to see the splendor of Your strength . . .[11]

Another example is *Ke'Ayal Ta'arog Al Afikey Mayim:*

Like a hind crying for water,
my soul cries for You, O God,
my soul thirsts for God, the living God;
O when will I come to appear before God! . . .
Why so downcast, my soul,
why disquieted within me? . . .
Have hope in God;

I will yet praise Him,
My ever-present help, my God.[12]

Although, as I said earlier, I bear resentment toward *some* teachers who did not respond to my doubts with the empathy and honesty I expected and wanted from teachers, for the most part I have positive feelings about my religious home environment and the yeshivot in which I had spent many months and years studying Torah. I had, and still have, affection for *some* of my teachers, who were to me positive models of *musar* (a high level of ethical sensitivity and behavior) and of genuine concern for the spiritual and Talmudic development of their students, me no less than many others. My own moral and ethical values have been deeply shaped by certain core values and teachings of Orthodox Judaism, even as I find other teachings and values in Orthodoxy to be morally problematic. I do not perceive myself as having rebelled against Orthodox belief and practice because they were emotionally repelling or overly burdensome. Of course, once I no longer accepted the doctrinal foundation of Orthodoxy, rebellion in behavior and emotional attitude became more possible and actual, though still not easy. Notwithstanding my "rebellion," I prefer to be a member of, and most frequently attend services and pray in, an Orthodox synagogue, and I am observant of a substantial amount of halakha—although not because I believe that God commanded these laws, or for any other theological reason. I am ambivalent toward traditional Judaism as a way of life. Some might say that I lack the courage to follow my beliefs (or lack of beliefs) to their logical conclusion. Perhaps. Or perhaps there can be many reasons why a person maintains the traditions and lifestyle, and certain values, of the religion and culture into which he was socialized, even though he no longer accepts the religious tradition's own claims for its authority over him.[13]

Notwithstanding the loss of the faith of my youth, my existential and intellectual preoccupations in my post-Orthodox state have always related to the religious, spiritual and ethical teachings of Judaism, to the Jewish people, and to the State of Israel.

Throughout my adult years I have tried to retain a strong Jewish identity and to understand as objectively as possible the historical development of Judaism. I have attempted to convey to my students something of my love of Jewish wisdom, tradition, and experience while not denying my intellectual and emotional ambivalence toward many of its teachings, values, and norms that I find either irrational or immoral. I have also tried to selectively extract from Jewish religious culture those elements and values I consider worth perpetuating among Jews and universally.

My involvement in Jewish study, teaching, and writing in an *academic* setting, and from an academic perspective, serves my personal need to maintain my deep-rooted connection to Judaism and the Jewish people, and to hold on to the pervasive sense of Jewish identity and identification that was so strongly inculcated in me in my childhood and early adulthood, while allowing me at the same time to be fully open to the ever-expanding understanding of what it means to be human and to be Jewish. This expansion of knowledge and self-understanding derives from ongoing advances in the humanities, the social sciences, the life sciences, and cosmology. My openness has brought me to look at Judaism critically, to be attentive to the intellectual and moral challenges posed to it by contemporary thought and science. This commitment to Jewish culture and preservation of Jewish identity, while being open to modern thought and being wary of excessive ethnocentrism, can generate intellectual and emotional tension and can be accompanied by a certain sadness. This is so because the core and grounding of my Jewish identity from earliest childhood was, as I have said, Orthodox belief, values, emotions, behavior, and community. All of these have weakened as a consequence of my skepticism, and their replacements have not been as intense, vigorous, joyous, and existentially meaningful as was Orthodoxy.[14]

Individuals who were socialized in an Orthodox community and ideology and who leave the ideological and behavioral fold often continue to view, or at least experience, themselves, via the perspectives and categories of the Orthodoxy that they left. They may feel themselves to be rebels, heretics, apostates, and traitors—negative terms—even though at the cognitive level they consider their present views to be truer than the Orthodox doctrines that they left. It is hard to break out of a mold even after one has broken away from the fold. One of my students was raised in an ultra-Orthodox Jewish environment. She eventually adopted the views of secular humanistic Judaism. She made it a point to define herself by what she believed in and by the values she affirmed, rather than through the lens of the community from which she came. She took offense when someone referred to her as a "nonbeliever," maintaining, quite rightly, that she is a passionate believer. It is just that she believes in different things than the members of the community which she left believe in.

I still have some difficulty doing what my student is able to do. I often experience and define myself as a rebel or heretic vis à vis Orthodox Judaism, which entails a certain emotional defensiveness, even though I consider my views to be more plausible and reasonable than those of Orthodoxy. Perhaps this is because I continue to participate in the world of Orthodoxy and, hence, am regularly reminded of my deviations from its beliefs and commitments.

In any case, my release from the constraints of religious and theological doctrines has given me an exhilarating freedom to explore and pursue ideas that are exciting, at times unconventional or controversial, and occasionally perhaps radical in their implications, for example, reassessing the concept of man's uniqueness as a creature in the image of God, in light of evolutionary theory and genetics. Such a reassessment may require radical revisions of long-held principles that are foundations of our moral and social order.

My existential biography spills over into my academic life and is expressed in one way or another in what and how I teach, research, and write.

My relationship to the Jewish texts that I teach is often ambivalent. On the one hand, I am drawn to them because they address significant issues of meaning, value, purpose, identity, and spiritual striving. Moreover, when I study and teach a biblical, rabbinic, or medieval text, I often find that the most pedagogically effective way to engage the students' interest and to be naturally enthusiastic in my teaching is to enter into the conceptual and emotional world of the text. In a certain sense, I suspend for a while whatever intellectual disbelief or emotional disaffection I would have were I to be examining and teaching the text from a critical and dispassionate perspective. Teaching becomes like theater in which I, and perhaps at times my students as well, are transported back in time and place. This is very much like the experience of studying Talmud or midrash in a yeshiva. I also have very positive emotional and cognitive associations with my yeshiva experiences, and teaching Talmud often triggers in me those feelings, which are easily picked up by my students. However, I know that my attitude toward these texts is no longer what it was when I was in yeshiva. Their moral and religious claims need to be proven as justifiable by reason, and often cannot be; their assumption that they have a priori authority over me as a Jew is one that I do not share, just as I do not believe that they are divinely revealed or inspired. It is my responsibility and my desire as a teacher to make my students aware of this nontraditional perspective on the texts and the tradition. The challenge I face is how to engender some of that emotional involvement in, and at times passion for, tradition while at the same time maintaining the critical distance and objective stance that truth and intellectual honesty require.

I face another challenge in relating to certain students. Because of my ortho-*praxis,* people often assume that I am ortho-*dox.* On occasion, therefore, I find that students who are in the process of becoming closer to Orthodox tradition seek me out as a resource, if not a model. I am uncomfortable with this role because I know who I really am, or at least I think that I do, whereas these students, I think, perceive me as something other than what I really am. I want to encourage them to draw closer to Jewish tradition and to Jewish learning, but not necessarily in the way in which Orthodoxy approaches it. I let the students know quite early in the relationship what my views are and that I think there are many avenues to God and to Judaism. I think that often this opens up for them directions that will be important as they explore their evolving relationship to Judaism and to their Jewishness.

———

I turn now to a discussion of the theological and philosophical question of the relationships between faith, revelation, and reason, an issue that was at the center of my own religious struggles and those of other people whom we will encounter in the pages ahead.

| Faith, Revelation, and Reason

MY FOCUS IS on the psychology of maintaining, or clinging to, implausible or even irrational religious beliefs. The relationships between religious belief, faith, and reason have been of interest to theologians and philosophers for many centuries, long before the separate discipline of psychology emerged in the nineteenth century. Closely related to the "faith and reason" issue was (and still is) the relationship between reason and revelation. Theological and philosophical reflections on the "faith/revelation and reason" issue can provide a useful background for addressing some of the psychological questions that are my primary interest.

What is meant by reason, what is meant by faith, and what kinds of relationships might there be between them?[1] The terms *belief* and *faith* are often used interchangeably, as well as in multiple senses, so it is important to be aware of what specific senses we have in mind when we use them.[2] Faith in God, for example, usually refers to a sense of trust and confidence in God's protection, or wisdom, or caring. It is primarily an emotion, or a long-term, stable feeling state. However, as with most emotions, it has implicit cognitive dimensions, the most obvious one being the idea or assertion that there is such an entity as God who has certain attributes.

How does the person who trusts in God know that there is a God? Or to put it another way, why does the person who has faith in God believe that there is a God in whom he can trust? He might believe in God because he was raised to believe that there is a God. He might have had certain personal experiences that he interprets as evidence for God. He might come to believe in the existence of God because he accepts certain religious texts as sources of truth. He might believe that there are firm logical proofs for the existence of God. He might believe in God because he accepts the wisdom and authority of certain individuals, such as religious leaders or theologians, who affirm that God exists. He might find that only by believing in the existence of God does his own existence have any meaning or purpose. In all of these cases of belief in God, there is either an explicit or an implicit assertion or "proposition" to the effect that God exists. Because he believes that God exists, he can have faith in God, in the sense of trust and confidence.

Some who believe in the existence of God might feel absolutely certain that he exists, experiencing no doubts whatsoever about this proposition. The "proofs" for the existence of God might be logically compelling to him. Or his personal experiences of what he feels to be God are even more compelling for him than any formal logical proofs could be. In fact, his personal experience of God may be so compelling that it overrides highly plausible arguments that the God in whom he believes, for example, a benevolent and omnipotent God, does not exist. Others, although believing, may harbor doubts or be open to the possibility that God may not exist.

Some theologians maintain that there is no merit to belief in God if God's existence could be proven, just as there is no merit in believing that two plus two equals four. We automatically assent to that which is proven beyond a doubt. They therefore feel that it is not desirable, and perhaps not possible, to prove in a formal way that God exists. The merit of belief in God is in relating to God as a certainty—even though there is room for doubts about his existence. Even if the existence of God could be proven, some teachings about God's attributes could not, such as, in Christian doctrine, the Trinity and the Incarnation, which one must believe with certainty on the basis of tradition and revelation. Other theologians feel that it is desirable to prove beyond a shadow of cognitive doubt that God exists. The true merit of religion is not in believing that God exists, but in having faith in God—placing one's trust in him—and in doing his will.

Reason can have several senses. It might refer to logical deduction or induction. In recent centuries it has often referred to the methods and findings of science or of scholarly research. It might mean "common sense" or well-established, properly functioning sensory and/or perceptual experience. Sometimes it refers to the accumulated wisdom of a religious or a philosophical tradition, or cultural consensus. There is a significant difference between using the term *reason* in the sense of a syllogistic deduction, or a scientific induction based upon a plethora of data, that has been frequently replicated by independent experimentalists, and using it in the sense of a cultural consensus about "the way things are."

And so, finally, "reason" is frequently used as a shorthand for what is reasonable. This usage is loose and rather culturally conditioned. For what is reasonable might be thought of as what is in accordance with common sense, but what is in accordance with common sense varies from time to time; for example, it varies with the popularity and influence of certain scientific, religious, or metaphysical ideas. Thus it may be reasonable to burn witches, or to take it for granted that the earth is flat, or that the design evidenced in nature requires a designer.[3]

My purpose in noting that there are different uses and senses of *faith, belief,* and *reason* is not to prefer one sense or usage over another, but to alert us to be aware of the specific sense and usage of these terms when we encounter them. A considerable amount of ambiguity and confusion can be eliminated if we are sensitive to the particular denotation of these words. People sometimes shift from one sense of these terms to another, without being explicit or even aware that they are doing so.

There are at least four attitudes toward what can or should be the proper relationship between religious belief and reason.

1. Reason can prove religious beliefs, such as the existence of God, or the divine authorship of the Pentateuch or the Koran, or the resurrection of Jesus.
2. Reason, in the sense of formal logic, may not be able to prove a religious proposition, but it can demonstrate that a religious proposition is not contrary to reason.
3. Reason is not fit to examine or critique religious beliefs, and the faith based upon them. Belief and faith are above or beyond reason.
4. There is no intellectually compelling argument as to why a believer needs to provide any rational justification for his beliefs.

Judaism, Christianity, and Islam developed theological approaches to their respective worldviews that emphasized the importance of reason in the religious life. At the same time, each of them had theologians or religious thinkers who downplayed, or even denigrated, the role that reason can and should play in the life of belief and faith. Both approaches appealed to their sacred scriptures to justify their views about reason.

For the three religions, the rationalistic-oriented theologians emphasized that the human being was the epitome of terrestrial creation, endowed with intelligence and rationality that set him apart from and above the animal world. This capacity was celebrated as a divine gift, and, as such, humans were obligated to actualize their intellectual potential, which entails the cultivation, use, and application of logical and rational skills. People should acquire knowledge about the world that God created and, to the extent possible, knowledge about God himself. The more one understood nature and its divinely ordained laws, and the more one understood what God is—or at least what God cannot be, such as multiple or corporeal, for the rationalists in Judaism and Islam, and why this is so—the closer one can become to God. Moreover, from this perspective, the laws and other norms that God revealed should in principle conform to reason, because reason is a characteristic of God, and so his teachings and commandments cannot be irrational. In addition, divine teachings and assertions about nature and history must be true, because truthfulness is another of God's characteristics. Because God endowed humans with the unique capacity to reason it is plausible to assume that he would want humans to exercise that capacity as they contemplated his laws and submitted to them. Not only should his laws be compatible with reason, but divine utterances about reality should be true. Would God endow me with reason and then ask me to believe in things that are unreasonable or false, or ask me to engage in irrational behaviors? Surely not.

In their works the theologian/philosophers discussed the nature of reasoning, of evidence, and of proof. For example, we acquire reliable knowledge through our sense perception, certain self-evident principles, logical inference, and reliable and authoritative transmitters of tradition.

According to Isaac Husik, Saadia Gaon, the ninth-century Jewish theologian, maintains that because investigation

> will give us a reasoned and scientific knowledge of those things which the Prophets taught us dogmatically ... it is ... our duty to confirm the truths of religion by reason ... [I]n reference to Biblical interpretation Saadia makes the general remark that whenever a verse of Scripture apparently contradicts the truths of reason, there is no doubt that it is figurative, and a person who successfully interprets it so as to reconcile it with the data of sense or reason will be rewarded for it. For not the Bible alone is the source of Judaism, Reason is another source preceding the Bible ... [4]

Saadia also states, "Any prophet whose teachings contradict reason must be rejected even if he performs miracles."[5]

However, even the rationalistic-oriented theologians maintained that for all of his capacity to reason, man often errs in his reasoning, and they enumerated various causes for these failures in the exercise of rationality. It takes time to hone one's intellectual skills and to acquire the knowledge to which they need to be applied. The necessary tasks of life do not always leave room for one to engage in philosophical and logical activities to the depth required for the ascertainment of truth, and some individuals are not endowed with the capacity for sophisticated reasoning.

Moreover, our reasoning is often distorted by desire and temptation, to the point that we will not even be aware of how subconscious motivations enable us to convince ourselves that certain things are true even though they are really false. Therefore, even as we extol reason, appeal to it, and give it a central role in our religious consciousness, we need to be aware of our capacity to fail to use it properly. Hence we must adopt a stance of humility even as we acknowledge our "rational superiority" over the animals.[6]

Rationalist-oriented theologians working within the Abrahamic religious traditions, in which divine revelation was central, maintained that because the exercise of reason may be inadequate or deferred, it was necessary for God to supplement human reason with divine revelation. But the two are fully compatible. Furthermore, human reason on its own could not ascertain certain religious principles or ritual requirements that were grounded in historical events. God's actions in history, a theme common to the three Abrahamic faiths, and one of the bases for God's demands of man, are known not by a process of reasoning, but either by personal experience, by way of transmission of traditions from ancestors to descendants, or by revelations that describe those acts of God in history.

Thus although the rationalist theologians acknowledge that there were certain beliefs and teachings that we might not arrive at exclusively by our reason, revelation cannot be incompatible with what we can prove or disprove by the proper exercise of reason.

For example, the Bible, and to a much lesser degree, the Koran, describe God anthropomorphically. But for Maimonides and Averroes logic demonstrates that God cannot be corporeal. Hence those descriptions of God cannot be understood literally. Maimonides devotes a major part of his theological/philosophical *The Guide of the Perplexed* to explaining how anthropomorphic biblical descriptions of God should be understood figuratively so that they can conform to his philosophical conception of God's incorporeality. Notwithstanding the hundreds or thousands of corporeal descriptions of God in the Bible and in postbiblical rabbinic literature, Maimonides considers the person who believes that God is corporeal to be a heretic.

Aquinas, too, maintains that in principle, reason and the creeds of faith cannot contradict one another:

that truth that the human reason is naturally endowed to know cannot be opposed to the truth of the Christian faith. For that with which the human reason is naturally endowed is clearly most true; so much so, that it is impossible for us to think of such truths as false. Nor is it permissible to believe as false that which we hold by faith, since this is confirmed in a way that is so clearly divine. Since, therefore, only the false is opposed to the true... it is impossible that the truth of faith should be opposed to those principles that the human reason knows naturally.[7]

Islamic rationalist philosophers, such as Averroes, make the same point with respect to reason and the Koran. He quotes the saying of God the Exalted in the Koranic verse "Summon to the way of your Lord by wisdom and by good preaching, and debate with them in the most effective manner" (Sura 16:125) in order to prove the following:

Demonstrative truth and scriptural truth cannot conflict.

Now since this religion is true and summons to the study which leads to knowledge of the Truth, we the Muslim community know definitely that demonstrative study does not lead to [conclusions] conflicting with what Scripture has given us; for truth does not oppose truth but accords with it and bears witness to it.

If the apparent meaning of Scripture conflicts with demonstrative conclusions it must be interpreted allegorically, i.e., metaphorically.[8]

The rationalists thus interpreted Koranic descriptions of Allah "seeing" and "saying" as metaphors or analogies necessary in order to communicate to the philosophically unsophisticated masses.

On the other hand, the nonrationalist-oriented, or even antirationalist-oriented, religious thinkers emphasized human limitations in the exercise of reason. Most of these non- or antirationalists considered the existence of God to be self-evident and accepted without doubt the authenticity of their scriptures and core traditions. Of concern to them (as it was, of course, to the rationalists as well) was the role of reason, if any, in relationship to divine law. They were opposed to attempts to provide rational bases for biblical or Koranic law. They argued that it is the height of hubris for humans to assume that they could fathom the depths of divine wisdom. If piety meant, among other things, obedience and submission to the will of God, it would be impious to make such submission contingent upon a rational comprehension of the divine will or command. God's right to command and our obligation to submit derives from the inherent nature of the divine-human relationship. God has created me and sustains me, and I owe all to him, my will, and my life if necessary. Therefore whether or not his teachings and commands make "sense" to me is irrelevant when I consider whether or not to accept his teachings and obey his commands. Moreover, humility and cognizance of my intellectual limitations dictates that it is foolish to use my reason as the yardstick to measure the rationality or the appropriateness of God's revelations or actions—as Job was told when God responded from the tempest to Job's "rational" argument that if God is omnipotent and just, then Job, who was innocent of sin, should not have suffered. God tells Job that it is hubris to think that a human can understand the ways of God. If we can't understand nature, which God created and controls, even though we directly experience it on a daily basis, how can we hope to understand God himself and his providence?

Another danger in the attempt to rely on our reason as a primary source of our religious beliefs, faith, and commitments is that when we fail to come up with a plausible reason for or explanation of a revealed teaching or an assertion about God or one of his actions, our belief, faith, and obedience might be weakened as a result. Moreover, in our quest for knowledge through the exercise of reason, we might become so enamored of our intellectual achievements that we will begin to view ourselves as akin to the divine, and our awe and reverence for God will be diminished.

The Authenticity and Authority of Accounts of Revelation and of Experiencing God

An obvious problem with belief in the truth and authority of scriptural accounts of divine revelation is the question of why one should accept the authenticity of revelation or of prophecy as recorded in ancient texts (or even in recent ones, such as the Book of Mormon) if he has not been socialized into a tradition that believes in the veracity of the alleged scriptural revelation. The skeptic says to the believer, "How do you or I, or anyone, know that the accounts of God and of divine action in the Bible or the Koran are true?" The skeptic probes further and tries to understand why the believer believes in the authenticity of the scripture that he claims is divinely revealed. How does religious socialization do its work, and what other factors may be involved in affirming the divine origin of scripture? Do not the contents of the claims— for example, that Yahweh transformed the waters of the Nile to blood, and later spoke to Moses on Mt. Sinai, that Jesus walked on the Sea of Galilee, that the angel Gabriel conveyed Allah's words to Muhammad—have to be verified by evidence? Because these are miraculous events that involve apparent suspension of "laws of nature," should not the burden of proof for their having actually occurred be upon one who asserts their truth? Moreover, the claims that the books that record these alleged events are themselves divinely revealed or inspired need to be substantiated with evidence. Indeed, the Hebrew Bible, the New Testament, and the Koran contain passages that indicate that whoever authored them was aware that part or all of their authenticity was challenged by skeptics in their own day. They include arguments or exhortations against doubters or deniers (e.g., Korah and his followers, who are punished for challenging Moses' claim to authority in the name of Yahweh; the doubting Thomas in the Gospel of John; the repeated criticism of the Meccan pagans and others who questioned the authenticity of Muhammad's revelatory claims).[9]

With respect to the claims of a believer that he had a personal revelation from or experience of God, why should someone who has not been privy to a personal experience of an encounter with the divine, believe in the validity and truth of the claims of the believer?

Believers offer several answers to these questions of the skeptics. The individual believer's potent personal experience of an encounter with God or of a revelation by him, coupled with the cumulative testimony of the experiences of many other believers over the ages, provide for the believer evidence of the reality of God and/or his revelation, and of the truth of beliefs and of the worthiness of faith based on these encounters and revelations. They do not need reason to validate them. Moreover, rational arguments that question or challenge the belief and the faith, and their grounding in God, are too weak to overcome the impact of the believer's sense of having encountered the divine.[10]

A devout and extremely intelligent Christian woman with whom I corresponded about her understanding of the relationship between her religious beliefs and her respect for reason wrote me at length about her "conversion" to Christianity and how she perceived the relationship between faith and reason in her own life. After describing some personal experiences that preceded and precipitated her acceptance of Christ she wrote the following:

> If He were just a theory, just a doctrine, with no experience of Him woven into us, I doubt that faith in Him would ever last long. I take my experience out of the drawer and marvel at it even today, and knowing what happened strengthens me when doubts come (which they do). Of course, it can't be proved that what happened to me was

more than psychological. But the Bible speaks of having "eyes to see" and "ears to hear." Once you believe God and He becomes real, the doubts of the intellect, while difficult and persistent and demanding answers, lose some of their power, because you have the sense that the part of you that doubts and mocks and postures as heroic for doing so is only the blind part, and that this part is not to be given as much credence as you gave it before you had an experience of God . . . There was a certain day where a transaction took place that changed my life irrevocably. I walked up to that day more or less unwittingly, and have not been the same since. In other words, my entrance into faith was through experience, and that has been its character ever since. I was not convinced by rational argument of things I had not believed before—instead, I saw them through another faculty entirely, and my reason has followed along in the wake of that experience, examining the evidence, sifting the facts, analyzing the possibilities of deception or contradiction . . . but always knowing itself to be in the presence of something greater than itself, something that it dare not try to mock or erase or entirely belittle. Reason has been eager to investigate whether my experience can be evaluated in an intellectual way and yet stand. But reason comes along behind, it cannot have the last word; it is mute even when it occasionally has the impulse to mock or to challenge, and speaks mostly when it has rational insight into the thing greater than itself (faith)—or into some aspect of it, since reason is unable to completely understand or explain . . . My inner life has become more real to me than my intellectual life, if I may distinguish them. Light simply explains itself—or doesn't explain, just shines. Once I had seen this sort of light pouring down on everything, my interest in intellectual things was to probe this mystery from the intellectual angle—not so much to prove that it could be true (although that is always interesting!) as to support by reason, if it's possible, why it is true. I was willing to assent to things that could not be proven on an intellectual basis because the results of believing that they were true had a power that surpassed comprehension . . . Nevertheless, the intellect is a God-given faculty. He shares it, created it, and prods its use in us . . . and I believe, increasingly, that it is possible to see with the mind, and to support with reason (though not necessarily to prove by means of reason) everything that is true. So I have slowly developed the notion of the intellect as the servant of the spirit. Here is the only role that I can allow it to have—but in that role my intellect can work, explore freely, think daringly, question, complain—be itself without censure. The doubts of the intellect are real, but the part of me that God has touched—which I call my spirit—has to allow these doubts a voice without allowing them "head." It seems, actually, that doubts, and paradox, and pain, all deepen faith, which without them might be easy or smug. Instead, faith and reason sometimes battle, but my being assents to one above the other. If I try to reverse their order, I am overwhelmed with loss, and in the end run back to my Father whose face was obscured by my experiments with thoughts that do not place everything in the context of Him. I can no longer live without Him, and have lost the desire to do so. From the point of view of the intellectual, I have sold out. Reason is not the ruling principle in my soul. But I would not have it any other way.[11]

How might a skeptic respond to, or analyze the appeal to, the power of personal experience of the divine and of the faith-related emotions that it generates and inspires?

There are two issues here. How would the skeptic—be he or she a philosopher, a psychologist, a historian of religion, or anyone else—who did not believe in the propositions explicit or implicit in a believer's affirmations, and hence in the plausibility of placing one's trust and confidence in God, as per Moses', Jesus', or Muhammad's teachings about him, explain the believer's experiences and interpretation of her experiences? The skeptic's explanation need not be addressed directly to the believer in an attempt to undermine the believer's beliefs about her experiences and their meaning. The skeptic, for example, a strict, nontheistic naturalist, might simply want to understand the experiential phenomena described by the believer from a perspective that does not invoke any concepts of God or of supernatural, miraculous events. He is concerned not with changing the views of any particular person but rather with the general psychology and epistemology of religious experiences and derivative beliefs and faith. Doing this is how many philosophers and psychologists of religion have earned their daily bread. Of course, their analyses, if convincing to the believer or to others, can undermine belief, and sometimes that was a motive of theirs as well, albeit not their primary one.

However, it has often been the case that the primary motive of the skeptic is more than just a "dispassionate" understanding of religious experiences and concomitant religious claims. In the long history of both interreligious and religious-secular dispute and conflict, the skeptic wants to undermine the believer's beliefs and faith and to assure that the believer will not be able to successfully transmit them to others such that those people will adopt them as well. This was often a reciprocal exchange—the believer and the skeptic each trying to undermine the worldview of the other. They might have been competing for political power, for resources, for a vision of the ideal society or of the future, and victory rather than mere understanding was the ultimate goal of each. This attempt by skeptics to undermine religious belief, and by religionists to undermine secular beliefs, has ethical, political, and cultural implications that go beyond just an interest in understanding religion and secularism. I will discuss some of these implications in chapter 7 and in a sequel to this book, and here want to address only the first interest of the skeptic, the attempt to understand the phenomenon of religious experience, such as the one described by my correspondent.

Skeptics use a range of arguments to challenge the veridicality of religious experience. They maintain that many reported religious experiences are nothing more than expressions of some pathology, such as delusions or an altered state of consciousness induced by a drug or an unusual physiological state. Some claim that the reported religious experiences and their underlying doctrinal assumptions serve common psychological needs, such as the need for love or for security, or the alleviation of a sense of guilt or rejection, and that the satisfaction of these needs suffices to account for religious experiences and beliefs without assuming the existence of God or the reality of a divine encounter or revelation. Skeptics also argue against the credibility of religious experiences and associated truth claims on the grounds that the experiences and beliefs of most religious people tend to be similar or identical to those described and espoused by the religions and religious communities into which they have been socialized, making it highly probable that what and how one experiences as a religious experience, revelation, or belief system is culturally determined rather than divinely begotten. Moreover, given the variety of religions, with their various unique experiential expectations and belief systems that often make contradictory and mutually incompatible claims, it is more plausible to explain religious experiences as products of cultural learning, and culturally learned suggestibility, than actual revelations of God.

At most, only one (if any) of the mutually incompatible and competing religious claims of the devout Jew or Christian or Muslim can be "true."

Some philosophers of religion, and even some theologians, maintain that there are certain truths about divinity and the transcendent that are shared by and underlie all religions, and to which all religions point, though each one in its unique way.[12] Abrahamic religious fundamentalists, however, do not accept this point of view. What grounds does the Jewish, or Christian, or

Muslim believer have to assume that his experience of God and his understanding of God's will is the one that is true? Aware of this competition, theologians of these three religions have spent much time (measured in centuries), effort, thought, ink, and powers of persuasion in trying to prove that their version is the only true one. (They often supplemented rational argument with coercion and violence when they failed to convince their opponents of their views.) The skeptic, though, is not convinced that the fundamental religious claims of any of the three faiths is true. The skeptic, maintaining the stance of an outside observer who has studied the history and psychology of how these religions developed and evolved in relation to their cultural environments and in relationship to one another, finds it much more plausible to understand their teachings, doctrines, institutions, rituals, and experiences from a naturalistic, nontheistic perspective,[13] even though he acknowledges that many aspects of religion are not as yet fully accounted for naturalistically. More recent explanations of religious experiences and beliefs, suggested by evolutionary psychologists and anthropologists, ascribe many of their features to innate human nature.[14]

Religious believers and theologians for whom personal or group religious experiences and/or claims of divine revelation are important bases for their beliefs need to address several challenges posed by skeptics of "the evidentiary force of religious experience."

When the beliefs are formulated as propositions about historical facts, or are derived from such propositions, how can they justify these beliefs in the absence of "objective" evidence for the propositions?

Religionists from each of the three Abrahamic religions are adept at "proving" the historical reliability of their sacred "revealed" texts and their beliefs derived from them, while denigrating the "proofs" proffered by the other two faiths. Most philosophers and psychologists today who do not subscribe to any of these three faiths tend to find all of the "proofs" to be tendentious and unconvincing,[15] as do religious thinkers of non-Abrahamic religions, such as Hinduism.

Often the goal of the theologians and religious apologists, especially in the modern era, is not to prove the propositions of the faith, but to demonstrate (or argue) that at least they are plausible and, hence, that the believer need not feel defensive about believing them. They might say, for example, that if God exists, created life, and cares for humans, it is reasonable to assume that he would have provided guidelines for humans as to how they should lead their lives. Thus, to believe in divine revelation is eminently plausible, maybe even more plausible than to believe in the existence of God but to deny his revelation. They might argue, for example, that if one believes in God and that there is more to reality than admitted by materialist naturalism, it is not at all unreasonable to believe that miracles can occur and have occurred. Even if one were to assume that miracles do not occur nowadays (an assumption that many religionists would deny), this is no way proves that miracles haven't happened in the past.

Theologians or religious apologists often have to justify beliefs when there seems to be a preponderance of evidence that the beliefs are false. This, of course, is an especially challenging task. It is one thing to defend a belief when there is no obvious, unambiguous evidence for it, but there is also no actual evidence or logical argument against it either. For example, with respect to claims that a miracle occurred, where a skeptic is not denying a priori the possibility that it could have, the believer would try to prove to the skeptic that it did, by providing credible eyewitness or other testimony to that effect.[16] It is another thing to have to account for, or explain away, actual evidence and arguments against a belief stated as a proposition. For example, modern biblical scholarship provides strong evidence that the Pentateuch was not written at the time that fundamentalist Jews and Christians claim that it was, and modern Koranic scholarship provides evidence that much of the Koran was not initially uttered when Muslims claim that it was. Moreover, there is strong evidence that both books were authored by human beings. For another example, "You," says the skeptic to the fundamentalist, "believe that the universe, including mankind, was created in six days. Scientific knowledge and reasoning provide evidence that the universe is billions of years old and that all living things, including humans, evolved over millions of years. How do you deal with this scholarly and scientific counterevidence to your religious propositions?" It is here in particular that fundamentalist Jews, Christians, and Muslims demonstrate "pseudocognitive acrobatics" as they contrive various explanations to account for problematic facts and logic or, failing that, then to discount them, as we shall be seeing in the chapters that follow. When they don't resort to such techniques, they will claim that "simple, innocent faith" or "the incomprehensible mysteries of the divine" or "leaps into the absurd" trump reason, and that they can live with the irrational if their faith is incompatible with reason. There are, we saw, medieval theological precedents for such an approach, especially in Christianity, in which conflicts between reason and doctrine were more acute than in Judaism or Islam.

Furthermore, given that fundamentalist Jews, Christians, and Muslims each believe that only their beliefs are true and many of the beliefs of the other two faiths are false, and given that each religion appeals to unique "authentic" personal or revelatory experiences of the divine, the religionist has to justify his claim that it is only his beliefs that are true and only his experiences that are authentic, whereas the beliefs of the others are false and their experiences inauthentic. For example, Jews believe that the laws of the Torah (Pentateuch) will never be abrogated and deny that Jesus was resurrected or is in any way divine; Christians believe that the rituals laws of the Torah were abrogated and Jesus was resurrected, and is God or God incarnate; Muslims deny that Jesus was resurrected, consider the belief that Jesus is God, or God incarnate, to be heretical, and believe that the Koran is the words of God and that Muhammad is the final prophetic authority, which Jews and Christians deny.

Why, asks the skeptic of each of these believers, is your personal or revelatory experience of the divine or of truths about the divine more reliable than those of the others? One Christian line of argument in response to this goes as follows:

> Alvin Plantinga . . . argues that it is perfectly justifiable for believers to maintain their exclusivist beliefs in the face of religious diversity. Believers may hold that their beliefs are true and that beliefs incompatible with theirs are false because their beliefs are warranted, perhaps by evidential reasoning, but also because the beliefs are properly basic [i.e., formed by properly functioning modes of perceptual, sensory, and cognitive experience]. Properly basic beliefs are formed in such a way that the believer is justified in taking them to be true and in believing that contrary beliefs held by others were not formed under proper epistemic conditions . . . In the face of the contrary beliefs held by others, it is not prima facie obvious that believers ought to abandon beliefs they take as justified.[17]

Of course the above argument is made by devout Jews and Muslims in order to justify their exclusive belief claims as well, as Plantinga is aware. The purpose of his argument, and that of the Jews and Muslims making analogous ones, is not to evangelize others but to make the believer comfortable that maintaining his belief is something reasonable and justifiable, when faced with the challenge that it is an arbitrary, nonrational choice given the fact that there are other, contradictory religious belief systems, to which reasonable and thoughtful individuals subscribe.

There are, of course, as I noted earlier, religious people who do not claim that their religion is the only true and authentic one. They may believe that there are multiple sources of knowledge about God and his will, and there can be multiple paths to experiencing God and living one's life in accordance with his will. They may see core commonalities in different religions, and they will usually understand their beliefs to not be assertions about actual historical events or even absolute propositions about the divine, but religious narratives and "myths" through which they experience reality in a spiritual way. They will say that because of their upbringing, religious culture, and personal experience, their particular religion—its narratives, myths, rituals, language, and communities—is most meaningful for them, although acknowledging that for others with different experiences and backgrounds, a different religion is the appropriate approach to God. What I am discussing, however, are religious people who are exclusivists in their religious claims and fundamentalists in the nature of their assertions about the origins and authority of their sacred scriptures.

Another ground for validating exclusivist religious claims is based upon the presumed unique positive life consequences of one's religion, a "pragmatic" truth. The kind of life that the revelation teaches and that is lived by the community of believers is superior along several dimensions, such as the ethical and the existential—providing meaning and purpose to life—to other "alleged" revelations or to nonrevelation-based worldviews. The fruits of the experienced encounter(s) with the divine suffice to validate it.

To this the skeptic responds with several arguments. First of all, there are many unethical laws, teachings, and values in all of the allegedly "revealed" religious texts and traditions. Of course such a claim can be made only on the assumption that there are criteria for the ethical and the moral that are independent of the teachings of the religious texts, and against which the latter can be measured. This is denied by some religious people. However, those who defend their religious beliefs by appealing to some external, revelation-independent standards of ethics and morality cannot ignore such criticisms from skeptics. The Hebrew Bible, for example, mandates the death penalty for males who engage in anal sex and for violation of the Sabbath. It mandates the extermination of certain ethnic groups. Its laws in the realm of personal status and other legal areas discriminate severely against women.

The New Testament, though rejecting most of the ritual obligations of the Old Testament, shares many of its values and attitudes toward homosexual behavior and women. It generates and justifies hatred of Jews, and it consigns those who do not belief in Christ to eternal damnation in Hell. While preaching the virtue of forgiveness on the one hand,[18] many of its passages express a desire for vengeance on those who do not accept its theses. The history of Christian behavior, such as anti-Semitism, the brutal suppression of "heresies," Catholic-Protestant wars, and Christian support of dictatorships such as the Catholic Church in Franco's Spain, belies any claims to Christianity's moral superiority.

The Koran teaches the inferiority of those who deny that Muhammad was a prophet of Allah and that the Koran is authored by God. Many Koranic passages instruct believers to kill "infidels" or at best to grant some of them a subservient status in Muslim societies. Husbands are permitted to physically strike their wives when they do not submit to their patriarchal authority, and the amputation of limbs is the penalty for certain crimes—see the Saudi Arabian penal code and practice. One need only observe the Muslim Middle East in the past few decades to get a sense of the moral and ethical depravity rampant in some sectors of the Muslim world. In the 1980s we witnessed the Iran-Iraq war in which millions died. More recently, in 2005–2008 we had in Iraq mutual Sunni-Shiite torture and murder of civilians—men, women and children, old and young—each Muslim sect committing its atrocities in the name of Allah and Muslim religious beliefs. Also in 2006 we witnessed the criminal actions of Hezbollah in Lebanon, waving the banner of Shiism, as it fired thousand of rockets and missiles at civilians in densely populated cities in Israel because the Islam it believes in teaches that the State of Israel and Jews who support it need to be exterminated. This Shiite jihad against Israel and Jews was incited and supported by many devout and pious Muslim clerics of Iran, some of whom deny or justify the Holocaust and would like to do what they claim Hitler either didn't try to do or left unfinished—annihilate the Jews. The president of Iran, with the frenzied approbation of millions of his coreligionists, repeatedly calls for the destruction of the State of Israel. And beyond the Middle East, although with its roots there, we have Al Qaeda–sponsored terrorism and mass murder in the World Trade Center in New York, and in train bombings in Madrid, and suicide (homicide) bombings in London, Bali, and numerous other cities around the world. Is it any wonder that a skeptic takes with a ton of salt the Muslim claim that the values its sacred Koran generates, and the communities it nurtures, are paragons of ethics and morality?

This is not to say that there haven't been nonreligious "religions" and worldviews that have been as immoral and unethical as some Muslim groups and states today, indeed even more so. Communism, Fascism, Nazism, and Western colonialism have all committed the gravest of crimes against humanity. But the skeptic is not trying to defend these nonreligious ideologies. He is just pointing to the evidence that religious claims to "authenticity" and validity on the basis of their alleged morality and ethics are preposterous.

This is also not to deny that many teachings of the Bible and the Koran, and many who live by these teachings, are morally and ethically sensitive, and that religious texts and traditions have much to teach us about how to become better human beings.[19] But this is far from sufficient to confirm the claim for any ethical superiority of religion over nonreligious worldviews.

The skeptic also points out that religions, and sects within a particular religion, often disagree on what is and is not considered ethical and moral. Abortion, stem cell research, capital punishment, distribution of wealth, gender equality, attitudes toward the "other," justifications for or against this or that particular war—on all of these ethical-moral issues of great concern today, one can find significant differences across and within religions. This diversity of opinions makes the claim that religion creates greater ethical and moral sensitivity and behavior so much the less convincing, given that the religions often can't even agree on what their own religious texts teach on the great moral and ethical challenges of the day.

The other claim of religionists, that religion provides existential meaning and purpose, is very often true. However, given the differences between religions as to what this purpose and what this meaning should be, the skeptic cannot help but wonder how this validates a particular religion's claim to being the only true and authentic one. The subjective experience of having one's life feel meaningful and "purpose-driven" by accepting and living by a religion is psychologically "true" for the believer/practitioner but does not speak to believers/practitioners of another religion, or of none. So it is a weak reed on which to rely for any claim to universal truth. Moreover, adds the skeptic, meaning and purpose are not unique to religion and religious people. Secular humanists, animists, polytheists, and other "ists," and the "isms" to which they subscribe, also provide meaning and purpose for millions of people around the world. Does that make their "isms" universally true? The Abrahamic monotheist says "No!" So why does he say "Yes!" to the universalist truth claim of his own "ism"?

Miracles are another ground for religious beliefs. Miracles—experienced by individuals or by a group—are, according to this view, best explained by assuming the existence and intervention of a divine being in the life of the individual and/or the community of the faithful. In the Orthodox Jewish context, for example, the claim is made that the survival of the Jewish people cannot be plausibly accounted for by natural historical processes. In the case of Christianity the miracles ascribed to Jesus—which the believer accepts as historical events—testify to his status as someone infused with divinely bestowed charisma, who knows what God wants of people.[20] For the Muslim, the reputed multiple appearances of Gabriel—an angel whose existence he does not doubt—to Muhammad testifies to the authenticity of his prophetic status and to the truth of his teachings.

To this the skeptic will say that he doesn't believe that the events that are alleged to be revelations or miracles ever occurred or he will say that the events that are pointed to as revelations from God, or miracles, can be explained in a naturalistic way.

From the perspective of the believer, however, either his personal experience or his trust in those who attest to the revelation and to the miracles is so deep that he accepts their testimony and interpretation of the scripture as absolutely reliable. This is especially the case when a believer has not been exposed in the early years of his life to an alternative view or interpretation of the beliefs. Once beliefs have been internalized by years of socialization in an unquestioning environment, they are difficult to undermine, even though to the skeptic there appear to be sound rational arguments that refute them, or make them highly improbable. They are, however, not impossible to undermine, as witnessed by the fact that many people raised religious eventually forsake their religious beliefs and practices. Whether and when it is morally desirable to encourage this process will be discussed in chapter 7, and how to do so will be addressed in the sequel to this book.

As we noted earlier, often believers will use reason to argue in favor of their core beliefs, but with the proviso that the arguments from reason are meant to be supportive of claims based upon personal experience of the divine, revelation, miracles, or the "fruits of faith" rather than fully determinative.

―――

An interesting example of the attempt to use reason to justify the claims of revelation that are rendered problematic by modern archaeology, scholarship, and science is the persistence in contemporary Jewish Orthodoxy of an appeal to the medieval Kuzari argument. According to Orthodox Jews, who accept as historical truth the Bible's account of the exodus from Egypt and God's revelation at Mt. Sinai, at least two million people witnessed these events. This number is based upon the account in Exodus according to which 600,000 adult males were at Sinai. Because women and children also witnessed the Sinaitic revelation, two million is a conservative estimate of the number of people present at Sinai, from the narrator's perspective.

Archeologists and biblical scholars find no independent evidence for these events other than the stories in the Book of Exodus, and scientists consider it impossible for such a large group to have survived in the Sinai wilderness for 40 years, unless of course they were sustained by miracles as the Bible maintains. Defenders of the historicity of the biblical account argue by appeal to reason and logic, that two million people could not have been deluded into a false belief about the occurrence of such miracles as the ten plagues and divine revelations to Moses and the Israelites. This is often referred to as the Kuzari proof, because it appears in Rabbi Yehuda HaLevi's twelfth-century influential theological apologia for Judaism, the *Kuzari*. When challenged with the skeptic's argument that there are no grounds for believing the biblical account that two million people witnessed these events, they adapt and elaborate upon the proof.

As proof for the truthfulness of the Exodus traditions, they argue that were it the case that these events did not actually happen as described, but that the Exodus stories were created sometime after the entry into Canaan by a few individuals, no one would have believed these individuals and their stories. Because the allegedly "fabricated" story about the Exodus and Sinaitic revelation included the claim that it had been witnessed by millions, any reasonable Israelite living in Canaan/Israel a few hundred years after the Exodus, would have asked, "If as you claim, millions of our ancestors witnessed and experienced that event, why are we first hearing about it from you, and haven't ever heard it from our parents, who would have heard it from their parents, and so forth, going back up to the time of the initial event?" Yet the traditions of the Exodus have been believed by numerous Jews to be true, for 2,500 or more years.

It is therefore concluded by Jewish (and Christian) defenders of the historicity of the biblical accounts of what transpired at Sinai that millions of Israelites had indeed experienced the revelation at Sinai, and had indeed transmitted their accounts of this experience to their children, and so on down the generations—from the time of the actual, initial event. This conclusion, they argue, is the only, or at least, the most reasonable, explanation for the fact that Jews throughout the ages have continued to affirm their belief in the historicity of the revelation in its biblical details. To assume that the story was fabricated, or was the figment of someone's (or a few people's) imagination, would require ascribing a highly implausible degree of gullibility to the millions who we know have accepted it as true for thousands of years. It is more plausible to believe that there had indeed been two million people who left Egypt. Having thus "established" that two million people really did claim to have experienced miracles in Egypt (e.g., the ten plagues) during the exodus from Egypt (e.g., the splitting of the Sea), and claimed to have experienced a divine revelation at Sinai, they argue that it is more plausible to believe that these miracles and the revelation actually occurred than that these two million people were hallucinating or delusional. We can also rely on the biblical account of God's special providence in providing for them during their journey in the wilderness by miraculous means in order to account for their survival.

Moreover, because neither Christianity nor Islam claim that the miracles or revelations that are the basis of their faiths were witnessed by more than a small group of individuals, the Jewish claim to the authenticity of its revelation narrative is much stronger than the claims of Christians and Muslims to the authenticity of their revelation narratives, because it is much more likely that a few individuals were fabricators, or delusional, or hallucinatory, than that two million were.

Skeptics offer several rebuttals to the Kuzari proof and variations on it. Myths of origin accrue details and become elaborated over time, so, for example, an original story about 600 ancestors might become 6,000, then 60,000, and so forth. Moreover, the Bible itself says that there were periods when the Israelites were unaware of their own early history. Furthermore, people are indeed very gullible, and masses of people often believe falsehoods or imaginative stories and myths spread by just a few people.[21]

The Kuzari argument was more convincing in the Middle Ages when the existence of God and belief in the possibility of divine revelation was almost universal in the lands of Abrahamic religion, at most doubted by a few philosophers. The argument was used in the context of debates between Jews, Christians, and Muslims as to whose traditions about the nature and content of divine revelation were the most reliable ones. Moreover, the primitive concept of God in the Exodus account was not too troublesome to believers. Either they accepted the anthropomorphic description of him as reasonable, or they interpreted it metaphorically. Moreover, there was little knowledge of how religions, myths, and legends evolve, and there was no field akin to modern biblical scholarship, which with good reason doubts the historicity of numerous biblical stories. Nor was there a field of psychology or psychiatry that could provide credible psychological explanations for experiences of revelation, of individuals, and of large groups.[22]

However, the Kuzari argument today, though still used in certain circles of Orthodox Judaism, is a specious one, for the reasons mentioned above and others. For example, because as a result of modern biblical scholarship we now understand that the anthropomorphic descriptions of God in Exodus and elsewhere in the Pentateuch meant for the most part what they literally said about God (although the Orthodox today deny that, as did Maimonides in the thirteenth century), are we to indeed believe today in the existence of the primitive God who strolled in the Garden of Eden, who descended from the sky to a mountain, or who needed Moses to teach him how to manage his anger? Moreover, to believe that God revealed himself and his Torah at Sinai, as Jesus, Peter, and Paul believed along with most of their Jewish contemporaries, means that one must believe or accept many incredible, implausible, and immoral stories and teachings in the Bible. Many possible naturalistic psychological, anthropological, and sociological explanations for the biblical Sinaitic revelation story, and other biblical stories, and for their being accepted as true by many Jews (and Christians) to this day, are more plausible than the Kuzari conclusion that the events described in the Bible actually happened as described.

—————

Having provided an overview of some of the issues in the historical and contemporary debates about faith, revelation, and reason, I continue to explore in the next chapter the tenacity of unreasonable beliefs of Orthodox, fundamentalist Jews.

CHAPTER THREE | Jewish Biblical Fundamentalism

WHY DO SO many modern Orthodox scientists, and modern Orthodox academics in fields of Jewish studies, continue to affirm the traditional doctrine that the Pentateuch was divinely revealed by God to Moses in the thirteenth century BCE (TMS, Torah to Moses at Sinai, also referred to as Torah Mi'Sinai) in the face of overwhelming evidence against it from the fields of modern biblical scholarship, comparative religious studies, psychology, anthropology, philosophy, and the natural sciences? Why do the modern Orthodox resist the multiple-source/post-Mosaic/human authorship view (MSPM)? After all, these Orthodox scientists and scholars are committed to empirically based, scientific and scholarly methods of examining and accounting for evidence. They apply rigorous logic and criteria for plausibility in their professional fields. Yet when it comes to TMS versus MSPM, they seem unable or unwilling to acknowledge the implausibility of their belief.

There are three separate explicit assertions in TMS: (1) divine authorship of the Pentateuch, (2) the Pentateuch is a unitary rather than a composite work, and (3) the Pentateuch was revealed around the thirteenth century BCE. Because the Pentateuch makes many assertions of a historical or factual nature—for example, that the earth and water existed before the sun existed— TMS implies that these assertions are true as well. If these assertions, even only some of them, are shown to be false, TMS itself must be false.

Some Orthodox Jews take issue with my premise and argue that TMS is very plausible. Others admit the implausibility of TMS but claim that it is still true. Others say that it is not possible to determine on rational or empirical grounds whether or not TMS is true. They accept its truth on faith, a faith that is not grounded in rational argument or empirical proof. I consider all of these approaches to be instances of clinging to an implausible belief in the face of powerful evidence against it.

A concise but very detailed summary of seven main lines of evidence against TMS and in support of the documentary hypothesis (the most widely accepted version of the MSPM thesis), based upon internal biblical analysis, is provided by Richard Elliott Friedman in his book *The Bible with Sources Revealed*.[1] I suggest that Orthodox Jews hold their Bible in one hand and Friedman's summary in the other, and follow the data and arguments he puts forth, item by item, proof by proof. If they do this, setting aside their preconceptions about authorship of the Pentateuch, I think many of them will be much less secure and assertive in their dogmatic affirmation of TMS.[2] Of course internal biblical analysis is only one of many lines of evidence and argument against TMS and in favor of MSPM.[3]

Who decides upon the criteria one should use in determining what is rational and plausible and what is irrational and implausible? The question is well formulated by the social theorist Lukes:

> When I come across a set of beliefs which appear *prima facie* irrational, what should my attitude be towards them? Should I adopt a critical attitude, taking it as a fact about the beliefs that they are irrational, and seek to explain how they came to be held, how they manage to survive unprofaned by rational criticism, what their consequences are, etc.? Or should I treat such beliefs charitably: should I begin from the assumption that what appears to me to be irrational may be interpreted as rational when fully understood in its context? More briefly, the problem comes down to whether or not there are alternative standards of rationality.[4]

I adopt both approaches. I define as irrational those religious beliefs that make assertions about history or nature that are contradicted by a preponderance of empirical evidence and/or are logically inconsistent. At the same time I accept the second attitude, to the extent of acknowledging that cultural, psychological, and ideological contexts can powerfully shape the religious believer's assessment of evidence and logic.

To determine the degree of rationality or plausibility of religious beliefs it would be useful for scholars of religion, psychologists, and philosophers to collaborate on developing a scale of measurement for assessing various religious claims and assertions. In the absence of such a scale, however, it seems to me, for example, that belief in the existence of God is more plausible (or less implausible) than belief in the specific claim that God revealed the Pentateuch to Moses in the thirteenth century BCE, in the Sinai wilderness, and hence that the laws, narratives, values, language, and so forth of the Pentateuch are of divine origin. This is why I am focusing on the implausibility of belief in TMS rather than on the belief in God, as I examine the tenacity of unreasonable beliefs.

As we have seen with the Kuzari argument, and will see more of later, many Orthodox Jews, modern and haredi, often appeal to reason in making their claim that *they* possess truth, and that believers in other religions, and nonbelievers, do not. They claim that their beliefs are more plausible or rational than those of Christians, Muslims, Mormons, and believers in all the other religions of the world. Given this appeal of theirs to reason rather than just to faith or religious intuition, rational criticism of their claims is especially appropriate, in addition to other justifications for subjecting religious beliefs and claims to rational scrutiny.

The phenomenon of clinging to implausible beliefs also occurs with certain academics or scientists who have strong vested interests, whether emotional, economic, or other, in a particular theory or point of view in their respective disciplines. Some proponents of secular ideologies, such as communism and psychoanalysis, have also manifested features of dogmatic fundamentalism by treating the works of Marx and of Freud as though they were inerrant sacred scriptures. Unlike fundamentalist Orthodoxy, however, the ethos of the world of academia and modern science, in principle at least, if not always in practice, is to remain open to revising, changing, or even discarding one's cherished theory if the arguments against it are logically and empirically compelling. Orthodoxies (Jewish or otherwise) assert that no evidence or argument can disprove their beliefs, which are immutable and eternal. This assertion of doctrinal immutability is often made notwithstanding the fact that a history of Orthodox doctrines will reveal significant changes over time, which is often not acknowledged as such by the contemporary believer who will retroject his current beliefs onto earlier authorities in the chain of tradition.

Some might accuse me of arrogance because I assume that I am more rational and intellectually honest than believers, at least with respect to the issue of belief in or rejection of TMS. I claim to reject TMS in favor of MSPM, based upon evidence and logic, whereas believers in TMS seem to ignore or deny evidence and arguments that I find compelling. Now, I know very well that many believers in TMS are much brighter than I am, and more knowledgeable than me in many areas of Jewish scholarship, science, and philosophy. Why then, I ask myself, do I reject TMS whereas they continue to believe in it? It is because I "face up" to the evidence and arguments against my early beliefs, rather than avoid addressing their full intellectual implications. If this is arrogance, it is not in assuming that I am "smarter" or know more than the believers, but in maintaining that I am more rational and intellectually honest than they are. Why, however, is this the case? Clearly, being very smart and knowledgeable is not the same thing as being rational and intellectually honest. Other factors come into play, as we shall see.

I want to understand why so many people with educational and socialization experiences similar to mine and equal or greater intelligence did not eventually reject Orthodox belief as I did. One way of explaining this phenomenon is to ascribe psychological and social motives for maintaining "implausible" beliefs to people who are otherwise very smart, knowledgeable, and rational in many areas of life.

In this vein, Robert A. Hinde (1999) writes the following:

> [W]hat is the basis of the ubiquity and persistence of religious systems? . . . The approach may boil down to an evaluation of religion, an enterprise which would seem both arrogant and absurd to the traditionally minded, who see no problem in the ubiquity of religious systems, except perhaps in their diversity. But, for those who regard transcendental explanation as inadequate, or feel that an appeal to supernatural explanations involves a sacrifice of intellectual integrity, the phenomena of religious observance must be aligned with what is known of other aspects of human psychological functioning.[5] (223)

People use the expression "I believe" in at least two different senses:(a) Some people mean that it is their opinion that the proposition about which they affirm their belief *asserts a fact or the occurrence of an event for which there is empirical evidence or logical proof;* (b) others who say "I believe" mean that *their personal experience or feeling informs them that the asserted fact is true or that the event occurred.* They do not claim that they can argue for its plausibility empirically or logically so as to convince others of the proposition in which they believe. Sometimes people are themselves unclear about what they mean. They may initially mean "I believe" in sense (b), but once having affirmed their belief they then go on to treat their belief as if it were of type (a), and, for example, expect others to affirm the belief as well.

Some people who believe in TMS do so in sense (a). They argue for its high level of plausibility using many different arguments or proofs, as we saw with the Kuzari argument. Not only do they believe the proposition of TMS, but they maintain that it can be proved.

If they are not aware of the evidence or arguments against it, or don't trust the sources or authority of those who bring that evidence, and if they trust the authority of those who teach TMS, then their belief in TMS is *psychologically* quite understandable. Even if their *logical reasoning* is flawed, but they are not aware of the flaws, and the flaws are not transparent, then although their belief may be *logically implausible,* it is not necessarily *psychologically implausible.*

My inquiry can be parsed into two related questions:

1. What are some of the emotional and social motives of the modern Orthodox for resisting the evidence and arguments against TMS and in favor of MSPM?
2. What are some of the psychological mechanisms and apologetics used by the modern Orthodox to enable them to hold on to the implausible dogma of TMS?

In analyzing these two questions I focus on the secularly educated modern Orthodox, Torah U'Madda community (Torah synthesized with Madda, i.e., with general secular knowledge) rather than on the "right-wing" Orthodox (haredi), anti-Madda group. My attempt to understand the motives for affirming implausible beliefs is most relevant to those individuals who have been exposed to evidence and argument against the belief, and may even struggle with it. This is much more the case with modern Orthodox Jews than with "right-wing" or "ultra," haredi Orthodox Jews. However, even many of the latter have had some exposure to modern challenges to the accuracy of the Bible from scholarship or science via the media or social interaction. Moreover, they are well aware of contradictions in the Bible, which could lead some of them to question its inerrancy and divinity (although they have sophisticated interpretive techniques dating as far back as two thousand years to resolve these contradictions).

"Modern" or "centrist" Orthodoxy isn't a well-defined and unambiguous sociological or theological category. I tend to use the terms in a broad sense, including, for the most part, individuals who affirm Orthodox (dox!) beliefs; consider halakha to be binding because its authority is divine, albeit as interpreted by rabbinic tradition; live an Orthodox lifestyle; and have an advanced secular education in the sciences (not restricted to mathematics, accounting, or computer science), humanities, academic Jewish studies, or professions like law and medicine. They maintain that many elements of general Western and American culture can enrich them religiously, for example, the pursuit of truth via philosophy and science. They claim to be open, indeed eager, to learn from all people who have wisdom and knowledge to impart, and to integrate these with their religious beliefs and commitments.

They participate in many general cultural activities, such as art, music, and theater. There are differences within this broad, catchall group, but it can be differentiated from much of the right-wing or haredi Orthodox (although among the latter, also, there are a good number who are secularly educated at the university level and beyond).[6] The haredi Orthodox do not see secular knowledge as a source of religious values, and when they engage in secular studies do so primarily for its instrumental worth of providing a profession or occupation with which to support oneself economically. They view Western art, music, theater, and literature as either a waste of time, or worse, as a threat to their religious values and way of life.

There has been of late some blurring of boundaries between modern and right-wing Orthodoxy. For example, the Union of Orthodox Jewish Congregations of America (http://www.ou.org) for decades had been associated with "centrist" or "modern" Orthodox Judaism. However, on their website there is a page on Jewish philosophy and belief with links to many essays on the websites of three other Orthodox organizations, at least two of which, Aish HaTorah and Ohr Somayach, are associated with "right-wing" Orthodoxy.

The Orthodox Rabbinical Council of America (RCA) emphasizes its "modern" or "centrist" Orthodox orientation (without using those terms) by its positive reference to secular studies and to its working, at the institutional level, with the entire Jewish community, including its synagogue organizations, presumably non-Orthodox as well as Orthodox. It also expresses its responsibility to the general society. These attitudes are not characteristic of right-wing Orthodoxy.

However, the RCA has collaborated with ArtScroll to publish a joint prayer book (Siddur). The ideology of ArtScroll, as reflected in its commentaries on the Bible and the Siddur is opposed to that of Torah U-Madda with respect to the value of secular and academic Jewish studies for the Orthodox Jew, especially at the university level. This, too, suggests blurring of the distinction between "right-wing" and "centrist" Orthodoxy.

Another modern Orthodox organization was *Edah* (now defunct). Its mission statement read as follows:

> The mission of *Edah* is to give voice to the ideology and values of modern Orthodoxy and to educate and empower the community to address its concerns . . . Fully committed to Torah, *halakhah* (Jewish law), and the quest for *kedushah* (holiness), *Edah* values open intellectual inquiry and expression in both secular and religious arenas; engagement with the social, political and the technological realities of

the modern world; the religious significance of the State of Israel; and the unity of *Klal Yisrael* (the Jewish people).

None of these modern or centrist Orthodox organizations openly and explicitly accept the basic approach and findings of modern biblical scholarship with respect to the origin and authorship of the Pentateuch. On the Edah Web site (http://www.edah.org/backend/coldfusion/display_main.cfm) one will find several articles by individuals, for example Tamar Ross and Barry Levy, who grapple with this issue to one degree or another; but Edah itself did not, to my knowledge, have the institutional courage to schedule major sessions at its national conferences, where the implications of biblical scholarship for Orthodox theology and halakhic commitment and change were addressed.

Although there are many similarities between the modern Orthodox and the haredi Orthodox in their beliefs and in the ways that they "protect" their beliefs, people in the haredi group are significantly less exposed to the evidence and arguments that would challenge their belief in TMS than are the modern Orthodox.[7] Therefore, it is less surprising that they affirm the traditional belief. They are either oblivious to the MSPM point of view or, in principle, reject the world of scholarship and science as reliable sources of insight and authority in matters that bear upon their religious beliefs.[8] However, people in the Torah U'Madda group, who accept and play by academic and scientific "rules of the game," are either aware of the details of the evidence and arguments against the TMS theory or at least know that the MSPM theory is the near universally held view among biblical and other scholars in academe.

Let us examine a few statements by modern Orthodox scholars about the nature of and grounds for their affirmation of TMS and their attitude toward the historical/critical or what is sometimes called the rational/scientific approach to the Pentateuch.

One scholar, aware that "most academic scholarship in Bible is conducted as if the fundamental tenets of Orthodox Judaism were false," describes these tenets, which he holds as "firm, unshakable convictions." He then writes the following:

> [I]t is held that failure to apply to Torah the same methods used in other academic disciplines ... constitutes an inconsistency. This argument is especially deployed against "highly regarded centrist *roshei yeshiva*" (rabbinic heads of yeshivot) who advocate the study of Western literature, philosophy and the like. When they insist that Torah is different from other disciplines they are accused of coming close to making a mockery of the entire enterprise ...

He argues in their defense:

[T]he argument makes sense if it means that what counts as truth and what counts as evidence is determined by the gatekeepers of a discipline, and that intellectual honesty requires us to forsake all knowledge that is not certified as part of the discipline we are studying at the moment. From a common sense perspective, however, inquiry that systematically ignores everything else we know (including the knowledge given us through revelation) is not honest. On the contrary: it is the height of perversity![9]

Another scholar writes the following:

We must study the biblical text with our open eyes and endeavor to respond to all of the problems with which it presents us ... On the other hand, we have axioms more precious to us than those of scholarship ... There are conclusions of scholarship which might come into conflict with some of those axioms ... when presuppositions and method lead to theologically difficult conclusions, we are left with *zarikh iyyun gadol* [the matter needs further intensive analysis], an uncomfortable, but not unprecedented posture ... the Orthodox graduate student or young scholar who feels a genuine urge to work in areas where the sets of presupposition clash [Orthodox belief and critical biblical scholarship] must be aware of the potential pitfalls, spiritual and academic, of such research. He or she must be prepared ... to conclude *zarikh iyyun gadol* [the matter needs further intensive analysis] or the equivalent, and to step back, spiritually whole.[10]

Similarly, another scholar, in defending the Torah U'Madda Orthodox philosophy and critiquing the anti-Madda Orthodox position, states that Torah U'Madda advocates should give "credence to science but insist ... on priority for Torah ... when push finally comes to shove and *madda* threatens inalienable Torah beliefs—for example, '*ikkarei emunah*' (fundamentals of faith) which resist any modification or reinterpretation. At all points everyone must be prepared to reject some of *madda*'s conclusions if necessary, even in the absence of a madda-based critique ..."[11]

Two other scholars who maintain that Orthodox intellectuals must study heretical works, which include modern biblical scholarship, also remind the reader that Orthodox Judaism does not permit a Jew to embrace heresy. In their defense of the Torah U'Madda philosophy they cite Maimonides in the *Sefer Ha-Mitzvot:*

We have been commanded not to exercise freedom of thought to the point of holding views opposed to those expressed in the Torah; rather, we must limit our thought by setting up a boundary where it must stop, and that boundary is the commandments and the injunctions of the Torah. This is the intent of the statement, "You shall not stray after your heart and after your eyes." In the language of the *Sifre,* "You shall not stray after your heart"—this refers to heresy . . . , and after your eyes"—this refers to licentiousness.

They then state the following:

Here the Rambam defines the biblical prohibition [of heresy] in terms of accepting heretical doctrine rather than entertaining thoughts with the potential of leading to such doctrine. It is no doubt true that if a person feels that the pursuit of a particular argument is seriously threatening his or her belief in what is clearly a cardinal principle of Judaism, there exists an obligation to take the intellectual equivalent of a cold shower, and the ruling in the *Mishnah Torah* underscores this obligation. Nonetheless, the fundamental prohibition is to embrace heresy . . .[12]

These scholars are not simply interpreting Maimonides, but accepting his formulation as obligatory. By taking "the intellectual equivalent of a cold shower," they mean that "if you feel you are in danger of coming to believe a heretical position, you may have to close the book" and engage in some other activities or distractions, and "go back to the disturbing book sometime later."[13] Given Maimonides' articulation of the Torah to Moses at Sinai doctrine in his cardinal principles of Jewish faith, he and they would forbid anyone to accept the validity of arguments against TMS, whatever their source. At the psychological point when argument or evidence against the dogma of TMS begins to seem overwhelming, one must turn away from the evidence or ideas and, I suppose, turn off or repress one's doubt so as not to embrace the convincing heretical view.[14] Indeed, one of the authors of this article recalls with gratitude how he as a youngster did just that, warding off heretical thoughts raised by the documentary hypothesis:

In my mid-teens, I experienced periods of perplexity and inner struggle while reading works of biblical criticism. While I generally resisted arguments for the documentary hypothesis with a comfortable margin of safety, there were moments of deep turmoil. I have a vivid recollection of standing at an outdoor *kabbalat Shabbat* [Friday evening prayer service] in camp overwhelmed with doubts and hoping that

God would give me the strength to remain an Orthodox Jew. What saved me was a combination of two factors: works that provided reasoned arguments in favor of traditional belief and the knowledge that to embrace the position that the Torah consists of discrete, often contradictory documents was to embrace not merely error but *apikorsut* [heresy].[15]

It seems to me that there is a psychological naïveté in the assumption that most *serious* Orthodox students (graduate or undergraduate) who, once being exposed in an academic setting to biblical scholarship, and as a result of such exposure, begin to question the Orthodox dogma or belief in TMS, can (or even should) squelch or suppress their doubts about the validity of the Orthodox belief by avoiding further reading or study in the area of biblical scholarship. I would surmise (and hope) that most Orthodox graduate students in Judaic studies are deeply committed to the pursuit of truth because of their acceptance of both the ethos of scholarship and the ethos of truth as a religious value. If so, they would be determined to explore in depth which explanation for the origins of the Torah is most plausible, TMS or MSPM, because they would consider the answer to this question to be central to the decisions they would be making about their most significant life commitments. They would not squelch their doubts about TMS that were raised by both biblical scholarship and by common sense. On the contrary, they would feel impelled to delve into biblical scholarship so that they could compare and contrast its explanations for the origins of the Torah with those of the rabbinic tradition.

One modern Orthodox philosopher affirms his belief that the Torah is the record of God's revelation to Moses while acknowledging that there are no rational grounds for such a belief: "Revelation is not a rational, but a supra-rational category . . . On the basis of reason I reject all revelation; on the grounds on which I accept revelation as a category of the supra-rational, I accept every word of the Torah as revealed, i.e. as having reached Moses from God, as the end-result of revelational experience."[16]

Mordechai Breuer, a prominent Orthodox Israeli Bible scholar, maintains the curious view that if the Pentateuch were a humanly authored document, then the views of biblical scholars that it is a composite work from multiple sources and different periods would be absolutely convincing. However, this is totally irrelevant to the Orthodox Jew, who knows that the Pentateuch was revealed by God to Moses and that God's style of writing and composition is not bound by the rules of human literary production.[17] Therefore, alternative, theologically acceptable explanations for the otherwise convincing evidence for the documentary hypothesis need to be generated.[18]

This is somewhat analogous to those in the right wing or haredi Orthodox world who argue that the fossils found by paleontologists—which would seem to prove that the world is considerably older than tradition says it is, and that species evolved rather than being created "off the shelf," so to speak—were deliberately placed by God in different strata of the earth so as to give the appearance of evolution. Why God did this is unclear, but one hypothesis is that he did so in order to test our faith in the truth of his Pentateuchal revelation that creation took place in seven days and included all animal and human species on the fifth and sixth days of that first week of the universe. Although "to test our faith" in the divine authorship of the Pentateuch is not Breuer's own explanation for why God wrote the Pentateuch such that it appears to have been authored over centuries by multiple humans, there is a formal and a psychological similarity between Breuer's acceptance of apparent multiple sources in the Pentateuch and haredi acknowledgment of the existence of dinosaur fossils. Both finally face the reality of disturbing facts (even for some fundamentalists, there are limits to how far denial can go) but insist on retaining traditional dogmas that are challenged by these very facts.

A propos of this line of reasoning, with respect to inferences from the findings of paleontology and geology, someone had posted the following on the Mada e-list of Jewish scientists: "With regards to the issue of the age of the universe this only proves that the world gives the appearance of great age; whether this appearance reflects reality is impossible to determine."

In response to which another scientist replied as follows:

It is also impossible to determine that the world was not created last Tuesday and we were all created with our memories intact [i.e., our memories of events that presumably occurred before last Tuesday are not evidence that they actually occurred since we may have been created only last Tuesday, but with these so-called "memories" of pre-Tuesday events implanted in our brains when we were created]. If you want to choose to be nihilistic about this you can have any universe you want. The conventional scientific argument assumes that physical laws have remained constant, a reasonable assumption since they have never been observed to change. You cannot disprove a 6000 year age universe, you cannot disprove a six hour age universe. However it seems perverse to me to give all these theories equal weight.[19]

Another scholar, though himself a Torah U'Madda adherent, is unconvinced by Breuer's argument that the reason why the Bible seems to be a composite of human documents is that God authored the Bible in a way that in effect makes it appear as such, but only to nonbelievers who analyze biblical texts by assuming that human literary conventions apply to them. Believers, however, do not necessarily apply such conventions to divinely authored texts, and hence they need not be upset by appearances to the contrary and can be assured that the Bible really has only one divine author. This scholar writes the following:

> Now a proposed solution to a problem is persuasive only to the extent that it can either be verified or falsified. What would persuade a rational observer that [the] proposed solution is either true or false? The answer, of course, is, nothing. Since [the] claim is that we do not know how divine writing works, it follows that we cannot know with certainty whether or not human literary conventions apply to divine documents...Since...[his] solution can neither be verified or falsified, his solution remains problematic and unconvincing. On such a slender reed, the Jew who confronts the modern study of the Bible will lean precariously if at all.[20]

Most people in the Torah U'Madda group who are willing to concede the problems posed by biblical scholarship and other disciplines for TMS defend their affirmation of TMS with terms such as *axiomatic; firm, unshakable convictions; insights from divine revelation; existential leaps of faith; inalienable Torah beliefs* and the like.

Why is it difficult for these modern Orthodox scholars to accept that for all of the respect and veneration they have for the traditions of Judaism, the tradition was wrong in its doctrine of TMS?

Part of the answer is that in general, beliefs are often affirmed even when they are highly implausible, irrational, or even absurd, because of their actual or presumed rewards for the individual and community who affirm and reinforce them. Moreover, the resistance to letting go of a belief, even in the face of strong evidence against it, is often due to the actual or imagined aversive effects of doing so, for the individual and the community. The believer is not always fully aware of these underlying fears and anxieties.

There are many rewards and positive reasons for "believing." Beliefs uphold a value system and bond a community. They also provide, for some, an "escape from freedom"—the freedom, often fraught with anxiety, of having to use one's own intelligence to make fundamental existential decisions about what one believes and how one will live. The believer can ignore, dismiss, or relate in a facile manner to the challenges of modern science and scholarship by assuming that the belief system, its religious norms, and its authoritative interpreters can appropriately and effectively respond to these challenges because the belief system is presumed to be ultimately grounded in the absolute truths of revelation. Even if the believer himself doesn't "know the answer" to a challenge, he assumes that the ideology does.

The social psychologist Jean-Pierre Deconchy, who has explored the relationships between orthodox belief systems and social control, points out that "every belief is an integral part of an individual or a social system outside of which it is hardly conceivable."[21]

Deconchy also notes the interesting phenomenon that "[a]mongst ideological systems, religious ideologies are probably the only ones which explicitly admit—even proclaim—the non-rationality of their essential beliefs" (422) as, for example, did the previously cited philosopher. Deconchy, in his study of dogmatic belief among Catholics is interested in "the characteristics of the sociocognitive field which enable these beliefs to remain 'tenable' despite their divergence from what is habitually referred to as 'rationality'" (429). He explores the relationships between the maintenance of irrational dogmatic beliefs and the degree and nature of social control exercised by the Catholic Church.

Although processes of social control are surely relevant to dogmatic belief in Orthodox Judaism, this is more so in the haredi communities than in modern Orthodox ones. Judaism today does not have an official, centralized, powerful, authoritarian hierarchy whose representatives can exercise a high degree of social control over doctrinal deviance. However, in haredi communities, the authority of the Hasidic *rebbe,* or of a prominent Torah scholar who heads a yeshiva, though unofficial, is still widely recognized and respected. His views on doctrinal and ideological issues influence his constituents, who in turn can monitor expressions of doubt by individuals and apply painful social sanctions against those who stray, not only in behavior but in thought as well. In the modern Orthodox community, the authority of even a distinguished rabbi is weak, especially with respect to doctrinal matters (in contrast with halakhic ones). In the modern Orthodox community, *psychological* factors play a more critical role in maintaining implausible beliefs, such as the belief in TMS, although these factors, too, are often related to informal, though not intense, social/communal pressures.

The fear of facing biblical scholarship is evident in the previously quoted attempt to squelch incipient doubt. Indeed, some prominent Torah U'Madda scholars, among them professors in Jewish studies, have advised university level and graduate students not to take courses in Bible lest they be exposed to the heresies of modern scholarship.[22] I suppose that they are unaware of the inherent contradiction between what they profess and do as academics and the advice they offer their students. They are also perhaps unaware of the futility of trying to suppress readily accessible knowledge, or of the conceptual, intellectual, and methodological links between their fields of specialization and the fields of biblical studies, philosophy, and other TMS-challenging disciplines.

Fear is reflected in the following comment, by a modern Orthodox critic of Breuer, about the need to be extremely cautious in dealing with this "dangerous" field of study:

> Orthodoxy owes a genuine debt of gratitude to [Breuer] for agreeing to address a very sensitive issue, namely the documentary hypothesis. He walks bravely where angels fear to tread...undoubtedly, risks abound with regard to the critical study of the Bible...Distinctions need to be made, perhaps, between private study and public discourse...between adults with no background in Jewish study and the mature rabbinic scholar who has "filled his belly" with *Shas* [Talmud] and *Poskim* [codes of Jewish law based upon the Talmudic-rabbinic tradition].[23]

Actually, this critic of Breuer is himself ambivalent about how to approach biblical scholarship for which he, like Breuer, seems to have much respect. He concludes his paper by saying that it is suicidal for Orthodoxy not to grapple honestly with the challenges of biblical scholarship to traditional belief in TMS.

––––––

What are some of the real or imagined adverse consequences that a modern Orthodox Jew may fear if he or she were to cease to believe in TMS and accept MSPM in its stead? Before, however, considering the fear that loss of belief may entail, it is essential to note that a primary motive for maintaining belief in TMS is the profound love that so many Orthodox people have for Orthodox tradition and for the Orthodox community, its values, its beauty, and its way of life. All of these are intimately linked to and guided by the Torah and its rabbinic interpretations and elaborations over several millennia. For most Orthodox Jews, belief in TMS lies at the core of their commitment to a life guided by Torah and enriched by it.

Giving up belief in TMS can be very painful, especially if one declares it publicly. Among its consequences can be loss of existential meaning and purpose, denial of one's past, the shattering of one's core self-identity, guilt, shame, disruption of family stability and relationships, social ostracism, and loss of professional or financial standing. This is especially the case for individuals who have invested their best energies in studying Torah or in teaching, preaching, and educating others in the faith. The more intensely one was committed to the dogma, the harder it is to admit that it is false.

With respect to the fear of social ostracism that an Orthodox individual might experience if he were to pursue academic biblical scholarship, Barry Levy writes the following:

> The Orthodox Bible student who chose to continue his education in a non-Jewish institution (or, even worse, from the popular perspective, in a non-Orthodox Jewish one) risked being disenfranchised and isolated from his community—*which remains a serious threat* [my emphasis]. And even if he completed his studies without leaving the fold, the risk of *de facto* excommunication was ever present, because in the final analysis, the assumptions of Bible scholarship are perceived by the Orthodox community to be foreign and hostile to its interests.
>
> As an observant Jew in his private life, the Orthodox Bible scholar . . . would seek to be part of an active, observant community, to worship in synagogues that welcome him, and to educate his children in schools that satisfy his religious and intellectual needs. But the North American Orthodox community and most of its constituent institutions have not favoured—more accurately, they often openly opposed—the involvement of anyone who shares the academic interests of the Bible scholar. All too frequently he is libeled privately and insulted publicly by his clerical rabbinic colleagues . . .[24]

In *Commentary*'s 1966 symposium "The State of Jewish Belief," the first part of the first question was, "In what sense do you believe the Torah to be divine revelation?"[25]

In a personally revealing and honest acknowledgment of the psychological grounds for his arational belief in *Torah min-ha-shamayim* (Torah from Heaven, i.e., TMS), Marvin Fox, a leader of the Torah U'Madda camp, responded as follows:

> I believe in the traditional doctrine of Torah min ha-shamayim, the teaching that the Torah is divine . . . No one can reasonably claim to understand how God reveals Himself to man. The very idea of revelation leads us to paradoxes which defy rational explanation . . . Yet we affirm in faith what we cannot explicate, for our very humanity is at stake. I believe, because I cannot afford not to believe. I believe, as a Jew, in the divinity of Torah, because without God's Torah I have lost the ground for making my own life intelligible and purposeful.[26]

A fear related to this fear of loss of meaning, and one that may be objectively true for many Orthodox today, is that to give up their beliefs may deny them the spiritual fulfillment for which they yearn. This is especially so for those who have been taught that there are no avenues for meaningful and authentic spirituality for Jews outside of Orthodoxy.

Some of the painful existential and emotional consequences of loss of faith are analyzed by Mintz in his book *Banished from Their Father's Table: Loss of Faith and Hebrew Autobiography:*

> The turning point in the biographies of these young writers is the moment of apostasy: the sudden realization that the received belief in the God of Israel—and therefore the authority of the Torah and the commandments—is no longer possible . . . The pathos of this event is underscored by the origins of these young men. Typically, they originated from the most devout and scholarly circles of Jewish society, and many distinguished themselves as child prodigies of Talmudic learning in whom the pride and resources of family and community were heavily invested . . . the experience of apostasy became . . . cruelly desolating.[27] It was not so much that the world of faith had been purposefully rejected but that at a certain point its plausibility had simply collapsed. The world that had once been thick with symbols and texts, sacred times and covenanted obligations, providential signs and redemptive promises, was, suddenly, not there. What had been lost, moreover, even if it was no longer tenable, was also no longer replaceable. . . . This intellectual and metaphysical negation was deepened by the loneliness that resulted from the break with family and community.[28]

Similarly, the nineteenth-century French philosopher Jouffroy describes the emotional impact of his loss of faith in Catholicism:

> This moment was a frightful one; and when towards morning I threw myself exhausted on my bed, I seemed to feel my earlier life, so smiling and so full, go out like a fire, and before me another life opened, sombre and unpeopled, where in future I must live alone, alone with my fatal thought which had exiled me thither, and which I was tempted to curse. The days which followed this discovery were the saddest of my life.[29]

The awareness that heresy can result in such pain and loneliness can deter the would-be heretic from admitting his heresy, even to himself, and from objectively weighing the evidence and arguments for the heretical view.

The Orthodox community's lifestyle, which is structured around halakha, is built upon the doctrine of TMS. Although some halakhically committed theologians and biblical scholars, such as Louis Jacobs,[30] Jon Levenson,[31] Baruch Schwartz,[32] James Kugel,[33] and maybe Abraham Heschel[34] have argued or demonstrated that halakhic commitment can be maintained without affirming TMS, this view does not prevail in the Torah U'Madda camp, which fears that if members of the Orthodox community lose their belief in TMS, this will eventually destroy the community. There is an assumption—perhaps justifiable—that the very existence and cohesiveness of the community depends upon the shared belief of its members in TMS and the halakhic imperatives and rabbinic authority that it and only it confers.

What are some of the other fears and anxieties attendant upon acknowledging that TMS is false?

First, the Orthodox have been socialized to revere and deeply empathize with the heroes and martyrs of the Jewish past who went so far as to sacrifice their lives for the sake of their faith in TMS and traditional Judaism. To deny the truthfulness of a core traditional belief is experienced as mocking or denigrating the sacred past (which has shaped the present individual's personality) and to render heroic acts filled with suffering and sacrifice as futile and meaningless in retrospect.

This compelling sense of betrayal of one's ancestors or relatives, and devaluation of their sacrifices, isn't mollified by a realization that the belief system that rendered the martyrs heroic, and which gave meaning to their lives and deaths, was significant for them, whether or not it is accepted now. Although our current disbeliefs don't retroactively affect the meanings that religious beliefs had for our parents, grandparents, and ancestors in the past, we may still feel deeply uncomfortable when we question the truthfulness of those beliefs for which they died.

This powerful and complex emotion, which feeds on an apprehension of prospective guilt or painful unease, is, of course, not a rational argument for the truth of the belief in TMS, but a psychological explanation for why it is so difficult for some believers to give it up.

An analogous situation might be that of a committed secular Zionist who fervently believed that it was noble to die in defense of the State of Israel, and who lost a child in one of Israel's wars. If he were to become a radical "post-Zionist" and question the justice and legitimacy of Israel's right to exist as a sovereign Jewish state, he might then feel that the "sacrifice" of his child on the altar of Zionism was not justifiable and that his child's death was devoid of any "redemptive" existential meaning. During the phase of thinking about whether or not to accept the claims of post-Zionism, the father would probably be strongly inclined to resist those claims because of a liminal awareness—not always surfacing to full consciousness—that to do so would undermine the consolation for and the justification of the loss of his child that his fervent Zionist beliefs provided.

Second, for some there is the fear of what they might do if they lost their faith in TMS. Will I become immoral and unethical? Sometimes this fear may be based on reality. This would be the case when the Orthodox Jew's moral behavior is indeed based upon and primarily sustained by the belief that the moral and ethical rules to which he subscribes are of divine origin, and that were these rules demonstrated to be of human origin they would no longer bind him. *Some* Orthodox educators teach that Orthodox belief is necessary in order for someone to be ethical, moral, and in control of one's baser instincts. This is especially the case with the haredi or right-wing Orthodox. Although most members of the modern Orthodox community interact regularly with non-Orthodox Jews and with non-Jews, and as such are well aware of the capacity of all people for moral and ethical values and behaviors, they too often tolerate the fact that many of the teachers of Jewish studies in modern Orthodox day schools in the United States are not themselves modern, but are right-wing Orthodox. The negative attitudes of these teachers toward the values and norms of non-Orthodox Jews and Gentiles are transmitted to children from modern Orthodox homes, who will sometimes internalize them and believe that ethics and morality are rare without Orthodox beliefs, which in turn will make them fear rejecting those beliefs. Similar attitudes, and consequences for inhibiting doubts about TMS exist among *some* of the religious Zionist Orthodox in Israel, namely those who are not respectful of secular Jews and proclaim that they are bereft of moral and ethical values.[35]

Even though many Orthodox Jews are moral or ethical, and temperate in their passions, for reasons and factors that are not dependent on their dogmatic beliefs, they may not be aware that this is the case. Furthermore, the Orthodox often teach that heresy does not really result from rational considerations. Its true, underlying motives are the desire to sin, to be licentious and so forth. The reasons offered for heresy by the heretic, they say, are only rationalizations and cover-ups for his real evil motives, whether conscious or unconscious. Therefore, the Orthodox Jew who is struggling with heretical thoughts will fear that giving in to heresy will be the first step in the eruption of his base impulses.

Third, because the belief in TMS links the individual to his family, giving up the belief might hurt family members, create friction and guilt, and weaken family ties or cut the "denier" off from his or her family entirely.

This, too, is often the actual consequence of admitting to family members that one no longer believes in TMS or other Orthodox dogmas. This is not, of course, always the case. There are many Orthodox families who continue to maintain loving ties and bonds between family members irrespective of what their faith/belief choices have been. This latter response is more the case with Sephardim[36] and Yemenites than with Orthodox Jews of Eastern European Ashkenazi origin.

In his autobiographical novel *Whither*, M. Z. Feierberg describes the anguish of the protagonist, Nahman, who right after Kol Nidre has publicly violated the solemn day of Yom Kippur by extinguishing a candle in full view of his saintly and beloved father and the entire traditional community gathered in the synagogue:

> Why had he blown out the candle? The thought of it depressed him terribly. How could he have brought such disgrace, such everlasting shame, upon his father, who was dearer to him than life itself? Cain had killed Abel, his brother, but he had killed his own father! Ah, what a dreadful thought . . . but had he really wanted to do it? No, he felt as though he had been forced to blow out the candle against his will . . . But . . . why must he profane what was holy to so many people?[37]

The wider the phenomenon of "heresy," the more "tolerable" to devout family members it might become. Twenty or so years ago it would have been shameful in the modern Orthodox religious Zionist community in Israel, to acknowledge that one's son or daughter was a *hozer bi'she'ayla*, one who questions the validity of Orthodoxy, or a *datlash*, a *dati leshe'avar*, a "formerly religious person." Nowadays, parents openly commiserate with one another about the "problem" or the phenomenon, and conferences are convened to discuss it because it has become so frequent that it cannot be swept under the rug. Nonreligious teens and adults who were raised in modern Orthodox families are much less frequently "banished from their father's table" than they were in the past, although there still are many instances of family rupture because of differences over religious belief. Moreover, I surmise that as the phenomenon becomes more prevalent, and given that parents usually love and respect their children, they will perceive and respond to their child's questioning or "deviant" point of view in a more respectful manner than traditional Judaism allowed.

Similar processes operate in the American modern Orthodox community. This does not mean that the child's "heresy" is not painful to the parent (or to religious siblings), but that it is better tolerated. The nature of the parent-child relationship in these cases is very much influenced by the personalities of both, and by the ways in which each is or is not sensitive to the feelings of the other. It is one thing for a child to say that he no longer believes in TMS. It is quite another for him to say that because he doesn't believe in TMS, he will turn on the TV in the living room of his observant parents' home on Shabbat. In fact, many parents are more concerned about their child's public behavior, and what message it conveys about his affiliation with the Orthodox community in which he was socialized and in which they live, than about private "beliefs" he might have, heretical as they might be, but which do not result in changed public behavior. Of course, this is a very non-Maimonidean approach to the importance of beliefs and doctrines in defining one's human worth and virtue. Many Orthodox Jews are not Maimonideans on this issue. However, notwithstanding the increasing tolerance of heresy, the heretic still causes pain and might feel ostracized and guilty.

Fourth, denying TMS will alienate one from the community of believers with whom one is deeply bonded and which provides social support and friendship. This too will often actually happen. However, many modern Orthodox communities follow a "don't ask, don't tell" policy. As long as you keep your heretical beliefs to yourself and publicly behave in a halakhically acceptable manner, you can be part of the community. Barry Levy, a thoughtful member and observer of a modern Orthodox community in Montreal, writes about the spheres of belief and of behavior:

> Despite the difficulties, Orthodox Jews have completed doctorates in Bible and pursued professional careers in this area; their thinking may indeed differ from that of some other Orthodox Jews. Sometimes they offer private admissions that their religious beliefs do not correspond fully with their religious behaviors. While accepting the legitimacy of critical attempts to explain the Bible, they refrain from applying their implications to their religious lives, thereby compartmentalizing the two spheres. They give each full rein in its designated area but do not allow them to interact. This position resembles somewhat the interrelationship of professional and religious life that one might expect of Orthodox plumbers or mailmen.[38]

Fifth, those who have jobs that involve the socialization of others into Orthodox Judaism, such as rabbis and educators, may rightly fear that if they were publicly to state their beliefs, they might be fired. In this case they do not necessarily fear the implications of heretical belief per se, but of its becoming public knowledge. At times, though, this will result in pressure on closet heretics holding public communal, rabbinical, or educational positions in the Orthodox community, to publicly state one thing while believing another. This can result in an erosion of one's sense of integrity and intellectual and emotional honesty.

Some of these five fears are based upon real consequences, whereas others may be exaggerated, and the feared aversive consequences of giving up the belief in TMS may not be inevitable. But for fears to influence what we think and how we behave, they do not have to be based upon reality.

As I said, sometimes the fears cause the doubter or heretic to conceal his doubts or heresies only from family or community, not to deny them to himself. However, often the fears are so powerful that they cause the incipient doubter to suppress his doubts or avoid exposure to evidence or arguments that would threaten the Orthodox belief such as TMS. Often the more one is threatened by counterevidence, the more fervently he will labor to convince himself and others of the truth of the dogma being challenged.

An aspect of this process is described by Moshe Leib Lilienblum in his autobiography:

> I absolutely did not want to be an *apikoros* (heretic), and when in my heart there arose a doubt about the truthfulness of some statement in the Talmud...I forced my intellect to believe [the Talmudic statement].... My mind was like a printing house in which one prepares for publication many free, uncensored ideas in order to resolve problems. However, prior to their seeing the light of day these ideas stand in judgment before the censor who decides which can go forth and which cannot... All of my intellectual powers were constantly trying to resolve the questions that burdened me oppressively. However, before I reached a final decision on my own about these matters I deferred to the authority of the Talmud or Maimonides.[39]

Given all of these fears attendant upon loss of faith, a proponent of Torah U'Madda Orthodoxy, sensing that he was wavering in his faith, would probably erect a strong set of psychological defenses to prevent the heresy from gaining a firm foothold in his consciousness in the first place. And if he eventually became convinced of the truth of MSPM, he would have difficulty admitting publicly to the repudiation of his earlier belief in TMS.

What defense mechanisms do the Orthodox employ to counter the powerful evidence and arguments against TMS that support MSPM?

Several approaches are taken by Orthodox believers.

1. As I said earlier, many will deny that their belief is implausible. An example of this approach is the book by Kelemen, *Permission to Receive* (1996).

Kelemen, interestingly, tries to prove that it is not implausible, and that it is indeed plausible, to believe in TMS. His audience seems to be people from the yeshiva world who have had some exposure to biblical scholarship and have come to question whether their Orthodox belief in TMS is implausible or irrational. Kelemen is defensive rather offensive. He is saying to his reader that you don't have to be ashamed about asserting your belief in TMS. He is superficially respectful of academic biblical scholarship and tries to use (very selectively) its views to bolster his argument. His logic is very flawed, but his stance is interesting for someone from the yeshiva world.

Some apologists for TMS attempt to discover secret codes in the Torah, which allegedly prove its divine origin.[40]

2. They may challenge the evidence against their belief and claim that the evidence for the alternative is weak. They will often disparage the disciplines and methods used in the academic study of bible and comparative religion.

Thus, for example, one of the most influential thinkers in the Torah U'Madda world wrote the following in the *Commentary* symposium:

> Higher Criticism is far indeed from an exact science. The startling lack of agreement among scholars on any one critical view;...the many revisions that archaeology has forced upon literary critics; and the unfortunate neglect even by Bible scholars of much first-rate scholarship in modern Hebrew supporting the traditional claim of Mosaic authorship—all these reduce the question of Higher Criticism from the massive proportions it has often assumed to a relatively minor and manageable problem that is chiefly a nuisance but not a threat to the enlightened believer.[41]

3. They may employ ad hominem arguments against the proponents of the competing, challenging belief, for example, accusing academic biblical scholars of being blinded by their evil inclinations, being anti-Semites, or being self-hating Jews. They will often assert that academic biblical scholars are unfamiliar with traditional rabbinic and medieval Jewish exegesis (which is sometimes the case, but there are numerous others who are fully versed in rabbinic and medieval biblical interpretation). If, say the believers, the biblical critics were aware of the traditional approaches to bible study, they would accept Torah to Moses at Sinai.

In doing so they ignore that although it is true that prior to the mid-twentieth century many leading Christian biblical scholars, such as Wellhausen and Eichrodt, were anti-Semitic and/or disparagers of Juaism, the Christian biblical critics applied their methods of analysis to the New Testament as well as to the Hebrew Bible. Jon Levenson has noted, "[The] fact that historical criticism has undermined Christianity no less than Judaism . . . is too often ignored [by Jewish critics of modern biblical scholarship]."[42] Also, many archaeologists whose findings challenge the historical accuracy of biblical accounts, and indirectly the theory of TMS, actually were motivated by a desire to corroborate the historical accuracy of the Bible and to support traditional doctrines rather than to discover evidence against them. Moreover, a good number of contemporary biblical scholars who take for granted the MSPM theory are strongly identifying, halakhically practicing, self-loving Jews.

4. TMS believers will often argue that the consequences of their belief system are positive whereas those of the alternative beliefs are negative. For example, they will claim that to deny TMS will destroy morality, weaken Jewish identity, and lead to the assimilation of Jews and to the demise of Judaism.

This assertion of mine about modern Orthodoxy might be countered with the claim that modern Orthodox leaders respect the non-Orthodox rabbinate and recognize vitality outside of Orthodoxy. Moreover, a critic might say that modern Orthodox academics for the most part have a sufficiently broad vision of the state of the Jewish people to realize that denial of TMS does not spell the death of Jewish life. After all, they know that non-Orthodox denominations of Judaism, which do not believe in TMS, have existed for more than a century and continue to serve major segments of the Jewish population. Their concern about preserving belief in TMS is not out of a fear of the demise of Judaism, broadly construed, but out of a fear of the weakening of the Orthodox Jewish community.[43]

My response to this criticism is to ask, in what sense do modern Orthodox leaders "respect the non-Orthodox rabbinate"? Do they consider the non-Orthodox understandings and practice of Judaism to be valid or merely a lesser of two evils—better to be a religious non-Orthodox Jew than to be a nonreligious Jew?

I think that modern Orthodoxy—if it is truly Orthodox in belief and in halakhic commitment—sees non-Orthodox denominations of Judaism, and, of course, a strictly cultural Judaism, as "false" but preferable to other possibilities, such as assimilation. If one believes in TMS and in traditional rabbinic Judaism, as modern Orthodoxy claims to do, then almost by definition those who do not accept the binding and ultimate authority of the Torah and of traditional halakha are in error and may be sinners. To argue, as some do, that not only the followers, but the leaders as well, of non-Orthodox denominations, are in the category of "infants taken captive among the idolaters" (*tinokot shenishbu*), in other words, those who have never been adequately exposed to the "truths" on which Orthodox Judaism is based, is disingenuous. So if the leaders and rabbis are aware of the beliefs and practices of Orthodoxy and still reject them, they are either in error or sinners—although sinners who also do many good things in that they may act as a deterrent to assimilation.[44] Some elements of modern Orthodoxy are still grappling with the degree to which they can accept non-Orthodox and nonreligious forms of Jewish identity and commitment as being "legitimate." On its Web site, the relatively new modern Orthodox rabbinical seminary Yeshivat Chovevei Torah (YCT) includes in its mission statement the following: "Promotion of *Ahavat Yisrael* (love of the Jewish people) in the relationship to all Jews and of respectful interaction of all Jewish movements."

However, YCT represents only the liberal segment of the modern Orthodox community but not all of the community. Moreover, given its commitment to TMS and to the authority of halakha, its dogmas will limit participation in nonhalakhic prayer and certain ritual performances. It and some other modern Orthodox Jews may "respect" the non-Orthodox and recognize their vitality—indeed, they may even acknowledge that modern Orthodoxy can learn aspects of Jewish spirituality from them—but the respect does not yet accord validity to the view of a rabbi who denies TMS.[45]

How essential, if at all, is an Orthodox belief system in maintaining worthwhile Jewish communities in the United States that will perpetuate themselves?

To be more specific, what are the necessary and sufficient conditions or ingredients for establishing and sustaining local Jewish communities that have the following characteristics?

- Its members are committed (as demonstrated in practice and in allocation of resources) to the significant study of Jewish literature and thought from the Hebrew Bible to contemporary writings (preferably, but not necessarily, including a commitment to study the Hebrew language).
- Its members practice a significant number of rituals rooted in and continuous with (but not precluding adaptations of) Jewish tradition.
- Its members constitute a strongly bonded, cohesive group of individuals and families who engage in ongoing mutual support and friendship throughout the life cycle, sharing its joys, rites of passage, and sorrows.
- Its members are caring, charitable, and compassionate toward one another and, to a lesser but significant degree, to Jews and to non-Jews elsewhere, especially those in need.

- The members of the group succeed in socializing their children to identify strongly as Jews, allowing for a variety of expressions of such Jewish identity, but all of which include at their core a high level of Jewish "literacy," ethics, and a sense of social responsibility.
- The members succeed in having their children choose to marry other Jews.
- The members succeed in having their married children join (or establish) local Jewish communities that have these same seven characteristics.

What beliefs/doctrines/dogmas are necessary to generate communities of the above kind? I admit that I do not have the answers to this question, but the claim that Orthodox dogma is a necessary condition needs to be explored empirically by sociologists who study Jewish religious communities and by historians of modern Jewry, and not be asserted as a self-evident truth.

5. As we saw before, some Orthodox, modern as well as right-wing, will avoid exposing themselves to the evidence and the arguments of scholarship. There is awareness that exposure might generate doubt and because the consequences of doubt can be dangerous and painful, it is better to remain ignorant of the counterevidence and competing theories. Some TMS believers will appeal to the authority of Torah sages whose views, for them, have greater weight than the findings and theories of professors in matters of belief.

Sternberg's comment, in his article analyzing the history of rabbinic responses to medical and scientific findings that contradict assumptions about medicine and science that are the basis for Talmudic halakha, is illuminating:

A third position taken by many Halakhic authorities is one of denial—to refuse to accept scientific statements (even quite standard ones) if they flatly contradict Talmudic doctrines which have Halakhic implications . . . As this denial might seem strange . . . we should pause a moment to understand what is involved. Science as a whole is a belief system, to the extent that it depends on trust, in the sense that no one individual can understand all the arguments from the first principles or reproduce the basic experiments which constitute scientific evidence for even the most fundamental and universally accepted tenets in most fields . . . The man in the street has no more direct experience with bacteria or quarks or buckyballs than he has with demons or the evil eye or astrology. To choose one system over another is ultimately an act of faith for most people. For someone reared entirely in the

Yeshiva world, the Talmud and its commentators represent the ultimate authority. Hence when there is a direct challenge to the veracity of statements of *Hazal* [rabbinic sages of the Talmudic period], especially when these statements have direct halakhic consequences, it is easy to understand how one may choose to deny the scientist's claims.[46]

6. TMS believers will assert that there are limits to what we can know or infer from reason and empirical evidence. This, of course, is quite true. But the point at which they will introduce this claim is not necessarily the point at which evidence and reason *can't* be plausibly applied but rather the point at which plausible evidence and reason become compelling arguments against TMS.

———

Does belief in TMS and related Orthodox doctrines have any negative *intellectual* consequences?

I think that it does. *This is not to deny the many highly positive ethical, spiritual, and social consequences of Orthodox belief and doctrine.* My focus, here, however, is on the *intellectual problems* that I think are engendered from the belief in TMS and by the mechanisms used to defend the belief in modern Orthodox education and socialization. The first of these is the dilution of commitment to the scientific, philosophical, and religious value of pursuit of truth and the related use of a distorted, contorted logic and apologetic. I am not suggesting that modern Orthodox scientists or scholars are any less competent or intellectually and scientifically rigorous *in their own fields of expertise* than their colleagues in those fields. I am referring rather to dilution of commitment to the pursuit of truth and to the distortion of logic in the study and evaluation of the Bible, and sometimes of other aspects of the study of Judaism as well, such as the history of the development of the Oral Law, and to the apologetics involved in attempting to reconcile the Bible with various scientific, geological, and archaeological findings or ancient Near Eastern texts.[47]

I also have in mind the educational consequences of the Orthodox approach for the ways in which their children will learn to think about religious and moral questions. The attempt to suppress serious exposure to biblical scholarship is futile with respect to young people who are intelligent, intellectually curious, and who take seriously the professed Orthodox belief in the value of *emet*—truth. Although some modern Orthodox day schools do expose their students to biblical scholarship, with a traditional "spin," the bright student will sooner or later see the spin for what it is—an attempt to indoctrinate rather than to educate—and he or she may become bitter at his teachers and school for underestimating his intelligence. Many Orthodox day schools do not even acknowledge the world of biblical scholarship despite the fact that their students are spending years studying the Hebrew Bible. Every so often these youth will encounter in the mass media, in their private reading, or later, in a college course references to and findings of biblical scholarship that contradict what they have been taught in their Orthodox day school. The attempt to discourage an honest confrontation with biblical scholarship in the case of college-age students is even more futile—again, at least for those young men and women who have internalized the value of truth and honesty in intellectual pursuits.

I do not mean to idealize university education or biblical scholarship as paragons of the objective pursuit of truth and of intellectual honesty. All human pursuits are fallible and tainted by subjective considerations and biases, often unconscious. Scholarship and science, however, for all of their flaws, at least attempt to make us more aware of these biases and to exercise control over them, and it is in the universities that these attempts take place, not in the confessional yeshiva with its certainties about divine revelation. The modern Orthodox send their children to university, and it is in the universities where critical biblical scholarship is pursued. I assume that the development of critical thinking skills is one of the goals of sending children to college, and it is to be expected, indeed hoped for, that they will acquire and apply these skills to matters of existential importance, such as the nature of one's religious commitments and spiritual world view, which, in Judaism, are impacted by one's views about the authorship, and hence the authority, of the Torah.[48]

In addition, the dogmatic, fundamentalist approach to the Pentateuch precludes from most modern Orthodox the possibility of understanding the true origins and development of the religion of ancient Israel and even of later Judaism.

Many of the modern Orthodox apply different criteria when making academic or scientific truth claims than they do when making claims about religious beliefs. Of them I ask, at what point do you switch from the scientific domain with its criteria to the religious domain with its criteria? And if religious affirmations are of an intrinsically different nature than scientific or scholarly ones, with the former not being subject to the same criteria of plausibility assessment or verification as are the latter, is it not inappropriate for someone to make a religious affirmation and then argue that it tells us objective "truths" about history, psychology, biology, cosmology, or other sciences?

Is the modern Orthodox affirmation that God revealed the Torah to Moses at Sinai a statement about an alleged objective historical occurrence, in which case it should be subjected to the criteria for plausibility that are applied by the modern Orthodox to other statements about historical events. Or is it a subjective affirmation that it is important and meaningful to the believer that he or she believe in TMS, but with cognizance that the belief is not subject to falsification or verification by the methods of science, scholarship, or philosophy? If the latter is admitted to be the case, then how can the modern Orthodox maintain that their belief is the only true and "authentic" one, which in principle all Jews (and indeed, all humans) are obligated to affirm, and that those who do not affirm it and the commandments (*mitzvot*) that follow from it, should, *at least in principle,* be punished, as mandated by the Bible and by rabbinic law?[49] After all, what may be subjectively meaningful to modern Orthodox Jews may not be so to others, who may have their own subjectively meaningful belief systems, or even none at all.

———

In presentations of my critique of modern Orthodoxy at various venues some people have been offended by my designation of modern Orthodox belief in TMS as "unreasonable." Others claim that I am ignoring the essential nature of belief, which is beyond the rational. For example, a prominent ethnographer of Orthodox Judaism wrote the following:

> I am moved to point out that [Schimmel's] call to believers to justify their belief in divine revelation at Sinai on rational or reasonable grounds misses the basic element of belief. As in the old maxim: Believe not what is, believe what is absurd. Beliefs of this sort are by their very nature beyond the rational...But of course, the case Schimmel cites is but one of many. He could have easily chosen any other set of religious beliefs held by otherwise rational people and asked the believers to reassess their faith in light of reason. And why? The "belief" in reason seems no less a dogma than any other. Reason cannot save us; it has not so far.[50]

I do not agree with this critic that most Orthodox Jews, modern or haredi, maintain that their belief in TMS is based primarily on "faith" or the "absurd" and not on "reason," as I have discussed earlier and elsewhere in the book. The appeal to faith is often a secondary claim, introduced when the logic of their appeal to reason is challenged.

One passionate correspondent said that my view is an affirmation of a nihilistic scientific materialistic bleak view of a godless, purposeless life:

[T]here is no room for God in the world of contemporary science. Certainly, the dogmas of modern biology preclude the existence of God.

. . . [H]umankind's existence is a lonely accident, a freak of nature, and we toil in an existential loneliness with meaning coming only from what we are able to invest in our lives. Our emotions are merely discrete neurotransmitter-induced brain states, and there is nothing before our lives and nothing after. It is no more rational to believe in God than it is to believe in Torah miSinai [TMS]. For the Orthodox scientist . . . science as a belief system is accepted neither uncritically nor absolutely, and a belief in God and Torah are accepted as part of a religious faith experience. I wonder if Dr. Schimmel is prepared to affirm the bleak view of life and of a Godless universe demanded by contemporary science . . .[51]

I regularly grapple with the moral and emotional implications of loss of religious faith. As I wrote earlier, I am acutely aware of the pain of loss of faith and meaning as I myself experienced it after many years of studying in yeshivot and being a firm believer in Orthodox teachings. This is why I feel that Orthodox, indeed, all religious thinkers, should be working on developing theologies that are responsive to the intellectual and spiritual challenges raised by modern science rather than engaging in avoidance behavior, sticking their head in the sand and clinging to beliefs that are no longer tenable in their traditional formulations. The challenges posed by the natural and the social sciences, and by biblical scholarship, to religion in general and Orthodoxy in particular derive primarily not from some malicious, dogmatic conspiracy of science and scholarship against religion, but from the hard earned findings of these disciplines.

———

Let me digress to consider a broader question: What are some of the ways in which apparent or real conflicts between modern science and premodern Judaism, or traditional Judaism in its modern expression, can be and have been addressed? The Association of Orthodox Jewish Scientists (AOJS) was established in 1948 with one of it purposes being to resolve apparent conflicts between science and Orthodox Judaism, and it has organized many conferences to address these issues.

How do modern Orthodox 'hard' scientists deal with apparent contradictions between biblical texts and modern biology and cosmology? On the one hand, the creation story of Genesis 1 describes vegetation, animal, and human life as coming into existence by divine utterances that take place on the third through the sixth days of a 6-day process of creation. There is no mention or suggestion of the evolution of one species from earlier ones in the biblical account. On the other hand, modern biology is based upon the facts and theory of evolution, and modern cosmology provides universally accepted evidence (by the community of cosmologists and those in related disciplines who have the expertise to know) for an Earth and a universe that are billions of years old. One would expect that, given the rigorous logic involved in mathematical thinking and in the research, application, and teaching of modern physics, 'hard' scientists would be logical (and honest) when pondering the conflicts between their religious belief in TMS and their scientific knowledge and try to resolve them.

Unlike the non-Orthodox, these Orthodox scientists consider the Genesis account to be of divine origin. Hence they cannot relate to it as to an ancient etiological creation myth imaginatively formulated by pre-scientific minds to explain why and how the world is as it is, insofar as people living 2,500 or more years ago perceived and experienced it. If contemporary Orthodox scientists were not fettered by their dogma of TMS, they could acknowledge that there is no reason to assume that an ancient creation myth needs to be compatible with modern science. However, their theology, and their fear of the existential and behavioral consequences of jettisoning their theology, induces them to engage in illogical and farfetched attempts to 'reconcile' the description of the origins of the universe, of Earth, and of humankind in Genesis 1 with the findings of modern science.

Several different strategies are used. A small number of Orthodox Jewish scientists interpret Genesis 1 literally (as do many more fundamentalist Protestant young-earth special-creationists) and assert, against the vast majority of biologists and cosmologists, that modern evolution and/or cosmology are factually incorrect. If the Bible, as they understand it, conflicts with prevailing scientific views, there must be something wrong with our scientific understanding. For example, one view is that "it is not difficult to criticise the theory of evolution to show up its weaknesses, its speculative nature, its circular reasoning. The so-called facts of evolution are . . . not facts at all but extrapolations from fragmentary data backwards in time to a dim and unknown past."[52]

At Touro College, which provides college-level academic training primarily for Jews who are more inclined to right-wing rather than to centrist, modern Orthodoxy,[53] some of the professors who teach science are openly hostile to evolution and teach creationism.[54]

Another argument put forth by some is that although the laws and principles of biology and of physics plausibly explain reality as we know it *today*, these laws were not necessarily operative in the distant past.

Many other Orthodox scientists reject these approaches and argue, based upon respectable precedents in traditional biblical commentary, that Genesis 1 should not and need not be understood literally, and hence, there is no conflict between it and modern science. Genesis 1 can be understood metaphorically, theologically, allegorically, morally or mystically: One can be a faithful Orthodox Jew while accepting the theory of the Big Bang and of the evolution of the solar system and life on earth, as events that have transpired over billions of years. However, these processes, from the Big Bang onward, are purposeful unfoldings of a divine plan and are *not* the result of 'random' processes in a strictly material world.[55] Evolution is theistically guided and reflects intelligent, that is, divine, design. These Orthodox scientists claim that the divine purpose and goal of evolution—cosmic and biological—was the creation of humans, and from humans, the designation of Israel as a chosen people. Inherent in this plan was the eventual revelation of the Torah to Moses at Sinai by the designer, who is identified with the God of the Bible.

I find it disconcerting to see how myopic, parochial, species-arrogant, and irrational some of these scientists can be. What they are claiming, in effect, is that God triggered the Big Bang event 14 billion years ago, which subsequently produced a universe of immense vastness filled with innumerable galaxies, stars, and planets, *in order to* bring into existence the planet Earth *so that* organic life should evolve on it, *for the purpose of* the evolution of human beings (who are but a small fraction of all living species), *with the goal* of selecting for a special relationship with him a specific group, consisting of a fraction of a percent of the entire human population. But if God is all powerful, why would he have used such an inefficient and wasteful process to achieve his ultimate goal?

A more recent version of this argument is the so-called anthropic principle, which, according to Nathan Aviezer, an Orthodox physicist, states that "the universe looks as if it had been specifically designed to permit the existence of human beings." According to Aviezer the anthropic principle demonstrates that the "seemingly impossible predictions of our Torah and our tradition are confirmed by science" (2007, 24).[56] To support his claim he quotes the paleontologist Stephen Gould, who wrote that "human intelligence is the result of a staggeringly improbable series of events, utterly unpredictable and quite unrepeatable.... It fills us with amazement that human beings exist at all" (quoted in ibid.).

Of course the same could be said about the olfactory sense of dogs, the eyes of many birds and animals, and numerous other manifestations of nature. In fact, Gould criticizes those who use the anthropic principle to claim that the laws of physics have been fine-tuned to produce intelligent life. The universe hasn't been fine-tuned so as to produce life, but rather life has evolved in response to and has been fine-tuned by properties of the universe. Life has adapted to physics rather than the laws of physics having been assigned certain parameters at the origin of the universe in order to culminate with intelligent human life billions of years later. Improbability, unpredictability, unrepeatability, and amazement do not imply divine design. Variation and natural selection have sufficed to produce innumerable instances of complexity that instill awe and that would have been considered improbable (and which were unpredicted before they occurred) and might be unrepeatable.

Even if the anthropic principle were valid it would imply only that there is divine design in the creation of the universe we know and of human beings; but it implies nothing about the truth and validity of the Torah and of Orthodox Judaism. Aviezer sees the anthropic principle as confirming the view of the Torah that the universe was created for the sake of humankind, which, in turn, gives a high degree of plausibility to the Orthodox belief in the divine authorship of the Torah, which makes that claim. But the Pentateuch is not unique among ancient literatures in asserting that the world was created with a divine purpose in mind and for the sake of human beings. Moreover, the anthropic principle, if true, could also be used to argue for the 'plausibility' that the world was divinely designed so as to create the mosquito that I just crushed with a swap of my hand, since this mosquito could not have come into being were the (alleged) statistically improbable physical parameters and properties of nature that underlie the presumed anthropic principle not to exist. Shall we then assign the mosquito a unique role in the divine plan? Some Orthodox thinkers might say yes.[57] How about a worm, or a brutal murderer, about whom the same could be said: they too could not exist if certain specific, unique parameters of physics did not exist. Was the world created by God *for* them? The anthropic principle can be used to argue that *whatever* exists 'must have been designed by a creator,' since, after all, it does exist, and its existence can only come about if certain physical constants or properties of the physical world exist. Surely, such a principle is not useful in bolstering specific claims for the truthfulness of Orthodox Judaism and the revelation of Torah at Sinai. In fact, the anthropic principle argument has been used by some Christians to make similar claims about the universe having been designed so as to bring about the coming of Christ and the

Christian faith. I am pretty certain that if they haven't already done so, Muslim scientists and theologians will soon join the bandwagon and use this presumed principle to validate their claim that the universe was designed for the revelation of the Koran and the prophetic role of Muhammad.

Aviezer is also an example of an Orthodox physicist who denies Darwinian evolution using "identical strategies [that] have been employed by Protestant fundamentalists in their attempts to discredit Darwinism, their logic being that if Darwinism is wrong, the Bible must be right."[58] Other Orthodox and non-Orthodox scientists have taken Aviezer to task for his misrepresentations of the theory and facts of evolution as well as for the logical inadequacies of his arguments.[59] What is troubling to me is that a distinguished, presumably logical physicist and devout individual can use specious arguments in order to protect his faith from being discredited. In a way this is a more egregious 'sin' (although it might be rooted in self-deception rather than deliberate deception) than when a distinguished rabbi who is not himself a scientist disparages evolution, as did Rabbi Moses Feinstein, the leading halakhic authority in mid-twentieth-century American Orthodoxy. He ruled that Orthodox yeshivot (day schools) that used secular science textbooks should tear out the pages that deal with evolution.[60]

Still other Orthodox scientists claim and attempt to demonstrate that not only is there no conflict between Genesis 1 and modern science, but when Genesis 1 is properly understood we can see that it actually *anticipates* and *incorporates* much of modern biology and cosmology.[61] Aviezer and Gerald Schroeder, who is also a physicist and whose books are popular and widely disseminated in the world of Orthodoxy and used by non-scientists to 'prove' or bolster the truth-claims of Orthodox Judaism, appeal to this argument. Shai Cherry (2006) has trenchantly analyzed their writings and revealed the flaws in their methods, assumptions, and 'logic.' He concludes that "Aviezer has shoehorned into nine verses of Genesis the Cambrian explosion, the Paleozoic and Mesozoic periods, the disappearance of Neanderthal man, the rise of modern man, and the Neolithic revolution [albeit not evolution]" (172). This is indeed quite a feat! It is surprising that for the past 2,500 or more years since the appearance of the Pentateuch this has gone unnoticed. Be that as it may, for Aviezer science is not a threat to Orthodox dogma. On the contrary, science supports and reinforces faith in God and in God's revelation of the Torah. Aviezer hopes thereby to reinforce the commitment of modern Orthodox Jews to the traditional faith and beliefs of Judaism.[62]

With respect to Schroeder's elaborate 'proofs' that modern scientific knowledge is embedded in the Torah, Cherry concludes that "by using a conceptual and historical hodgepodge of biblical, midrashic, Aristotelian, and kabbalistic sources, Schroeder opportunistically constructs a Creation narrative whose ostensibly literal interpretation roughly corresponds to the scientific account of the physical universe."[63]

As we have seen and will see more of later, when someone's religious beliefs and values are threatened, he will go to great lengths to protect and preserve them, allowing his emotions to overcome or distort his reason—no matter how rational and logical that person might be in his other pursuits including scientific ones. Each of the aforementioned attempts at resolving the apparent conflicts between Torah and science are either logically flawed, incapable of disconfirmation, misrepresentations of scientific knowledge or theory, or inconsistent with other beliefs or assumptions of the Orthodox system that they are trying to defend.

What motivates the attempts of these scientists to reconcile Genesis 1 with modern science? In addition to the motives that impel Orthodox think-ers (and non-thinkers) to deny modern biblical scholarship, there is the desire to allay doubts about the truth of Orthodox dogmas that are raised by some potential *baalei teshuva* (non-Orthodox Jews evincing an interest in becoming Orthodox) who have been exposed to modern biology and cosmology. For people on the threshold of Orthodoxy, conflicts between science and Torah can be an obstacle to crossing that threshold. *Kiruv* (outreach) organizations need the Aviezer, Schroeder, and other science-Torah reconcilers in order to succeed in their recruitment efforts.[64]

It must be noted, however, that in a recent survey of the teaching of science in twelve modern Orthodox yeshiva high schools Rena Selya found "there is little conflict between contemporary modern Orthodox Judaism and Darwinian evolution. In many Jewish high schools, teenagers study the ideas and evidence of evolution by natural selection."[65] A good number of the parents of these teenagers are doctors and scientists, and they aspire to have their children admitted to prestigious colleges. The study of science at an advanced and sophisticated level in high school is valued for its intrinsic worth and because it is often a condition for admission to good universities (many of these families are aiming for the Ivies). Selya points out that in earlier decades such a positive attitude towards the teaching of the theory of evolution was less common. In the modern Orthodox yeshiva that I attended in the 1950s there was a disconnect between what we were studying in the morning sessions—Bible and Talmud—and our afternoon class in biology. Although the official motto of Yeshiva University High School was, and still is, Torah and Madda—the synthesis of Torah with secular studies—no attempt was made by the school to address the questions, doubts, and confusions some of us were experiencing as we pondered how to reconcile our biblical studies with the biology we were being taught. The school did not censor the biology textbook we were using, and did not instruct our gentile teacher to avoid discussion of evolution. But it definitely was educationally derelict in that it avoided engaging us in an open and honest discussion of the conflicts that were generated by our dual curriculum. It was only when a group of us (I was the instigator) pressed the issue did one of the younger members of the faculty agree to meet with those of us who were interested in discussing the topic of evolution, *after* regular class hours (which were from 9 A.M. to 6 P.M.).

Selya notes that even where evolution is taught in yeshiva high schools today, more or less in the same manner as it would be taught in a public or private secular high school, the possible religious and philosophical implications aren't always discussed in class. If they are discussed (usually by the rabbis who teach Jewish Studies rather than by the science teacher who may not even be Jewish, or if Jewish, not necessarily Orthodox), God is included in the evolutionary process (e.g., as the hidden guiding force, or the intelligent designer), and evolution is presented as being compatible with Orthodox Judaism. In a few instances where the scientist teaching biology was also a rabbi, or the rabbi teaching Bible was also a scientist, a conscious effort was made to incorporate into the curriculum sophisticated and thoughtful articles on the Torah-science relationship. It seems that there is less fear of teaching evolution in most modern Orthodox high schools than there is in teaching modern biblical scholarship.

However some of the schools that Selya surveyed had a decidedly dismissive attitude toward evolution even though they taught it. For example, in one school students were told to study about evolution only for the purpose of taking the State exam in biology, and after having taken the exam they were encouraged to forget what they had been taught about it. In another school, one rabbi publicly tried to disprove evolution on ostensibly scientific grounds, claiming that God had placed fossils on earth in order to test our faith.[66]

Another example of the conflict between traditional Orthodox beliefs and modern science is in the implications of modern evolutionary theory and neuropsychology for three traditional Jewish concepts: the "soul" as an entity distinct from the body, human beings being created in the "image of God," and "free will." These concepts, as traditionally understood (albeit in more than one way), are no longer plausible as descriptions of humans and of human nature.[67]

There are at least six ways one can respond to the challenges that modern biology and psychology present to Jewish religious assumptions about the essence of being human, and values that derive from those assumptions.

At one extreme, one can deny or ignore the scientific evidence and plausible scientific theories that derive from that evidence. People who do this continue to insist on the "truth" of the traditional understandings of what it means to be human, and hence of the norms that tradition derives from those accepted "truths."

At the other extreme, one can accept a secular, naturalistic-physicalist view of the human being and conclude that Judaism no longer provides compelling guidance in trying to develop an ethical-moral value system because its fundamental assumptions about the nature of the human being are wrong.

A third approach is to look respectfully, though critically, to Judaism (and other religions as well, which face similar challenges) for ethical wisdom, based upon its thousands of years of reflecting upon human nature and human society, and appropriate whatever values are consistent with contemporary scientific understandings of the human being. Even as one discards the ob-solete notions of "image of God," "soul," and maybe even "freedom of the will," one can maintain that much of the social and psychological wisdom of religion remains valuable today. This approach looks to religious tradition for guidance and insight but is not bound by tradition's religious anthropology and its claims to authority. Such an approach will inevitably find some teachings of Judaism to be ethically and morally *un*acceptable, and will reject what cannot be justified by appeals to reason and scientific knowledge.

A fourth approach is to retain the *terms* "image of God," "soul," and "free-will" but no longer as expressing objective realities, but as useful shorthand descriptors of certain aspects of human personality, thought, experience, and behavior that are really better conceptualized and understood by modern psychological and biological constructs.

A fifth approach is to acknowledge that although humans are no more created "in the image of God" or ensouled than are earthworms or great apes, it might be useful to talk, or even think, about humans *as if* they were created in the "image of God," had souls, and could exercise free will because this will help sustain many desirable ethical and moral values. These "beliefs" work, in a pragmatic sense, and this endows them with a utilitarian value, even if they are not "true" in an empirical sense.

A sixth approach is to redefine the meaning of these three concepts in ways that are fully consonant with modern psychology and biology, while at the same time retaining the belief that humans are still different in kind from the rest of nature and have a special relationship with a transcendent, creator God. Some evangelical Christians have adopted this approach.[68]

Jewish theologians have much constructive theology to do if they want to make Judaism relevant to Jews for whom the life sciences are sources of truth about what a human being is, and of the existential meaning of being human, no less than are religious traditions, values, and concepts.

———

Some individuals maintain that dogmas, such as TMS, play only a peripheral role in the religious consciousness of the Orthodox and that "Torah is the metaphor we use to organize our lives in a very confusing world. To . . . try to discover how people deal with discrepancies in the system is to ask a question that is only of concern to the far right. Most observant Jews outside of the Haredi community feel no need to work out the internal conflicts and find the issue intellectually rather uninteresting."[69]

If this comment is correct, that except for the Haredi community the issue of TMS is "intellectually rather uninteresting," I wonder, why did my Internet postings and presentations on this topic generate a significant amount of interest, passion, and debate among a range of Orthodox Jews, including distinguished representatives of the modern Orthodox scholarly community? I think that although many Jews who conduct their lives behaviorally and ritually in accordance with Orthodox halakha do not reflect on the doctrinal and theological foundations of the Orthodoxy that they practice and love, this is not the case with the more sophisticated intellectual leaders of the movement, rabbis or academics, who write extensively and thoughtfully on these issues. It is the very nature of the thoughtful person to reflect on *why* he or she does or believes *that which* he or she does or believes. This is especially the case for people who are responsible for transmitting their religious heritage to the next generation, in their role as rabbis or as teachers, in an open environment in which there is a marketplace of competing ideas to which the young generation is constantly being exposed. Moreover, Orthodoxy is regularly challenged by the non-Orthodox and the secular Jewish world and feels compelled to defend its theological and doctrinal views in response to these challenges. Most of the Orthodox rabbis, scholars, and scientists—even when they perceived my tone and tenor as being arrogant, self-righteous, condescending, unfair, and so forth—did not ignore or dismiss the issues I raised. On the contrary, they rather vehemently, and, in some cases, writing at considerable length, criticized the substance of what I had written and the claims I was making on any number of points with which they disagreed. In addition, not a few people from Orthodox backgrounds expressed their appreciation for my raising questions that they felt were not being adequately addressed in the Orthodox schools they were attending or had attended, or in the Orthodox communities in which they lived.

———

I turn now to a discussion and critique of several influential Orthodox Jewish theologians who have discussed the belief in TMS and to a widely used Orthodox commentary on the Pentateuch based upon that belief.

Dani Statman (1998) has analyzed the grounds for observing the halakha in the thought of the Orthodox philosopher Eliezer Goldman. Goldman maintains that God does not manifest himself in history or in nature [or, perhaps, if God does, humans in any case are unable to discern these manifestations]. The Bible and rabbinic literature, which are replete with descriptions of divine manifestations in nature and in history, need to be radically reinterpreted to be in accord with this view. The religious person keeps commandments (*mitzvot*) as a way of worshipping God, and these observances are what endow a person's life and actions with meaning, insofar as they derive from (and presumably reinforce) a sense that beyond the actual world that one experiences there exists a transcendent being. Faith and religious awareness, and the decision to observe the *mitzvot* are one and the same thing. One doesn't keep the *mitzvot* in order to achieve some other religious or mystical goal. The religious experience is itself embodied in the decision to keep the *mitzvot* and in the very doing so.

If God does not manifest himself in either nature or history then there can never be a real conflict between the findings of science and religious faith, which is indeed Goldman's view.

What, however, would be the implications of Goldman's view for the religious person's approach to modern biblical scholarship? If God has not manifested himself in history, then there could be no contradiction between its findings and religious faith, and, indeed, Goldman maintains that there is no reason why a religious person shouldn't participate fully in such scholarship.

As Statman points out, the difficulty with such an approach, for a religious person for whom observing the *mitzvot* of the Torah and the halakha is crucial, is twofold. First of all, how does one know what are the commandments that one should perform? Presumably it is those that are part of the religious traditions of Judaism. But how does one know that those traditions indeed convey the will of God? Presumably through some sort of divine revelation. But isn't divine revelation a manifestation of God in history? This contradicts Goldman's central thesis. Statman notes Goldman's statement that one of the things that he regrets is not developing a theory of revelation.

But even if there were a theory of revelation compatible with a purely transcendent conception of God, the religious believer who would want to choose to obey the halakha as his or her mode of divine worship would have difficulty doing so if, as Goldman maintains, modern biblical scholarship can be embraced. Statman (1998) asks the following:

> Let us assume that bible scholars will succeed in determining not only the estimated date of composition of a specific chapter of the Bible, but also the precise identity of the human author ... [for example] the author of the section of Leviticus that specifies prohibited foods [i.e., the basis of most of the laws of *kashrut*], and in doing so will disprove the belief that it was composed (or transmitted) by Moses. Or what if they will find the extrabiblical source from which that section was copied without any significant change or editing. Will the believer who accepts these conclusions still be able to claim that when he fulfills the demands of this Pentateuchal section he is *worshipping God?* Will there still be *religious* significance to a meticulous observance of these laws? In what sense?[70]

I would like to venture a psychological explanation for why Goldman posits the theology of commandments that he does, which is very difficult to sustain on rational grounds. He is an individual deeply committed to traditional Judaism's halakhic lifestyle. Confronted with conflicts between the profound religious meaning that observing *mitzvot* has for him and the findings of the sciences and of biblical scholarship that render highly implausible the cognitive foundations of such a commitment, and unable or unwilling to reject either science/biblical scholarship on the one hand, or a life of *mitzvot* on the other, he develops a theological and philosophical theory that "allows" him to hold on to both.

I would venture a similar psychological analysis to explain the views of the Orthodox scientist and philosopher Yeshayahu Leibowitz (1992), for whom Judaism is essentially obedience to the commandments of the Torah (in accordance with their rabbinic interpretation). "For the believing Jew ... the holiness of Scripture does not hinge on beliefs, views or outlooks about the nature or the sources of the material found in the Bible and about its historical and scientific value."[71] Attempts such as that of Maimonides to understand the nature of God or of revelation should not play an important role in religious life, nor should one try to understand reasons for the biblical commandments or justify obedience to them on the basis of some human interest that they might serve. All that is important is for the Jew to worship God by obeying the halakha which is part of the Oral Law, and indeed it is the Oral Law itself that endows the Scripture with its holiness.

In analyzing and critiquing Leibowitz's approach to Scripture, Avi Sagi concludes that "the factual question, namely whether this text was given at Sinai, remains unanswered, as does the question of how to contend with the problem of biblical criticism ... the achievement that is entailed by the release of Scripture from factual contexts remains incomplete, as it fails to answer the believer's basic questions concerning the status of the Sinai revelation" (441). If Scripture does not deal with the factual, then maybe there was no revelation at Sinai, so why should a Jew obey the Oral Law, which is based upon the assumption that there was such a revelation? To say that the Oral Law itself is an expression of the divine will, will only lead to the following question: If these norms are not based on a revelation at Sinai as recorded in the Pentateuch, on what basis should a Jew assume that the expositors and transmitters of the Oral Law knew, and know, that their halakhic norms are what God wants the Jew to do? The inadequacy of Leibowitz's logic in trying to justify obedience to biblical and rabbinic law is glaring. How can such a brilliant person not see the obvious flaws in his arguments? Something psychological has to be going on.

The bottom line of Goldman and Leibowitz's approach is that science and biblical scholarship are "kosher," even as pig and shrimp remain "non-kosher," *because God prohibited them.* They are not satisfied with an obligation to obey biblical and rabbinic law that is not based upon a belief in their divine origin and authority.[72]

When we compare Goldman and Leibowitz's approaches with those in the ultra-Orthodox world who deny the validity of "evidence" from science and biblical scholarship, we find that notwithstanding their diametrically opposite attitudes toward science and scholarship, their theological and behavioral conclusions are identical—the mitzvot in the Torah and the commandments of the halakha are divine and should be observed because of that.

More internally consistent, but less emotionally satisfying resolutions for their conundrum, would have been either to accept the findings of science and biblical scholarship (that were convincing) and admit that the Torah's prohibitions on eating some animals are man made (the view, e.g., of Reform Judaism) or to ignore science and biblical scholarship (and many other disciplines) and continue to affirm that God revealed the entire Pentateuch to Moses and it was God who forbade the forbidden foods and who commanded the execution of adulterers, Sabbath transgressors, and idolaters (the view of the ultra-Orthodox).

As I pointed out earlier, in the past two or three decades there has been some blurring of the distinction between modern Orthodox Judaism on the one hand, and "traditional" (or "right-wing," "haredi," or "yeshivish") Orthodox Judaism on the other. One sign of this is the widespread use of the ArtScroll edition of the Torah in numerous synagogues that are "modern Orthodox," in that many of their members are well-educated secularly across a range of scientific, scholarly, and professional disciplines. Many of the rabbis of these synagogues are members of the Rabbinical Council of America (RCA), the largest modern Orthodox rabbinical association.[73] In other words, every Saturday morning these secularly well-educated Orthodox Jews are following the weekly reading of the Torah portion from an edition of the Pentateuch that includes the following comments:

> Rambam, or Maimonides, formulated the Thirteen Principles of Faith, which are incumbent upon every Jew...
>
> 8. I believe with complete faith that the entire Torah now in our hands is the same one that was given to Moses, our teacher, peace be upon him.
>
> ... [T]he attitude of one who approaches a book as the immutable word of God is far, far different from one who holds a volume that was composed by men and amended by others over the years. As we begin the study of the Torah, we should resolve that this recognition of its origin and immutability will be in our consciousness always.
>
> In several of his writings, Rambam sets forth at much greater length the unanimously held view that every letter and word of the Torah was given to Moses by God; that it has not and cannot be changed; and that nothing was ever or can ever be added to it. Indeed, the Talmud states emphatically that if one questions the Divine origin of even a single letter or traditionally accepted interpretation of the Torah, it is tantamount to denial of the entire Torah (Sanhedrin 99a).[74]

A similar approach is taken by the influential yeshiva Aish HaTorah, based in Israel, with branches elsewhere. Aish HaTorah is very much involved in *kiruv,* outreach to individuals who are not familiar with traditional, Orthodox Judaism. Like the author of the ArtScroll commentary, in their Discovery Seminars they state that "[t]he Torah was originally dictated from God to Moses, letter for letter" and that "the great success of Jewish tradition is the meticulous transmission of the Torah text." They then ask, "But actually how accurate is it? How do we know that the Torah we have today is the same text given on Mount Sinai?" and provide a detailed "proof" that the widely accepted Masoretic text of the Pentateuch that we have today corresponds with near absolute fidelity to the presumed "original" Torah Moses received at Sinai from God.[75]

It is not uncommon for right-wing orthodox writers as well as for Aish HaTorah and some other Orthodox *kiruv* (outreach to Jews) organizations to make false assertions and claims. I assume that most of the time these false assertions and claims are based upon a sincere ignorance of contemporary academic scholarship in biblical and Jewish Studies. Sometimes, however, there seems to be a conscious manipulation and distortion of facts, as can be seen, for example, in "revisionist" accounts of recent Jewish history by some Orthodox "right-wingers" as richly documented by J. J. Schacter.[76] For example, notwithstanding ample historical evidence that the illustrious rabbi Naftali Zvi Yehuda Berlin (Neziv), the head of the renowned Yeshiva of Volozhin, allowed, in the late nineteenth century, albeit against his will and in response to tremendous external pressure, the introduction of secular studies into that school, many rabbis in the right-wing/haredi world today insist on denying this. They might fear that knowledge of this fact might lead some members of their community to question their policy of prohibiting secular studies in the confines of contemporary haredi yeshivot (and outside of it as well).

The English translation of the memoirs of Rabbi Barukh HaLevi Epstein provides another example. Rabbi Epstein, the nephew of the Neziv, and a great Torah scholar himself, mentions in his memoirs that his aunt, the Neziv's wife, used to read (or perhaps study), the Mishna, in addition to Jewish devotional texts. The Mishna is a second-century rabbinic text that deals primarily with halakha, Jewish law, and is the foundation of the Talmud, which for nearly two millennia had been off limits to women. In the English translation of these memoirs, the mention of the Mishna is deleted. Why? Because the issue of whether or not women should be permitted to study Mishna is still debated today in ultra-Orthodox circles. Either the publisher supports the view of those opposed to such study, and hence would not want it to be known that the great Neziv allowed his wife to study Mishna, or perhaps the publisher, to maximize sales of the memoirs and to play it safe, does not want to offend any potential buyers by including such a "heretical" fact. In both of these examples, historical truth is distorted or falsified for ideological reasons.[77] Some of the falsifiers justify their approach with the claim that objective history is not an important value. What is important is the way in which the presentation of history will impact on the reader. It is appropriate and justifiable to distort history if a legitimate religious end will be achieved by such distortion. The end justifies the means.

A similar mentality seems to be operating in some of the Aish HaTorah Discovery Seminars, such as those that claim to have discovered hidden codes in the sequencing of letters in the Pentateuch. One young man, in an essay describing his loss of faith in Orthodox Judaism, describes his personal experience with this Aish HaTorah approach, and his reaction to it:

> One thing kept me mostly Jewish-observant throughout all this—the codes. Despite everything else, their statistical validity could simply not be argued with . . . I found some information from the other side, about the possible bias in the experiment and evidence against its espoused chronology . . . I read some more . . . did some of my own experiments, and finally came to the sorry conclusion that there is absolutely no decent evidence for predictive codes in Genesis, or indeed anywhere else in the Bible . . .

Upon reaching this conclusion, he wrote to one of the rabbis who had led the seminar on the biblical codes:

> "In case you are about to discard this letter, I should say one more thing—I am an intelligent, honest, God-seeking person. If you find that hard to believe, well, I suggest you contact me and I'll outargue you (and if you win such a debate, well, I'll go back to being *frum* [religious and observant] again. But if I win, I expect you to give up your job) . . . So why am I writing this to you? Part of me wants to make it my mission to expose your organization's intellectual deficiencies. But . . . I recognize that Aish HaTorah is on the front lines of keeping Jews in touch with all these things I admire, so I don't actually want to be a thorn in your side. But I'm sure you're aware of the halakhic prohibition against doing a sin for the sake of a *mitzvah.* Maybe you apply a *heter kiruv* [dispensation for the sake of bringing Jews closer to the religion] here, but I don't think even an Aish *heter* permits distorting the truth for the sake of Torah Judaism." Perhaps not surprisingly, I never received a reply.[78]

To return to the ArtScroll commentary on the Torah, with reference to the rabbinic and Maimonidean teaching that those who deny the divine origin of even a single letter of the Torah will have no share in the world to come, the editor of the commentary, Nosson Scherman (1993), writes the following:

This harsh judgment is quite proper, for if a critic can take it upon himself to deny the provenance of one verse or letter of the Torah, what is to stop him from discarding any part that displeases him? Modern times illustrate this all too clearly. And logic dictates that man cannot tamper with the word of God, not merely because man's intelligence is of a different, infinitely inferior order, but because God and His wisdom are perfect, and, by definition, perfection cannot be improved. (xx)

Scherman is alluding to modern biblical scholarship, which he rejects absolutely because it denies Maimonides' eighth principle. One hundred and fifty years of thoughtful and assiduous study of the Bible by legions of scholars, many of them Jewish, and some of them experts in rabbinic Judaism and medieval Jewish philosophy, are to be ignored because of a Talmudic teaching that Maimonides incorporated into his creedal formulation. Scherman and his ilk, who accept Talmudic teachings as authoritative, maintain that a person who (like me) was socialized into and knowledgeable in the Talmudic-rabbinic tradition and who deliberately rejected its teaching about the divine origin of every single letter of the Torah has no share in the world to come. In other words, someone who would accept *the most modest of scholarly claims*—that one word (or even one letter) of the Pentateuch was inserted by a human rather than dictated by God—will be consigned to eternal oblivion or may even be subjected to horrible postmortem punishments (according to some interpretations of the expression, 'has no share in the world to come').

This ArtScroll theology is analogous to the doctrine of Southern Baptists and some other Christians who exclude Jews from Heaven and consign them to Hell because they do not accept Christ as Savior.

Scherman relies on Talmudic and Maimonidean authority for this claim. The assumption is that Talmudic rabbis of the first to fifth centuries CE, Maimonides, and other medieval Jewish scholars who agreed with Maimonides would hold the same views today that they held when they lived. However neither I nor Scherman can know whether or not those rabbis and scholars would indeed have ignored biblical scholarship or other disciplines that would have questioned the accuracy of their beliefs and views, had they been aware of them, which, of course, they could not have been. Modern methods of biblical study, archaeology, and modern science did not exist in their times. In effect, then, ArtScroll's belief about the origin of the Torah, although ostensibly grounded in Talmudic and Maimonidean teachings, is very different from that of the Talmud and of Maimonides. Scherman is aware of (and could be notably more aware of) much that they were not aware of (and could not have been aware of). Given Maimonides' openness to truth even when the expounders or discoverers of those truths were not Jewish, such as Aristotle, it is more, rather than less, probable to assume that he would have revised his views about the authorship of the Torah were he familiar with modern scholarship and science. Indeed, as Marc Shapiro has demonstrated,[79] Maimonides himself didn't believe his own eighth principle in the absolute and extreme formulation in which Scherman cites it. He was well aware of variations in Torah scrolls that were used by different Jewish communities, all of whom were considered to be devout adherents of rabbinic Judaism. What he wrote for certain audiences for polemical or pedagogic purposes was not necessarily what he took to be the actual, factual, truth.

Does what Tirosh-Samuelson writes about the historical attitude of numerous great rabbis, such as Maimonides, toward philosophy, apply equally well to biblical scholarship and science?

> "Wisdom" is the Jewish category that refers to the pursuit of truth accessible to all human beings by virtue of their being rational. Under that rubric, Jews have acquired knowledge about the world and about God from a variety of sources and traditions. The pursuit of truth, the truth that constitutes the love of wisdom—that is, philosophy— transcends ethnic or cultural boundaries. Indeed, the Jewish Wisdom tradition presented herein shows that to love God Jews must be willing to examine all truth claims; if found to be true, these claims are part of Judaism, because what is true is what is Jewish. Philosophical activity, therefore, is inherently Jewish.[80]

Some Jewish philosophers, in line with the pragmatism of William James, argue that the consequences of beliefs need to be taken into account in assessing their truth value. The "truth" that is more important than the "truth" of who actually authored the Torah is the effect of believing TMS versus believing MSPM on the survival of the Jewish people or of the Orthodox Jewish community. Is it indeed the case, as Tirosh-Samuelson asserts, that "Judaism" has, and should continue, to examine all truth claims and accept them if they were found to be true? Perhaps certain truths are incompatible with Judaism, and if Judaism is to survive they need to be rejected. Or, perhaps, in line with her claim, the value of truth is central to Judaism, and Judaism is adaptive, so that newly discovered truths can be incorporated into Judaism, which assimilates them and evolves into a new form that retains what is compatible with these truths and rejects what is not.

This raises two questions worth pursuing, but which I cannot pursue here: What have been the meanings of the word *emet* (usually translated as "truth") in Judaism from its biblical usages until today, and how central is *emet* and the pursuit of *emet* to Judaism's self-definition and self-understanding?[81]

Returning to the ArtScroll Pentateuch, in his commentary on the first three verses of Genesis chapter 1, Scherman makes the following points:

> As Ramban [Nachmanides] notes, even after reading how the world and its central character, Man, came into being, we still do not understand the secret or even the process of Creation. Rather, the work of Creation is a deep mystery that can be comprehended only through the tradition transmitted by God to Moses, and those who are privileged to be entrusted with this hidden knowledge are not permitted to reveal it. (2)

In other words, Scherman, writing at the end of the twentieth century, and all of the readers of his commentary know no more about the process of creation than did Nahmanides who lived in the thirteenth century. Is that really true? I doubt that Nahmanides would agree with Scherman. Surely there are still numerous, perhaps unknowable or insoluble, scientific (or kabbalistic), mysteries about the process of creation. But we do know a lot about it—the approximate age of the universe and of the earth; the relationship between sun, moon, stars, and Earth; the origins of the oceans, of plant and animal life and their speciation; and the evolution of humans. We know enough to know that the author of chapter 1 of Genesis knew a lot less than we know. However, Scherman uses Nahmanides as a way of avoiding acknowledging what we do know about the process of creation, because to acknowledge what we do know would threaten his belief in the perfect and inerrant knowledge of God, to whom he ascribes chapter 1.

Scherman, however, does have some certain knowledge, as indicated by his italicization of the word *do:* "What we *do* know is that Adam and Eve, the forerunners of humanity, had the mission of bringing about the fulfillment of God's commandment. They failed, and were driven into exile . . ."(ibid.).

So at the close of the twentieth century, Scherman believes that Adam and Eve are the forerunners of humanity. Do the Orthodox scientists and philosophers and lawyers and doctors who are using his Torah commentary also believe this? Some do and some do not. Those who do are like the fundamentalist Christians who reject evolution and cosmology because they contradict the creation narrative of Genesis. They are on the side of William Jennings Bryan in the Scopes "Monkey" Trial. As for those who don't, why don't they object to using Scherman's commentary in their synagogues?

Scherman writes the following:

Ramban comments that the Torah relates the story of the six days of Creation *ex nihilo* to establish that God is the sole Creator and to refute the theories of those who claim that the universe is timeless or that it came into being through some massive coincidence or accident. This is implicit in the narrative of the first six days, for Scripture gives no specific details regarding the process of Creation, just as it makes no mention of the angels or other incorporeal beings. The story of Creation tells of when the major categories of the universe came into existence only in very general terms, because its primary purpose is to state that nothing came into being except at God's command. . . . (3)

Did Nahmanides mean to say that nothing in the creation account can be explained, and that nothing was to be taken literally, or rather that even though the account provides a general, and true outline of the order of creation, it doesn't explicitly provide us with the kabbalistic interpretation of God's creation of the world?[82] If the former, then why does Nahmanides go on to explain in some detail the creation account of chapter 1, using, Heaven forbid, his *knowledge of Greek science and philosophy* to do so? Nahmanides can use Greek science and philosophy, but ArtScroll cannot use modern science and scholarship.

With respect to the creation story Nahmanides, in his comment on "And there was light," says, "Know that the term "day" as used in the story of the creation was, in the case of the creation of heaven and earth, a real day, composed of hours and seconds, and there were six days like the six days of the workweek as is the plain meaning of the verse" (28) Nahmanides also reconciles the apparent contradiction between Genesis 1:11–12 and Genesis 2:5–6, both of which deal with the creation of vegetation, in the following manner:

In my opinion, in accordance with the plain meaning of Scripture, on the third day (Genesis 1:11–12) the earth did bring forth the grass and the fruit trees in their full-grown stature and quality as He commanded concerning them. And now (Genesis 2:5–6) Scripture tells us that there was no one to plant and sow them for future purposes, and the earth would not produce until a mist would come up from it and water it, and man was formed who would work it—to seed, to plant, and to guard. This is the meaning of "the shrub of the field . . . had not yet grown." It does not say "the shrub of the ground" for only a place which is cultivated is called "field."[83]

In other words, Nahmanides understands the time frame and the order of creation in its plain scriptural sense, although the verses also allude to additional mystical or symbolic senses, which do not, however, negate the "plain" meaning.

Nahmanides thus believes, among other things which modern science refutes, that the world as we know it was created in 144 hours ($6 \times 24 = 144$) and that vegetation existed on earth before there was a sun.

It is not at all surprising or unreasonable that Nahmanides, living in the thirteenth century, who knows nothing about evolution or cosmology, thinks this way.

Scherman, however, who I assume has heard of Darwin, evolution, Einstein, and the Big Bang, misuses Nahmanides by quoting him selectively and misinterpreting him in order to avoid the obvious problems that the creation story, as understood by Nahmanides himself, presents with respect to the duration of creation, the order in which the entities were created, and their relationships. Scherman surely knows that modern science refutes much of chapters 1 and 2 when they are understood in accordance with their *peshat,* in other words, their "plain" sense. However, he cannot acknowledge that the creation account is false because his Torah is inerrant, and he also doesn't want to give explicit credence to modern biology and science.

Moreover, Scherman contradicts himself. If creation is really a mystery, then why is he so sure that Adam and Eve are the forerunners of humankind? Why isn't the story about them also a mystery? He wants to read that story literally. Why not, then, read the rest of the account literally as well, and affirm that the earth, the oceans, and vegetation preceded the existence of the sun? Scherman skirts these issues, because he has no convincing way of reconciling his belief in the truth of the biblical creation accounts with his awareness that they are contradicted by science.

The culmination of Scherman's obscurantism (which reflects the obscurantism of the segment of Orthodox Judaism from which he emerges) is on page 53, at the end of Genesis 11. He provides a chart with the heading "Chronology/Time Line—Adam to Jacob." It begins with Adam, who lived from the years 1 to 930, and concludes with Jacob, who lived from the years 2108 to 2255 (according to the traditional Jewish calendar). In other words, Jacob was born 2,108 years after the creation of the world. If there had been a tiny little note somewhere on this chart indicating that these dates are the dates according to the biblical narrative, which cannot be taken literally because we now know that the world is somewhat older than 5,768 years (the age of the world according to the traditional Jewish calendar), and that no humans were around 2,108 years after either the Big Bang or after Earth was formed, all would have been well (not really all—because the very historicity of Adam, and even of Jacob, can be reasonably called into question, although I would not expect that much from ArtScrollers). But I was unable to locate such a note explaining this. In other words, Scherman, and the editors of the ArtScroll Commentary on the Torah, seem to believe that the first eleven chapters of Genesis are to be understood "literally," at least insofar as their account of the chronology of the creation of the world, of Adam and Eve, and of the subsequent generations through the patriarchs is concerned.

Scherman's English is sophisticated, but his thoughts are simplistic. Anyone who watches a few science or nature programs on public television or who reads the *New York Times* or a comparable newspaper or magazine would know that the Genesis creation story is scientifically incredible.

Scherman professes humility—we finite, limited mortals can't understand God, or creation—but this humility masks the arrogance of the fundamentalist who is certain of the truths of his certainties, and that all who disagree with him are wrong, misguided, or heretics who have no share in the world to come.

A heated debate transpired in the pages of *Tradition* (1981, 1982), a leading journal of modern Orthodox thought, in response to a highly negative review of ArtScroll publications by Barry Levy (1981). In his response to critics of his review, Levy (1982) claimed that the ArtScroll commentaries on the Bible "misrepresent the sacred literature of normative Judaism" (374). Levy challenged modern Orthodoxy, which appeals to "those individuals who have toiled in the study of Torah and the human sciences and who are ready to seek after and serve God with nothing less than the full range of their intellects" to call upon those individuals who possess a "narrow Orthodox mentality," such as the authors and supporters of ArtScroll, to "abandon their claims of superiority" and to be made to "recognize their intellectual inferiority" (375).[84] Steven Bayme (1982), another prominent modern Orthodox intellectual, severely criticized ArtScroll, which "pretends that one may study sacred texts with no references whatsoever to historical method, literary criticism, or scientific scholarship." As one of numerous egregious examples of ArtScroll's pretending that modern scholarship does not exist, he cites its historical introduction to the Book of Esther, which dates the Declaration of Cyrus to 370 BCE, based upon the Talmudic "historiography" of the Persian period, which accords it only fifty-two years of existence, rather than to approximately 537 BCE, based upon the unanimous opinion of modern historians who accord more than 200 years to the Persian period. Bayme notes that the social reality of ArtScroll, which received the imprimatur of major rabbinic and synagogue organizations that were historically identified with modern Orthodoxy, and its use in many Orthodox day schools,

> connotes that modern Orthodox and right-wing Orthodoxy have virtually coalesced. If this means the demise of the ideals of Torah U'Madda in favor of a compartmentalized Orthodoxy whose members are quite sophisticated in their professional enterprises yet close their minds to modern scholarship when they think Jewishly, then we must pay the price of acknowledging that Orthodoxy and modernity are indeed incompatible. (372–373)

Both Levy and Bayme identify themselves as modern Orthodox, and I cite them as internal critics of an ideology and of a movement that they feel has abandoned its original commitment to a serious and honest engagement with modernity. I am not suggesting that they would support my critique of modern Orthodoxy, which goes much further than theirs.

I suppose that there are many who enjoy the ArtScroll Torah for its graphics and for the wealth of traditional rabbinic and medieval biblical commentary that it summarizes and anthologizes in elegant English prose, but who ignore its dogmatic fundamentalism. But there are many others in these synagogues who are comfortable with or even intensely committed to the yeshiva world's dogmatic fundamentalism reflected in the ArtScroll translation of and commentary on the Torah. It seems as if these people who assiduously use critical thinking in their professions and scientific research suspend it when they leave their offices and laboratories for the synagogue, or whenever they are operating in the mode of "religious" consciousness, wherever they might be.

———

What is the cognitive fuel that powers the persistence of the Orthodox person's reading and study of the Torah from the rabbinic perspective that it is an organic, internally consistent, absolutely coherent work? Two contributing factors, especially for those raised and schooled in Orthodoxy from childhood, are the sophisticated and ingenious traditional interpretations, based upon the rabbinic dual Torah theory—the Pentateuch was accompanied at Sinai with an Oral tradition of interpretation—which has a history of 2,000 years, and the lack of exposure to any way of approaching the Torah other than through the traditional lenses. Intelligent, often brilliant Jews, who were masters of the Torah and of the entire Bible, diligently scrutinized the text and noted many (maybe even most) of the linguistic anomalies, contradictions between laws and between narratives, doublets, different designations of God, inconsistencies in the way in which God (and other aspects of the Israelite religion) are described and construed, and the conflicts between biblical concepts and rationalist philosophy. Because they all assumed the truth of both TMS and the tradition that the Oral Law was given to Moses at Sinai along with the written Torah, they labored assiduously and impressively to resolve all of the problems raised by the above phenomena, enlisting and expanding upon the Oral tradition to help them do so.

The advent of modern critical scholarly study of the Torah, with Spinoza's *Tractatus Theologico-Politicus,* did not reveal to the faithful much that was new in the sense of questions about the Torah, and most traditional Jews were not even exposed to the new critical approach. The vast literature of midrash (rabbinic biblical exegesis) followed by medieval biblical commentary "answered," often plausibly—if one accepted TMS and the Oral Law theory—any question or doubt raised by the Torah text. Because the Orthodox person has deep reverence for and stands in awe of traditional rabbis, teachers, and scholars, it either does not occur to him to challenge most of their explanations, or if he thinks of doing so, he will not do so to the point of challenging the bedrock premises of their theology of TMS and Oral Law. When the different interpretations of the biblical text are mutually exclusive, he may say that one interpretation or resolution of a textual problem seems more convincing than another. This is legitimate within the belief system. Even when doing so, he will still accord reverence and respect for the opinion that he rejects, in accordance with the rabbinic notion that differences of opinion between scholars who are committed to the basic theology and commitments of rabbinic Judaism, are all "the words of the living God." The accumulated literature of traditional biblical interpretation is vast, fascinating, inspiring, and intellectually challenging, and holds tremendous power over the believer.

But this would probably not suffice to explain the insistence of so many that the only proper and rational way of reading and understanding the Torah is through the rabbinic modes of doing so. Most people in the Orthodox world, especially, but not only, the right-wing Orthodox community, have never been exposed to any other way of reading and thinking about the Torah. Whenever they pick up a Torah, they approach it with the only method with which they are familiar. Hence they have no alternative way of understanding it. It is their exclusive paradigm. Even I, growing up in the United States and schooled though high school in modern Orthodox institutions waving the banner of Torah U'Madda (Torah and General Knowledge), never heard about the documentary hypothesis from any of my teachers. I clandestinely learned of it from reading books my older brother brought home from his college classes, then from my own search for material, and from being told about the critical approach from an older friend.[85] Indeed, I was afraid to raise the subject with teachers, especially when I later studied in more right wing yeshivot, for fear of being suspected of being a heretic, or of harboring heretical thoughts. It is extremely difficult to get someone who has been used to only one way of reading, thinking about, interpreting, and explaining a text (or, for that matter, an experience, or a datum) to do so in another way—especially in a way that contradicts the basic assumptions of the paradigm in which he has been trained and socialized. I am speaking here primarily about the *cognitive* difficulty of switching to another paradigm of interpretation. Earlier I discussed the emotional and social tensions generated by such a new way of looking at the Torah and its authorship.

An analogy to the above is the competing Ptolemaic and Copernican theories of the workings of the solar system. Astronomers raised on the Ptolemaic system naturally attempted to fit all new data, even that which at first seemed to be inconsistent with the system, into the old paradigm. Overall, they did so successfully, making necessary adjustments to the theory so that it could accommodate and assimilate the new astronomical observations. However, at some point, some astronomers realized that the Copernican theory was the much more parsimonious one, and better accounted for the data, old and new. It must have been a wrenching cognitive experience for those who for most of their life had looked at the heavens through a metaphorical Ptolemaic telescope to late in life abandon it for a Copernican one. There were also emotional, social, and theological anxieties that the Copernican theory generated, given the widely accepted belief, based upon commonsense observation and biblical texts that the sun moves in the sky and the earth is the stationary center of the solar system. Of course, someone raised on the Copernican system would find it very difficult to understand the Ptolemaic one and would wonder how anyone could have ever believed that—just as I, in my periods of arrogance, wonder how anyone could possibly believe in TMS, even though I myself believed in it until I was twenty-three years old.

———

Jonathan Sacks, Chief Rabbi of the United Kingdom, with a Ph.D. in philosophy from the University of Cambridge, is an articulate and sophisticated modern Orthodox defender of the doctrine of TMS. In his article "Fundamentalism Reconsidered," he critiques the theology of contemporary Conservative Judaism that considers the Torah to have been divinely inspired but not to have been dictated or revealed in its entirety by God to Moses.[86] He also defends the Orthodox approach to the Pentateuch from the criticism leveled at it by modern critical-historical Biblical scholarship, which sees the Torah as a humanly authored work:

Orthodoxy involves belief in a proposition denied by non-Orthodox Jews, namely, that the Five Books of Moses are the unmediated word of God. They are, that is to say, *revelation*... The belief in Torah as revelation is not simply *a* fundamental of Jewish faith. It is *the* fundamental. For were it not for our faith in Torah, how could we arrive at religious certainty about the creation of the world, the meaningfulness of human existence, the justice of history and the promise of messianic redemption? Our knowledge of these things, fragmentary though it is, is derived neither from logic nor science but from our faith in Torah and its Divine authorship. In this sense, therefore, Orthodoxy *is* fundamentalist...

Religious belief... always requires faith. But faith is not a denial of the evidence of the senses. It is trust in something beyond the senses... There was something beyond the human hand that first inscribed the words of the Mosaic books. That something... was God.

Sacks's liberal views within the spectrum of Orthodoxy is reflected, as but one example of many, in his acknowledging that there can be more than one plausible way to explain events described as miracles in the Bible, and that someone who lacks the faith that he has can explain them (or, presumably, the biblical accounts about them, if the skeptic doesn't believe that they actually occurred as described) without recourse to God.

For Sacks it is the desire for "religious certainty about the creation of the world, the meaningfulness of human existence, the justice of history and the promise of messianic redemption" that compels belief in the Torah as divine revelation. Why, however, I ask, must we assume that religious certainties, or, for that matter, nonreligious certainties, are either necessary or possible for humans to acquire? Why can't we acknowledge our finitude and our cognitive limitations, and adopt a stance of intellectual humility? Perhaps the world, even if created by a God, wasn't created to serve humankind? Perhaps there is no "ultimate meaning" to human existence? Perhaps there is no justice in history? Perhaps a messianic redemption might never transpire? Or perhaps the opposite of all of these indeed is the case, as the faithful would have it. Can't we acknowledge that we don't really know, and can't really know, and from this stance develop a religious or an ethical/moral culture and society that realizes that its religions and its ethical/moral values, and institutions to guarantee them, are human constructions created by humans in order to improve the human condition to the best of our ability? Scriptural fundamentalists seem to have greater difficulty with existential uncertainty and moral ambiguity than do nonfundamentalists.

Sacks differentiates between two aspects of Protestant fundamentalism's attitude toward the Bible and that of Orthodox Judaism, biblical *authority,* and biblical *inerrancy and literalism.*[87] Orthodoxy, he argues, does not rely on the Bible itself for religious authority (unlike the "fundamentalist" Karaites, whom the rabbinates considered heretics), but on its *interpretation by authoritative experts based upon tradition,* and the tradition "has the same authority as revelation itself." With respect to the Bible's literal sense and its inerrancy, Orthodoxy does believe that the Torah is true and free of error, and some Orthodox apply this notion to *factual information* in the Bible, such as that the world was created in six days as described in chapter 1 of Genesis. However, there are many Orthodox who do not read the Bible as a source of factual information but as a source of instruction, a book of commandments. "Torah . . . is not an assemblage of facts: it is a set of rules and models of how Israel should live and be blessed. It does not set out primarily to answer the question, "What happened?" but the question, "How then shall I live?" (11). These truths of the Torah are not arrived at by a literal understanding of the Bible, but by a variety of figurative or metaphorical understandings of what lies behind the simple literal sense of its words.

Sacks notes the following:

> Leo Strauss, in his *Philosophy and Law,* made the very telling point that the Enlightenment, in its assault on religious traditions generally and Biblical faith specifically, never truly engaged with the concept of revelation. It merely took its non-existence as given, and proceeded to interpret the Bible accordingly, as if it had proved what in fact it had merely assumed. The traditional belief in revelation, meanwhile, was neither refuted nor refutable. For that reason, Orthodoxy, unchanged in its essence, was able to outlast the attack of the Enlightenment and all later attacks and retreats. (11)

Why is the basis of traditional Jewish belief, the Orthodox assertion that the Pentateuch was revealed at Sinai, not refutable if it is an historical claim which can be refuted, or if even only *some* of the assertions in the Pentateuch are refutable? And if the impossibility of refuting the assertion that God revealed the Pentateuch is the reason that it outlasted all attacks from the Enlightenment onward, is this a proof of its credibility? Why is it more credible than many nonrefutable assertions or claims for revelation made by other religions, cults, or individuals?

It seems to me that Rabbi Sacks's beliefs and arguments are not as different in their underlying structure from Protestant fundamentalists as he thinks they are.[88]

Is there any kind of evidence, arguments or experience that might induce Orthodox Jewish fundamentalists to change their beliefs about TMS? I raised the following questions on several electronic discussion groups and in other venues.

1. Why do you believe in Torah Mi'Sinai (TMS)? (Reasons can run the gamut from philosophical, existential, psychological and anything else you would consider to be the grounds for your affirming this belief.)

2. How do you explain the fact that the vast majority of biblical scholars in academia consider the Torah Mi'Sinai theory to be extremely unreasonable?[89]

3. How do you deal with the evidence provided by biblical scholarship and related disciplines that challenges the traditional Torah Mi'Sinai theory?

4. Is there any kind of evidence that you could imagine which would lead you to change your belief from the Torah Mi'Sinai (divine revelation to Moses) theory to a multiple source/human authorship/post-Mosaic theory? If there is, could you provide some examples of the kind of evidence that would get you to change your view?

I in turn was asked what kind of evidence would induce me to change my present view and convince me to revert back to the TMS view that I rejected after having once believed in it fervently. I find it difficult to imagine such evidence, but at a minimum it would have to be such that its cumulative effect would be to make the TMS theory (and all that such a theory or belief implies) more plausible than a non-TMS theory. For example, if the following evidence and/or arguments were presented, I would probably reconsider *some* aspects of my present beliefs:

1. The discovery of a complete scroll of the Pentateuch that was dated with a high degree of certainty (using accepted methods of dating ancient scrolls, whether carbon dating, archaeological dating, etc.) to the thirteenth century BCE.

2. The discovery of human bones that could be demonstrated to have been several hundred years old at the time of the death of the person whose skeleton was found.

3. References to a mass exodus of several million Israelites from Egypt in the thirteenth century, in nonbiblical literature from the thirteenth century BCE, that was independent of the biblical account of the Exodus.

4. Extrabiblical evidence, for example, artifacts or human remains, that several million people spent forty years in the Sinai wilderness in the thirteenth century, many of whom died there.

The above would prove not that the Pentateuch was revealed by God but only that it was a unitary document already in the thirteenth century BCE and that some of its statements about historical events are most probably true.

I am still waiting for such findings to present themselves. It is easier for me to imagine returning to my earlier belief system, not so much on the basis of "evidence" or "proof," but because doing so might at some future time in my life serve important existential, psychological, and emotional needs I might have.

Many individuals responded to or addressed the questions I had raised, mostly from the Orthodox world, but from other Jewish orientations as well. I summarize and paraphrase a few of those that I found to be of most psychological or intellectual interest.

One determined defender of Orthodox belief insisted that belief in TMS had little to do with reason or empirical evidence.[90] One first decides whether or not he is willing to believe that God revealed the Torah to Moses, and this axiomatic choice then determines the way in which he assesses alleged evidence for or against the doctrine. There is sufficient wiggle room to account for the alleged counterevidence to TMS to make belief in TMS reasonable once one has accepted it on faith. For example, if one accepts TMS and the biblical assertion that miracles occurred during the forty-year period of Israelite wandering in the desert, such as divine provision of manna as food, it is not surprising that archaeologists haven't found remnants of typical, non-manna food in the Sinai desert traceable to the millions of Israelites who traversed it.

With respect to the rejection of TMS by almost all academic biblical scholars, this defender of the faith writes, "This is a defense mechanism to allow people to live an 'irreligious' life style. After all, if you do not attack the Biblical revelation as 'unreasonable,' then the next question is: Why are you not observant? . . . A person who chooses to be non-observant must either attack the Sinai experience or decide that they are going to defy G–d."

Another respondent argued correctly that the fact that numerous people believe something to be true is not proof that it is true. He then asserts that the fact that most academic biblical scholars reject TMS and affirm MSPM proves nothing and is a question that requires no answer on the part of a believer.

This argument, though, ignores the specific reasons for which numerous people believe what they do. If the reasons are convincing to thoughtful people who have subjected the evidence and arguments for them to intensive critical scrutiny, then numbers do count, especially when those people are especially qualified to assess the evidence.

Several respondents assumed that I was not familiar with or knowledgeable about traditional Judaism. They seemed to have difficulty imagining that a person with an intensive traditional education and background would reject the basic beliefs of the tradition. They did not seem to be aware of how common such rejections were from the late eighteenth century onward, through today, and that many Reformers, Maskilim ["enlightenment thinkers"], scholars of Jewish studies, secular Zionists, socialists, communists, agnostics, and atheists had been intensively schooled in traditional Judaism, which they rejected in late adolescence or adulthood. In fact, some of the greatest and most brilliant academic scholars of rabbinics and postrabbinic traditional Jewish thought and literature had undergone such a journey from tradition to "heresy," as defined by the upholders of tradition. Those who are unaware of, or who deny, this history of knowledge-based heresy tend to explain the decline of traditional Judaism over the past two centuries almost exclusively by social or economic factors, which resulted in little or no access to intensive traditional Jewish education for so many Jews (which surely did play an important, but not an exclusive, role in this decline). Thus people who were not traditional in belief and practice were such, they claim, only because they had been deprived of the "proper" education, and not because of any valid substantive problems with traditional theology. A kindly respondent offered to direct me to Orthodox rabbis in the Boston area, where I live, who would be able to educate me about traditional Judaism.

Those believers who are aware of and acknowledge the fact that many individuals who had intensive traditional education became "heretics" find it difficult to assimilate this fact, because they are so certain about the truthfulness and value of their beliefs and way of life, which makes it difficult for them to see how it is that rational and learned others may not share their certainties. It also is very threatening for them to acknowledge that such people opted for heresy, because it presents a challenge to their own beliefs and commitments.

Some believers respond to this challenge, for example, by attributing the "heresy" to the "evil impulses" of the knowledgeable heretic. A frequently cited formulation of this view is that of Rabbi Elhonon Wasserman, who, after presenting the "argument by design" as proof that the world was created by a God, asks how it can be that intelligent people will deny the existence of God. It seems that Wasserman was not familiar with the specific refutations of this proof for the existence of God that were put forth on logical grounds by philosophers such as Hume, because he considers the argument by design to be so absolutely persuasive that it provides no room for any rationally based doubts about it. How then to explain the fact that there are many intelligent people who are atheists? He explains as follows:

> Now, of course, we shouldn't be astonished that so many great philosophers had difficulty believing that the world was created by a Purposeful Creator. Their minds were surely great, but their desire to gain benefit from the pleasures of this world overcame their ability to think straight. Such a powerful bias can divert a person's mind to the point that he can say two plus two does not equal four, but five...
>
> The foundations of true faith are simple and unquestionable for anyone who isn't an idiot. It is simply impossible to doubt their veracity. This is only true, however, on the condition that one does not allow oneself to be bribed. One must be disinterested in and free from the desires and allures of this world, and his own personal desires [for gain].
>
> If so, the root of God-denial lies not in the distortion of the intellect in and of itself. It lies in the heart, i.e., in one's desire to gain benefit [from this world], which distorts and blinds the intellect...
>
> One must simply remove the obstacles that stand in the way of believing. It will then come naturally, of itself.[91]

Others claim that heresy is a form of mental illness—and hence the heretic's "arguments" and objections to tradition needn't be seriously addressed. That is why Nahman, the heretical protagonist in *Whither,* is called Nahman *HaMeshuga* (the crazy one).

My questions assumed that there are good reasons to deny TMS and that beliefs and affirmations about TMS could be and should be subject to empirical and logical analysis, an assumption to which some objected. As one person asked, how can any event of the past be subject to empirical validation or invalidation if we cannot experience it directly, test it, or predict it? Why then is belief in TMS less believable than belief in the Big Bang, which, if it occurred billions of years ago, we cannot directly experience, test, or predict?

The claim that the occurrence of past events is not subject to empirical proof, and hence to verification or falsification, eliminates in one fell swoop every discipline that explores the past. In fact, it eliminates any possibility of claiming that any past event has actually happened, even a minute ago. This is a specious argument when taken to its extreme. Those who raise it to defend their intuitive or faith-based belief in TMS in the absence of evidence for it, and in the presence of evidence against it, do not, after all, also deny events of a day, a week, or a year ago, which are not presently experienced, are often not testable, and are not predictable.

When claiming that an event has occurred we always deal with inferences and plausibilities based upon all we know about the laws of nature, including human nature, which we assume have been constant for, at a minimum, 10,000 years, which is more than enough time to cover the time span referred to in biblical historical narratives. (There are some recalcitrant Orthodox believers of the haredi rather than the modern variety who invoke concepts such as the change of the laws of nature and/or of human nature within the past few thousand years to defend their belief in the veracity of biblical or rabbinic statements that contradict current scientific and medical knowledge.[92]) We may not be able to affirm with absolute certainty that an event occurred, but we do have some criteria for assessing degrees of reasonableness about historical claims. Some of these criteria also involve prediction of future events—for example, if such an event occurred in the past, then we can predict that we will discover some artifact or document, which is then indeed found.

The specious Kuzari argument, which I discussed earlier, was put forth by numerous defenders of the belief in TMS. The argument has strong appeal to a good number of extremely bright believers and seekers, and many people, past and present, have written volumes in attempts to defend it (and others in attempts to refute it).

Does the very fact that I and others need to reflect on the arguments raised by supporters of TMS in order to demonstrate their weaknesses indicate that the belief is *not* implausible or irrational? Perhaps it does. On the other hand, a psychiatrist who would try to convince his paranoid patient that his delusional beliefs are absurd would have to work very hard at it, too, and the paranoid patient would come up with what are on the face of it coherent and plausible justifications for his delusions—as long as his very premise that he is being persecuted is not dislodged. He can be extremely ingenious and creative in "proving" that events and actions that to the nonparanoid person have no bearing on the paranoid person are indeed directed at him by his persecutors. Does this imply that the beliefs of the paranoiac are plausible?

I am not equating belief in TMS or other religious beliefs with paranoia or mental illness. I am pointing out that people can be very rational and logical in their arguments and beliefs, and explain away all challenges to them, as long as they do not question the foundational beliefs from which the others are derived or to which they are intimately linked.

One believing respondent wrote that he is always open to the challenge of proving to himself that arguments *against* TMS are *invalid.* This reflects more openness than that of most haredi Orthodox people and institutions, and a few modern Orthodox as well, who will refuse to listen to or to teach what the proponents of heresies such as MSPM have to say. This believer is following the rabbinic dictum "Know what to respond to the heretic," which is conventionally understood to mean that the believer should prepare himself to be able to refute heretical views. To do so, he has to be familiar with them and the rationales upon which they are based. He should not, however, study them for any intrinsic value or merit that they might have because, being heretical, they have no positive value or merit.

Some respondents assumed that providing psychological and/or sociological explanations for why people affirm TMS automatically implies that the belief is nonrational. Hence they were offended by my psychological/social inquiries. But this is not necessarily the case. As William James argued in *The Varieties of Religious Experience,* rational arguments supporting a belief need to be assessed on their own merits independently of whatever psychological motives a believer might have for accepting the belief and the arguments supporting it. My rejection of the doctrine of TMS is based on the *rational arguments and empirical evidence* against it, not on the fact that belief in the truth of the doctrine serves certain psychological and social needs of the believers. These needs are invoked not to discredit or disprove the doctrine per se, but to understand the motives of the believers in retaining their belief in its truth.

One respondent honestly acknowledged the following: "I think a rejection would shake the quiet basis of my life. In essence, I currently feel safe in my life with the knowledge that all is for the best since G–d is in control. Losing faith in Torah MiSinai is in my mind almost equivalent to losing faith in G–d which would hurt my emotional balance. This is another reason I would probably reject almost any evidence." He anticipated that his behavior would also change dramatically: "When I was younger I imagined if I could somehow be sure there was no G–d then I would go out and do every sin I knew ... sort of flip side to Pascal's wager. Of course, the habit of keeping the Torah is quite strong, but if I truly lost my faith in Torah MiSinai I would have lost my reason to be stringent and I'm sure I would rapidly "slip" into a non-religious lifestyle."

This linking of morality exclusively to the belief in Torah Mi'Sinai, which we discussed earlier in this chapter, was strikingly expressed by another respondent: "If Torah isn't from Sinai—then ... we would lose the basis of our moral structure, our family structure and the rules and mores of human behavior. I have no idea what such a society would become—but anything would be possible. Only as long as Torah Mi'Sinai is valid can we demand Jewish moral behavior, which has become the basis of most of the modern acceptable mores in the world." This woman assumes that Jews (and in fact, all people) should lead their lives in accordance with the moral code of the Torah. She also assumes that the Torah's moral code is the sole grounds for morality. Of course, both of these assumptions are problematic. With respect to the first, there are teachings in the Torah that many people would consider to be unacceptable guidelines for contemporary behavior.

With respect to the second, she seems to be anticipating the question of the presence of moral codes in non-Jewish societies. If TMS is the only grounds for "morality," such that rejection of it would result in total moral anarchy, how does one explain the fact that most of the world's population does have moral rules, even though they do not believe in TMS? Hence her assertion that the world's moral rules are themselves based on the Torah's teachings, which have influenced the non-Jewish world.

This might be argued for those cultures and societies that have been influenced by the Bible, but it leaves out Indian, Chinese, Japanese, and numerous other civilizations that have moral and ethical codes and values, but which were not influenced by the Torah and never even heard of it.

One respondent, a physicist, stated that he would only be willing to consider a non-TMS view if he had been told by the rabbinic scholar/teacher whom he most venerated that some early outstanding religious authority, such as Maimonides, had accepted such a view. But his belief would not be affected in any way by the modern study of history or of literary techniques of analysis. For him, the authority and trustworthiness of the person who is espousing a belief is a more important consideration in determining whether or not to accept it than are the actual arguments or evidence for or against it.[93]

In chapter 6 I will discuss in greater depth psychological explanations for the tenacity and durability of several fundamentalisms, including Orthodox Jewish fundamentalism. I turn now, however, to a consideration of Christian biblical fundamentalism.

| Christian Biblical Fundamentalism

I N THIS CHAPTER I will discuss three expressions of Christian biblical
fundamentalism, the doctrine of biblical inerrancy, the belief in the physical resurrection of Jesus, and the theology and practices of snake-handling
sects.

———

Christian fundamentalists, whose core doctrines are the "inerrancy" and the
"infallibility" of the Bible, provide an example of the tenacity of implausible
beliefs. Implausible religious beliefs are maintained even, or in some instances,
especially, when one's religious values and beliefs, and sense of identity are
under attack. The threats to biblical fundamentalists are real. They come from
modern biblical scholarship, philosophical naturalism, cultural and moral
pluralism, and the implications of the facts and theory of evolution for the
fundamentalists' theological, religious-anthropological, and ethical worldviews. Among these Christian fundamentalist beliefs and doctrines, as formulated by one prominent and influential evangelical Protestant theologian,
Wayne Grudem, are the following:[1]

1. All the words in the Old and in the New Testaments are the words of God. Anyone
who believes that even one word of Scripture is not from God, does not believe in
God. Anyone who disobeys any word from Scripture has disobeyed God. (33)

As we saw earlier, the Talmud makes a similar statement with respect to the
Pentateuch, which is reiterated in Orthodox Jewish fundamentalism, as in
the *Artscroll* introduction to its commentary on the Torah. The authors of the
Artscroll commentary on the Torah and the authors of the *New Scofield Re-*
ference Bible (a widely used Christian fundamentalist Bible commentary) share

many attitudes toward and interpretations of the Pentateuch, although they differ in that *Artscroll* reads the Torah from the perspective of one variant of the theology of postbiblical rabbinic Judaism, whereas *Scofield* reads it from the perspective of one variant of Christian theology. Neither of them read it from the perspective of modern historical-critical biblical scholarship, except in those instances in which the latter does not conflict with their theology. One wonders if these Jewish and Christian fundamentalists are aware of how much they share, not only in their dogma about the origin and inerrancy of the Pentateuch, but in the implausibility of their interpretations of it.

2. *"All of the words in Scripture are completely true and without error in any part"* (40). And *"{t}he inerrancy of Scripture means that Scripture in the original manuscripts does not affirm anything which is contrary to fact."* (42)

Because almost all fundamentalists read the Bible in English translations, primarily but not only the King James Version, rather than in the original Hebrew (Old Testament) and Greek (New Testament), and there are variant readings of ancient manuscripts of both Testaments, and different English translations of them, the question arises as to which "words" of Scripture are the actual, original words of God, that are inerrant. The fundamentalist answers, "However, even though no one has access to these 'original manuscripts' for over 99% of the words of the Bible, we *know* what the original manuscripts said" (45).

The notion of "original manuscripts" is a hypothetical construct, the argument being that there must have been at some point an original manuscript of each and every book of the Bible to which ultimate inerrancy is ascribed. Of course, it is quite possible that no such entity for many parts of the Bible ever did exist, because many of the biblical narratives, laws, poems, prophetic oracles, sermons, and other sections were first transmitted orally for years, decades, or centuries before being committed to writing, and several different individuals might have recorded different versions of the same narrative, law, and so forth. At some point one or another of these different versions became the Bible of the canon, as we know it, and this canonization did not eliminate all traces of variation in the manuscript traditions.

3. *One does not have to be a biblical scholar in order to understand the Bible correctly. The Bible is clear (and one of the "proofs" of this is that the Bible says of itself that it is clear). "The clarity of Scripture means that the Bible is written in such a way that its teachings are able to be understood by all who would read it seeking God's help and being willing to follow it."* (52)

In making this argument, the fundamentalist theologian often assumes an organic unity across the entire Bible. For example, one proof of the doctrine of the "clarity of Scripture" goes as follows: In Deuteronomy Moses says to Israel, in the name of God, "These words which I command you this day shall be upon your heart; and *you shall teach them diligently to your children,* and shall *talk of them* when you sit in your house, and when you walk by the way, and when you lie down, and when you rise" (Deut. 6:6–7). Grudem concludes from this "that God expected that *all* of his people would know and be able to talk about his Word with proper application to ordinary life situations" (pp. 50–51). The phrase "these words which I command you" is taken to refer to the entire Bible, even though the entire Bible had not yet been composed at the time when these words were uttered. Once the Bible was completed, the phrase could be taken out of its local context and applied to the entire canon.

This approach is similar to rabbinic midrash, which also sees an organic unity across the Hebrew Bible, so that a verse from *Psalms* or *Job* or anywhere else—that in its "contextual sense" is not referring, for example, to a story or a law in another biblical book—is assumed to be so. However, the rabbinic users of this midrashic method were often (though not always) aware that their interpretation by "cross-referencing" did not necessarily reflect the original intent of either of the two passages used in the cross-referencing. *The New Scofield Bible* lists thousands of such "cross-references" as one tool for harmonizing what appear to be contradictions of fact or belief between biblical passages, in a contorted though often ingenious attempt to resolve the contradictions without appealing to the heresies of modern critical biblical scholarship, convincing and relatively parsimonious as they might be.

This doctrine of "scriptural clarity" or transparency goes back to the early Protestant attack on the claims of the Catholic Church that it alone was authorized to interpret the Bible. One way of weakening that claim to and source of authority was the doctrine that scripture alone is the source of religious authority. The Bible was meant to be a guide to everyman, and hence everyman is capable of reading it, understanding its truths and teachings, without the mediation of others, as long as the reader is approaching it with proper pious intent. The Holy Spirit will assure the correct understanding. Of course such a doctrine could and did lead to havoc, because the fact of the matter was that many apparently pious people reading the same Bible frequently disagreed about its "plain sense," contributing to the proliferation of Protestant denominations, sects, and subsects. Each claimed to be the sole authentic readers of the text, and often condemned other Christians as, at the least, being erroneous, or at the worst, being heretics, with gradations of disparagement in between these poles. One denomination or sect would say to another: Your reading is wrong because your sinful inclinations, or your less than pure intentions, have clouded your ability to see the meaning of the text that is apparent in its full clarity to me. In fact, however, fundamentalists, although dogmatically claiming that the biblical text is more or less self-evident in its meanings, developed their own authorities and commentaries, among the most prominent of which is the *Scofield Reference Bible* (original 1907 edition, and the *New Scofield Reference Bible,* 1967). The interpretations in these commentaries, rather than being models of clarity and straightforwardness, as one might expect on doctrinal grounds, are often quite complex in the concepts they use, in their elaborate biblical theologies, such as dispensationalism,[2] and the theories and principles of biblical interpretation that follow them, and in the extensive and complicated "chaining" and cross-referencing of numerous biblical verses to one another, in order to arrive at the allegedly "simple" meaning of the text.

Dispensationalism refers to the theory of biblical theology and interpretation that posits "progressive and connected revelations of God's dealings with man." During each dispensational period or age man "is tested in respect to his obedience to some specific revelation of the will of God."[3] One widely used fundamentalist scheme divides history into seven dispensations, beginning with Innocence, when Adam and Eve were first placed in the Garden of Eden and commanded not to eat from the Tree of the Knowledge of Good and Evil. Later stages include the age of Law, the age of Grace, and the final age of the Kingdom. This complex theory/theology has social and theological implications, but also serves as an instrument for "resolving" challenges to the theory of inerrancy by reconciling or harmonizing contradictory biblical texts by assigning one passage to one dispensation and another passage to a different one.[4] Barr notes that "the task of fitting this general scheme into the detail of the biblical text requires an extremely complex apparatus of distinctions, discriminations and explanations . . . [Dispensationalism] is a remarkable achievement of the mythopoeic fantasy."[5]

The authors of *Scofield* surely have high IQs, because to follow such a scheme is intellectually demanding. Once again we see that very smart people can believe very stupid things—perhaps a guiding mantra of this book.

Without going to the extremes of postmodernist literary theory,[6] which negates a single, authoritative, determinate meaning of any text, it should be evident to anyone who reads the Bible that there are hundreds of passages whose meaning is unclear, or at least susceptible to several plausible, and often mutually exclusive, interpretations, putting the lie to the doctrine of "scriptural clarity."

The doctrine of "biblical clarity" does not always mean that the Bible is to be understood "literally." When a literal reading of a biblical text is contradicted by scientific facts accepted by a fundamentalist, many a fundamentalist will read the biblical text nonliterally. Fundamentalists today who accept (as most do) the Copernican view that the earth revolves around the sun, rather than that the sun moves around the earth, interpret the passage in Joshua 10:12–15 that the sun stood still (implying that the sun moves) in response to Joshua's command that it do so during a battle, in a nonliteral sense. The plain, literal sense of the passage is that the battle had begun at night, with a surprise attack, and extended into daytime. Joshua wanted to prolong the daylight hours, so he stopped the sun in its tracks for a while, giving him time to defeat the enemy. But the fundamentalists who accept the Copernican theory that the sun does not move and believe that the Bible is inerrant cannot explain the story in this manner. Instead, they resolve the dilemma posed by a literal reading of the passage by offering a nonliteral one. Joshua, they contend, wanted the darkness of night to be extended, because darkness was to the advantage of the Israelites. The expressions in verses 12 and 13, which are translated in the *New Revised Standard* version of the Bible as "Sun, stand still at Gibeon" (v. 12) and "The sun stopped in midheaven" (v. 13), are (according to these fundamentalists) not about the sun stopping in its tracks but about something that prevents the rays of the sun from illuminating the battlefield. Joshua commanded the sun to stop shining (i.e. to 'stand still' from shining, not to stop moving). The answer to Joshua's prayer was a hailstorm that stopped the sun from shining by blocking its rays—in effect prolonging the darkness of night.[7] This interpretation is clearly forced and counter to the original intent of the passage and the meaning of the Hebrew. One cannot help but wonder how *The New Bible Commentary Revised* (another fundamentalist commentary) is oblivious to its absurdity and to the absurdity of numerous analogous flights from the literal when the literal cannot be sustained in the face of the factual. For this fundamentalist commentator, the doctrine of biblical inerrancy is supreme and supersedes the doctrine of "clarity" or the commonsense interpretation. For several centuries after the Copernican theory was put forth, there was sufficient doubt about its veracity so that traditional readers of the Bible did not feel compelled to interpret "let the sun stand still" nonliterally. When the evidence for Copernican theory became overwhelming this new reading became necessary.

There might still be in some obscure location a few fundamentalists who are either unfamiliar with Copernican theory, or who are unconvinced by it, or who reject it because they are committed to a literalist understanding of the Bible. If the Bible says the sun stood still, implying that under normal circumstances the sun moves, then Copernicus must be wrong. The Bible is always right.

There is thus an inner logic to the illogicality of fundamentalism—once you accept the premise of inerrancy as an unassailable doctrine, and its theological primacy, all else needs to be sacrificed to maintain it, including plausibility and consistency of interpretation.

Of course the fundamentalist commentator[8] would probably argue that because inerrancy is clearly true, his interpretation is more plausible than the literal one that would lead to the even more implausible conclusion that the Bible is errant. The issue becomes for him not so much which interpretation of a particular text is more plausible, but which one is less implausible in the broader context of his belief system. Because inerrancy is treated as axiomatic (even though fundamentalists attempt to prove it by logical argumentation), from his perspective, he is correct that his interpretation is less implausible. It would seem, therefore, that it is futile to try to convince such a fundamentalist of the implausibility of his view by critiquing specific textual interpretations, or even a pattern of inconsistent interpretations.

There are, however, other approaches that might be more productive in undermining faith in fundamentalism, if that were an objective. I will mention some of these in chapter 6, but that is not the primary purpose of this book. When and whether it is appropriate to undermine fundamentalist beliefs will be addressed in chapter 7, and an in-depth analysis of how to do so in a sequel to this book. My aim here is more along the lines of Barr's, but from a psychological rather than a theological perspective (although I do hope that some fundamentalists, or those hovering on the borders of fundamentalism might be influenced by this book of mine). Barr writes the following:

> I do not find any of its [fundamentalism's] intellectual arguments to have validity except in very minor respects. But this book is not written for the sake of controversy with fundamentalists. I did not write in order to produce arguments that will make them feel they are wrong or cause them to change their minds. I am interested, not so much in altering their opinions, as in understanding an intellectual structure that will be little affected by arguments anyway. My purpose is thus to understand fundamentalism as a religious and intellectual system and to see why it functions as it does.[9]

The inconsistency of interpretation of fundamentalist commentaries is in the fact that many biblical passages, such as the physical existence of Hell and its fire and other torments, are interpreted literally—and dogmatically so. Because there is no way that anyone, scientist or layperson, can disprove the existence of Hell, there is no need to interpret it nonliterally. Moreover, the literalist interpretation of Hell provides a strong instrument of control over the lives of the flocks of the fundamentalists by their leaders.

The deeper question, as to why people who are intelligent and rational in many spheres of experience "lose it" when it comes to their theology, is answered by understanding the social and psychological motives that underlie their commitment to fundamentalism in the first place, some of which we have already discussed and more of which we will discuss later.

As with the Copernican theory so, too, with the age of the earth and evolution, we see fundamentalist ambivalence about when to read a text literally and when nonliterally. A good number of fundamentalists today deny evolution, especially human evolution. They have not yet accepted a nonliteral understanding of the counter-scientific account of the creation of the oceans, the celestial bodies, vegetation, animals, and humans. Some other fundamentalists long ago accepted the evidence from the geological record that the age of the Earth was at least millions of years (current scientific estimates put it as approximately 4.5 billion years). They reinterpreted the Genesis 1 account of creation in six days to accommodate eons, ignoring the simple, clear, commonsense meaning that to the ancient author 6 days of morning and evening meant just that. Some fundamentalists have conceded that science has plausibly arrived at "truth" about the origin of some of those entities, such as the celestial bodies, but not about the origin of humans.[10] So they will be nonliteralists with respect to the celestial bodies acknowledging that the earth came into existence after the formation of the sun, as established by modern cosmology. If so, they can no longer understand the placement of the sun, moon, and stars in the firmament to have taken place after the creation of Earth on the first day. But that seems to be what the Bible says. So they interpret the events of the fourth day to mean that the celestial bodies had actually been created on the first day, prior to the creation of Earth, but only became visible on the fourth day (or stage, if they equate day with an eon or stage) of creation. Yet they will still maintain that humans didn't evolve from an earlier primate and that women were created from a rib taken from Adam and shaped by God, because "the Bible tells them so."

Barr sums up this inconsistent approach:

[F]undamentalist interpretation does not take the Bible literally, but varies between taking it literally and taking it non-literally. This variation is made necessary by the real guiding principle of fundamentalist interpretations, namely that one must ensure that the Bible is inerrant, without error. Inerrancy is maintained only by constantly altering the mode of interpretation, and in particular by abandoning the literal sense as soon as it would be an embarrassment to the view of inerrancy held.[11]

With respect to biblical miracles, too, fundamentalist biblical interpretation is riddled with inconsistencies, convoluted attempts at harmonization, and ambivalent attitudes. It tries to explain many miracles "naturalistically" while at the same time maintaining that it is in God's power to perform supernatural miracles and that he has sometimes exercised this power in the past. This might be because many fundamentalists, interestingly enough, are highly educated engineers and scientists, and not uneducated ignoramuses, as some stereotypes of them would have it. In fact, one feature of many fundamentalist theologians is a commitment to rationality and to the notion that the inerrancy of the Bible, and many of its assertions, such as the resurrection, can be "proven" on strictly logical and/or evidentiary grounds. They do not appeal to "blind faith" or to nonbiblical spiritual intuition as the grounds for their belief, although, as we saw above, they accord the Holy Spirit a role in helping the believer ascertain the true meaning of the text. The proofs for their Christian beliefs, so they argue and believe, come from human reason, which proves the revelatory status of the text and its inerrancy, and once that has been established, other Christian beliefs and values derive from, and only from, the text itself.

It is fascinating and sad to see the minds of these fundamentalist inerrantists in action. Hundreds of books, thousands of pages, myriads of hours, and millions of brain cells are devoted to defending, on ostensibly rational grounds, contradictions in the Bible, inconsistencies in their own dogmas, circularity in their reasoning, absurdities in their conclusions,[12] cruelty in their doctrines,[13] and selfishness in their social visions. They scurry to and fro with their inane "logic" and "proofs," defending themselves against criticism instead of acknowledging their errors. Some of them militantly crusade against (verbally—not physically) leading academic scholars of the Bible, biologists who teach evolution, and school boards who want our children to receive a proper scientific education in biology. Many of these fundamentalists are "smart." Why then are they so "stupid"? Why is rationality so fragile? We will attempt to answer this question in chapter 6.

How Do We Know That the Entire Bible Is God's Words?

How does a fundamentalist know that "all the words in Scripture are God's words"? Let us return to Grudem, the systematic theologian of fundamentalism who systematically sets forth the proofs for this assertion.[14]

1. This is what the Bible claims for itself.

Stage 1 of the argument tries to prove that the Bible makes the claim that it, in its entirety, is the word of God. A complex chain of many (weak) links is constructed in order to substantiate this. Grudem begins by citing numerous Old Testament passages that say or clearly imply that they are divine revelation, or the words of God. For example, many Old Testament prophetic oracles are introduced by the phrase "Thus says the Lord," and many Old Testament laws, transmitted by Moses to the people of Israel, are attributed to God's revelation and are often referred to as "the words of the Lord" or some variant thereof.

Grudem believes that the actual words of the entire Bible were "approved" by God, word for word, even though many of these words were initially formulated by humans, in their own idiosyncratic language and style, whether in response to a divine revelation, or even on their own initiative for some mundane end, or even for an evil purpose. So when, for example, Korah, the sinner who rebels against Moses, makes certain "evil" statements, which he uttered by his own free will, the initial utterance was not God's. However, once God approved the inclusion of this story with the utterances, in the Bible, these words become God's words. This is similar to the rabbinic notion that Yahweh dictated the entire Pentateuch to Moses, who was acting simply as a scribe without any input of his own to the final document, and to the Muslim belief that all the words of the Koran are from Allah, including those that are attributed to sinners. Most Christian fundamentalists prefer the concept of "verbal" inspiration (all of the words of the Bible) or "plenary" inspiration (i.e., the entire text of the Bible)—the Bible as being *in-spired* ("breathed into") by God, rather than a dictation theory.[15]

Grudem acknowledges the following:

> [T]hese verses by themselves [such as "Thus says the Lord" or "the words of the Lord"] do not claim that *all* the words in the Old Testament are God's words, for these verses themselves are referring only to specific sections of spoken or written words in the Old Testament. But the cumulative force of these [hundreds of] passages . . . demonstrate that within the Old Testament we have written records of words that are said to be God's words. These words constitute large sections of the Old Testament. (34)

So far so good. How do we get from this to the idea that the OT makes the claim that in its entirety it is the words of God? "When we realize that all of the words that were part of 'the law of God' or the 'book of the covenant' were considered God's words, we see that the whole Old Testament claims that kind of authority" (34). Without getting into the full fallaciousness of this argument, of arguing from the *part* to the *whole,* and of misinterpreting the referents of "law of God" and "book of the covenant," which refer only to specific sections of what later became the Pentateuch or, in some cases, to nothing in the Pentateuch at all, but to some other ancient oral and/or written Israelite traditions, there is the "minor" problem that the Pentateuch, and most of the rest of the Old Testament, didn't even exist as a "book" or "books" when those phrases were used. Of course, the fundamentalist who rejects the views of nearly every serious biblical scholar that the Pentateuch (and several other OT books) are edited, anthologized composites of multiple earlier sources (and hence can be inconsistent and contradictory), and that the Pentateuch as we have it did not exist prior to the late sixth century BCE, can be oblivious to these problems with his theory and conjure up whatever scenarios he wants to, as long as the net outcome will be the doctrine to which he is a priori committed.

With respect to the New Testament, chronologically early works of the New Testament that refer to some New Testament writings as the words of God are taken to refer to the entire New Testament, including works that had not yet been written. For example, 2 Peter 3:15–16 refers to Paul's letters: "Our beloved brother Paul wrote to you according to the wisdom given him, speaking as he does in *all his letters.* There are some things in them hard to understand, which the ignorant and unstable twist to their destruction, as they do *the other scriptures.*"

This suggests that at the time of the writing of this letter attributed to Peter (but not written by him, according to many nonfundamentalist New Testament scholars), Paul's letters to various Christian communities were being read at some worship services, as were sections of the Old Testament (i.e., "scriptures").

Now if we turn to 2 Timothy 3:16, in which Timothy is reporting Paul's charge to him, we read that "all scripture is inspired by God (literally, God-breathed)[16] and is useful for teaching, for reproof, for correction, and for training in righteousness." So Peter compares Paul's letters to "scripture," and Timothy says that "all scripture" is God-breathed. How do we get from this to the idea that the entire New Testament is inspired or God-breathed?[17] After all, much if not most of the New Testament was written after Peter, Paul, and Timothy were dead.

No problem is insurmountable for the dedicated fundamentalist:

These two passages taken together indicate that during the time of the writing of the New Testament documents there was an awareness that *additions* were being made to this special category of writings called "scripture," writings that had the character of being God's very words. Thus, once we establish that a New Testament writing belongs to the special category of "scripture," we are correct in applying 2 Timothy 3:16 to that writing as well, and saying that that writing also has the characteristic Paul attributes to "all scripture": It is "God-breathed," and all its words are the very words of God. (35)

Now this first weak link in the chain of argument has been used only to "establish" that, at least in the fundamentalist reading and cross-textual gymnastics, the entire Bible claims of itself that it is the word of God.

So what? Grudem is aware that "claiming" is not "proving." So how do we get from one to the other?

> It is one thing to affirm that the Bible claims to be the words of God. It is another thing to be convinced that those claims are true. Our ultimate conviction that the words of the Bible are God's words comes only when the Holy Spirit speaks *in* and *through* the words of the Bible to our hearts and gives us inner assurance that these are the words of our Creator speaking to us. Apart from the work of the Spirit of God, a person will not receive or accept the truth that the words of Scripture are in fact the words of God.
>
> But for those in whom God's Spirit is working there is a recognition that the words of the Bible are the words of God . . . as people read Scripture . . . they hear their Creator's voice speaking to them in the words of Scripture and realize that the book they are reading is unlike any other book, that it is indeed a book of God's own words speaking to their hearts. (36)

There are some problems here, insofar as Grudem is trying to prove to me, and to everyone who is reading his systematic theology, that the entire Bible is the words of God.

He is appealing to subjective, individual, religious experience to make a claim that he wants everyone to accept. *I* [Grudem], and fundamentalists like me feel, when reading the Bible, that the Bible is authored by God. This proves that it is. Therefore, *you* (i.e., all mankind) should acknowledge that this is true (especially if you don't want to end up in Hell), even though when you read the Bible you don't experience what I and my fellow fundamentalists experience.[18]

However, even people who "experience the Holy Spirit" when they read the Bible might experience it only when reading certain sections and not others. So perhaps only those sections are the word of God. Or perhaps whatever section one reads is the word of God only on the days when the individual experiences the Holy Spirit while reading it, but not on days when she does not have such an experience. It is a rather common experience of many religious people reading the Bible to experience the Holy Spirit intermittently or sporadically rather than consistently. Or perhaps the same biblical section is *simultaneously* the word of God and not the word of God as when two people read the same section at the same time, one of whom experiences the Holy Spirit while doing so and the other does not.

Let us look at another somersault. Grudem has "proved," at least to his satisfaction, that the entire Bible is the word of God. But he doesn't want to stop there, given his peculiar, but influential fundamentalist stance within the fundamentalist movement. He argues that at the most fundamental level the proof that the entire Bible is the words of God cannot rely on any authority or argument, higher than, or external to the Bible itself, which is the ultimate authority for all beliefs. He even has to qualify the proof from the Holy Spirit experience. "It is important to remember that this conviction that the words of Scripture are the words of God does not come *apart from* the words of Scripture or *in addition* to the words of Scripture" (36). Moreover,

> the words of Scripture are "self attesting," they cannot be "proved" to be God's words by appeal to any higher authority. If we make our ultimate appeal, for example, to human logic ... to prove that the Bible is God's Word, then we assume the thing to which we appeal to be a higher authority than God's words and one that is more true or more reliable. Therefore, the ultimate authority by which Scripture is shown to be God's words must be Scripture itself. (37)

As an aside, I must admit that I am somewhat confused here. Grudem is using a multipaged, multichained sequence of ostensibly logical arguments of systematic theology to prove his doctrinal claims about the Bible, while at the same time denying the authority of logic to prove these claims.

It has not escaped Grudem's attention that there is some circularity in his argument above, and he takes this challenge head on.

> Someone may object that to say Scripture proves itself to be God's words is to use a circular argument: We believe that Scripture is God's Word because it claims to be that. And we believe its claims because Scripture is God's Word. And we believe that it is God's Word because it claims to be that, and so forth.

It should be admitted that this is a kind of circular argument. However, that does not make its use invalid, for all arguments for an absolute authority must ultimately appeal to that authority for proof; otherwise the authority would not be an absolute or highest authority. The problem is not unique to the Christian who is arguing for the authority of the Bible. Everyone either implicitly or explicitly uses some kind of circular argument when defending his or her ultimate authority for belief . . . [for example,] "my reason is my ultimate authority because it seems reasonable to me to make it so." (37–38)

Granting, for argument's sake, that circular reasoning is necessary for "proving" any claim for ultimate authority, does that make the use of circular reasoning valid? No. What it should do is lead Grudem and others who make "claims for *ultimate* authority," to cease and desist from making such claims, and humbly acknowledge that such claims are arbitrary and cannot be verified.

Having acknowledged that all claims to ultimate authority are in principle circular, but still making such a claim for and about the Bible, Grudem, relentlessly "logical" and "rational" in his systematic theology, takes up the next obvious question: On what grounds should one choose, from the competing, mutually exclusive claims to ultimate authority that are made by different religions, the one that is really "true"?

How then does a Christian, or anyone else, choose among the various claims for absolute authorities? Ultimately, the truthfulness of the Bible will commend itself as being far more persuasive than other religious books (such as the *Book of Mormon* or the *Qur'an*) or than any other intellectual constructions of the human mind (such as logic, human reason, sense experience, scientific methodology, etc.). It will be more persuasive because, in the actual experience of life, all of these other candidates for ultimate authority are seen to be inconsistent or to have shortcomings that disqualify them, while the Bible will be seen to be fully in accord with all that we know about the world around us, about ourselves, and about God. (38)

First of all, it needs to be noted that not all of the supposed claimants of ultimate authority that Grudem lists actually make such a claim. Many scientists are simply content to go about doing their research making discoveries without claiming "ultimate authority" for what they do, discover, or theorize. So, too, with many philosophers, who may question all claims to "ultimate authority" without claiming that philosophy has "ultimate authority." Philosophy is a method to try to get people to better understand the nature of their thinking and its pitfalls. Similarly, many psychologists try to understand human thought processes without suggesting that psychology is an ultimate authority. So far, "reason" seems to be a pretty good source of wisdom, but not the only source. One need not claim that reason has ultimate authority in order to appreciate its value. Moreover, there are many Christian theologians who do not make claims for the "ultimate authority" of the Bible even as they enlighten us on many aspects of our humanity by explicating Christian historical experience and Christian religious literature.

Can anyone guess how a Muslim might respond to Grudem's argument? If he is as hard core a textual fundamentalist with respect to the Qur'an, all he needs to do is substitute "How then does a Christian choose..." with "How then does a Muslim choose...," and then in the places in the above paragraph where it says "Bible," substitute for "Bible" "Qur'an," and—voilà!— he has conclusive evidence that the Qur'an is the true ultimate authority. And as we shall see in chapter 5, a similar argument is indeed made by many Muslims to "prove" that the Qur'an is the actual words of God, the source of all truth, wisdom, knowledge, morality, and so forth.

Fundamentalists tend to have an either/or approach to Christian truth. If the Bible is wholly inerrant and wholly infallible in its teachings, then and only then does it have any religious value and authority. If it is shown to be errant, or fallible, even to the slightest degree, it no longer is a source of religious significance and has no claim on our belief or behavior. Such an either/or approach lends itself to intolerance of non-Christians, and even of nonfundamentalist Christians. Everyone except fundamentalists are guilty of the sin of denying God, and are denied the salvation achieved only by belief in Christ's atoning death as they understand it, and will be consigned to eternal damnation in Hell. This is similar to many Islamic teachings about the ultimate fate on Judgment Day of those who do not accept Allah, Muhammad his prophet, and the Koran, Allah's inerrant, infallible revelation to mankind via Muhammad. Jewish fundamentalism is more tolerant, inasmuch as it allows for salvation, without conversion to Judaism, for those who accept and live by the seven Noahide laws.[19]

Fundamentalists share, of course, many other implausible, irrational, or nonconfirmable beliefs and assertions of the New Testament and of traditional Christianity, albeit with their own particular theological perspective on them. Among these are the belief that Mary was a virgin even though she conceived and gave birth to Jesus, because Jesus had no human father; God incarnated himself in Jesus; Jesus was both fully God and fully human; after his death Jesus was physically (bodily) resurrected; the resurrected Jesus ascended to Heaven; Jesus will return to earth in the future to judge mankind; and the righteous will enjoy eternal reward in Heaven, and the wicked will suffer eternal damnation in Hell.

Some of these beliefs and doctrines have been reinterpreted by liberal theologians to make them more credible and reasonable to the modern mind. Fundamentalists, however, resist these trends, as do many if not most theologically conservative Christians.

The Physical Resurrection of Jesus

Based on various New Testament sources, fundamentalists believe that Jesus was physically resurrected. Many traditional Christian believers who do not identify themselves as fundamentalists and who are not considered by historians or sociologists of religion to be fundamentalist Christians also believe that Jesus was physically resurrected. The fundamentalists tend to assert their belief with certainty, passion, deprecation of nonbelievers, and evangelical zeal. Nonfundamentalists who believe in the physical resurrection of Jesus might acknowledge its implausibility but believe that it is not so inherently unreasonable that it needs to be rejected outright. They might embrace the belief in a spirit of hope or longing, rather than certainty. If indeed Jesus' death was not final, then the death of others, especially the righteous, might not be final either. Agnostics, atheists, most non-Christians, and many Christians, as well, maintain that belief in the physical resurrection of Jesus is so implausible and improbable that they consider the belief in it and religious commitments based upon it to border upon or enter the realm of the irrational.

What is the basis for the belief of the fundamentalist Christian, who preaches the physical resurrection of Jesus with absolute assurance and zeal? It rests on several assumptions:

1. God exists and can miraculously bring a dead person to physical life.
2. The New Testament says that this is what happened to Jesus, and because the Bible is true and inerrant, this is what happened.

According to the fundamentalist reading of the passages that assert Jesus' resurrection and report sightings of Jesus after his death, Jesus was *physically* resurrected. (Other Christians, however, interpret the same texts as referring to some form of nonphysical, spiritual, postdeath existence. Yet others interpret these texts as spiritual metaphors, which are not to be understood in any sense that is close to the literal.)

3. A careful examination of the "historical evidence" from the first century, which includes the New Testament accounts and the teachings and activities of the early followers of Jesus, proves that Jesus was resurrected. Not only is the assumption that there was an actual resurrection the most plausible explanation for the known facts, relative to other explanations of the textual and historical sources, it is in an absolute sense a highly plausible explanation for them.

Skepticism with respect to this belief began as soon as the claim was made, and this is recognized in the New Testament itself, which brings several "proofs" to rebut the skeptics' denial.[20]

The debate continues to this day, engaging the intellectual attention of theologians, philosophers, and historians, as well as psychologists.[21] The first assumption, that God exists and performs miracles, is the domain of theology and philosophy of religion. The second assumption, biblical infallibility and inerrancy, is also in the domain of theology. The third assumption relates to the methodology of historical research, the nature of historical explanation, and the historical reliability of New Testament texts.

Psychology enters the debate by trying to explain why people experience visions of those who have died. How do their prior beliefs generate and shape their visions, and how do their visions affect their beliefs? Although it is conceptually useful to identify these four domains of discourse (theology; philosophy of religion; historical method and explanation; psychology) with respect to belief in the resurrection, in the actual belief structure of an individual, and in debates about belief, they are interconnected. Thus, for example, one's theological premises will affect one's approach to historical explanation; one's assumptions about human psychology will affect one's theological beliefs.

One of the staunchest, articulate, and persistent spokespersons for the fundamentalist view of resurrection is philosopher of religion William Lane Craig, a Fellow at the Discovery Institute[22] and active in the Campus Crusade for Christ. In the past few years, philosopher Antony Flew[23] and historian of early Christianity Bart Ehrman have been prominent critics of Craig and his views. Craig has debated both of them, and other academics, on many university campuses.[24]

I will not present here a full account of Craig's arguments for the historicity of the resurrection[25] but will focus only on the main arguments against the plausibility of belief in it and Craig's response to them.

The theme of the Craig–Flew debate was "Does God Exist?" and Craig uses the alleged resurrection of Jesus as a proof for the existence of God, because only God would be capable of physically resurrecting someone who had died.

How does Craig prove that Jesus was resurrected? He presents several historical facts from which he infers the resurrection:

> Fact 1. On the Sunday following his crucifixion Jesus' tomb was found empty by a group of his women followers.
> Fact 2. On separate occasions different individuals and groups saw appearances of Jesus alive after his death.
> Fact 3. The original disciples suddenly came to believe in the resurrection of Jesus despite their having every disposition to the contrary.
>
> The simple fact is that there just is no plausible, naturalistic explanation of these three facts. And therefore, it seems to me, the Christian is amply justified in believing that Jesus rose from the dead and was who he claimed to be....[26]

These three "facts" are not as self-evidently factual as Craig takes them to be. The reliability of these gospel accounts to serve as history is questioned by numerous scholars, not least because of contradictions between the various New Testament accounts of the events following Jesus' death. The assertion of Fact 3, that the disciples had every disposition not to believe in the resurrection, is false. On the contrary, belief in the possibility of resurrection was widespread among first-century Jews.[27]

Even if evidence for the truthfulness of these three "facts" was strong, Craig's assertion that the *only* plausible explanation for them is a supernatural one is absurd, as there are many naturalistic explanations that could account for them. For example, Kent cites ample evidence from psychology and psychiatry to establish that individuals suffering deep grief at the loss of a beloved one will often have hallucinations in which they encounter the deceased, in their mind, in a way that makes them feel that he or she is physically present and communicating with them. This could account for the experiences reported by Mary Magdalene and other grief-stricken disciples of Jesus. Paul probably suffered a "conversion disorder" on the road to Damascus, during which he saw a risen Christ, "and out of the mystical component of this psychological trauma he passionately believed that Jesus had been resurrected from the dead by a unilateral act of God."[28] *Even if the proposed naturalistic explanations are not very plausible,* they are still *more* plausible than the supernatural one, given that we have no *credible* evidence that any other human being was ever resurrected,[29] either before or after Jesus died.[30]

Flew argues that "we need to have far and away stronger evidence for the actual occurrence of a truly miraculous event than we need to have for an ordinary non-miraculous event," and Craig's evidence for the miraculous event does not come anywhere near to meeting this criterion. (Of course a simplistic, circular reasoning fundamentalist might interject—this is all the more proof of the uniqueness of Jesus. Ever since his resurrection no one else has been resurrected.)

The personal history or psychological makeup of antagonists in a debate should not affect our evaluation of the validity of their arguments. However, personal history and psychology may offer insight into their choice of one argument or view over another when neither can be definitively proven. This is often the case when there are differences of opinion in the humanities, religious studies, and the social sciences, in which plausibility or reasonableness rather than formal proof is the yardstick we use to assess truthfulness.[31] They might be relevant to understanding the way in which an individual responds to arguments and evidence that challenge his views. Personal history and psychological makeup often impact on the passion and emotions that accompany argumentation and debate. This is the case for all people, fundamentalist and nonfundamentalist alike. Although I will put neither Craig nor Ehrman on the couch, lacking as I do intimate knowledge of their histories and psychologies, it is interesting to learn a few autobiographical facts that they have chosen to share with the public, specifically with respect to their relationship to Christian fundamentalism.

Craig and Ehrman had similar childhood and young adult experiences. As teenagers both became devout Christians, with a strong personal faith in Christ, and this born-again spiritual experience led both of them to Wheaton College, a Christian liberal arts school. Craig's studies at Wheaton reinforced his commitment to Christianity and his conviction of the historicity of the resurrection.

> Of course, ever since my conversion, I believed in the resurrection of Jesus on the basis of my personal experience,[32] and I still think this experiential approach to the resurrection is a perfectly valid way to knowing that Christ has risen. It's the way that most Christians today know that Jesus is risen and alive.... God became a living reality to me. The light went on where before there was only darkness, and God became an experiential reality, along with an overwhelming joy and peace and meaning that He imparted to my life.[33]

Ehrman eventually took a different path after first attending Moody Bible Institute and then going on to Wheaton.

> I used to believe them [the resurrection and other conservative evangelical beliefs about Jesus and early Christianity] with my whole heart and soul. I used to preach them and try to convince others that

they were true. But then I . . . became a historian of antiquity . . . After years of studying, I finally came to the conclusion that everything I had previously thought about the historical evidence of the resurrection was absolutely wrong.

One of the intriguing and still mysterious aspects of belief is why it is that so often two rational, intelligent individuals who have had similar educations, read the same books, and studied the same "arguments" for and against a belief or worldview arrive at vastly different conclusions about the belief. They do not suspend judgment about whether or not the belief is plausible, but adopt strong positions of either affirmation or denial, and devote intellectual, emotional, and behavioral resources for many years of their life in support of their respective beliefs. I cannot provide a definitive answer to this question but do speculate about it in chapter 6, which deals with psychological explanations for the tenacity of beliefs, even—or, perhaps especially—of "unreasonable" ones.[34]

In response to Craig's claim for the reliability of the Gospels as historical sources, Ehrman says, "But how good are they as historical sources? Unfortunately, they're not as good as we would like. The Gospels were written 35 to 65 years after Jesus' death . . . not by people who were eyewitnesses, but by people living later . . . Where did these people get their information from?" Ehrman's explanation is that those who followed Jesus and continued to believe in him after his death created stories about him in order to convince others to join them in their faith. Storytelling about the miraculous deeds of God or gods, heroes, and prophets, especially in antiquity, was an important way of propagandizing for a faith, and especially when someone was trying to encourage people to give up the faith of their fathers and adopt a new one. The new converts in turn converted others, using the stories they had been told, adapting them and adding others, as appropriate to the needs of the newer recruits.[35] This accounts for the irreconcilable discrepancies in the stories about Jesus that are found in the Gospels. Because the stories were authored long after Jesus' death, were not unbiased historical accounts, and are inconsistent, they are historically unreliable sources for information about Jesus' life and for what occurred to his body and to his followers after he died. Ehrman further argues:

> Even if these stories were the best sources in the world, there would still be a major obstacle that we simply cannot overcome if we want to approach the question of the resurrection historically rather than theologically . . . Miracles are so highly improbable that they're the least possible occurrence in any given instance. They violate the way

nature naturally works . . . Historians can only establish what probably happened in the past, and by definition a miracle is the least probable occurrence . . . The resurrection has to be taken on faith, not on the basis of proof.

In the course of the debate Ehrman speculates on other naturalistic scenarios that might account for Craig's (disputed) facts, and points out that he could conjure up many more, some of which are very implausible. However, they are still more probable than the supernatural explanation of resurrection, given the rarity of resurrection in known human history and experience.

In rebuttal Craig presents a complicated (to someone not familiar with probability theory and calculus) set of mathematical equations to argue that the resurrection explanation is not at all improbable.

Fundamentalists with a mathematical or scientific background frequently use the tactic of arguing or bolstering their case with elaborate mathematical and scientific concepts and procedures, whose accuracy cannot be judged by most of their intended audience. This is the case, for example, with Jewish outreach "evangelists" such as Aish HaTorah who try to win Jewish souls to their version of Orthodox Judaism by proving that the Torah is a divine revelation because after rather complex statistical analyses of patterns of letters and words in the Hebrew Bible, they "discover" hidden Bible codes that have allegedly predicted historical events. Of course, they then have to develop a theory as to why previous generations did not need such proofs for their beliefs, and indeed could not have known them, because the field of modern statistics didn't exist. They have an answer to this conundrum as well—the Torah speaks to each generation in terms of the concepts of its age and the challenges to faith of the culture in which it is embedded. In an age of sophisticated science and mathematics, in which people place their trust, it makes sense that science and math will be used to prove the divinity of the Torah. Some of the proponents of "creation science" and "intelligent design" use similar techniques, as does Craig in his proof for the resurrection.

Craig continues:

Dr. Ehrman . . . assumes that the probability of the resurrection . . . is very low. But here, I think, he's confused. What, after all, is the resurrection hypothesis? It's the hypothesis that Jesus rose supernaturally from the dead. It is not the hypothesis that Jesus rose naturally from the dead. That Jesus rose naturally from the dead is fantastically improbable. But I see no reason whatsoever to think that it is improbable that God raised Jesus from the dead. In order to show that that hypothesis is improbable, you'd have to show that God's existence is improbable. But Dr. Ehrman says that the historian cannot say anything about God. Therefore, he cannot say that God's existence is improbable. But if he can't say that, neither can he say that the resurrection of Jesus is improbable. So Dr. Ehrman's position is literally self-refuting.

Although Ehrman does not explicitly point it out, there is a flaw in Craig's argument. Granting for argument's sake that if God exists it is not at all improbable that he *could have* resurrected Jesus, it is still highly improbable that God *actually did so* if the only evidence is the empty tomb, the disciples' subsequent visions of Jesus, and their new convictions about him. Given the fact that, as Craig would himself admit, God has not resurrected any[36] of the billions of people who have lived and died before, during, and after the life and death of Jesus, the probability of God actually resurrecting anyone, including Jesus, approaches zero, based upon how God operates in the world. Craig cannot argue that Jesus was unique, because that would be circular. He wants to prove Jesus' uniqueness by the fact that he was allegedly resurrected, so you can't prove his having been resurrected by appeal to his uniqueness.[37] Even the most outlandish explanations for the empty tomb, the visions and conversion experiences that do not invoke God's resurrecting action, are vastly more probable than the resurrection explanation. Moreover, one needn't look far for a plausible, naturalistic explanation that is not outlandish.

Ehrman rebuts that Craig has shifted his ground in the course of his argument. He began with "historical proofs"[38] and then fell back on theological assertions. "[Craig's] . . . concluding inference that God raised Jesus from the dead . . . is a theological conclusion. It's not a historical one. It's a statement about God."

In the course of the debate, in response to one of Ehrman's points, Craig acknowledged differences between earlier gospel accounts of the resurrection (e.g., Mark) and later ones (e.g., Luke). Ehrman seized on this point to challenge Craig, knowing that he was committed to the doctrine of biblical inerrancy: "If Bill is claiming to be a historian, then I think it's important to evaluate his whole relationship to the historical documents that he's appealing to. Does Bill think that the Gospels he relies upon for all his information have any mistakes in them at all? If so, could he tell us two or three of those mistakes?" Craig, even when pressed, ignored or evaded this question. If he were to cite "mistakes," he could no longer claim inerrancy. If he claimed inerrancy, he was no longer examining the sources as a historian, even though he was claiming to bring "historical proof" for the resurrection from a critical examination of the sources.

Ehrman takes him to task for this: "Bill did not deal with the inconsistencies that I pointed out among our accounts . . . I want him to come clean and tell me, does he think that the later accounts are inconsistent and does he think there are errors in them—yes or no?"

Craig stonewalls.

Ehrman concludes, "I do think, though, that what we've seen is that Bill is, at heart, an evangelist who wants people to come to share his belief in Jesus and that he's trying to disguise himself as a historian as a means to that end. . . . The appearances of Jesus may just as well have been visions of Jesus as they were physical appearances of Jesus because people did and do have visions all the time."

Craig had claimed that a naturalistic explanation can't explain the appearances of Jesus.

Ehrman responded, "People have visions all the time. Once people come to believe Jesus' tomb was empty, they come to believe he's raised from the dead, and they have visions. I'm not saying I think this happened. I think that it's plausible. It could have happened. It's more plausible than the claim that God must have raised Jesus from the dead."[39]

Craig remains tenacious in his unreasonable beliefs even though he is a highly trained and knowledgeable philosopher capable of formulating complex logical and mathematical arguments.[40]

Is it possible to plumb the psychological depths of Craig and Ehrman, or of any individuals in order to understand why one believes and the other does not?[41]

Pascal Boyer in his *Explaining Religion,* after a lengthy anthropological and evolutionary psychological analysis of why certain "religious" concepts and beliefs are "natural" to humans, asks the following:

Why do some people believe and not others? I have described religion in terms of cognitive processes that are common to all human brains, part and parcel of how a normal human mind functions. Does this mean that non-believers are abnormal? Or to put a more positive slant on this question, that they managed to free themselves from the shackles of ordinary cognition? . . . I think this question is very likely to remain unresolved . . . All we can describe are trends in groups . . . (318–319)

I am more optimistic than Boyer about accounting for why, of two individuals raised to believe, for example, in fundamentalist Christianity (or Judaism or Islam), one remains a believer and the other does not, as I discuss in chapter 6. However, I feel that intellectual humility is required when attempting to explain a particular person's adherence (or rejection) of a religious worldview, in situations in which that person has been exposed to arguments against his view and to alternatives to it. We must listen carefully to how the person himself understands why he believes what he does before delving into explanations that appeal to unconscious factors of which the person is not aware.

In explaining religious beliefs, whether of groups or of individuals, appeal to "unconscious" factors can be appropriate as long as the explanation that is offered is plausible. This has not always been the case with certain highly speculative and psychologically reductive accounts of religion and religious beliefs, as, for example, Freud's *Moses and Monotheism.*

Indeed, as noted earlier, "Orthodox" psychoanalysis and "Orthodox" Marxism themselves, and their faithful followers, exhibit many features of religious fundamentalism and fundamentalists. Some of their explanations of religion and of human psychology are embedded in conceptual systems that do not allow for disconfirmation of their assertions. They can be as dogmatic about their beliefs, and as passionately so, as are rigid religious fundamentalists.

The phenomenon of clinging tenaciously to beliefs has also been seen in some scientists who cannot get themselves to abandon theories in which they have invested their lives and careers long after the data that refute those theories have resulted in their being abandoned by most of their scientific colleagues. This is, however, psychologically motivated rather than the result of inherent logical flaws in empirically grounded scientific theorizing and scientific explanatory systems. In contrast, in the case of most religious and other ideological fundamentalists, in addition to psychological factors that account for the tenacity of their unreasonable beliefs, the belief systems they cling to are themselves riddled with logical flaws, which, paradoxically provides the fundamentalists with 'justifications' for holding onto their beliefs in the face of evidence and logic against them. I elaborate on this in chapter 6.

The Beliefs of Serpent Handling Sects

A relatively small Christian fundamentalist sect, located mainly in Appalachia, engages in ritual handling of venomous snakes as part of its worship services.[42] The sect was established around 1910 by George Went Hensley, a newly converted Christian. The tradition is perpetuated primarily by successful family-based socialization of the young generation into the belief system on which it is based, rather than by recruitment of new members from outside the practicing congregations. Serpent handlers do not seek publicity because they are often mocked or criticized, especially when practitioners are injured or killed by the venom, and because the practice is illegal in some jurisdictions. Many members of the sect have been injured, and at least one hundred cases of death by the snake venom have been documented. Snake handling congregations have only a few thousand members and in numerical terms are an insignificant component of American fundamentalists, of which there are millions. However, their way of using the Bible to support what to an outsider would seem to be an irrational practice, based upon irrational beliefs, is not all that different from the way the Bible is used by "mainstream" fundamentalists. It therefore provides an interesting case example of fundamentalist thinking. William James might even argue that precisely because it is behavior of the extreme it gives us a clearer grasp of the underlying psychology of fundamentalist thought than do more "moderate" expressions of fundamentalism,[43] although James's view that there is a continuum, rather than a fundamental difference between "moderate" and "extreme" religious experiences, is contested by some.

Hood, Hill, and Williamson use the concept of "*intra*textuality" (in contrast to "*inter* textuality") to describe the thinking patterns and psychology of religious fundamentalism in general, and apply it specifically to the snake handlers. Intratextuality refers to a certain structure and process of thinking in which a person (or group) has a sacred text that he believes contains within it all knowledge and truth about ultimate reality, as well as guidelines for how one should lead one's spiritual, God-obeying life. It is the ultimate and final source of all morality and ethics. There is no source outside of the sacred text that has more authority than it. Each element of the text can cast light on another element, and there can be no inconsistencies in the sacred text.

Intratextuality is another way of referring to inerrancy, infallibility, and "sufficiency"—the sacred text suffices to inform us of all we need to know about how to lead our lives in obedience to God's will. What their model emphasizes is that if an "outsider"—including social scientists—wants to understand the psychology of the fundamentalist, he must do so "from the inside." This means paying close attention to what fundamentalists say about themselves and their reasons for believing and behaving as they do, and understanding the central role that the sacred text plays in their life and how they make use of it.[44]

Hood et al., in their analysis of snake handlers (and other fundamentalist groups), help us get inside the fundamentalists' "intratextual head."[45]

I will frame my discussion around three questions:

1. Why do snake handlers believe that it is their Christian obligation to engage in this dangerous behavior?
2. What religious objectives do snake handlers believe are accomplished by snake handling?
3. How do snake handlers account for the fact that many of them are injured and some are killed by the bite of a snake, which they are handling in obedience to God's command?

Hensley had been a member of a fundamentalist group, Church of God (COG), in which a passage from the Gospel of Mark had played an important theological role. Just before the resurrected Jesus was to ascend to Heaven he appeared to his disciples and said the following to them (KJV, Mark 16:15–18):

> v. 15. ...Go ye into all the world, and preach the gospel to every creature.

> v. 16. He that believeth and is baptized shall be saved; but he that believeth not shall be damned.

> v. 17. And these signs shall follow them that believe; In my name shall they cast out devils; they shall speak with new tongues;

> v. 18. They shall take up serpents; and if they drink any deadly thing, it shall not hurt them; they shall lay hands on the sick, and they shall recover.

Hensley understood the word "shall" in verses 17–18 to mean that if one wanted to be certain that he is a true believer and hence among the saved and not the damned, he must perform the four actions preceded by "shall." (Because drinking a deadly thing is preceded by "if," he did not consider it mandatory but optional.) The COG to which he belonged did not "take up serpents," and eventually Hensley was deeply troubled by this. It suggested that they were not true believers. Moreover, how could he know that he was a true believer unless he did so? Was he not risking damnation by ignoring this mandatory sign of true belief?

> His decision was to risk his life in order to have rest from his spiritual burden. Thus it was that he set out on probably the first religious snake hunt in modern civilized history.
> In a great rocky gap in the mountainside he found what he sought, a large rattlesnake. He approached the reptile ... knelt a few feet away

from it and prayed loudly into the sky for God to remove his fear and to anoint him with the "power." Then suddenly with a shout he leaped forward and grasped the reptile and held it in trembling hands.[46]

This was a life-transforming experience for Hensley. He came down the mountain holding the rattlesnake and began to evangelize, challenging those who want to be true believers to add taking up serpents to their repertoire of Christian rites. Hensley and his followers were eventually forced out of the COG and became a small itinerant sect. When he was about seventy-five years old, in 1955, he died from the bite of a rattlesnake he was handling while preaching at a service in Florida.

Although the vast majority of fundamentalists, for one reason or another,[47] do not consider the handling of venomous snakes to be their Christian duty, there is a definite "logic" to Hensley's view if one believes that "the Bible says what it means," and that it should be one's infallible guide to holiness. Whatever might have been the original, contextual meaning of the Markan passage, it gives the taking up of serpents the same status as casting out of devils and speaking in tongues, which were part of the worship service of COG, and other Pentecostalist, fundamentalist denominations. Hensley could plausibly argue that he was consistent in his reading of verses 17–18 and in his application of them to his Christian life, whereas others were not.

Fundamentalists differ in their attitudes toward personal experience of the Holy Spirit. Some fundamentalists, although acknowledging the value of subjective religious experience, minimize its authority. For them it is a handmaiden to the Bible. It can often help to illuminate the "commonsense" meaning of a Biblical passage but cannot supplant Scripture. Its essential subjectivity is a threat to the authority that derives from the "objectivity" of scripture. Hence they look askance at Pentecostalists, for whom the personal experience of the Holy Spirit dwelling in them, which results from prayerful meditation in dialogue with a biblical text, is accorded great authority. Pentecostalists, in turn, disparage fundamentalists who downplay the power of the Spirit.

Here is how an experienced serpent handling preacher puts it:

Praise the name of the Lord, you can go to all the colleges you want to, and you can learn the Bible from Genesis to Revelations. You can learn the words that's in there. Anybody with any education at all can read those words, but they can't bring any understanding to those words unless they've got the power of God... I didn't go to college to learn how to preach God's word, but I declare to you that I've got a degree... I've got a BA degree... I went to the college of kneeology.

Praise the name of Jesus. The BA degree I've got is the Born Again experience.[48]

That was the kind of experience that Hensley had when he handled serpents and which his followers experience as well. Once you've had that powerful subjective experience, you know that serpent handling is God's way, and it is difficult to be convinced otherwise. Hood et al. put it this way:

> Once revelation of an absolute truth is obtained, particularly of such a truth as serpent handling, a believer cannot be persuaded otherwise by any reason or debate from other recognized authorities on scripture.[49] To enlightened serpent handlers, such so-called authorities and skeptics are simply blinded from spiritual truth by Satan and by their reliance on worldly knowledge and wisdom. According to the believer's worldview of meaning, critics simply cannot see truth, and hence they resist it. (121)

Psychoanalysts used to make a similar accusation, or analysis, of why their opponents "resisted" the truths that Freud had revealed. Of course, for the critics who are skeptical of the serpent handlers' beliefs and behaviors, it is the serpent handlers who "simply cannot see truth and hence they resist it."

Once the serpent handler experiences the power of God in him and the spiritual discernment that it confers, as a consequence of the intense experience of ritual handling of a poisonous snake, it confirms his understanding of the passage in Mark. Because he also believes in Scripture as God's revealed word, he will find corroboration for his certainty about the necessity of serpent handling for salvation from other biblical texts. The passage in Mark, validated by the actions of the believer, serves as the primary authoritative text, to which the rest of the Bible becomes the handmaiden. He will also find in the Bible verses that clarify other aspects of the ritual and its effects. Let us see how this process works.

Williamson interviewed nineteen serpent handlers from the Southeast.[50] The handlers cite a variety of biblical texts to explain what he refers to as "the fundamentals of religious serpent handling," which are the mandate to handle, the power to handle, the danger in handling, and the confirmation of blessing on believing handlers. All of the interviewees link their belief in these fundamentals, either explicitly or implicitly, to biblical passages.

One handler believes that Jesus engaged in serpent handling, and Jesus is a model for how he should behave. Now, you can search high and low in the New Testament and you will not find any reference to Jesus handling serpents. So on what basis, then, does the handler know that he did? Because for the handler Jesus is God, and in the book of Job (written long before Jesus lived and the New Testament was written) we read about God that "His spirit had garnished the heavens, His *hands* formed the crooked serpent" (Job 26:13), the handler concludes that Jesus had handled serpents because, after all, "he wouldn't be a just God to tell us to do something he wouldn't do himself" (124).

I must admit that the logic here escapes me. Leaving aside the dubious premises that Jesus is God and that the book of Job is describing some kind of physical act of handling snakes,[51] if Jesus/God will only command people to do that which he himself does, how would the serpent handler explain God's command to humans to be fruitful and multiply? Did Jesus/God engage in sexual intercourse? Perhaps Jesus did (we really don't know), but I doubt that the handler would think that God did or does, or that a divine Jesus did.

All of the snake handlers, some of whom are quite skilled and have had many years of experience (if they weren't, most of them would be dead, given the frequency with which they handle snakes), do not ascribe their ability to do so to a natural learning process. It is rather a gift of God to the obedient. In addition to the Markan verse, they cite Luke 10:19, in which Jesus tells his disciples, "Behold I give unto you power to tread on serpents and scorpions, and over all the power of the enemy; and nothing shall by any means hurt you." There is much in this verse, when understood literally, to support the handlers' assertion that their ability is God-given. Some logical problems, however, still remain. The verse refers to "treading" on serpents, not to handling them. Moreover, there are many non-Christians (in India and in circuses and in zoos) who tread on or handle poisonous snakes without being harmed. How do they accomplish that feat if they are not obedient Christians? If they have acquired the skill by practice, why shouldn't practice suffice to explain the Christian handlers' ability to survive the experience?

Snake handlers are well aware that the mandate and the power to handle snakes does not guarantee that they will not be injured or killed by a bite. Hood et al. report the following:

In our 10 years of field research, we have known fewer than five handlers (among scores of others) who have been successful in escaping the fang of the serpent. With frequent handling over the years, most have suffered at least one or more painful bites; some of these have led to twisted hands, gnarled and missing fingers, atrophied limbs, near-death experiences, and even the loss of beloved family members to death. Yet, for these enlightened believers, the reality and meaning of their worldview dictate that they continue as obedient followers of the Lord. To do this they must continue to study the text. (122)

One text they study is the verse in Ecclesiastes 10:8, "He that breaketh the hedge, him a serpent will bite." A hedge around a field kept out dangerous snakes; breaking the hedge enabled snakes to enter the field and harm a person working there. This verse is widely understood in Jewish and Christian biblical commentary to be a metaphor for the idea that God will punish those who violate his commandments. Obedience to God's commandments (the hedge) protects a person from harm (the serpent). Disobedience removes that protection.

The snake handlers, who would agree with this message of the verse, read other messages in it as well. The hedge is the protective spirit of God. If for some reason that protection is removed, you will, literally, be bitten by a serpent. Being a snake handler does not in and of itself guarantee that God's spirit will be there to protect you from injury. There can be several reasons why God removes his protective hedge against injury from his devoted followers. Even devoted followers can sin, and sometimes their sin is directly related to their engaging in snake handling, or it can be sins in general:

> "You see, God's the hedge, and maybe we moved out of the will of God . . . There can be sin there." The sins of pride and haughtiness can result in disapproval from God . . . Sometimes believers enjoy the blessing of serpent handling so well that they fail to heed God's warning that the time has come for returning the serpent to the box . . . (129) . . . "You really have to have your life in order when you go in that box—or you better have—because that could be instant death." (127)

The "beauty" of this way of thinking is that it protects the belief system no matter what happens to the snake handler. If you don't get bitten, or even if you get bitten but are not harmed by the bite, the power of God was with you. If you do get bitten and injured, then the power of God was not with you. There is nothing inherently illogical about making such an assertion— on the contrary, it is quite "logical," even though it cannot be confirmed or refuted by experience. The theology covers all bases. This is not unique to the theology of snake handlers. It is characteristic of almost all systematic Jewish, Christian, and Muslim theologies, as well as of classical psychoanalysis— there is an explanation for every possible event that might appear to challenge the system.

On those occasions when a handler was not harmed, we have testimony to God's power. Corroboration of this is found in the story about Paul in Acts 28: 3–5, in which we are told that the ship on which Paul had been sailing to Rome was shipwrecked in Melita. The "barbarians" (i.e., the natives of the island) treated him well and kindled a fire to protect him and the other passengers from the cold:

> And when Paul had gathered a bundle of sticks, and laid them on the fire, there came a viper out of the heat, and fastened on his hand.
>
> And when the barbarians saw the venomous beast hang on his hand, they said among themselves, No doubt this man is a murderer, whom though he hath escaped the sea, yet vengeance suffereth not to live.[52]
>
> And he shook off the beast into the fire, and felt no harm.

In this story Paul is not "taking up" or handling serpents as a sign of obedience to God. Its purpose is to demonstrate that God miraculously saved him from the serpent that was attracted by the heat. It is close enough, however, to Mark 16 to confirm that God saves the obedient from venomous snakes, to apply it to serpent handlers.

However, for those occasions when handlers are harmed we have numerous biblical verses that link sin to punishment, which snake handlers cite (as indeed anyone who reads the Bible can do) to reinforce the "sin" explanation for why the handler might have been injured.

Sin, however, is not the only possible reason.

The handler might have been injured or killed as a sign to unbelievers. Skeptics of snake handling argued that the handlers were engaging in deception—the snakes' fangs or venom had been removed. However, if a handler was harmed, this might have been God's way of answering the skeptics—see, we snake handlers are not deceivers; these snakes are deadly poisonous. The logic seems to be that God chose this particular handler to be harmed this time so that God's power will be confirmed on subsequent occasions when this handler (if he survives) or other handlers are not harmed. Moreover, when the unbeliever sees that a handler is bitten and seriously injured he might be so impressed with the handler's obedience to God, in that he was willing to undertake such a risk, that this will convert him. The net effect of these interpretations is that fear of injury, and the frequent reality of it, are no reason to desist from snake handling. On the contrary, they provide all the more reason for engaging in the practice.

It is not unusual for religions to teach, and for believers to believe, that there are times when the righteous and innocent need to suffer for some divine purpose, and not as punishment for their sins. Indeed, this is perhaps the core concept of the Christian doctrine of Christ's atoning death. He suffered for humankind's sake. Judaism, Christianity, and Islam extol the martyr who is willing to die in order to witness for God. So it is not strange that a snake handler should be willing to suffer and even die if this will be a "sign to the unbelievers," bringing some of them to Christ, or if it will strengthen the belief of those who waver in their faith. It is even a privilege.

But didn't Jesus, according to Mark 16, say that those who handle snakes will not be harmed? Go back to that passage and read it carefully—because it does not say that. Or at least it can be interpreted as not saying that. It first says that believers in the risen Jesus will be saved and not damned, which refers to postmortem experience, and then it says the following:

> v. 17. And these signs shall follow them that believe; In my name shall they cast out devils; they shall speak with new tongues;

> v. 18. They shall take up serpents; and if they drink any deadly thing, it shall not hurt them; they shall lay hands on the sick, and they shall recover.

The phrase "it shall not hurt them" can be interpreted as referring only to the clause that immediately precedes it, the drinking of a deadly thing, and not to the one before that, about taking up serpents. So Jesus never guaranteed that no harm would come to a handler. Injury and even death do not contradict what the Bible said.

What about drinking deadly things? God has not commanded that—it is an "if," not a "shall." I suppose that the snake handler would say that if a true believer drank snake venom or some other poison as a sign of his obedience, he might survive that experience as well. However, if he wouldn't, there could be justifiable reasons for that. Maybe he thought he was obedient but he really was not. In any case, no one is required to subject him- or herself to that test, because it is not commanded.

A third explanation for why a handler might get injured or die relies on the well-known last refuge of believers who can't seem to make sense of why a compassionate and just God allows for what appears to be unjustifiable and cruel suffering, or of apparent contradictions between their beliefs and their experience, or, especially in Christian theology, of contradictions between its beliefs themselves. It is a divine mystery, and we mortals are not capable of comprehending the ways of God. God has willed it thus, or has taught thus, and I have faith in him, so I humbly accept what he has done and taught, even though I cannot explain it in any rational or moral way.

We have seen how snake handlers use the story about Paul to confirm that God blesses believers by protecting them from serpents. They cite other "serpent" verses to support this idea. In Exodus 7:9–12 Aaron casts Moses' rod before Pharaoh and it is transformed into a serpent. Pharaoh's magicians do the same. Moses' rod/serpent swallows up those of the magicians. This story is not talking about being protected from serpents, but about who has more power, Yahweh or Pharaoh, because that was the basic issue in the redemption from Egypt story. Pharaoh refuses to recognize Yahweh and obey his command to free Israel, Yahweh's people, so that they could worship him. Yahweh's power as expressed in the rod/serpent of Moses is more powerful than Pharaoh's power. But at another level of interpretation, one could say that God's power protects Moses and Aaron from the danger of being bitten by the magicians' serpents, confirming the thesis of serpent handlers that God protects believers not just from evil in general, or enemies of God, but from actual serpents. Descriptions of the miraculous acts of the apostles, as in Acts 2:43, are cited as implicit justification for the general belief in the power of believers and the blessings and protection they receive, which is then applied to snake handling.

The ingenious, creative, albeit often stretched, use of intratextuality has a certain charm to it and is not unique to fundamentalists. It is a common hermeneutic of rabbinic midrash and Christian bible commentary and homiletics. In fact, traditional Christianity and the New Testament itself read their beliefs and values about Jesus and Christ into the Old Testament, even though few non-Christians see them there.[53] It is only because snake handlers act in a very dangerous way upon this particular belief that they appear strange, or weird, or pathological to outsiders. But, aside from the danger of their rite, is it any less rational to believe that handling snakes in obedience to God is a sign of holiness, given Mark 16, than to believe that when one eats from the wafer and drinks from the wine of the Eucharist, that one is imbibing the flesh and blood of Christ?[54]

Although snake handlers rely on many biblical texts to affirm and confirm their belief that snake handling confers blessings on believers, they also rely on personal religious experiences, as did Hensley, the founder of the sect. These experiences reinforce the believer in his practice, and also convince others of its truth and merit. Here is the testimony of one person who "converted" to the sect after observing rites of snake handling: " You could just see these people. You could see the expression on their face that they were really getting a hold of something. And I said, 'Lord, how *great* that must feel.' It wasn't the idea of handling a serpent. I wanted to feel what those people were feeling."[55]

Snake handlers cling tenaciously to their beliefs and practice, appealing to Scripture and to experience to do so, even though most people, and most Christians, would consider the belief and practice to be irrational. However, if we get into the mindset of the believer and *suspend our disbelief in the premises of his faith,* it doesn't appear to be all that irrational. Maybe the premises are irrational (to me or to you)—the authority of the Bible and the intratextual way of reading and interpreting it—but once those are accepted, this belief and practice (and many other Christian ones) are often derived from those premises by appeals to logic, textual interpretation, and evidence, as imperfect as they might be.

How would an "outsider," such as a psychologist or a sociologist, account for snake handling? Do social scientific explanations of the practice, and of its tenacity, add any insights to those provided by explanations that snake handlers themselves provide to explain their behavior? In chapter 6, I look at a variety of social, psychological, cultural, and historical explanations for the tenacity of unreasonable religious beliefs and practices in general, of which snake handling is but one. First, though, I invite you to examine with me aspects of Muslim scriptural fundamentalism.

CHAPTER FIVE | Muslim Koranic Fundamentalism

L IKE ORTHODOX JEWS and fundamentalist Christians, Muslims, both
Sunni and Shia, who adhere to traditional Islamic teachings and beliefs,
affirm a set of propositions about "history" and "reality" that from a *critical
scholarly* and a *naturalistic scientific* perspective are highly unreasonable. Their
version of the origins of Islam, the life of Muhammad, the source of the
Koran, and the Hadith (traditions presumably transmitted by Muhammad's
companions about what he said, did, and approved of), maintains that the
Koran was authored by God and dictated by an angel named Gabriel to
Muhammad over a period of twenty-two years (610–632 CE). Islam begins
with Muhammad's preaching of these "divine" revelations to fellow Arabs in
Mecca, now a part of Saudi Arabia. Muslims claim that Koranic and "authorized" Hadith traditions are objective, historical reports of real events dating
to the lifetime of Muhammad. Islamic tradition acknowledges that there were
numerous non-Koranic traditions attributed to Muhammad that were false or
erroneous, and there developed a subdiscipline of Islamic scholarship that was
devoted to differentiating the "reliable" or "authentic" traditions from the
unreliable ones. Some modern scholars consider many of traditions that came
to be accepted as "reliable" to be unreliable as well, including many that were
incorporated in the Koran itself. In fact, an increasing number of non-Muslim
(and some Muslim) academicians maintain that many of the Koranic and
Hadithic reports of events are fictitious and legendary, and were composed
after the death of Muhammad in order to establish a religion that would unify
a rapidly expanding Arab empire.

Ibn Warraq, in his book *Why I Am Not a Muslim,* analyzes the Koran and
presents many arguments against the idea that it is a divine work. The points

he makes could undermine the faith of many a Muslim believer who was open enough to consider the evidence and arguments against his belief. "Ibn Warraq" is a pseudonym. At one time he feared that his life might be in danger were his identity known,[1] not only because his heretical views might influence the devout to forgo their faith, but because having been born and raised a Muslim, he is considered by many Muslims to be an apostate, publicly proclaiming his apostasy and calling others to do the same, and hence deserving of death. This was the case with Salman Rushdie, upon whom a fatwa was issued calling on Muslims anywhere and everywhere to kill him for having published his novel *Satanic Verses,* which was deemed by some Iranian (and other) Muslim clergy to be heretical. Ibn Warraq writes that "as soon as I was able to think for myself, I discarded all religious dogmas... and now consider myself to be a secular humanist." It was, however, the Rushdie affair that galvanized him to write this book, which "attempts to sow a drop of doubt in an ocean of dogmatic certainty by taking an uncompromising and critical look at almost all the fundamental tenets of Islam."[2]

Why the great Muslim fear of blasphemy and apostasy to the point that some Muslim scholars maintain that one who commits these sins should be put to death by any Muslim, in some instances even without a formal trial? There are differing views within Islam as to whether, when, and to whom the death penalty for apostasy should be applied. One justification for such a harsh penalty is the Muslim state's responsibility to assure the spiritual health and welfare of its inhabitants. Apostasy can produce moral, religious, and social instability in a Muslim community. Moreover, the apostate might influence others negatively and thus jeopardize their entry into Paradise and facilitate their entry to Hell in the hereafter.[3]

Ibn Warraq's chapter "The Koran" (104–162) should be read by any Muslim who wants to know the arguments against traditional Muslim beliefs offered by "heretics" (and by scholars), whether in order to refute them or in order to consider whether they are valid. Of course, many Muslims are not interested in reading something that challenges their beliefs. They may consider it forbidden to do so because challenges are inherently heretical and must be avoided as spiritually polluting, or because they might lead to heresy and apostasy, which are grave sins.[4] Many Muslim religious leaders suppress freedom of thought and expression, especially critical thinking and serious scholarship about the origins of the Koran and of Islam, because they fear— correctly so—that it might generate doubts about traditional dogmas and doctrines. In addition to the spiritual harm this might cause to their followers, it would also weaken their own authority and power.

Toby Lester, in a controversial article, reported on the deep Muslim hostility toward, and fear of, critical examination of the origins and history of the Koran.[5] He points out that assumptions of contemporary scholars, such as the very notion that the Koran has a history, are deeply threatening.[6] One such scholar goes so far as to state that "The Koran is the charter for the [Muslim] community, the document that called it into existence . . . Islamic history has been the effort to pursue and work out the commandments of the Koran in human life. If the Koran is a historical document [i.e., rather than divine], the whole Islamic struggle of fourteen centuries is effectively meaningless."[7]

I don't think that the past products of a religious culture that resulted in positive human experiences are rendered "meaningless" when the theological or doctrinal premises on which that culture was based are found to be groundless in subsequent generations. However, those who want to maintain intellectual integrity while at the same time preserving the positive effects of the religious belief system that is no longer intellectually tenable need to revise and reformulate their religion so as to make it compatible with the best of contemporary knowledge. Many Jews, Christians, and, more recently, Muslims as well, grapple with this challenge of modernity to traditional religion, with varying degrees of success. Many, however, do not, and remain committed to archaic beliefs.

Imagine the psychological trauma that devout, traditionalist Muslims would experience if, for example, they discovered, and accepted as convincing, what scholars know to be the case—that the Koran (as well as the Hadith and the Sharia, Islamic law) is deeply indebted to Jews and Jewish texts and teachings, in addition to the Bible, such as the apocrypha and rabbinic midrash,[8] for many of its laws, stories, and beliefs. These, however, are presented in the Koran as divine revelations from Allah rather than as borrowings, adaptations, derivatives of or reactions to Judaism and its traditions,[9] which itself, like all religions, is a human product. Although the Koran does acknowledge a relationship to the Bible and accepts some of its prophets as genuine conduits of divine revelation, it sees Muhammad as the final and greatest prophet and the Koran as the final divine revelation. Traditional Islam claims that the Jews and the Christians distorted, added to, and deleted from the original prophetic revelations to Abraham, Moses, and Jesus. It does not consider the Hebrew Bible or the New Testament to be sacred texts inasmuch as they reflect the falsification rather than the true transmission and report of much of divine revelation.[10]

Muslims consider it highly offensive for someone to treat the Koran (or to speak of Muhammad or of Islam) with disrespect. Yet, many of them—

especially but not only when they are in the majority—see nothing improper in speaking with contempt about nonbelievers and in treating their sacred texts disrespectfully. Many Muslims disparage Judaism and Christianity just as the latter disparage Islam.

Anyone, devout Jew, Christian, or Muslim, living in a Western democracy needs to be willing to accept the right of anyone to criticize his or her religious beliefs and the sacred texts in which they are formulated. Freedom of religion and freedom of speech include not only the right to practice and preach one's religion openly, as long as one does not violate the rights of others in doing so, but also the right to preach against any and all religions as well. Muslims have no right (from the standpoint of a neutral observer) to object to non-Muslims' critiques of Islam and its sacred scriptures, given that they do the same to Jews, Christians, infidels, and atheists. The Koran and the Hadith are replete with critiques and disparagement of non-Muslims.

The critical scholarly community sees the Koran as a human product of particular historical periods and processes. Some scholars even go so far as to consider early Islam to be an offshoot of Judaism, or one of its sects.[11] Of course, the trauma of truth for traditional Muslims would occur even in the absence of the proven dependence of Islam on Judaism. Because Islam claims that aspects of the Bible are true, and it acknowledges its own continuity with earlier revelations to Jews and Christians, it is not always troubled by similarities between it and the Bible—or even between it and some rabbinic and Christian traditions. However, it cannot tolerate the academics' claim that Muhammad or other humans authored the corpus now known as the Koran and that he or they "borrowed" whether consciously or unconsciously, ideas, values, teachings, and traditions, from any person or group. Such an assertion denies the divine authorship of those sections of the Koran, and their divine revelation to Muhammad via the angel Gabriel. To acknowledge that many of the "authentic" traditions of the Hadith are also borrowed or adapted from Judaism or Christianity threatens the Muslim belief in the integral relationship of the Hadith to the Koran and the real-life Muhammad. Modern scholarship attempts to demonstrate a plausible, naturalistic, historically grounded explanation for the origins of the Koran. This adds further force to the basic implausibility of the traditional belief that it came from Allah and renders it superfluous as an explanation for how the Koran as we know it came to be.[12]

The very fact of the Koran's not being revealed by God would be enough to cause deep anguish and anxiety for the devout believer. But the Jewish/ Judaism dependency adds insult to injury. It is not surprising, therefore, that *even otherwise highly intelligent* Muslims react with fearful fervor against the emerging scholarly insights about the bedrock principles of their faith.

One way of dismissing critical Koranic scholarship is to attack the scholars' real or presumed malicious motives for engaging in the enterprise in the first place.[13] There is, actually, more than a grain of truth to the notion that there is a long Western history of critiquing the Koran and Islam, often referred to as "Orientalism," which was motivated and even shaped by Christian disdain for Islam, the West's imperialist and colonialist denigration of Muslim culture, and other less than objective considerations.[14] However, there is a limit as to how far a devout Muslim can rely on impugning the motives of scholars, especially when, as is increasingly the case, these factors are less significant than in the past. Many contemporary scholars have no "Orientalist" axes to grind, and some of them may be Muslims who are ready and eager to revise their understanding of Islam in accordance with the insights of scholarship, and wish to promote rather than destroy Islam as a religion and a religious culture. Ultimately it is the evidence and the arguments and their relative plausibility that need to be addressed. Moreover, even if the proponent of a critical or possibly negative view of the Koran and of Islam is motivated by conscious or unconscious hostility toward them, the facts and the hypotheses put forth to defend such a view need to be addressed on their own merit. After all, the Muslim apologist for tradition is biased in its favor just as the non-Muslim critic of Islamic tradition might be biased against it, so it is to evidence and logic that all of the disputants must ultimately turn, at least as long as they claim to be using reason in making and validating their respective truth claims.[15]

Thus there is little to be gained in the long-term search for truth from the psychologically understandable if misdirected fulminations of, for example, S. Parvez Manzoor, a Swedish Muslim critic of Western Koranic scholarship:

> At the greatest hour of his worldly-triumph, the Western man, co-ordinating the powers of the State, Church and Academia, launched his most determined assault on the citadel of Muslim faith. All the aberrant streaks of his arrogant personality—its *reckless rationalism,* its world-domineering phantasy and its sectarian fanaticism—joined in an unholy conspiracy to dislodge the Muslim Scripture from its firmly entrenched position as the epitome of *historic authenticity and moral unassailability.* The ultimate trophy that the Western man sought by his dare-devil venture was the Muslim mind itself. In order to rid the West forever of the "problem" of Islam, he reasoned, Muslim

consciousness must be made to despair of the *cognitive certainty of the Divine message revealed to the Prophet.* Only a Muslim confounded of the historical authenticity or doctrinal autonomy of the Qur'anic revelation would abdicate his universal mission and hence pose no challenge to the global domination of the West. Such, at least, seems to have been the tacit, if not the explicit, rationale of the Orientalist assault on the Qur'an [my italics].[16]

For Manzoor, the critic of Islam is a "reckless rationalist," Muslim Scripture is "the epitome of historic authenticity and moral unassailability," and unconfounded Muslims possess "cognitive certainty of the Divine message revealed to the Prophet."

Manzoor argues that Jewish and Christian critics of Islam and the Koran were inconsistent and hypocritical in their approach. They were willing to accept the theological and doctrinal assumptions of their respective religions but not those of Islam. To believe that God revealed himself to Muhammad was absurd, whereas to believe that he revealed himself to Moses or Jesus was not. Although this bias did, and does, exist, there are many scholars, from the Enlightenment until today, who apply the same naturalistic, nontheological assumptions to their analyses of the Hebrew Bible and the New Testament as they apply to their analyses of the Koran. Indeed, they are often self-consciously adapting the tools of modern critical biblical scholarship to the Koran, while taking into account the significant differences between the Bible and the Koran. Rather than trying to single out Islam and the Koran for historical contextualization and development, literary and linguistic analysis, and nontheologically based assumptions about their origins and authority, they are simply treating them as they would treat any text and religious movement—whether of the seventh- or eighth-century Orient (when the Koran was authored), the first and second century Palestine (when the New Testament was formed), or the sixth and fifth century BCE Babylon (when the Pentateuch was most probably redacted).

Manzoor and other defenders of traditional Islamic faith and its belief in "miracles," such as Mustafa Akyol, correctly point out that many modern scholars and scientists work from naturalistic premises that a priori exclude the possibility of miracles, such as divine revelation or the conception and birth of Jesus by the Virgin Mary, who is revered in Islam. The devout Muslim (and many devout Jews and Christians as well) denies this naturalistic premise.[17] It is therefore difficult if not impossible to challenge a devout Muslim's beliefs by appeal to the laws of nature:

Yet, that is also exactly where they are wrong. In fact, science doesn't tell us that miracles can't happen. It only tells us that miracles don't happen now. It shows that the natural world around us is operating within constant laws of physics and chemistry. Thanks to these laws, fire always burns, the dead never arise, and nobody walks on water. However, science can't tell us that this was always the case in history nor that this necessarily will always be so in every instance in the future.

The belief that this was always the case in history does not come from "science," but from a philosophy called naturalism. Naturalism holds that nature is all there is and there are no supernatural entities, such as God, to have influence over nature. This philosophic view is a belief, not a testable, observable fact. Therefore, when people object to the virgin birth or other miracles told in the Qur'an, they are doing so not because of science, but because of their faith in naturalism.[18]

Earlier I discussed the intellectual weakness of this argument, which is resorted to by Jewish and Christian fundamentalists as well. Is there any way to dislodge Manzoor, Akyol, and other Muslims possessed with the same Islamic faith and certainties of their "unassailable" beliefs? It isn't an easy task, but given that some believers do become "apostates," or at least open to doubt and respectful of it, there is hope.

Truth must be allowed to speak openly and freely if the West is to prevail over the fundamentalism of Islam. Unfortunately there are influential Muslims in the United States who are deemed moderate and tolerant by the media, and may indeed be so at present when compared to other Muslims here and in other countries, but who pose a long-term threat to core values of American democracy. For example, Imam Zaid Shakir, an African American convert to Islam, was profiled in a *New York Times* article as one such middle-of-the-road, moderate preacher and leader, to whom thousands of Muslims flock for guidance. Although Shakir eschews the use of violence to transform America into a Muslim country, he hopes that one day the United States will be ruled by Sharia and asserts (probably correctly) that this is the view of any honest Muslim.[19] Mr. Shakir, who had led a mosque in New Haven in 1992, once wrote that "Islam presents an absolutist political agenda, one that doesn't lend itself to compromise, nor to coalition building." He had supported the Taliban in Afghanistan, and notwithstanding his having given up on violent revolution as a strategy for bringing Muslims and Islam to power, now says, "To be perfectly honest, I don't regret anything I've done or said."[20]

Mr. Shakir is entitled to believe and preach as he does as long as he does not violate the laws of the United States. However, the fact that he has the legal right to do so does not mean that his view that Sharia, Islamic law, is the most desirable legal system by which to govern society, should be respected, quietly tolerated, and go unchallenged. He might no longer be preaching violence—whether on theological or practical grounds—and he might not be preaching coercion or deception. However, insofar as he attempts to teach and preach, and hence convince others, that Sharia law, grounded in alleged divine revelation and interpreted by a Muslim religious leadership, is superior to the Constitution and Bill of Rights of the United States and to legislation by humanly elected representatives, his views and those of other Muslims who sympathize with him must be aggressively discredited.

I do not mean to suggest that all of the legal, moral, and political principles and the actual laws of the United States are always more just or desirable than anything in the Sharia. It can be reasonably argued that Jewish halakha, Islamic Sharia, and Catholic canon law and moral theology might in many instances be considered more just, compassionate, practical, socially desirable, and economically fair than some principles and laws of our capitalist democracy. To the extent that we and/or our elected representatives are convinced of this, we can learn from those religious legal systems and incorporate some of their wisdom into our legislation (or, for that matter, even amend our Constitution, if we see fit to do so). Legal systems should learn from each other, and secular legal systems, such as ours, have a long history of borrowing and adapting legal principles and laws from religious ones, such as from the Hebrew Bible's legal collections. However, the process of such borrowing and adaptation should be based on the essential notion that in our democracy laws are created by humans for humans and do not derive their authority from God. Moreover, there are many Sharia (and halakhic and Christian) principles and laws that run counter to our Constitution and to the fundamental values of our representative democracy, as well as our widely accepted moral and ethical values, which are often reinforced by our laws. For example, the definition of adultery as occurring when a married woman has consensual sexual relations with someone other than her husband, even if he is single, but as not occurring when a married man has sexual relations with an unmarried woman, which is the case in Jewish and Muslim law, goes against our notions of gender equality before the law. If someone can come up with a plausible explanation to justify such a gender distinction in the law,[21] he can try to convince our legislatures to accept it and embody it in law. However, to claim that sufficient justification for this legal distinction is that it is divinely revealed, and hence should be the law of our land, is unacceptable.

In order for our freedoms to be protected, it is essential that the truths about the origin and development of the Koran and of Islam be widely disseminated in the press and the media. When courses on religions of the world are taught in schools[22] and universities, as they should be, it is important to approach the study and the history of religion with academic rigor and critical tools of analysis. We should not be politically correct or overly sensitive to the "feelings" of religious adherents and to the demand that we show "respect" for religion(s) to the point that the best of contemporary scholarship (which is always subject to revision and reevaluation based upon new evidence and/or more compelling analyses of its subject matter) is ignored or relegated to a minor role in our teaching. The stakes are too high for democracy to shy away from asserting its principles, its rights, and its promise—albeit far from fully materialized—for a just and compassionate society.[23] If religions can and do critique secular democracy, secular democracy has every right and duty to critique religion. Although I am discussing Islam here, the same applies to fundamentalist versions of Judaism, Christianity, and any other religion or ideology that would seek to undermine the fundamental principles and values of the Declaration of Independence, the Constitution, and other foundational documents of our democratic society and political-social contract.

Hopefully, Muslims living in the United States and in other societies that believe in a free marketplace of ideas and in the pursuit of truth will eventually be exposed to critiques of their faith.[24] Some will reject the critiques and retain their traditional Islamic beliefs. Some will reject the major tenets of Islam and many of its unethical and unjust values such as homophobia, gender inequality (including, for many Muslims, the right to beat one's wife in certain circumstances, but not for her to beat her husband in analogous ones),[25] and religious intolerance. Some will reinterpret Islam in ways that will enable them to integrate modern thought, science, and scholarship with it.[26]

To return to Ibn Warraq's book, I will discuss nine of his points.[27]

1. The Arabic of the Koran is far from perfect, which goes against the doctrine that it is impossible for anyone to produce a work as literarily beautiful and perfect as the Koran. "... while many parts of the Koran undoubtedly have considerable power, even over an unbelieving reader, the book, aesthetically considered, is by no means a first rate performance ... there is a good deal of superfluous verbiage ... the connection of ideas is extremely loose ... there is no great literary skill evinced in the frequent and needless harping on the same words and phrases ...."[28]

2. Many verses that were in earlier versions of the Koran are missing in the present "canonical" version, and many verses in the present version have been

added to whatever might have been earlier versions of it. This fact, says Ibn Warraq, "makes nonsense of Muslim dogma about the Koran...there is no such thing as *the* Koran.... When a Muslim dogmatically asserts that the Koran is the word of God, we need only ask, 'Which Koran?' to undermine his certainty" (108). Some of these deletions and additions seem to be related to political or theological controversies in the years after the death of Muhammad.

3. The Koran abounds in contradictions. One way in which theologians and Koranic commentators have dealt with this embarrassing fact is to develop the doctrine of "abrogation," which means that God abrogated a prior revelation with a subsequent one. "The doctrine of abrogation...makes a mockery of the Muslim dogma that the Koran is a faithful and unalterable reproduction of the original scriptures that are preserved in heaven. If God's words are eternal, uncreated, and of universal significance, then how can we talk of God's words being superseded or becoming obsolete...?" (115)

4. Many doctrines of the Koran are intellectually and/or morally flawed. For example, Islam has borrowed and incorporated elements of polytheism, positing the existence of angels, genies, demons, and other beings that are neither gods nor human but hover somewhere in between.[29]

With respect to the existence of *jinn* (genies), who are neither human nor animal, who engage in a variety of activities, and are punished for some of them, they are

> as vividly real in the world of the Koran as are demons and unclean spirits in that of the New Testament... the Koran tells us that the genies were created of fire. Unlike the evil spirits of the Gospels, they are not all bad: they were created to serve God (Q51:56), and while many will end up in Hell (Q11:119), there are Muslims among them (Q72:14); this came about when some genies overheard a recitation of the Koran, and were so impressed that they went off to preach the message to their fellows (Q46:29). In addition to this presence in the Koran, the genies are also strongly entrenched in Egyptian folk beliefs...[30]

The popular belief in genies, which the Koran embraced, even penetrated Islamic jurisprudence, leading to absurd (if you don't believe in genies, but perhaps "rational" if you do) legal discussions:

> Since... demons frequently assume human shape, the jurists assess the consequences of such transformations for religious law; serious arguments and counterarguments are urged, for example, whether such beings can be numbered among the participants necessary for the

Friday service. Another problematic case that the divine law must clarify: how is one to deal with the progeny from a marriage between a human being and a demon in human form . . . What are the consequences in family law of such marriages? Indeed the problem of *munakahat al-jinn* (marriages with the jinn) is treated in such circles with the same seriousness as any important point of the religious law.[31]

Indeed, in an infamous judicial proceeding against a lecturer at Cairo University, Nasr Hamid Abu Zayd, that wound its way through the Egyptian legal system from 1992 through 1996, the belief in genies—or rather Abu Zayd's apparent disbelief in them—played an important role in convicting him of apostasy and mandating that he divorce his wife, as required by Islamic law (which he avoided doing by leaving Egypt).

What was Abu Zayd's crime/sin?

Did Abu Zayd then go so far as to deny the very existence of the genies? What he did was to explain that the reason for their presence in the Koran was that they formed part of the culture of the Arabs at the time when the book was taking shape. It was only by appealing to existing Arab conceptions of communication between genies and humans that the notion of divine revelation could be made intelligible to them. This is not an explicit denial of the existence of genies, but it is certainly hard to imagine that someone who speaks of them in this way could actually believe in them. Such skepticism would not shock many people in the West: one can be a mainstream Christian without believing in demons and unclean spirits. But in his own religious community, Abu Zayd, though he has his supporters, could not be described as mainstream.[32]

Inasmuch as belief in angels, jinns, and other spirits are remnants of polytheism, their prominence in the Koran give the lie to the Koranic and Muslim claim that the religion the Koran propounds is a pure, rarified, superior monotheism that came to replace the allegedly primitive polytheism[33] of the Arab tribes of Muhammad's day.

Ibn Warraq, in line with the predominant view of contemporary philosophy, and even of much theology, denies the validity of traditional proofs for the existence of God, such as the argument by design, which is appealed to in the Koran several times.

On the moral level, he argues that Koranic monotheism is dogmatic and intolerant, and advocates the use of force and violence to impose its belief system and practices on others. "We know from the Koran itself the hatred preached at all kinds of belief labeled 'idolatry' or 'polytheism' . . . implicit in all kinds of monotheism is the dogmatic certainty that it alone has access to the true God, it alone has access to truth. Everyone else is not only woefully misguided but doomed to perdition and everlasting hellfire."[34]

5. Although the Koran speaks of both human free will and divine predestination, it is predestination that is the more dominant view. Those who do not believe in Muhammad and his divine message were either predestined to be sinners, or Allah led them astray. This doctrine has its foreshadowing when God first creates the human race. As one Muslim tradition tells it, "[W]hen God . . . resolved to create the human race, He took into His hands a mass of earth, the same whence all mankind were to be formed, and in which after a manner pre-existed; and having then divided the clod into two equal portions, He threw the one half into hell, saying, 'These to eternal fire, I care not,' and projected the other half into heaven adding, 'and these to Paradise, I care not'" (129).

This predestinarian view of human action, coupled with punishment for the sinners, is morally problematic. Why are people being punished for actions over which they have no control?

6. And what a punishment is in store for those who do not believe in Muhammad and his message! The Koranic description of Hell (which is similar to the Christian one and probably borrowed much from earlier Christian works) includes passages describing how nonbelievers will suffer the flames of an eternal fire, or how their skin will become infected with pus-oozing sores, or how they will be scalded with boiling water, or how their skulls will be crushed with instruments of iron, or how their innards will be destroyed, and more such sadistic, barbaric punishments. As a nonbeliever reading the Koran I was struck (and after a while, bored) by the almost obsessive repetitiveness of its admonitions and threats to nonbelievers about the furnaces of Hell that will be fueled and stoked by Allah on and after Judgment Day.[35]

So much for the Koranic doctrine of a compassionate, merciful, just, and ethical Allah.

Perhaps this partially explains the barbarity of many Muslims in their recent civil wars, in Lebanon, Palestine, Iraq, Iran, Pakistan, Afghanistan, and elsewhere. Muslims torture, behead, and desecrate the bodies of other Muslims (and, of course, of non-Muslims as well). If Allah can punish sinners with such methods, the argument might go, why can't we, his "devoted" followers, do so as well when we are fighting "heretics" or enemies of our version of and claims for Islam? Why wait until they die? In medieval

Christendom, too, there was extensive barbarity in the treatment of heretics, witches, infidels, Jews, and Muslims, perhaps "inspired" or at least legitimated by the descriptions of Hell and its tortures in Christian theological and devotional works. Barbaric treatment of enemies is also attested to in some books of the Hebrew Bible of ancient Israel, but there was no well-developed idea of Hell and divine torture in it as punishment of sinners.

7. The Koran describes and records Allah's revelations to Muhammad. Muhammad, we are told, was chosen to be the "final" prophet. He follows a succession of individuals mentioned in the Hebrew Bible and the New Testament, either explicitly as prophets or understood to be so in Koranic tradition. Among them are Noah, Abraham, Ishmael, Moses, and Jesus. The revelations to Muhammad constitute the "seal of prophecy" in human history.

Assuming that Muhammad had certain experiences that he understood to be revelations from God, whether directly or mediated via the angel Gabriel, why should his reports of this be taken as evidence that God (assuming he exists) did indeed reveal himself to Muhammad? According to the Koran itself, these revelations occurred in private. Perhaps Muhammad was delusional? Or perhaps he was a person of intense piety, who, when in a state of religious ecstasy, "heard" words that he believed to be from God but that were really generated internally? In a cultural milieu that accepts that God or gods communicate with humans, for Muhammad to believe he heard God or God's angel speaking to him would not necessarily be psychopathological or psychotic, but it would render his interpretation of his experiences highly questionable.

The argument against the credibility of Muhammad's testimony as to the source of his "revelations" was one often raised by Christians and Jews against the veracity of the Koran and hence of Islam. Jews and Christians, respectively, argue that there is greater evidence for the veracity of their traditions of revelation. As we have seen in our discussion of Jewish defenses of the historicity of the revelation at Sinai and Christian defenses of the historicity of the resurrection, their claims are no more credible than those of Muslims about Muhammad and the Koran.

8. The Koran accepts the historicity of many biblical narratives (although it often renders them inaccurately) and builds upon them. Because modern critical biblical scholarship plausibly demonstrates the legendary or mythological character of many of these stories, the Koran's veracity is impugned. Among the stories appropriated by the Koran is the creation of Adam and Eve as the first humans. This and other Koranic depictions of the creation of the world and of humankind are contradicted by the modern sciences of cosmology and evolution. Those Muslims *who are Koranic literalists,* of which

there are hundreds of millions, should be apprised of the incompatibility of the Koran, which they revere as the literal word of God, with scientific knowledge of the twenty-first century.

9. Although the Koran does not ascribe the active performance of miracles to Muhammad[36] (although the claim that God communicated his messages to Muhammad via the angel Gabriel is a claim for his *miraculous experiences*), there are several references to divinely performed supernatural miracles in the Koran. One of these is the night journey describing how God miraculously transported Muhammad from Mecca to Jerusalem (Sura 17:1). Another miracle accepted by the Koran, as we saw earlier, is the Christian belief that Jesus was born of Mary even though Mary was a virgin. "How, O my Lord, shall I have a son, when no man has touched me?" asked Mary. He said, "Thus: God creates whatever He wants, when He decrees a thing He has only to say, "Be," and it is" (Sura 19:20–22). Moreover, the Koran itself is considered to be the miracle par excellence (Sura 29:48–49). The Koran (like the New Testament and rabbinic, if not biblical, Judaism) asserts another miracle to come, that on a future Judgment Day dead people will be bodily resurrected.

To the extent that belief in supernatural miracles is implausible or irrational, the Koran asserts that which is implausible or irrational.

Of course, many Jews and Christians, as well as Muslims, argue that if an omnipotent, creator God exists, as they affirm that he does, then it is not irrational to believe that this God can suspend what appear to us, because of their regularity, to be immutable laws of nature, and bring about events that have no "naturalistic," or no obviously naturalistic, explanation. To this day many members of the three religions heatedly debate (or mock or disparage) one another with respect to whose miracle claims are true and whose are false, or which are plausible and which implausible, with each faith community casting doubt on some of the miracle claims of the other two faiths. All three faiths, however, accept that some supernatural miracles have occurred and will occur in the future (e.g., resurrection of the dead).

In addition to the above-mentioned miracles believed by Muslims, there are many statements in the Koran about natural phenomena that are incompatible with our current state of scientifically based knowledge, such as the description of the creation of the world in six days (Sura 32:4) and the formation of humans from clay (Sura 15:26), which are based upon the biblical creation legends of Genesis.

The effect of these critiques is to cast serious doubt on the Islamic claim that the Koran is a book authored by God, an expression of eternally superior wisdom, an infallible guide to ethics and morality, and worthy of unquestioned authority in the governance of human affairs.

Of course, every one of the arguments presented by Ibn Warraq is refuted, or its force denied, by one or another traditionalist theologian or Muslim commentator on the Koran. Among the defenses of tradition are the following arguments. Apostates and other nonbelievers do deserve eternal punishment in Hell, and those who deny this are presumptuous and arrogant in assuming they know better than Allah what is just and unjust punishment. The existence of variants in Koranic texts was a result of the errors of some individuals in reciting and/or recording the original words that were revealed, or of deliberate falsifications by some people who were hostile to the true faith. The early Muslim authorities who decided upon the "accepted" text were aware of the variations and the reasons for them, examined them, and, with divine guidance arrived at the final correct version. Contradictions between Koranic passages are resolved by exegesis, so that, for example, one passage refers to a particular situation or event and the one that contradicts it to a different one.[37] The doctrine that Allah predetermines our fate, or knows in advance how we will act, while at the same time granting us free will to make decisions, is not problematic because the nature of divine knowledge and divine will cannot be compared to human knowledge and will. So though to the human intellect divine predestination or divine foreknowledge seems to be incompatible with free will and with moral accountability, this is only because we mortals cannot comprehend the mysteries of the divine. As far as the doctrine of abrogation, the "proof" of its validity lies in the fact that if one accepts that the Koran is divine, and that God cannot contradict himself, then he must have abrogated some verses that contradict others (in the absence of other ways of explaining away the contradiction). What appears to us as though the immutable Allah has "changed his mind" reflects our ignorance of the divine nature. Miracles occur either because Allah has the power to suspend the laws of nature that we experience, or because they were preprogrammed by Allah into natural laws, from the time of creation, and hence are "natural" rather than suspensions of the laws of nature. As far as the existence of spirits and genies—just because we do not see them does not mean that they do not exist. There are numerous "things" whose existence we accept even though they cannot be seen by the naked eye, such as viruses and electrons. The claim that certain Koranic teachings are immoral assumes that the critic has criteria for morality independent of the Koran, by which he is judging the Koran—or rather judging Allah. On the contrary, it is Allah in his Koran who tells us what is moral and what is not. If Koranic morality differs from morality derived from non-Koranic sources, it is the non-Koranic moral norms that need to be discarded.

When weighing the arguments and the counterarguments, *in their aggregate,* with respect to the question of whether or not the Koran in its entirety, or in part, is the word of God, the criterion of plausibility over-whelmingly favors the critical over the traditional view.

The ways by which Muslims resist critical study of their religious texts and challenges to their beliefs are similar in many respects to the ways by which Orthodox Jews (haredi, and the haredi-leaning modern Orthodox) and fundamentalist Christians defend their text-based irrational beliefs. Although the fundamentalist adherents of each one of these three religions deny the basic truth claims of the other two, there is much overlap in the arguments they use in defending themselves against critiques and threats—whether critiques by the other two religions or, even more threatening today, critiques from secular culture, from scientific disciplines, and from the academic study of religion.

As with Orthodox Judaism and fundamentalist Christianity, the cluster of core traditional Muslim beliefs/assertions generates additional irrational, improbable, and unconfirmable assertions and beliefs. Because these Muslims maintain that the Koran is the immutable, eternal (or for some theologians—deemed heretics by others—the created) word of God, they assert that Koranic statements (and other early Islamic traditional statements that they revere) about life, human nature, and world history are "true" in a factual, propositional sense.

How, for example, are the facts of evolution dealt with? Some Muslims consider evolution to be compatible with Islam, maintaining, as do many Jews and Christians, that God is the intelligent designer, using evolution as the vehicle for the design of the world and of mankind. They might also claim that Koranic verses that on the surface appear to contradict evolution can be interpreted to be compatible with it. They might even argue that the Koran actually refers to evolution, along the lines of argumentation of those who see *modern* embryology, geology, cosmology, and physics—including relativity—in the Koran as well.

However, many Muslims vehemently deny both evolution and the notion that Koranic verses are in any way compatible with evolution. The Web site http://www.darwinism-watch.com/index.php is devoted to such a view.[38] It expresses the Muslim equivalent of the views of creationist, fundamentalist, literalist Christians, who deny the fact of evolution and consider the "belief" that it occurred to be heresy. Some American Muslims call for joining forces with Christian antievolutionists in trying to prevent the teaching of evolution in the public schools. For all of the conflict between Islam, Christianity, and Judaism, many fundamentalists from the three camps perceive acceptance of evolution to be a threat to the inerrancy and authority of their respective sacred scriptures and hence to their religious faith. When a Muslim reads the

Koranic passages that talk about how Allah created the world and mankind, more or less literally rather than metaphorically, he correctly sees them as contradicting evolution, just as the Christian or Jew who reads Genesis in a relatively literalist way correctly concludes that its account is incompatible with the modern biological account. The "irrationality" of the Muslim, the Jewish, and the Christian reader is not in their claim that the Koran or the Bible can and should be understood more or less literally, but in their belief in the divine origin and authority of these works in light of evidence against that belief, and in their denial of the scientific evidence of the past 150 years from biology and cosmology.

As I discussed earlier, the idea that numerous biblical passages were meant by their original authors to be understood literally is very plausible. In fact, it is often the metaphorical, or symbolic, or mystical, or philosophical reinterpretations of these biblical passages—even in the service of rationality, as, for example, was the case with Maimonides—that are much less "rational" or plausible readings of the original, contextual intent of the biblical authors. Whoever authored Genesis 1–2:3 might have very well believed that the world was created in six actual days, and that humankind was created on the sixth of these days. It is also possible that he might have thought otherwise, but whatever this "otherwise" in his mind might have been, he surely wasn't thinking about modern theories of cosmology and evolution. On the other hand, some fundamentalist readers of the Bible and the Koran take their "literalism" to an absurd extreme, to the point of denying the metaphoric sense of words and phrases that were meant as metaphors in the original intent and usage of the authors.[39]

The Muslim fundamentalist can have his choice of irrationalities—either to irrationally believe that the Koran knew about the specifics of the facts and processes of evolution, or to irrationally believe that evolution has never occurred.[40]

Another option for a believing Muslim is to accept evolution as a fact, and to maintain that the Koran is not concerned with science but with faith, values, and meaning. Such a Muslim, if he generally accepts the methods and findings of modern science, as many devout Muslims do, would not read the Koran literally, especially when to do so would conflict with the firmly established "truths" of science.[41]

The belief in miracles to validate the truths of Islam is linked, ironically, to ostensibly "rational" arguments in defense of those claims. We have already seen how common analogous moves are in Christian and Jewish polemics and apologetics. For example, we read in a widely distributed *A Brief Illustrated Guide to Understanding Islam* that "[i]f we would like to know if a religion is true or false, we should not depend on our emotions, feelings, or traditions. *Rather, we should depend on our reason and intellect* [emphasis mine]. When God sent the prophets he supported them with miracles and evidence which proved that they were truly prophets sent by God and hence the religion they came with is true."[42]

In addition to the appeal to reason and intellect via the evidence of miracles in support of Islamic faith, defenders of the faith "prove" the divine origin of the Koran with the claim that the Koran and Hadith contain "scientific" or "medical" information that could not have been known in the seventh century on the basis of scientific and medical knowledge current at the time. The Koran and Hadith, we are told, inform us, for example, whether explicitly or by inference, of facts about human embryonic development, geology, meteorology, and brain structure and function that anticipated medical and scientific discoveries that weren't made until recent centuries. For example, with respect to embryonic development, the Koran states the following:

> We created man from an essence of clay, then We placed him as a drop of fluid in a safe place, then We developed that drop into a clinging form (*aloqah*),[43] and We developed that form into a lump of flesh (*mudghah*),[44] and We developed that lump into bones, and We clothed those bones with flesh, and later We developed him into other forms— glory be to God, the best of creators!—then you will die and then, on the Day of Resurrection, you will be raised up again.[45]

The point of this passage is to inform the listener or reader, who might be skeptical about God's power and about a future resurrection at which time mankind will be judged, that just as God, in his power and unique ability, enables humans to be created through divinely regulated insemination and embryonic development, so, too, can he re-create humans at a future time.[46]

Centuries, if not millennia, before the seventh century CE it was well known in the Middle East that semen (the fluid) is necessary for procreation, and that the embryo and fetus develop in stages. One does not need divine revelation to infer that somehow the "liquid" develops in a "safe place" inside the mother's body, into a flesh-and-bones human being.

Aristotle had already systematically observed chick embryos and recorded different stages in their development. With respect to humans, some of this information could be acquired in many ways (in addition to speculation), such as by examining fetuses that were expelled or extracted when women had premature births at different stages of pregnancy, or from women who died while pregnant. The accumulation of medical and anatomical knowledge about fetuses from these sources revealed different stages of embryonic development and different shapes and forms of the fetus. In fact, the "stages of development" described in the Koran and Hadith are derivatives of Greek and Indian teachings. The Koran at best makes use of the knowledge of embryology that had been known from at least the time of Galen, 450 years prior to the writing of the Koran.[47]

Notwithstanding the rather vague description of embryonic development in the Koran passage cited above, some Muslims try to "prove" the divinity of the Koran by claiming that the Koranic passage provides a detailed description of embryonic development that corresponds to what is now known by modern embryology, and that there was no way a human being living in seventh-century Arabia could have known what the passage states, other than via divine revelation.

Here is one part of the "proof":

> The next stage mentioned in the verse is the *mudghah* stage. The Arabic word *mudghah* means "chewed substance."[48] If one were to take a piece of gum and chew it in his or her mouth and then compare it with an embryo at the *mudghah* stage, we would conclude that the embryo at the *mudghah* stage is similar in appearance to a chewed substance. This is because of the somites at the back of the embryo that "somewhat resemble teethmarks in a chewed substance."[49]

The author of this guide to Islam asks, "How could Muhammad have possibly known all this about fourteen hundred years ago, when scientists have only recently discovered this using advanced equipment and powerful microscopes which did not exist at that time?" and responds by quoting an embryologist who stated, "The only reasonable conclusion is: these descriptions were revealed to Muhammad from God. He could not have known such details because he was an illiterate man with absolutely no scientific training."[50]

One questioner on an Islamic website asks, "How do I really know the Qur'an is the word from Allah? What conditions and criteria must a scripture meet in order to be worthy of divinity?" To which the following reply is given:

> Let us examine the Qur'an more closely. Starting with the content, could the knowledge therein have been within the reach of any human source, i.e., the Prophet Muhammad, his contemporaries, or the whole human civilization and for several centuries ahead?

How could a book revealed at that point of history refer—in precise terms—to scientific phenomena and historical events—prior and subsequent—that were unknown or misunderstood before their subsequent verification?

These Qur'anic references cover such a wide spectrum of topics as the nature of space, relativity of time, the shape and motion of the earth, the role of mountains, water for life, the water cycle, the sources of rivers and groundwater, sea depths, embryology, and proper health practices, prophecies fulfilled (after revelation), etc.[51]

It is almost beneath the dignity of rational discourse to respond to such illogical so-called logical arguments. Unfortunately, however, irrational as the "proof" is, it can, for the naïve and ignorant, reinforce their belief in the divinity of the Koran. Given that some Muslims who believe in the divinity of the Koran are dangerous to people who do not share that belief (as well as to some who do share their belief), I sacrifice my dignity to point out the illogicality of some such "proofs" with the hope that this might undermine those Muslim believers' belief—assuming the believers will read books like mine.[52]

The *Brief Illustrated Guide to Understanding Islam* is distributed by the Embassy of Saudi Arabia in the United States. The Saudi government has been financing and spreading its Wahhabist version of Islam in numerous countries around the world. It funds mosques and religious schools to inculcate its primitive, anti-Western, intolerant Islamic ideology.[53]

The danger, then, posed by Ibrahim, and Saudi-supported promulgators of the faith like him who believe in the divinity of the Koran, is that some naïve and unsophisticated people who read his book (and numerous books and websites like it) will take them seriously. This of course implies that the very belief in the divinity of the Koran carries within it seeds of danger. It does.[54] Many of the beliefs and values explicitly taught or implied in the Koran, Hadith, and Sharia, such as restrictions on freedom of speech and religion, mutilation of the body as punishment for certain sins or crimes, hatred of non-believers, and violent "jihad" in defense of Islam, pose a threat to the people and institutions of the United States and other Western democracies.

Sadly, so much of the Koran and of Islam is interpreted and lived today in a way that is intolerant of non-Muslims, and that promotes and perpetuates theocratic and authoritarian forms of government and intolerance toward and oppression of non-Muslims, women, and homosexuals. Muslim religious leaders and millions of their followers, in this country and throughout the world, see themselves in a clash of civilizations with Western values. They might not represent the majority of Muslims, but they are an influential minority. Their views have been well summarized by El Fadl, a distinguished professor of Islamic law at the University of California:

> The theologically-based attitudes of these Muslim puritans [Osama Bin Laden, the Taliban, the Wahhabis of Saudi Arabia, and the Jihad organizations] are fundamentally at odds not only with a Western way of life, but also with the very idea of an international society or the notion of universal human values. They display an intolerant exclusiveness, and a belligerent sense of supremacy vis-à-vis the other. According to their theologies, Islam is the only way of life, and must be pursued regardless of its impact on the rights and well-being of others. The straight path (*al-sirat al-mustaqim*) is fixed, they say, by a system of Divine laws (*shariah*) that trump any moral considerations or ethical values that are not fully codified in the law . . . A life devoted to compliance with this legal code is considered inherently superior to all others, and the followers of any other way are considered either infidels (*kuffar*), hypocrites (*munafiqun*), or iniquitous (*fasiqun*) . . . Naturally, the rightly-guided are superior because they have God on their side.[55]

This is not to say that there aren't those who believe in the divinity of the Koran who also believe in democratic values and principles, or at least in tolerance of non-Muslims and in nonviolence. There definitely are many such Muslims, El Fadl being one of the strongest proponents of the view, that *certain interpretations* of the Koran, the Hadith, and other Islamic sources, are compatible with democracy.[56]

If the views of El Fadl or other moderate, progressive or reformist Muslims were the norm among Muslims, the belief that the Koran is divine would not be dangerous to nonbelievers, because the norms and values that they derive from that belief are benign or even in many ways socially desirable. Even though the belief is unreasonable in light of science and scholarship, as long as they respect the right of others to hold and live by different beliefs it isn't necessary to challenge it (unless, of course, one is engaging in the scholarly/academic study of the origins of the Koran and of Islam, in which case the academic is supposed to follow reason and evidence wherever they lead, even if they lead to "heresy" and to the undermining of the religious beliefs of the devout).

El Fadl bases his argument for democracy on six basic ideas that he draws from his understanding and interpretation of Islam:

My argument for democracy draws on six basic ideas:

1. Human beings are God's viceregents on earth;
2. this viceregency is the basis of individual responsibility;
3. individual responsibility and viceregency provide the basis for human rights and equality;
4. human beings in general, and Muslims specifically, have a fundamental obligation to foster justice (and more generally to command right and forbid wrong), and to preserve and promote God's law;
5. divine law must be distinguished from fallible human interpretations;
6. the state should not pretend to embody divine sovereignty and majesty.[57]

The idea that human beings are God's vice-regents on earth and that they have a fundamental obligation to preserve and promote God's law derive from El Fadl's belief in the divinity and authority of the Koran, which I personally consider to be false. However, the values and norms for Muslims in America, which El Fadl ascribes to on the basis of his religious beliefs, are consonant to a sufficient degree with those of secular democrats so that he can be considered to be an ally in a common cause. I respect his brilliance as an expert in Islamic law and theology, and his passionate endeavors to convince other Muslims that Islam, when understood at what he would consider to be its level of "deep structure," espouses democratic values and tolerance.[58] The fact that I consider it irrational for El Fadl to believe what he does about the origins of the Koran is of interest to me as a psychologist who wants to understand why highly intelligent and educated people maintain certain irrational beliefs. However, it is not relevant to my concern about the dangers we face from Muslim clerics and leaders who are antidemocratic.

However, unless and until the views of El Fadl and others who think like him prevail and become dominant in the world of contemporary Islam, non-Muslims will have to do battle against the intolerant believers. One way of doing so, among others, is to undermine a major underpinning of their antidemocratic values, their belief in the divinity of the Koran and hence its ultimate authority.[59]

Let us return to Ibrahim's "proof" of the Koran's anticipation of modern embryology as demonstrated by its comparison of an embryo to a piece of chewed gum. I experimented with a piece of gum, chewing it for different periods of time, and different configurations emerged, not all of which bore much resemblance to an embryo (although they did have indentations superficially similar to the somites of an embryo).[60]

Not only does the Koran add nothing to what was known about the development of the embryo by the seventh century, it repeats errors about reproduction that were commonly believed. For example, in Sura 86:6–7 we read that "He [man] is created from a drop emitted [i.e., the semen]—Proceeding from between the backbone and the ribs [i.e., the loins]," or, in Haleem's translation, "He is created from spurting fluid, then he [man] emerges from between the backbone and the breastbone [the mother's womb]."[61] Although both of these modern Koranic translators/interpreters explain these two verses in a way that would not make them contradict what we now know about the source of semen, the passage should most probably be understood as echoing the view of Hippocrates that the semen begins in the brain, travels down the spinal chord, passes through the kidneys, and from there continues its downward journey into the testicles and finally the penis, before being emitted or spurted out.[62]

Another proof for the alleged divinity of the Koran, based upon its presumed knowledge of nature that was unknown to all others before the modern period, is its statement that Allah has made the earth as a bed and the mountains as pegs (Sura 78:6–7). This pithy and poetic verse "of course" anticipates modern geology's theory of how mountains formed and of plate tectonics.[63]

The Koran, we are told, anticipated modern cosmology because it states that "the heavens and earth were one connected entity, then We [Allah] separated them" (Sura 21:30). Mr. Ibrahim goes on to quote a geologist, who states, "Somebody who did not know something about nuclear physics fourteen hundred years ago could not, I think, be in a position to find out from his own mind . . . that the earth and the heavens had the same origin."[64] In other words, the author of this Koranic verse has to be God, because no one else could have made such a statement. The fact that the statement could be made out of speculation, or that many premodern myths of cosmogony make similar statements about the earth and heaven having once been a single entity that were later separated, does not seem to occur to those who cite it as proof of Koranic divinity.

Scientific experts are cited in support of these and similar claims, along with graphs, equations, and other impressive visual accoutrements of scientific exposition, which of course lends credence to them in the eyes of the credulous reader. However, what this more plausibly suggests is that the scientific experts were either quoted partially, or out of context, or were Muslims (whether by birth or by conversion) who feel a need to harmonize their scientific knowledge with their own belief in the Koran as the revealed word of God. Or perhaps the experts were not fully lucid when they made their statements. Or scientists can be logical with respect to science but illogical when it comes to religion, but are not aware of this cognitive schizophrenia and feel compelled to harmonize the two components of their self, the scientific and the religious, and will go to absurd lengths to do so.[65]

Perhaps the apologist sincerely believes that the Koran does contain this scientific information, but it wasn't until recently that humans were enabled to decipher it there. Analogously, some Jews and Christians claim that the Bible was aware of modern scientific knowledge, such as the Big Bang or evolution, which is encoded in the Bible in esoteric and/or symbolic form. Modern science is only discovering the details and the processes that are alluded to and embedded in the biblical or Koranic texts. Some of this "modern" knowledge had already been known to a select few, saints, prophets, and sages of the past. This is not biblical or Koranic literalism, which denies evolution and the Big Bang but rather biblical or Koranic (i.e., divine) omniscience and esoteric coding.

I do not think that all, or even most, of the Muslims (and Christians and Jews)[66] who make these kinds of specious arguments are aware of their irrationality. They are not for the most part deliberately and consciously trying to convince the reader/listener with arguments and proofs that they know are riddled with logical holes or that are circular or highly implausible. After all, the form of their arguments is appeals to reason, so they seem to respect the force of reason in establishing plausibility. Yet one often finds that the need to validate their religious beliefs is so powerful that even when they are presented with arguments and evidence that seriously challenge those beliefs, they will continue to conjure up new counterarguments and proofs for their religious view. The smarter they are, the more adept and creative they are in rebounding with a revised "logical" defense of their beliefs. Arguing with a fundamentalist believer who appeals to reason often feels like trying to convince someone who is pathologically paranoid that his suspicions are based on delusions rather than on reality. He might momentarily retreat, but will not really budge, always raising some new "rational" argument in support of his paranoid belief, far-fetched as it might be to the attending psychiatrist. I am using paranoia as an analogy, and not to imply that fundamentalist believers are paranoid, although at some point one begins to wonder whether there is not some deep pathology in their stubborn insistence on the truth of their beliefs in the face of strong evidence against them.

The presumed medical knowledge of premodern authorities, be it the Bible or postbiblical Talmudic sages, plays a similar role today in the case of some fundamentalist Orthodox Jews. They either want to convince non-Orthodox Jews of the divine origin or divine inspiration of Orthodoxy's basic texts and revered teachers (outreach) or want to prevent "doubting Thomases" from within their own community from dropping out of it by reinforcing their faith through "rational" arguments. One form is "Our sages of the past could have known X only if they were privy to divine revelation or inspiration, because X was not known to science and to medicine until long after these sages lived and taught. Therefore, our texts and the teachings of our sages are 'true.' Moreover, being divine in origin, they should be accepted as authoritative." Such an argument has also been used in an attempt to silence other, less "fundamentalist" Orthodox Jews who maintain that religious texts and authorities might have erred at times when they wrote about scientific or medical matters. The notorious (within the rather small confines of the ultra-Orthodox or haredi Jewish world) "Zoo Rabbi" affair included an attempt to suppress publication or distribution of Rabbi Nosson Slifkin's alleged "heretical" books, in which he stated (correctly) that some earlier revered authorities had asserted that postbiblical, Talmudic teachings on medicine and "science" are not necessarily true, and that it is possible to be an "authentic" Orthodox Jew and believe that evolution has transpired, or that the world is older than six days, in apparent contradiction to a literal reading of Genesis chapter 1.

Assertions of premodern privileged knowledge about the origin of semen and other aspects of reproduction are used to provide false "rational proofs" by some ultra-Orthodox rabbis, just as they were for devout Muslim defenders of the faith.[67]

A leading rabbinic scholar writes as follows:

[T]he source of all the knowledge of the Sages is either from Sinaitic tradition (received at the Giving of the Torah) or from Divine inspiration. That they were in contact with such sources in undeniable. How else could we explain numerous examples where the Sages had scientific information which no scientist of their time had? . . . How did they know that "a drop exudes from the brain and develops into semen" without having known that the pituitary gland, located at the base of the brain, emits a hormone which controls the production of semen . . . Either they had a tradition directly teaching them [this fact], or they knew [it] by applying principles which were part of the Oral Torah regarding the inner workings of the world. Thus they knew . . . that there was a relationship . . . between the brain and male reproduction.[68]

In response to the above claim, one critic points out the following:

> what the Sages believed is inconsistent with scientific findings. The
> Sages believed that a drop from the brain became semen. This is false.
> Nothing from the pituitary gland becomes semen. The pituitary
> gland does signal to the testicles to produce testosterone, but the latter
> does not originate in the brain . . .
>
> In addition, there seems to be a good counterargument to [this]
> argument . . . How could our Sages possibly have had a Divinely en-
> dowed science if they believed things that are now known to be false?
> They believed, for example, in six days of creation, in the discrete
> creation of species, in an animal that grew out of the ground (and later
> in birds that grow on trees), and in lice that came to be without
> reproduction. Doesn't this show that what our Sages knew (or only
> believed) of science they must have gotten in ways other than by
> Divine endowment? . . . [69]

He concludes with the understatement, "To summarize, this attempt to
argue for the truth of the infallibility of our Sages on scientific matters is less
than convincing."[70]

Another critic points out quite correctly that statements about physi-
ology and other natural phenomena that are attributed to the rabbinic sages
in the Talmud "are all either things that non-Jews also knew, or they are
being conveniently re-interpreted to match modern science, or they are actually false, or all three."[71]

To return to Islam specifically, another proof for the divine authorship of
the Koran often brought by Muslim apologists is referred to as *Ijaz al Koran,*
the *inimitability* of the Koran. It is based upon several obscure Koranic
passages, among which are the following and a few similar ones: "If you have
doubts about the revelation We have sent down to Our servant, then produce
a single sura [chapter] like it—enlist whatever supporters you have other
than God—if you truly think you can. If you cannot do this—and you never
will—then beware of the Fire prepared for the disbelievers, whose fuel is men
and stones" (Koran 2: 23–24).[72]

For many traditional Muslim commentators, the challenge put forth here
refers to aspects of the excellence and uniqueness of certain literary and
linguistic features of the Arabic of the Koran when it is compared with the
Arabic of pre-Koranic poets. In order for the argument to be appreciated and
convincing, one would need to know Arabic, and know it well enough to
compare and contrast Koranic style with other classical Arabic writings.
A thoughtful Muslim would realize that one cannot use this argument to

convince a Westerner who does not know Arabic of the uniqueness of the Koran. However, some contemporary Muslim apologists or missionaries expand the meaning of the challenge considerably beyond the uniqueness of Koranic literary style and linguistic virtuosity.

This challenge, according to the apologists, has yet to be answered. After all, says one defender of the faith, "[e]ver since the Qur'an was revealed, fourteen centuries ago, no one has been able to produce a single chapter like the chapters of the Qur'an in their beauty, eloquence, splendor, wise legislation, true information, true prophecy, and other perfect attributes. Also, note that the smallest chapter in the Qur'an (108) is only ten words, yet no one has ever been able to meet this challenge, then or today."[73]

Sura 108 consists of ten words in the original Arabic. In Haleem's translation, it reads as follows: "We have truly given abundance to you [Prophet]—pray to your Lord and make your sacrifice to Him alone—it is the one who hates you who has been cut off."

Another Muslim scholar responds on his website to someone's question of how he can be certain that the Koran is a divine revelation as follows:

> As to the form of the Qur'an—i.e., linguistic and literary features—any strict comparative analysis identifies the Qur'an to be not only superior to any other text—preceding or following . . . but also to be a perfect, flawless and the most eloquent composition. This perfection can be witnessed and proved on the levels of the individual words (semantics), sentence (grammar and rhetoric), and whole surahs (chapters).
>
> Thorough examination of the Qur'an shows that each of these elements was selected and phrased in the most appropriate manner to fulfill the most precise meaning and most effective impact, whether cognitive, psychological, passionate, or phonic, on the reader or listener. The Qur'an challenges mankind, Arabs and non-Arabs, to the end of time, to produce anything like or compared to itself.[74]

Now what more compelling proof for the divinity of the Koran can there be than this?! Nothing written by man or woman in all of world literature, since the "revelation" of the Koran, equals the beauty, eloquence, and so forth of Sura 108 or of any other Koranic passage. It should be noted that it is not the Koran itself that has said this—it challenged those who refused to believe in Mohammed's alleged revelation to "produce a single sura *like it*," without specifying which attribute(s) of the revelation were unique.

Is the apologist oblivious to the circularity and, dare I say, stupidity of his assertion? What criteria of beauty, eloquence, splendor, wisdom, and so forth are being used to compare the Koran with human writings?

The implicit, distorted "logic" seems to be as follows: The Koran is the most sublime, wise, perfect, and so forth work because *it says that it is* (as interpreted by the apologist). Hence, it must be the case that no passage by Dante, Shakespeare, Milton, Goethe, or from any of the millions of volumes in the Library of Congress, can match it on any of these attributes. Therefore, we should be convinced of its divine authorship (which we believe in, in any case, which is why we believe that what it says about itself must indeed be true).

Why do some bright and educated Muslims put forth such specious arguments to defend their belief in the divine authorship of the Koran? Let me suggest here two reasons, and I will consider others in chapter 6.

1. They sincerely believe that the "proof" is logically valid. Why do they believe this? There are at least two explanations for this phenomenon:

   a. We are all imperfect reasoners and often believe or affirm things that we think are logically demonstrable when there is actually an error in the logic. Sometimes the difference between a logically valid and a logically invalid proof or argument is quite subtle and difficult to ascertain. In this sense, the Muslim is no different from anyone else who makes logical errors.

   b. Because the believer maintains his belief for a variety of reasons, motives, or causes, which for him make it very compelling (emotionally and/or rationally), he is more easily convinced of the validity of a particular specious proof or argument than a neutral observer would be. To the neutral observer, the alleged proof might be obviously illogical, but to the believer, it is much more difficult to perceive and/or accept the illogicality of the proof, given the support for the belief from other sources in his life experience and other arguments for his belief.

Thus the apologist might not see the flaws in his circular or specious argument. Because he is a fervent believer, when he reads the Koran and compares it with other writings, coming to it with his prior assumptions about its divinity and the nondivinity of the other writings, he actually experiences the Koran as the most beautiful, wise, eloquent, truth-bearing, and so forth writing he has ever encountered. It is like a parent who considers her ugly daughter to be the most beautiful child in the world, or the infatuated lover who considers his beloved, as imperfect as she might really be, to be the epitome of beauty, wisdom, virtue, and perfection. The devout Muslim loves his Koran and his Islam with a passion that blinds him to the imperfections that others see in it, and to the beauty, wisdom, and splendor in other works that exceed that of Koranic passages. Non-Muslims—and more rational Muslims—can be more objective in their assessments of the actual worth, and the relative worth, of the Koran, when compared with everything else that has been written by humankind.

2. Another factor that might be at play in the use of specious arguments is that "the ends justify the means." The believer might know that the proof is specious, but because he believes that it is important that the person he is trying to convince or evangelize should accept the belief, he is willing to use an argument he knows to be false, for the greater good of getting the other person to accept the belief. It is not important to the persuader that the persaudee's acceptance of the belief be based upon valid logic—what is important is that it be accepted.

Is it proper from the perspective of Islam (or for that matter, from that of Judaism and Christianity as well) to tell a deliberate lie if one believes that by doing so he will convince a skeptic or a nonbeliever to accept the religious "truth" and be saved from eternal punishment, or that he will save a believer who has begun to have doubts about the truth of what he believes, from a slippery slope to skepticism and apostasy? Perhaps it is. If so, this might explain why a Muslim embryologist can affirm that the Koran provides accurate embryological information that has been discovered by biologists only in the past two centuries. He may very well know that this is not the case, but he says that it is because he wants to convince those who question the divine origin of the Koran of its divinity and to save them from the fires of Hell that await the non-Muslim or the apostate at the Day of Judgment.

Here is another "proof" of the divinity of the Koran. One of the opponents of Muhammad, an evil unbeliever, forbade him from praying. God said, "If he does not stop, We will take him from the *naseyah* (front of the head), a lying, sinful *naseyah*" (Sura 96:15–16). Mr. Ibrahim, of *A Brief Illustrated Guide to Understanding Islam,* asks, why did God specifically refer to the front of the head as that which lies? The reason, he says, is because the "front of the head" refers to the prefrontal area of the cerebrum, and it is this area that is "responsible for planning, motivating, and initiating good and sinful behavior and is responsible for the telling of lies and the speaking of truth" (16–17). Given that it is only in the past century that science has learned about this function of the prefrontal area, we have proof that God wrote the Koran. This "proof" is buttressed with a beautiful, multicolored picture of the brain and its various sections, with each section named and its function briefly noted in the picture.

Is there no other plausible explanation for the phrase "lying, sinful *na-seyah*"? Ali translates *naseyah* not as "forehead" but as "forelock" (as does, for that matter, another translation of the Koran that was published in Saudi Arabia, which distributes Ibrahim's *Guide*). Ali is not foolish like Ibrahim, and doesn't ascribe "lying and sin" to the sinner's hair. He comments, "The forelock is on the forehead, and is thus symbolical of the summit and crown of the man's power or dignity. To be dragged by it is to suffer the lowest dregs of humiliation."[75]

The introductory page to Ibrahim's *Guide* lists six science editors, all with the designation Professor. I do not know where or what they teach, but I suppose some of them are legitimate scientists with legitimate academic titles and positions. In their capacity as "science editors" of this *Brief Guide to Understanding Islam*, they approve of all of Ibrahim's proofs for the divinity of the Koran. This further illustrates how highly educated and bright people can believe very foolish things and be oblivious to simple logic and standards of proof when it comes to issues of faith and belief.

Historically, there were, of course, much more sophisticated defenders of traditional Islamic belief—after all, there were great medieval Muslim rationalist philosophers and theologians. As we saw in chapter 2, many Muslim philosophers and Koranic commentators were deeply respectful of reason. They believed that Allah is rational and so his Koran must be rational. They interpreted certain Koranic passages in metaphoric or symbolic ways, especially those that they considered to be irrational if understood literally or that contradict one another. Many medieval Muslim (and Jewish and Christian) theologians considered the study of nature to be a religiously meritorious activity, or even a religious obligation. They felt that such study will enhance one's awe and love of God, and that it shows an appreciation for his creation. Some premodern Muslim cultures made significant contributions to our knowledge of nature. However, Islamic culture of the past few centuries has lagged far behind the West in science.

With all due respect for historical Muslim rationalist theology, what was intellectually sophisticated philosophical theology in the conceptual world of premodern Islam is no longer intellectually compelling today, including the claim that the Koran was "composed" and revealed by God. Such a claim cannot pass muster in light of modern categories of historical thought, critical Koranic scholarship, philosophy, and scientific criteria (of the social and the natural sciences) for testing the plausibility of religious truth claims, and for claims about reality based upon statements in sacred scriptures. The same can be said of Maimonides' rationalist theology, which affirms the divine origin of the Torah, and of Aquinas's scholastic theology, and con-

temporary conservative Christian theology, which accept elements of traditional Jewish belief, and adds to them additional unsupportable or irrational
beliefs, such as the physical resurrection and divinity of Jesus.

There are more intellectually sophisticated Muslim defenders of the
doctrine of Koranic divine authorship today than the likes of the author and
editors of *A Brief Illustrated Guide to Islam.* These defenders of the faith are
wise enough to discern and avoid specious proofs, although at the end of the
day their beliefs about the divinity of the Koran are also fundamentally
irrational. Be that as it may, the Muslim tradition of both a literalist and a
scientifically omniscient and inerrant reading and understanding of the Koran
remains widespread and powerful for hundreds of millions of Muslims, similar
to how fundamentalist Christians read the Bible and some ultra-Orthodox
Jews read the Hebrew Bible and rabbinic teaching. The masses are more influenced by simplistic but "scientifically credentialed" preachers and apologists
with their simplistic readings and specious proofs than they are by dense and
complex theological/philosophical arguments. Indeed, numerous Muslim
preachers and teachers are not experts in serious Muslim philosophical theology, whether traditional or modern.

———

I turn now to further discussion of reasons for the tenacity of unreasonable
beliefs and of psychological mechanisms that support such beliefs.

<table>
<tr><td>CHAPTER SIX</td><td>Acquiring and Protecting
Unreasonable Beliefs</td></tr>
</table>

I HAVE EXAMINED some of the manifestations and features of Jewish, Christian, and Muslim fundamentalism, especially in the sense of belief in the divine revelation of a sacred scripture and its absolute and ultimate authority, not only for the believer, but for all mankind. In the course of doing this we have seen the lengths to which fundamentalists go to convince themselves or others of the truth of their beliefs, and some of the ways they protect their beliefs, and themselves, from empirical and logical challenges. To me and to many others, their beliefs are very implausible or irrational, and to guard their beliefs, they invoke far-fetched and inconsistent arguments and proofs. I would now like to expand upon my earlier discussions and present more systematically some explanations for why fundamentalists cling so tenaciously to their apparently unreasonable beliefs, and the way their minds work as they defend them.

Fundamentalist Jews, Christians, and Muslims share more than they would probably want to admit in terms of their motives for belief and their belief-protection strategies. However, there are differences between the three groups of Abrahamic fundamentalists, in terms of their specific beliefs and their motives for and defenses of them. Each group needed to be understood in its particularity when trying to explain its religiocognitive map and religious behaviors, which is why I devoted separate chapters to Judaism, Christianity, and Islam.

However, just as there are similarities between the three religions with respect to their views about the relationships between faith, revelation, and reason, so, too, there are commonalities with respect to motives for beliefs and defenses of them. In fact, as we shall see, there are similarities between the structure and defenses of belief systems of Abrahamic fundamentalists and the structure and defense of belief systems of nonliterate, animist tribes studied by anthropologists. There are similarities as well in the structure and defenses of secular ideologies such as orthodox communism and orthodox Freudianism. Marx, Freud, and Mao, and their works, were treated by some "believers" with a reverence and were ascribed an authority that was akin to fundamentalist religiosity, and in some instances with a passionate fanaticism as well. Contradictions within their works were reconciled, and there was always an explanation available within the conceptual scheme of these secular "faiths" to explain any apparent logical or empirical challenge to their assertions or predictions. I will, however, not be examining these secular ideologies, because the focus of this book is on the Abrahamic religions.

Acquiring and Protecting Religious Beliefs

How do people acquire religious beliefs? Most often it is through a process of socialization that begins at birth, in one's family and in the religious community into which one is born. The individual imbibes the ideas, beliefs, values, sights, sounds, touches, and fragrances of the religion, and one practices its rituals for many years, long before he has sufficient cognitive ability to think about them critically.

Pascal Boyer, on the basis of findings and theories from anthropology, evolutionary psychology, and cognitive science, maintains that in order to explain the origin and maintenance of religious ideas, beliefs, rituals, and values, we cannot rely exclusively on environmental factors such as culture and socialization. We need to explore innate, cognitive systems that do their work, without our awareness, in several different "inferential systems." These systems relate, for example, to the nature of "agency" we ascribe to others (including some physical objects), our "intuitive psychology" (the assumptions we naturally make about what other people think and feel, and by extension—what "spirits," or deities, think and feel), our moral expectations (such as fairness), and our social and group needs. The systems explain aspects of experience. These innately wired systems also set limits on which specific religious concepts, beliefs, and practices will "survive." Rather than trying to account for "religion in general," we need to understand how these various inferential systems work in very particular situations and settings to address specific, concrete questions, challenges, or problems that humans encounter in cognitive, emotional, and social spheres of life. It is the aggregate effect of these that produces the specific religion of a particular individual or group. These "inferential systems" also set limits on the range of religious ideas, feelings, and behaviors that humans develop. The innate inferential systems are shaped by environmental influences, and develop and differentiate into many specific belief and religious sytstems.[1] Boyer provides a useful corrective to theories of religion that do not take account of human biology.

Returning, however, to powerful environmental factors, when infant, childhood, and early adolescent religious experiences have for the most part been positive, as they very often are, their resilience is easy to understand. Moreover, religion provides many people with meaning, purpose, hope, joy, serenity, resilience, consolation, identity, and social support.

With respect to the widely accepted functions served by religion, Boyer raises insightful and sometimes penetrating questions. For example, the claim that religion provides consolation seems to underestimate the fear and anxiety that religion can generate, with doctrines such as eternal damnation in Hell. To the claim that religion satisfies human curiosity about the origins of the universe, Boyer notes that most people unschooled in theology or philosophy do not expend too much intellectual or emotional energy on trying to explain the origin of things in general, and this curiosity differs from culture to culture. (Indeed, if this were of great concern to people, I wonder why more religious people in the United States aren't studying physics, cosmology, and evolution.) Moreover, some religious explanations of natural phenomena raise as many questions as they answer. In response to the claim that religion explains why human existence entails so much evil and suffering, Boyer maintains that in many religions, especially "primitive" ones,there is much less of a concern about the existence of evil and suffering in general than about particular instances of evil and suffering. To the claim that religion provides a moral code, there are the obvious cases of religion advocating actions that many people would consider to be highly immoral (e.g., burning heretics at the stake). To the claim that religion forges group solidarity, there are numerous instances of religion becoming a divisive rather than a unifying force in many groups.[2] Most students of religion, however, would still maintain that religion does provide meaning, purpose, hope, consolation, identity, social support, and so forth even after taking into account Boyer's reservations.

When people are socialized in a relatively isolated or self-contained religious community and are not directly exposed to alternative lifestyles or worldviews—as is the case, for example, with certain Jewish Hasidic groups, Bible Belt, serpent-handling Christian sects, and Muslims raised in exclusively Muslim societies—there is little reason for them to, or little chance that they will, examine their religion critically. Everyone they know, respect, and love and who loves and cares for them, accepts the religious worldview, so why should it be questioned or challenged? Even if they begin to note certain discrepancies between some of what the religion teaches and the reality that they experience, the religion usually has ways of explaining these discrepancies from within the system itself. The fundamentalist Jew believes that God loves the Jewish people. So why do the Jews suffer so much? Perhaps they have sinned and are being duly punished, just as a loving parent sometimes has to punish a child who has misbehaved. The serpent handler, too, invokes sin to explain why some handlers die from the venomous bite of the snake that they handle as a sign of their faith in Jesus. All three faiths believe that God is omnipotent and benevolent, so why do the innocent suffer? God's ways are mysterious, or the suffering of innocents atones for someone else's sins, or the innocent person will reap such rewards and pleasure in the afterlife that the suffering in this world is insignificant.

The power and attraction of religious convictions manifest themselves as well in their adaptability to apparent disconfirmation of beliefs by modifying the beliefs or generating new and novel ones that are incorporated into the belief system. This happens, for example, when prophecies or messianic expectations fail to materialize. Instead of concluding that the beliefs were false, the religious person will often conclude that there had been a misunderstanding of the belief system or that new factors have come into play which account for the apparent failure. Sometimes these adaptations or innovations are the work of religious leaders and theologians, sometimes of laypeople. They eventually spread and are incorporated into the religious worldview of the individual adherent. In the seventeenth century some devout Jews believed that Shabbetai Tzvi was the Messiah. Unfortunately, he converted to Islam, which is not exactly what had been expected of a Jewish Messiah. Many of his followers developed an elaborate theology to explain how this was a necessary stage in the ultimate redemption Tzvi was supposed to bring about. The disciples of Jesus hadn't expected him to be crucified. When he was, they developed the notion of his having been crucified in order to atone for the sins of mankind. They expected him to return in glory to earth in their lifetime. When that didn't happen, they developed the idea of, and belief, in a second coming of Christ.[3] A similar phenomenon occurred in the belief system of the Shia sect of Islam, which has been expecting the appearance of the Mahdi, the hidden twelfth Imam (a messianic-like figure) for many centuries, who hasn't yet shown up.

Another way of acquiring a religious belief system is through "conversion" or "persuasion." A person who was not raised religious adopts in adolescence or adulthood a religious worldview, for example, a "born-again" Christian in evangelical Christianity or a *baal teshuva* (returnee) in contemporary Jewish parlance, referring to a Jew who was not raised Orthodox but adopted Orthodoxy. These individuals often cling to their newfound religion as tenaciously, and with even more fervor, as those socialized from birth. In these cases it is not the emotive power of early socialization experiences that accounts for the commitment and the resistance to challenge, because they didn't experience early religious socialization. Rather, it is a combination of the rational, emotional, and values appeal of the newly adopted religion along with the newly acquired sense of meaning and purpose and the caring community that it provides, which is what motivates the born-again or converted Christian, Muslim or Jew. Sometimes there is also an element of rebellion against one's parents or against the community in which one was raised.

The convert to any new faith, or the Jewish baal teshuva has a special motive for warding off threats to his new belief system. The processes of conversion and of "baal teshuva-ing" often entail a considerable amount of tension with parents and friends "left behind," so to speak. Sometimes the convert/returnee sacrifices a lifestyle that had provided material satisfactions and pleasures and personal freedom when he adopts a new religious lifestyle that restricts the satisfaction of hedonistic impulses, imposes a rigorous behavioral discipline, and limits intellectual curiosity and autonomy. So when the convert or returnee perceives a threat to his newly acquired religious worldview and lifestyle, the well-known process of cognitive dissonance resolution comes into play. He needs to justify the sacrifices he has made and the pain he experienced and caused to others. Therefore, he has to ward off these threats with whatever unconscious cognitive mechanisms and conscious cognitive skills he can draw upon. Many of the staunchest defenders of the faith are the converts, born-againers, and returnees.

In their classic study of the reactions of millennial or messianic religious believers to disconfirmations of predictions they had made based upon their beliefs, Festinger and his colleagues[4] were specifically interested in how these disconfirmations resulted in increased efforts at proselytizing for the cult. However, it is not only the failure of predictions that can produce intensified commitment and proselytizing, but any threat to one's religious beliefs, especially to newly acquired ones. Many of those involved in Jewish "evangelical" movements, by which I refer to Orthodox Jewish institutions, such as Ohr Sameah and Aish HaTorah, that are engaged in *kiruv* (bringing those far from Orthodox Judaism closer to its "certain and absolute truths" and lifestyle) are themselves *baalei teshuva* (the plural of baal teshuva).

Moreover, many individuals raised as Orthodox Jews who have attended college or who are autodidacts are well aware of the threats to their Orthodoxy from modern science, philosophy, and biblical scholarship. Some try to ward off these threats by way of repressing doubts. Others choose the path of isolating themselves and their families as much as is feasible from the encroachments of modern thought. Still others, however, see it as their mission to aggressively fight the battle for God and against "ignorance" or *kefira* (heresy) by reaching out to, preaching to, and persuading the non-Orthodox to join the fold. Sometimes they engage in the morally questionable practice of deception in the arguments they use to persuade. At times their deception may be unintentional because they have already engaged in self-deception and sincerely believe the flawed arguments they use when they try to "convert" others. On other occasions, however, they are aware of the deceptive arguments they employ but perhaps believe that the ends of kiruv justify the means.

Whence this passionate commitment to defend and to spread the faith? The simplest explanation for outreach efforts is that they are motivated by the traditional value that all Jews are responsible for the spiritual (as well as material) well-being of one another. In addition, many people who experience a way of life that they find meaningful and enjoyable like to share it with others—people can be altruistic. However, given the evidence for increased commitment and proselytizing in the face of threats to one's belief system, it is reasonable to assume that this phenomenon exists in Orthodox outreach as well. Is it possible that some of the most passionate Orthodox devotees of outreach are themselves harboring doubts about the beliefs that they are trying to preach to others? Moreover, increased commitment as a response to doubt needn't be reflected only in outreach, but in other manifestations as well. Perhaps unrelenting, passionate, defenders of the faith—ever eager and ready to take up the cause of defending Orthodoxy against all who question its validity—might be suppressing their own doubts, conscious or unconscious, with their zeal. Some religious people are threatened by their own doubts, or by the heresy or apostasy of others, or by the mere existence of other religions, or by secular indifference to religion, whereas others are not. My sense is that it is usually those who feel threatened who feel a need to missionize, or to condemn, or to coerce, or to engage in polemics and apologetics.

Festinger et al. describe the mentality of religious conviction, especially when much has been invested in it:

> We have all experienced the futility of trying to change a strong conviction, especially if the convinced person has some investment in

his belief. We are familiar with the variety of ingenious defenses with which people protect their convictions, managing to keep them unscathed through the most devastating attacks.

But man's resourcefulness goes beyond simply protecting a belief. Suppose an individual believes something with his whole heart; suppose further that he has a commitment to this belief, that he has taken irrevocable actions because of it; finally, suppose that he is presented with evidence, unequivocal and undeniable evidence, that his belief is wrong: what will happen? The individual will frequently emerge, not only unshaken, but even more convinced of the truth of his beliefs than ever before. Indeed, he may even show a new fervor about convincing and converting other people to his view. . . . (3)

Festinger posits five conditions "under which we would expect to observe increased fervor following the disconfirmation of a belief" (3). I will list these conditions and indicate how they are applicable to Jewish "evangelicals," in the sense of apostles to fellow Jews.

1. A belief must be held with deep conviction and it must have some relevance to action, that is, to what the believer does or how he behaves. (4)

Orthodox Jewish evangelicals meet this condition of deep doctrinal conviction. They resolutely affirm the divinity of the Pentateuch and of the rabbinic oral traditions of its interpretation. Orthodox Judaism also demands rigorous adherence to numerous ritual (and ethical) behaviors.

2. The person holding the belief must have committed himself to it; that is, for the sake of the belief, he must have taken some important action that it is difficult to undo. In general, the more important such actions are, and the more difficult they are to undo, the greater is the individual's commitment to the belief. (4)

This condition is easily satisfied by the baalei teshuva who have abandoned one lifestyle and worldview for that of Orthodox Judaism. It is less often the case with those socialized Orthodox from infancy. However, given the demands of halakha, Jewish religious law, which entails rigorous adherence to hundreds if not thousands of behavioral obligations and restrictions, any committed Orthodox Jew takes "important actions," and these are difficult to undo—or rather, to cease doing—because of the guilt and social stigmatization that would ensue.

It should be noted, though, that for most Orthodox, halakhically committed Jews, raised as such from early childhood, the "yoke of the law" is not as burdensome as it appears to an outsider because living one's life under the yoke has been a natural experience from infancy, to which one has adapted. More importantly, for many or most such Jews, the "yoke of the law" is actually experienced as a very positive experience. It is the vehicle for doing God's will and becoming close to him. The "law" or, perhaps better, the *mitzvot* (commandments) are embedded into the very fabric of the religious life, which can be replete with family warmth, positive emotions, and intellectual satisfactions when Orthodoxy is functioning at its best. Actions undertaken out of love are also difficult to undo.[5]

3. The belief must be sufficiently specific and sufficiently concerned with the real world so that events may unequivocally refute the belief. (4)

This condition is harder to establish for Orthodox Judaism, as we will see below. However, because Orthodox Judaism maintains that God is omnipotent and benevolent, and that he loves the Jewish people, the real-world events of the ongoing suffering of hundreds of millions of innocent children (and innocent adults as well) as a consequence of poverty and disease, throughout the world,[6] and of the horrific sufferings experienced by the Jewish people historically, and more recently in the Holocaust, would seem to refute the belief in divine omnipotence and benevolence.

4. Such undeniable disconfirmatory evidence must occur and be recognized by the individual holding the belief. (4)

Orthodox Jews are very attuned to the reality of suffering. They do not deny it or idealize it, as some Christians do. Indeed, much of Jewish prayer refers to the history of Jewish suffering and pleads with God to prevent it from recurring. Moreover, the Orthodox Jewish ethos (and the non-Orthodox Jewish ethos as well) is permeated with the justifiable sense of having been victims of unwarranted persecution and of continuing to be so today, especially in the Arab and Muslim wars against the State of Israel and against Jews.

Festinger explains this:

> The first two of these conditions specify the circumstances that will make the belief resistant to change. The third and fourth conditions together, on the other hand, point to factors that would exert powerful pressure on a believer to discard his belief. It is, of course, possible that an individual, even though deeply convinced of a belief, may discard it in the face of unequivocal disconfirmation. We must, therefore, state a fifth condition specifying the circumstances under which the belief will be discarded and those under which it will be maintained with new fervor. (4)

5. The individual believer must have social support. It is unlikely that one isolated believer could withstand the kind of disconfirming evidence we have specified. If, however, the believer is a member of a group of convinced persons who can support one another, we would expect the belief to be maintained and the believers to proselyte or to persuade nonmembers that the belief is correct. . . . (4)

This condition is amply satisfied by Orthodox Judaism, which consists of robust communities whose members provide one another social and ideological support. In addition to these, the Orthodox Jewish evangelical movements have created their own institutions and mini-communities to support the baalei teshuva, whom they have attracted, and to support the students and rabbis of their seminaries, where much of the persuasion (emotional, social, and intellectual) takes place.

Given these five conditions, Festinger explains "why increased proselyting follows the disconfirmation of a prediction . . ." (25):

> If more and more people can be persuaded that the system of belief is correct, then clearly it must, after all, be correct . . . It is for this reason that we observe the increase in proselyting following disconfirmation. If the proselyting proves successful, then by gathering more adherents and effectively surrounding himself with supporters, the believer reduces dissonance to the point where he can live with it. (28)

Festinger's analysis plausibly accounts for *part* of the motives and passions of the proselytizing activities of Orthodox Jewish evangelicals, in whom the five conditions have been met.

One way of reducing or eliminating dissonance that is generated by facts or arguments that challenge a belief system is to anticipate and neutralize them by what I would call "preemptive theology." Preemptive theology often originates only after a threat or challenge has been posed. Initially, it was reactive theology. Once, however, the theological response to the challenge is formulated, it then serves to preempt the threat for the next generation of believers who will be exposed to the same or similar threats.

———

There are similarities in how the Abrahamic religious belief systems, with very sophisticated systematic theologies, have "answers" to all of the challenges to them and how the less systematized and formalized beliefs and practices of the illiterate animistic Azande tribe in the Sudan did the same. The great English anthropologist Evans-Pritchard studied and analyzed the Azande worldview, which includes belief in the efficacy of magic, sorcery, witchcraft, and oracles. With respect to the failed predictions of oracles or the contradictions between the predictions of two performances of an oracle, Evans-Pritchard asks the following:

> What explanation do Azande offer when the oracle contradicts itself? . . . They are not surprised by contradictions; they expect them. Paradox though it be, the errors as well as the valid judgments of the oracle prove to them its infallibility . . .
>
> But when faith directs behavior it must not be in glaring contradiction to experience in the objective world, or must offer explanations that demonstrate to the satisfaction of the intellect that the contradiction is only apparent or is due to peculiar conditions. The reader will naturally wonder what Azande say when subsequent events prove the prophecies of the poison oracle to be wrong. The oracle says one thing will happen and another and quite different thing happens. Here again Azande are not surprised at such an outcome, but it does not prove to them that the oracle is futile. It rather proves how well founded are their beliefs in witchcraft and sorcery and taboos. On this particular occasion the oracle was bad because it was corrupted by some evil influence. Subsequent events prove the presence of witchcraft on the earlier occasion. The contradiction between what the oracle said would happen and what actually has happened is just as glaring to Azande eyes as it is to ours, but they never for a moment question the virtue of the oracle in general but seek only to account for the inaccuracy of this particular poison . . .
>
> Moreover . . . there are other reasons which would equally account for its failure. It may be that the particular venture about the success of which a man was consulting the oracle was not at the time of consultation threatened by witchcraft, but that a witch intervened at some time between the consultation and the commencement of the undertaking.
>
> Azande see as well as we that the failure of their oracle to prophesy truly calls for explanation, but so entangled are they in mystical notions that they must make use of them to account for the failure. The contradiction between experience and one mystical notion is explained by reference to other mystical notions.[7]

In his detailed analysis of reasons for the persistence of Azande belief in magic, Evans-Pritchard gives twenty-two (!) possible reasons as to why the Azande do not see the futility of their magic (475–478) and notes that "it will be evident to the reader that some of these reasons only apply to the use of important medicines, others to all magic and to mystical beliefs in general." He defines "mystical notions" as "patterns of thought that attribute to phenomena supra-sensible qualities which, or part of which, are not derived from observation or cannot be logically inferred from it, and which they do not possess" (12).

Many of the reasons that Evans-Pritchard lists for the Azande's not perceiving the futility of certain practices and the falseness of certain beliefs, could also be applied to an analysis of why, for example, devout Jews, Christians, and Muslims pray to God that he heal the sick, notwithstanding the lack of evidence that prayer is effective in bringing about recovery from illness,[8] or why they seek blessings from saints even though the blessings do not materialize. Or why and how Abrahamic fundamentalists maintain religious beliefs that "are not derived from observation or cannot be logically inferred from it," even when the beliefs are contradictory, or when experience does not confirm the efficacy of practices that are mandated by the beliefs and which the beliefs say will be efficacious.

Here are seven of Evans-Pritchard's reasons for why the Azande do not perceive the futility of practices derived from their beliefs, and their analogues in the thought of fundamentalist Jews, Christians, and Muslims. These reasons explain why the Azande do not notice when a belief appears to be contradicted by experience or logic, or how the Azande explain such contradictions.

Evans-Pritchard is providing an explanation primarily for the way in which the Azande do not notice, or resolve, challenges to the expectations they have of the efficacy of magical rites (which imply or are based upon certain beliefs). I am adapting his model primarily to Abrahamic *beliefs* rather than *rites*. The theologies of the Abrahamic religions for the most part prohibit, condemn, or discourage magic, sorcery, and witchcraft, and theurgy. Hence religious practices, rituals, and rites are not necessarily understood to be directly theurgic. However, in reality, many fundamentalists do perceive them as such and perform them in the expectation, or at least in the hope, that they will stimulate God to respond to their requests that accompany the performance of the religious practice. In this sense, they are close in their mentality to the Azande.

1. Witchcraft, oracles, and magic form an intellectually coherent system. Each explains and proves the others.

Petitionary prayers for healing are sometimes followed by recovery and sometimes followed by death. In the case of recovery, God listened and responded. The positive outcome proves God's love and power, especially when the recovery is statistically unexpected. In the case of death, the all-knowing and powerful God listened to the prayers but decided that the patient had committed certain sins for which he deserved to die, or that he was righteous, and God, who especially loves the righteous, wanted his soul to be close to him in Heaven. Or God wanted him to die for some good reason, which we trust that God, who is omniscient, knows, but which we, who are not, cannot fathom. Whatever the outcome subsequent to the prayers and rite, for example giving charity, there is an explanation for it in the system. Sometimes the outcome is not only *explained* by the system, but "proves" the explanation. Why would a loving, omnipotent God allow the innocent child to die? He must have wanted the child's soul to return to him while still in its state of purity and innocence. This "proves" how much God loves the innocent and pure—he wants their souls to be released from their bodies so that they and he can be close to each other. Moreover, because God is just, the departed are enjoying their soul existence in the presence of God. This kind of logic can be found in some systematic theology, but even when it is not formulated systematically, it characterizes the way many religious people think and the way many priests, imams, pastors, and rabbis speak. There is no outcome subsequent to petitionary prayer that can disconfirm the belief system. People continue to pray. Social anthropologists have coined the term *secondary elaboration* to describe the characteristic of the theoretical thought of the traditional cultures, in which "there is a notable reluctance to register repeated failures of prediction and to act by attacking the beliefs involved. Instead, other current beliefs are utilized in such a way as to 'excuse' each failure as it occurs, and hence to protect the major theoretical assumptions on which prediction is based."[9]

In the context of arguing that *the affirmation of belief* is often more important to religion than *actual belief in the content* of an official doctrine, Daniel Dennett gives the example of the Catholic doctrine of transubstantiation during the sacrament of the Eucharist:

> [W]hat could you do to show that you really believe that the wine in the chalice has been transformed into the blood of Christ? You could bet a large sum of money on it and then send the wine to the biology lab to see if there was hemoglobin in it (and recover the genome of Jesus from the DNA in the bargain!)—except that the creed has been cleverly shielded from just such concrete tests. It would be a sacrilege to remove the wine from the ceremony, and, besides, taking the wine out of the holy context would surely untransubstantiate it, turning it back into ordinary wine. There is really only one action you can take to

demonstrate this belief: you can *say* that you believe it, over and over, as fervently as the occasion demands.[10]

For similar reasons, you cannot *disprove* the claims of the creed. It is remarkable that so much blood was shed in Christian history over creeds whose claims could be neither confirmed nor disconfirmed by any empirical method.

In addition to the theological explanations that validate all outcomes that follow prayer, praying behavior is probably reinforced by the fact that in Skinnerian operant conditioning terms, it is rewarded on a variable ratio schedule—every so often, in an unpredictable manner, prayer is followed by recovery—which tends to make behaviors resilient to extinction. Of course, people also engage in petitionary prayers in order to provide hope to themselves, or a sense of control when faced with a situation over which they seem to have no control, or in order to express their feelings of love and compassion for the person who is ill, or in order to ease their pain when they witness their loved ones suffering.

2. Azande often observe that a medicine is unsuccessful, but they do not generalize their observations. Therefore the failure of a single medicine does not teach them that all medicines are foolish. Far less does it teach them that all magic is useless.

The apparent failure of one prayer does not lead to the generalization that all petitionary prayer isn't effective. Far less does it teach that the performance of religious rites in general—doing God's will—doesn't result in health or prosperity. The health or prosperity might be delayed, or even deferred, to a spiritual hereafter in Jewish, Christian and Muslim belief (even to a hedonistic physical hereafter in some popular Muslim beliefs), but belief in God's reward for prayer and religious practices remains firm.

3. The results which magic is supposed to produce actually happen after rites are performed. Vengeance-magic is made and a man does die. Hunting-magic is made and animals are speared.

Sometimes petitionary prayer is followed by recovery from illness, or by success in some endeavor, or in defeat of one's enemies. Analogous to this is the belief that a murderer who is not apprehended and executed by a human court will eventually die, by God's order, an early and unusual death at the hands of an animal or a brigand. Some do. Thus belief in God's justice is vindicated in the face of what appears to be an amoral world.[11]

4. Contradictions between their beliefs are not noticed by Azande because the beliefs are not all present at the same time but function in different situations. They are therefore not brought into opposition.

This is primarily the case with laypersons, who are aware of many of the beliefs of their religion but do not evoke them in their thought and consciousness systematically and simultaneously. Today as I celebrate some success or good fortune, I might focus on God's magnanimity and not pay attention to the fact that even as I celebrate my good fortune, others are experiencing misfortune. My belief that God is fair and just and loves others, not only me, is not in my mind as I rejoice. God's magnanimity to me and apparent lack of magnanimity to others, or God's presumed fairness and his apparent lack of fairness in that he is good to me but not to others, are not brought into opposition.

However, systematic theologians are usually aware of these contradictions and oppositions between simultaneously held beliefs and doctrines, or beliefs and experience, and indeed, one of their major objectives and enterprises is to resolve them. Sometimes they do so plausibly, often they do so implausibly. Aquinas's *Summa Theologiae* is one of the greatest such systematic attempts in Western Christian thought.

5. A Zande is born into a culture with ready-made patterns of belief which have the weight of tradition behind them. It seldom occurs to him to question them. He accepts them, like those around him, with more or less faith according to their importance and his upbringing. Many of his beliefs being axiomatic, a Zande finds it difficult to understand that other peoples do not share them.

This is especially the case with those fundamentalist Jews, Christians, and Muslims who live in isolated communal enclaves, who exhibit the same lack of critical self-reflection as the Azande, and who are baffled when they learn that not everyone believes as they do. However, given the ubiquity of the "outside world" that is becomingly increasingly difficult to ignore because of the easy accessibility of information via twenty-first-century technologies of communication, these enclaves of the Abrahamic faiths will be under increasing pressure to defend their axiomatic beliefs rather than accept them uncritically. One sees this in recent years in the proliferation of forums and blogs in which fundamentalist Jews, Christians, and Muslims are battling to defend their beliefs against attack. Moreover, the relative anonymity of the Internet has provided an opportunity for doubters from within to voice their doubts openly and it is fascinating to follow some of these postings and discussions. Religious doubters who would not have the inclination or the courage to raise the questions they do about the beliefs in which they were socialized, or about the wisdom, and hence the authority of the religious leaders of their communities or seminaries, in a manner that would expose their identity, are doing so in blogs. My sense is that this freedom of expression is going to have strong repercussions in weakening the hold of fundamentalist spiritual and communal leaders over their flocks. Whereas in the past a doubter who was afraid of exposure would have to clandestinely acquire and read a forbidden book and hide it under his bed, and who would be wary of sharing his doubts with others, can today have easy access to a library of forbidden books, articles, and thoughts from a computer anywhere, and be part of a thriving community of doubters. Some Jewish fundamentalists have for this reason placed a ban on computers, or at least on connectivity to the Internet.

6. There are always stories circulating which tell of the achievement of magic. A man's belief is backed by other people's experiences contained in these stories. In certain myths and folk-tales the efficacy of magic is vouched for in olden times. Their fathers would not have used medicines unless their value was certain.

Abrahamic fundamentalists, who believe what they read in their sacred scriptures, have an extensive literature of legends and hagiographies describing the miracles and wonderworks performed by or for heroes and saints of old. The Hebrew Bible, the New Testament, and the Koran and Hadith (traditions about Muhammad and his companions) are replete with accounts of the miraculous, and new miracle stories have been added to the repertoire ever since. Legends and miracle stories are produced and flourish today. Contemporary Orthodox Hasidim vouch for the miracles performed by their current tzaddikim or rebbes, and contemporary miracles are officially validated by the Catholic Church, and more are validated by the gullible masses of believers. Miracles, when performed by humans (though ultimately attributed to God) are the Abrahamic siblings or cousins of "primitive" magic. Past and present miracles are "evidence" for the truth and effectiveness of one's faith and practices. If you have been taught from childhood, and still believe, that your ancestors, and even some of your contemporary leaders, have been miracle workers or beneficiaries of divine miracles, it is hard to question the beliefs that they have passed on to you.

7. Zande beliefs are generally vaguely formulated. A belief to be easily contradicted by experience and to be easily shown to be out of harmony with other beliefs must be clearly stated and intellectually developed—e.g., the Zande concept of a soul of medicine is so vague that it cannot clash with experience.

Abrahamic fundamentalist theologies, especially when systematized by theologians or religious philosophers, try to be precise rather than vague in defining their beliefs and core concepts and in charting their relationships. One reason for this is apologetics and polemics, often internal. Sunnis and

Shiites each have to explain to their adherents what differentiates them from the other, as do Catholic and Protestant Christians, and within Protestantism, the Anglicans from the Baptists, from the Methodists, from the Lutherans, and so on and so on. Fundamentalist Orthodox Jews have been less concerned with systematic theology because Judaism has been relatively open to diverse beliefs, within accepted parameters of certain basics, and has been more concerned with conformist behaviors. However, even in Orthodox Judaism, there have been times when, and there are groups for whom, acceptance of certain doctrines or dogmas has been considered important in deciding who is "in" and who is "out," and when that happens, there is a need for a certain precision. This was especially the case with Maimonides, for whom correct belief was essential to immortality, and Maimonides has his followers today, who check for hints or whiffs of heresy in their midst.

However, for all of the precision and intellectual sophistication of Abrahamic theologies, in contrast to Azande belief systems, the ultimate nature of Abrahamic God talk remains vague at a basic level. Some philosophers who analyze religious language argue that it never really makes any statements about an observable reality. Either it is emotive or it is meaningless:

> [A]ll metaphysical language, including the metaphysical language of religion and value, was cognitively meaningless. The claims that God exists, or that he is good (or that he does not exist, or is not good) are neither true nor false; they say nothing that could be true or false, because all such utterances are unverifiable by sense experience. So the language, despite its appearance, cannot be used to express truths or possible truths about the world. Because such language is uncheckable in principle, it asserts nothing. And because it asserts nothing, there is nothing for reason to assess or faith to believe.[12]

This argument is probably true for some religious terms, but not for all. Theologians themselves, however, will often say that human language is incapable of describing the reality of God; it is always metaphorical. Some say that God cannot be known in his essence but only by positing what he isn't—his "negative attributes." He isn't many; he isn't corporeal; he isn't emotional; he isn't created; he isn't bound by time; his knowledge is nothing like human knowledge; and he cannot be comprehended. If God talk is always metaphorical, or is always about what he isn't rather than about what he is, then God talk is essentially vague. So, too, with the central religious concept of the soul and beliefs/assertions about its origin, location, and destiny. Even the doctrine of free will is problematic when one tries to pin it down concretely and specifically. This vagueness, of course, provides a resilience to the concepts. It is hard to disconfirm the existence of God, the nature of God's revelation, the qualities of a nonphysical soul, the workings of free will, and the alleged relationships between all of these and what they assert about experience and reality if they haven't been defined precisely. So Abrahamic theologies and Azande beliefs share the quality of vagueness as well.

Evans-Pritchard further analyzes why it would be extremely difficult for the Azande to give up their faith in witchcraft and witch doctors, even in the face of apparently disconfirming experience. His analysis applies as well, with some distinctions, to certain Abrahamic fundamentalists:

> All their [Azande] beliefs hang together, and were a Zande to give up his faith in witch-doctorhood, he would have to surrender equally his faith in witchcraft and oracles ... In this web of belief every strand depends upon every other strand, and a Zande cannot get out of its meshes because it is the only world he knows.[13] The web is not an external structure in which he is enclosed. It is the texture of his thought and he cannot think that his thought is wrong.[14]

There are two points being made here. The first is the interconnected strands of the Azande's "web of belief"; the second is that witchcraft is the only world the Zande knows. For the Abrahamic fundamentalist, his entire worldview is premised on the divine authorship, inerrancy, and infallibility of all of his sacred Scripture, Bible or Koran. If even one sentence, or even one word, is admitted to be errant, or fallible, or of human authorship, the entire system collapses. That is why someone who denies that even one word of the Bible or of the Koran is from God is considered a heretic. Today he might deny just one word, but tomorrow he might deny an entire chapter of the Bible or a sura of the Koran. Eventually he will deny the authority of the entire Scripture, and hence of the religion's elaborate laws, rituals, and creeds because all of these base their claim for authority on the revelatory status of the Scriptures. The next step on the slippery slope is not only to deny the absolute authority of the texts and teachings but to deny the authority, and maybe the wisdom and even the virtue, of the religious leaders and institutions that teach, interpret, and enforce the scripturally based laws, rituals, and creeds. Thus, in the fundamentalist mentality there is a justifiable fear of and anxiety about what might appear to an outsider to be a minor, insignificant concession to biblical or Koranic critical scholarship. The individual fears the collapse of his belief system; the leaders fear that as well, but also the collapse of their authority.

As far as awareness of only one thought system, the Abrahamic fundamentalist who has not been exposed to an alternative worldview, like the

Azande, cannot imagine an alternative way of interpreting the world than that provided by the faith in which he was raised. However, as I noted above, nowadays this total isolation is rarely sustainable into adulthood. Contemporary Abrahamic fundamentalists are aware of the existence of alternative belief systems and theories that challenge their own, even though they might not be intimately familiar with the philosophical, scientific, empirical, and rational bases of these alternative theories. They can contemplate "heresy," and it is all the more threatening because they know it to actually exist in the broader world in which they live and with which they interact. Some contemporary Abrahamic fundamentalists are intimately familiar with alternate worldviews, which they examine and consciously reject. This makes them all the more psychologically intriguing. It is difficult to understand, for example, how one can continue to assert a belief in TMS, or in biblical or Koranic inerrancy, in the face of the overwhelming evidence against them from biblical and Koranic scholarship and other disciplines, to which one has been exposed, if evidence and rationality were the primary sources and sustainers of belief. Clearly they aren't. Other mechanisms are at work, such as emotional attachment and fear of existential chaos.

For the fundamentalist, as for the African traditionalist, "established beliefs have an absolute validity, and any threat to such beliefs is a horrific threat of chaos. Who is going to jump from the cosmic palm-tree [or the cosmic Torah or Koran] when there is no hope of another perch [or meaningful belief system] to swing to?"[15] Are the Azande stupid because they cannot see that the oracles, in which they believe, actually tell them nothing reliable about the future that they presumably predict? Not at all:

> And yet Azande do not see that their oracles tell them nothing! Their blindness is not due to their stupidity, for they display great ingenuity in explaining away the failure and inequalities of the poison oracle and experimental keenness in testing it. It is due rather to the fact that their intellectual ingenuity and experimental keenness are conditioned by patterns of ritual behavior and mystical belief. Within the limits set by these patterns, they show great intelligence, but it cannot operate beyond these limits. Or, to put it in another way; they reason excellently in the idiom of their beliefs, but they cannot reason outside, or against their beliefs because they have no other idiom in which to express their thoughts.[16]

We have seen that there are absolutely brilliant Abrahamic fundamentalists. Their brilliance is often manifested in their excellence in engineering, mathematics, and the pure, hard sciences, or in law and philosophy. Their brilliance is often manifested in their apologetics and the ingenuity of their biblical commentaries. But, as we noted, some very smart people (even Isaac Newton) can believe very stupid things, without themselves being "stupid."

Indeed, many brilliant and highly educated believers in the divine revelation of the Pentateuch or of the Koran argue the merits of their belief in sophisticated philosophical and theological language. This gives the appearance of rationality to their belief. But this is an illusion. These beliefs entail more than just a belief in the occurrence of a single, a few, or multiple episodes of divine revelation. It means affirming as true all of the teachings and stories of the Pentateuch or the Koran. Although there is considerable leeway within the Jewish, Christian and Muslim fundamentalist traditions for nonliteral, rationalistic interpretations of many of the miraculous events described in the Pentateuch, and in the Bible as a whole, or in the Koran, there are limits to how far these rationalizing tendencies do go and can go. All Abrahamic scriptural fundamentalisms involve believing that certain events actually occurred in the past, which scientists consider to have been impossible based upon the known physical laws of nature and the findings of biology, geology, archaeology, and linguistics.[17] Moreover, naturalistic explanations for the origin and content of the Scriptures are more plausible than the fundamentalist ones. So for all of the intellectual acumen of defenders of scriptural fundamentalism and their invocation of apparently sophisticated philosophical arguments, the bottom line is that their beliefs are irrational *in light of contemporary knowledge.*

I once heard an Orthodox rabbi discussing the attitude of the *halakha* (Jewish religious law) to the *apikoros* (heretic). He was arguing that it is proper for the Orthodox to show respect and love for those who left Orthodoxy or who are not Orthodox, even though, from the perspective of many in the Jewish tradition, the views of the non-Orthodox person are *false and irrational.* The halakha, at least in its twentieth- and twenty-first-century Orthodox formulations, extends a hand of tolerance and love to all Jews, even those whose *faulty reason* or inadequate knowledge of tradition has led them astray. This triggered in me the following thought experiment about who is rational and who is not, the Orthodox believer or the non-Orthodox nonbeliever.

Imagine a group of scientists, academicians, philosophers, lawyers, and others whose professional and occupational worldview are based upon a respect for and commitment to scientific, rational, and empirical thinking. As Americans, they also cherish the values of democracy, equality, and justice. They organize a club, open to individuals of similar values.

The club receives an application for membership from an individual, and they interview him in order to ascertain whether he shares their worldview. He is asked to summarize his worldview. He tells them that essential to his worldview are the following beliefs and tenets:

God appeared on a mountain and invited a man to ascend the mountain. On this mountain God gave the man a book known as the Torah and taught it to him for forty days, during which period the man fasted.

The book that God gave the man includes, among other teachings, the following ideas:

- It is permissible to buy and sell human beings as slaves.
- Men can divorce women, but women cannot divorce men.
- A male who engages in homosexual behavior (anal sex) should be put to death.
- A person who eats a lobster should be whipped.
- God has established and maintains a special relationship with a tiny nation that is dearer and more important to God than are the rest of the inhabitants of this planet.

The club assigns a committee of world-renowned specialists in the study of ancient Near Eastern texts to examine the Torah, which the applicant has claimed was given by God to the individual who ascended the mountain, sometime around the thirteenth century BCE. The specialists conclude that the book has all the signs of being a composite document, of human origin, influenced by ancient cultures, composed centuries after the time when the applicant for admission to the club believes it was written and delivered.

The members of the club vote not to admit the applicant because his views are irrational, or at least highly implausible, and because from their point of view, *he* is an *apikoros,* or heretic, who denies the foundational scientific, rational, and democratic beliefs and values of the members of the club. They decide, however, that as long as the applicant will not do anything harmful to society, and indeed does many good things for society, they will not take any action against him, and will even allow him to attend their meetings as an observer in the hope that he will eventually come around to a more rational and democratic worldview, at which time he can reapply for membership.

Are Orthodox leaders, when judging from their theological or religious law perspectives, what is the proper attitude to adopt toward non-Orthodox "heretics," capable of discerning that the perspective of the scientific/empirical non-Orthodox club is significantly more plausible and rational than theirs?

Some fundamentalists who adhere tenaciously to their beliefs, even when the data contradict their propositions, say that their attitude toward their beliefs is no different from the attitudes of scientists, who do not immediately reject a theory when they discover new data that disconfirm it. But this is a specious analogy.

What differentiates the attitude of the scientist toward his explanation of reality and to his beliefs about how nature works from the attitude of the fundamentalist? Horton asks this question with respect to the comparison of the scientific approach to dealing with data that contradict theory with the approach of the Azande to their belief in oracles even when experience would seem to disconfirm the oracles. His contrast between scientific and Azande approaches to the effect of new data on beliefs and theories applies as well to scriptural fundamentalists:

> And yet, the spirit behind the scientist's [and I would add, the scholar's] actions is very different. His pushing of a theory and his reluctance to scrap it are not due to any chilling intuition that if his theory fails him, chaos is at hand. Rather, they are due to the very knowledge that his theory is not something timeless and absolute. Precisely because he knows that the present theory came in at a certain epoch to replace a predecessor, and that its explanatory coverage is far better than its predecessor, he is reluctant to throw it away before giving it the benefit of every doubt. But this same knowledge makes for an acceptance of the theory which is far more qualified and far more watchful than that of the traditional thinker. The scientist is, as it were, always keeping account, balancing the successes of a theory against its failures. And when the failures start to come thick and fast, defence of the theory switches inexorably to attack on it.[18]

Evidentialism and Religious Beliefs

Throughout this book I have been assuming that rationality and reasonableness, pursuit of truth, and recourse to "facts" and empirical evidence should be the appropriate criteria for adhering to or adopting believers systems. I have pointed out that Abrahamic fundamentalist believers either deny these assumptions or do not abide by them when scrutinized, even when they claim to accept them. In some cases fundamentalists nominally accept the assumptions but have different criteria for reasonableness, truth, and evidence than do almost all critical biblical scholars (and an increasing number of critical Koranic scholars as well) or scientists. Are my assumptions valid or compelling? What is it about "reason" or "empirical evidence" that gives them priority over other claimed sources of truth?

With respect to the role that "evidence" should play in forming and maintaining religious beliefs, one Orthodox Jewish philosopher[19] critiqued my view that Orthodox Jews should accept the overwhelming scholarly evidence for the multiple-source post-Mosaic origin of the Pentateuch and abandon their assertion that it was revealed by God to Moses in the thirteenth century BCE. He wrote to me:

> I share your view that many Orthodox people (or "intellectuals")—and I include myself—have not developed certain sorts of evidence-based reasons for holding on to their beliefs. Some of us don't even know much about biblical studies or archaeology; I regard my own knowledge as limited—it's not my field. . . . I would classify your arguments as, with some qualification, an example of what philosophers call "evidentialism". . . Evidentialism was expressed in a particularly strong form by the nineteenth century writer W. K. Clifford: "It is wrong, anywhere and everywhere, to believe anything on insufficient evidence." Clifford pointed to negative social and intellectual consequences of beliefs lacking evidence. It was against this evidentialism that William James . . . argued that in some cases we do and should base our beliefs on our "passional nature" . . . Essentially he is trying to do away with the distinction you assume between rationality on the one hand and psychological explanation on the other. That a belief gives my life existential meaning is not just a psychological fact, it expresses a rational ground.[20] . . . Some beliefs will be reviewed only in the most exigent circumstances. When Marvin Fox declares that his very humanity is at stake, that life would lose its intelligibility and purpose if he vacated his religious commitment, he's giving, for my money, a much more impressive and compelling reason for retaining his beliefs than any of TMS's critics are giving for abandoning it . . .[21] A person has only one life to live, and as James argued, it's irrational for him or her to live it without hope, meaning, etc., all because of the current state of scholarly evidence, which itself might be overturned. To say that "objective" reasons for belief can't include considerations like Fox invokes, would make a mockery out of the deepest held convictions human beings have . . .

The Orthodox philosopher argues cogently for a philosophical position that it can be rational to maintain beliefs even in the absence of positive evidence for them. He also maintained that sometimes it can even be rational to maintain beliefs for which there is counterevidence, if those beliefs serve a valid human need, such as giving meaning and purpose to one's life or sustaining a community worth sustaining.

I do not disagree with many of the antievidentialist arguments to the effect that many of our "operative" beliefs and assumptions about reality and about our values cannot wait for airtight evidence and reasoned argumentation before we can justifiably use them to guide our lives.

I would ask, however, whether there are limits to the degree to which evidence that *contradicts* beliefs can be ignored by the believer when he becomes aware of it. Are biblical scholarship and other disciplines that challenge or refute assertions made in the Torah, or made, or implied, by the rabbinic construct that the Torah was revealed by God to Moses at Mt. Sinai, forever irrelevant to the maintenance or formation of one's religious beliefs, commitments, and way of life? Indeed, the philosopher is well aware that "the toughest challenges to religion today, or at least Orthodox religion today, come from the empirical disciplines: history, archaeology, biblical scholarship, neuropsychology, genetics, artificial intelligence, and the like."[22]

Belief in TMS, in the Orthodox world—including in the modern Orthodox world—is accompanied by belief in the doctrine that along with the revelation of the Pentateuch to Moses was the revelation of an Oral Law to him, which provided guidelines for the interpretation of the Pentateuch. Rabbinic/halakhic authority,[23] and numerous interpretations of the Pentateuch, are based upon this dual Torah doctrine of a written and an oral TMS.[24] The Orthodox belief in a "double TMS" thus carries with it much more "baggage" than just the ritualized recitation or affirmation of a sentence in a doxology. It entails a wide-ranging commitment to read, understand, and believe numerous biblical texts in ways that strain credulity and plausibility.

To express this in an extreme way, to teach the Torah as it is taught from Orthodox doctrinal assumptions is to engage in ongoing falsification of its meanings. To teach, in light of biblical and archaeological scholarship, that *most of the narratives of the Torah describe actual historical events,* is to teach a falsehood. To teach, *with the certainty that accompanies the fundamentalist assumptions about the Torah that Orthodoxy makes, that God wants us to do what the Torah says that God wants us to do,* is to often teach dubious, and sometimes morally problematic, norms and values.[25]

Are the tough challenges to Orthodox Judaism from history, archaeology, and biblical scholarship simply to be ignored by Orthodox educational institutions, including modern Orthodox ones?

This is what occurs daily in Orthodox schools, including modern ones, such as Yeshiva University, the "flagship" of modern Orthodoxy and Torah U'Madda ideology.[26] It is one thing to read the Torah judiciously and selectively, mythically, metaphorically, or devotionally, and use it as a resource for conveying certain beliefs and values, as do many non-orthodox Jews (and some Orthodox ones as well). It is quite another to read it as the *ultimate authority* for how Jews and mankind should lead their lives, interpreted through the prisms of rabbinic thought.

Moreover, is it reasonable to teach Torah as TMS without expecting or encouraging students who are being taught to think critically in their general studies to apply those same critical skills to the assertions of the tradition? And if the students do challenge the tradition because they become aware of biblical and other scholarship, as one would expect of a significant portion of students of high intellectual caliber in modern Orthodox day schools, what is the modern Orthodox response to their critical examination of the beliefs that Orthodoxy is attempting to indoctrinate?[27]

Reason as an Evolved Tool for Species Survival

In addition to the philosophical critique of *evidentialism,* there is another ground for questioning the priority of reason in deciding what we should believe and how we should live our lives. The human capacity to use reason is, after all, nothing but an evolutionary adaptation that enables our species to survive. Moreover, human reason is far from perfect. We make all kinds of logical errors in a variety of contexts. Reasoning skills do not come naturally, but require disciplined training, often of many years' duration, and for numerous people they never come at all. Most human beings believe things that do not meet the criteria of logical deduction or scientific induction, or even plausibility. We frequently make inferences about events of the past, or predictions about the future, which on strictly logical or probabilistic grounds do not make much sense, and we act in accordance with these erroneous assessments or expectations. Ancient and medieval philosophers pointed to the deficiencies of human reasoning in ascertaining "truth," and modern experimental psychologists have demonstrated these deficiencies in numerous contexts. Simply put, human "reasoning" doesn't live up to all that its devotees have claimed for it. It is nothing but a flawed, imperfect evolutionary tool that has been conducive to our survival as a species until now. There is no guarantee that it will continue to serve this function in the years ahead (just as our affinity for sugar helped us survive in the past but might not be conducive to our health today). Indeed, some of the most impressive products of human reason, such as nuclear physics—one of the pinnacles of reason's achievements—may yet prove to be the instrument for the destruction, rather than the survival, of humanity.

Consequently, if at times nonrational, intuitive, experiential, emotional, or even irrational beliefs and behaviors are more effective than "reason" for a particular individual or group in enabling them to survive, physically or culturally, then "reason" has no a priori claim on how they should lead their lives. Reason is only an instrument to be used when it is the best instrument available. If falsehood, self-deception, and psychological mechanisms of denial are better for certain purposes, so be it. "Reason" is not divine; it is not more or less "human" than are emotions, or self-deception. If self-deception, or denial, or faulty reasoning, or deliberate lying can, for example, make an individual less depressed, happier, more fulfilled, and even more humane, whereas reason would lead to nihilism, despair, depression, or inhumanity, then we need not assume that one should blindly follow reason and logic and empiricism to wherever they might lead. Why not take a Jamesian pragmatic approach to the "truth" or to religious experience and apply them to beliefs and doctrines as well? Whichever worldview bears better fruits is the one that we should, or at least can defensibly, adopt as "truer." An argument can be made that *in some circumstances and for some people, for some of the time,* the "objectively false" myths and assertions of religions serve mankind better than do the fruits of "critical thinking." There is no reason, therefore, that the presumed "truths" discovered by "objective reasoning" should have a favored status in guiding our lives. Naturally, because reason has evolved as a survival mechanism, it probably is in our interest to use it frequently, when it is shown to be advantageous to do so. Most religious fundamentalists are not averse to using modern technology and modern medicine, the fruits of reason and science. However, it is not appropriate to challenge the desirability or the utility of religious beliefs simply because they may be implausible or irrational. One would have to demonstrate that such beliefs are in the long run detrimental to human welfare, relative to the human welfare that would result by following only well-established "facts" and indisputable "reasons."

Interestingly, the claims of some fundamentalists actually work against their own religious interests. They assert that pursuit of truth is a lofty religious value and that there are "absolute truths" that can be ascertained by man through the exercise of reason. Yeshivat Aish HaTorah with its Discovery Seminars, Kelemen in his books *Permission to Believe* and *Permission to Receive,* and Rabbi Israel Chait in his elaborate and tightly knit defense of the Kuzari proof of Torah Mi'Sinai[28] maintain that it is possible to prove, by logical argumentation and empirical evidence, the truthfulness of the basic dogmas of Orthodox Judaism. We have seen similar arguments by some Christian and Muslim fundamentalists. Judaism, with its strong emphasis on Talmudic logic, argumentation, and proof, has a tendency to respect the rational. It seems that some Talmudic scholars transfer this approach to theology. If reason is so important and useful in understanding and determining Jewish law, then why not in theology as well?

In chapter 2 we saw that many theologians claim that religious traditions and beliefs cannot be incompatible with human reason. They say that mankind's uniqueness and very essence is in his capacity for reason, which was bestowed on humans by God. Religious thinkers who make such claims are, paradoxically, endowing "reason" with a preeminence that is not given to reason by secular, naturalistic, evolutionary accounts for its existence, functions, and force. The rationalist religionists, by making these lofty claims for reason, set themselves up for defeat because so many of their beliefs and assertions about history and nature cannot meet widely accepted standards of reason, logic, and empirical confirmation. It is a better strategy for such fundamentalist religionists to remove reason from the pedestal on which they have placed her, than for them to try to defend their beliefs with the tactics and strategies of reasoning.

So, by acknowledging the limitations of reason, have I conceded defeat to the fundamentalists who are antirationalists or limited rationalists? No. The issue is not whether reason, scholarship, and science are flawless tools for understanding and interpreting reality, and for living in and controlling reality for human benefit. It is rather whether, all things considered, they are preferable to a nonrational or irrational fundamentalist religious approach to life and reality. One must make a cost-benefit analysis comparing the effects on human welfare of maintaining a nonrational, or arational, or implausible religious worldview, with the costs and benefits of maintaining a nonfundamentalist worldview, whether religious or secular, in which reason and empirical evidence are given priority over other alleged sources of knowledge and insight.

The rationalist need not claim that reason and empiricism are the only sources of valuable human knowledge and insight. Art, music, poetry, fiction, and religious myth—much of which are not generated by, and do not appeal to, reason or to the empirical for their value to humanity—can be deeply appreciated by the rationalist for the richness they endow on human experience and the emotional and psychological insights and wisdom that they often convey. Imagination is a natural human faculty no less than is reason. Only when the humanities, including religions, make assertions about human nature, or about reality, in a propositional form, which can be subjected to rational analysis or empirical test, and those assertions fail to withstand that analysis or to meet that test, does the rationalist give reason and science epistemological priority over the humanities and religion.

We need to ask, does a particular fundamentalist religious worldview enhance the welfare of the individual believer or of the believing group? What is its impact on the welfare of people who do not subscribe to it? There are no single or simple answers to these questions. The same questions would have to be asked of the "rationalist," empiricist worldview. One of my motivations for writing this book is my belief that *there are many negative consequences of certain fundamentalist groups and their worldviews, both for their own adherents (who would most probably dispute this assertion) and for nonadherents.* This is not to deny that there are some people who profess rationalism and empiricism whose worldviews and prescriptions for living are also, from my perspective, detrimental to human welfare. However, unlike many fundamentalist beliefs that directly generate undesirable attitudes and actions, the detrimental views and behavioral norms of some rationalists and empiricists are not derived from the principles of rationalism and empiricism per se. An unethical version of social Darwinism does not necessarily follow from Darwinian biological theory, whereas the justification (and in some fundamentalist regimes, the practice as well) of killing blasphemers does derive directly from the belief that God commanded blasphemers to be put to death. Even if rationalism and empiricism do sometimes directly generate wrongdoing, I do not discuss this phenomenon here because the focus of this book is on understanding religious fundamentalism.

Truth and Attitudes toward Truth

What role does and what role should the "pursuit of 'truth'" play in the acquisition and maintenance of beliefs? Who decides what is "true"? One's views about "truth" affect one's beliefs and defenses of them.[29]

Let us look at ten attitudes toward "truth" that might support one or another of the mechanisms for rejecting the findings of modern biblical and Koranic scholarship when they threaten or refute the traditional belief in the divine source, inerrancy, and infallibility of the Bible or the Koran. We have seen explicit or implicit expressions of some of these attitudes in earlier chapters. This categorization summarizes and adds to what we have seen. In my explication and illustration of these attitudes I focus primarily on the Orthodox Jewish fundamentalist belief in TMS, a divinely authored thirteenth-century BCE Pentateuch, and its rejection of MSPM, multiple-source-post-Mosaic human authorship of the Pentateuch. However, similar attitudes toward truth are manifested by Christian and Muslim defenders of the divine authorship of their sacred Scriptures. I refer to the Islamic belief that the Koran was dictated to Muhammad by Gabriel, who received it from Allah, as the "Koran from Allah" (KFA) theory. This is in contrast to the scholarly approach that the Koran is of human authorship, whether by Muhammad and/or his followers.

Some believers might adopt several attitudes toward truth that function as mechanisms of defense against challenges, if the attitudes are not mutually exclusive. However, even if some of the attitudes are incompatible with others, the believer might alternate from one to another depending upon the nature of the threat or challenge to his belief, and the situation in which he is called upon to defend it.[30]

1. It may be true, but I choose not to confront that truth for reasons unrelated to the issues of truth.

For example, the believer in TMS does not claim that MSPM is definitely false. He could entertain the possibility that it might be true. He might feel, however, that were he to "confront that truth" and conclude that TMS were false, he would no longer be able to function as a leader who provides important spiritual and pastoral care to his religious community. He considers his leadership role to be more important than the "truth." Therefore, he does not delve deeply into the evidence in order to definitively resolve for himself the truth or falsehood of TMS or of MSPM because there is no benefit to be gained from doing so, and there might be a loss.

2. I am indifferent to the truth.

This attitude maintains that "truth" is not a particularly compelling value or goal. Many people live their lives without any strong interest in ascertaining philosophical, theological, political, historical, or scientific truths. They can lead meaningful, productive, and enjoyable lives in their blissful ignorance. Among fundamentalist Jews and Muslims, there are some who simply don't care much about the "truth" of TMS or of KFA. They simply accept it as part of their socialization experiences, but it is not a prime motivator in the way they lead their life. This attitude might characterize the majority of religious believers in all religions, and the majority of people in general.

Academics and religious and intellectual leaders who are supposed to specialize in "truth seeking" and "truth teaching" tend to unreasonably project their strong interest in "truth" onto others.

Moreover, as Pascal Boyer and others point out, the scientific method for ascertaining "truth" is far from natural to the human mind. Indeed, if it were natural, one would have expected it to emerge thousands of years ago rather than just a few centuries ago. Often the "explanations" of physical phenomena provided by religions have seemed more plausible to the average person's cognitive apparatus than have scientific ones, which are often counterintuitive. This has been the case even though the religious explanations have almost invariably been proven wrong with the advance of science.[31] This is similar to religious versus scholarly explanations for the origin of sacred scriptures.

3. I have a different vision of the truth.

This is similar to the point made earlier, that the consequences of beliefs are determinants of their "truthfulness," a notion that was attributed to William James and the pragmatists. "Truth" is not determined exclusively or even primarily by logic and "facts" but by effects. If belief in TMS contributes to Jewish continuity and belief in MSPM would lead to the demise of the Jewish community, then TMS is true and MSPM is false—in the sense that it is rational and plausible for the believer to decide that he or she will base his or her worldview and way of life on the assumption of TMS. Similarly, if continuity of the Islamic "ummah" depends on affirming KFA, then this is the "truth" that counts and is properly the foundation on which the believer will lead his or her life.

4. I believe in different forms of knowledge.

Here the believer in TMS or in KFA maintains that knowledge, and the "truths" that knowledge provide, can have multiple origins. Although logic, facts, and scientific methods are useful and often valid sources of knowledge and hence of "truth", revelation, intuition, or communication with the divine—whether directly or via the mediation of a religious figure, such as a prophet, a Hasidic rebbe, a charismatic, a saint, or an angel—are also valid sources of knowledge and truth, especially about transcendental matters. Belief in TMS or in KFA is based upon one or more of the latter sources rather than on the former, and I am justified in maintaining that the prophet or charismatic or angel is no less and probably even more reliable than is the philosopher, scientist, or historian of the ancient Near East or of the Arabian peninsula of the sixth and seventh centuries.

5. I have no need to resolve this particular contradiction even though I appreciate that you may have such a need.

In this case the believer acknowledges that there is what appears to be a logical or an empirical contradiction to his belief but it is not sufficiently significant to create conflict or discomfort at a conscious or unconscious level and therefore to require some final resolution. This attitude is reflected in the expression often used in the world of the yeshiva, "one doesn't die from a question." The theory of evolution contradicts the creation story of Genesis 1 or the Koranic assumption of six days of creation in Sura 25:59. So be it. At some time in the future either I the believer, or someone else, will come up with a resolution of the contradiction. Or perhaps in my lifetime no one will come up with a convincing resolution of the contradiction. So be it. Just because my belief in TMS or in KFA is contradicted today by science, or archaeology, or our knowledge of Egyptian or of Arabian history, doesn't justify my jettisoning the belief.

6. I compartmentalize well.

Here the believer has developed a mechanism of compartmentalization to the degree that he doesn't experience as a contradiction to his belief that which someone else would consider to be a contradiction. (Alternatively, he experiences it as a contradiction, but the contradiction does not result in intolerable conflict. It doesn't matter: He can separate perhaps his acknowledgement of a contradiction from his feelings about maintaining a contradiction).[32] The individual operates in two modes of consciousness that don't interact with or impact one another. When the believer is in the synagogue pointing to the Torah and proclaiming, "This is the Torah that Moses put before the people of Israel, in accordance with the word of the Lord," he vicariously experiences the moment of divine revelation at Sinai as depicted in Exodus and interpreted by the rabbis, and feels himself reliving or reentering that moment. This is what belief in TMS is for him—a recurring return to the revelatory experience that he believes occurred and that invests his being with meaning. When he is not in the synagogue, he does not consciously or explicitly affirm his belief in TMS but allows it to remain latent. In his secular endeavors he might not encounter any challenges to this belief if, for example, his profession or occupation is irrelevant to belief or disbelief in TMS, as most are. Or he will avoid engaging possible challenges to his belief in TMS if he senses that he might encounter them. In this way his religious beliefs and experiences are set apart from his other thoughts and actions, to a greater or lesser degree, depending upon his ability to use the mechanism of compartmentalization.

7. *This is true enough for my purposes.*

Here the believer is satisfied with what for him constitutes a reasonable degree of plausibility for the belief in order for him to affirm it and feel comfortable living his life in accordance with it. This is a position, for example, taken by many theists who believe in God and can provide some arguments to justify their belief, but who acknowledge that they have no incontrovertible proof or evidence for God's existence. In the case of TMS, or of KFA, the believer maintains that there are a variety of arguments in support of it, and even though these arguments do not provide absolute certainty, they provide what is for him a satisfactory level of reasonableness.

8. *The authorship issue does not materially affect me.*

This attitude can be divided into at least three approaches, any of which suffices for the believer to be committed to Orthodox life and practice. One approach is to believe that the Torah was revealed in its *entirety* to Moses (i.e., traditional TMS) but to be willing to accept either (or both) of the next two approaches as adequate for his commitment to orthodoxy as a "backup' to TMS if TMS becomes too implausible. The second approach is to believe that the Torah was revealed, in *part* to Moses and *in part* to Jewish spiritual leaders who lived after Moses. The third approach is to see the Torah's continuous interpretation and expansion over the generations as an ongoing unfolding and elaboration of the divine essence or elements and behavioral norms of whatever might have been the original core of Torah. The believer is comfortable with any of these approaches because all three of them consider the *mitzvot* (commandments) in their halakhic formulations to be authoritative products of a divine revelation. Therefore it really isn't important for him to know precisely who authored the Pentateuch, as long as he sees it as divinely inspired in a significant way.

The second approach goes against Maimonides's eighth principle that the entire Pentateuch (minus perhaps a few verses) was revealed to Moses, but it has been expressed by some medieval Jewish commentators on the Torah. Variants of the third approach are accepted by many contemporary Jewish theologians and Bible scholars, such as Abraham Joshua Heschel, Louis Jacobs, James Kugel, and Baruch Schwartz (and perhaps Tamar Ross).[33]

Another version of this attitude toward "truth" says that I can accept that "historically" TMS is wrong and MSPM is correct, in terms of how the Torah in its present form actually came to be and, more "heretically," might even maintain that no part of the Torah has been divinely revealed. In fact, I might even be an agnostic or an atheist, with a strong Jewish identity, and feel that because the Jewish people historically accepted the Torah as being divinely revealed, and have constructed their lives and communities around the Torah, and generated a rich culture of more than two thousand years based upon the assumption of TMS, and because I want to continue in this tradition and be part of the continuity of this people, I will lead my life *as if* the belief in TMS were true. Another motive might be more personal. The *"as if"* approach allows me to enjoy certain emotional and spiritual experiences that I cherish. This *as if* approach would probably generate a considerable amount of cognitive and emotional dissonance. However, there are such ortho*praxists* in the Jewish world, some of whom are quite adept at and comfortable with separating their cognitive beliefs from their emotional experiences, and are fully aware that they are doing so. They do not feel any need to "prove" to themselves or to others that the traditional doctrines and dogmas are "true" in order to justify their traditional Orthodox lifestyle.

As Muslims undergo a process of secularization, analogous phenomena can be expected to develop (and have already to some extent) among Muslim "heretics" who find much of Islamic literature, culture, values, and community worth preserving and nurturing. They will privately (or even publicly) deny KFA, but continue to live lives imbued with many Muslim values and practices.

9. I have rationalizing mechanisms to reconcile the evidence for multiple, human authorship or alleged scientific errors in my sacred Scripture, with my beliefs in their divine origin and inerrancy.

This approach denies that there is actual evidence against TMS, or against KFA, and/or maintains that logical and empirical evidence that *appears* to contradict TMS or KFA can be refuted. Internal contradictions in sacred Scripture, which abound, threaten the belief in their divinity and inerrancy. Therefore, a major part of midrash, Muslim Hadith, medieval biblical and Koranic commentary, and medieval Jewish, Christian, and Muslim apologetics and philosophy are devoted to resolving contradictions within the Torah, within the New Testament, and within the Koran. Contradictions between the Torah and "reason" as understood by rationalist philosophers, such as Maimonides, were also resolved in a variety of ways, for example, by nonliteral interpretations of verses in the Torah that describe and attribute to God human qualities and attributes.

Because for the Jewish fundamentalist believer the Torah cannot contradict reason or reality, and reason or reality must conform to the Torah, the presumed contradictory empirical evidence must be imprecise or false, and the logical arguments that challenge what is asserted by or implied by the Torah must be flawed. For example, in the case of belief in TMS, which would imply that several million Israelites sojourned in the wilderness for forty years, that the sun came into existence after there was vegetation on earth, and that humans were created as is, rather than having evolved from nonhuman animals, the believer will deny the reliability of data from archaeology and biology.

Sometimes the believer will argue that the reality we know today is different from the reality of the past so that what the Torah describes as having happened in the past conforms to reality at that time, even though it does not conform to reality as we now know it.

A more extreme mechanism of rationalization is the idea that true reality is determined and defined by the Torah, rather than by our senses or reason. If the latter contradict the Torah, then we are being deceived by our senses and reason.

Some believers will interpret the Torah symbolically, metaphorically, or allegorically. Although the Torah seems to be referring to the same reality that we experience, it really is referring to something else. Hence it cannot be contradicted by reality because it says nothing about history or the natural world. The difficulty for the Orthodox believer with this approach, which, however, has a long history in traditional Judaism, is that once you maintain that Torah texts need not always be understood literally, or at least according to their plain, contextual meaning, the question arises as to why one cannot follow this approach in interpreting the *laws* of the Torah. If the words of the Torah don't necessarily mean what they seem to mean according to their plain, contextual sense, then we needn't observe the *mitzvot* (commandments) if we can provide a symbolic, allegorical, or metaphorical understanding of what might appear to be a law but which needn't be understood as one. Such an approach would of course undermine the commitment to halakha, which is the hallmark of Orthodox Judaism and of believers in TMS. A similar problem is faced by Muslims who interpret some Koranic narratives symbolically or metaphorically, which could undermine the authority of those sections of the Koran that mandate norms of behavior or of belief.

Another approach is to argue that the Torah was not revealed by God to Moses for the purpose of teaching us history or science but to teach us a set of values and a way of living. Because the Torah is not a history or science text, it does not provide any historical or scientific information. Hence the Torah cannot be contradicted by history or science and vice versa, because they are not discussing the same topics or addressing shared concepts and concerns.

10. *I do not require revealed knowledge to conform to the same standards or methodological integrity or heuristic consistency as knowledge empirically derived or derived from sense data. For example, you and I discuss some metaphysical problem. We use logic and reference to classical philosophical positions. I hold you to a standard of logic, and you hold me to a standard of accurate citation. In contrast, I walk into an intensive care unit. I see a patient and instinctually prepare to resuscitate him. The sense data that prompted that response are insufficient to allow me to claim that I knew he was about to sustain a cardiorespiratory arrest, but sufficient to cause me to prepare and to respond to that event. The acceptable noise-to-signal ratio required in each circumstance is different: low in the first and high in the second.*

With respect to belief in TMS versus MSPM, the believer in TMS may be content with a lesser degree of logical or empirical plausibility than the believer in MSPM. Perhaps this is analogous to Pascal's Wager. Because the perceived consequences of rejecting TMS are considered to be very grave, it is worthwhile to "believe" it—or to behave as if it were true—without demanding a high standard of proof or evidence for it.

In response to my attempt to understand the psychology behind the tenacity of unreasonable beliefs, a perceptive correspondent of mine noted the following:

But the ultimate psychological answer [as to why certain believers in TMS do not give up their belief in the face of logic and empirical evidence that contradict it] is, I think, the simplest one. People do not believe out of logic, they believe out of bakwemlichkeit (comfort and convenience) and they will change only when the libidinal cost of maintaining a belief system exceeds the cost of relinquishing it. They seek serenity from religion as much as anything else, and will resist systemic forces that call the structure of their belief into question. This is a psychological, not a sociological or a *logical mechanism*. What follows psychologically is that I may be able to distinguish, and keep separate, the maintenance of a belief which I already have from the act of adopting or refuting an intrusive belief or line of inquiry which I have no psychological need to pursue ... A fundamental characteristic of religious belief is its embodiment of visions of virtue as well as of visions of truth. And all things being equal, it is very difficult for people to change areteic instincts even under the most compelling barrage of logic.[34]

Why Gods Persist

In his excellent book *Why Gods Persist,* the biologist Robert Hinde analyzes how and why people continue to affirm religious (and other) beliefs even when faced with evidence or strong arguments that contradict them, and he provides examples from many religions.[35] Hinde distinguishes between the maintenance of religious *systems* and the maintenance of beliefs in the *individual.* Throughout this book we have seen many examples of belief protection, and now using some of Hinde's concepts, I look more closely at instantiations of the "hows" in Orthodox Jews. Many parallels in Christianity and Islam will be obvious. My focus is on the individual, with full realization that the beliefs of individuals are related to and influenced by the social context and cultural systems in which they have been socialized and live.

Hinde notes that religious beliefs that are flexible rather than rigid may be more readily maintained because the believer can modify aspects of the belief while retaining its core, as he understands it. This is one of the advantages of vagueness in the articulation of a belief that we saw earlier—vagueness allows for flexibility and reinterpretation.

For example, the fact that within Judaism there have been multiple conceptions of God—ranging from the anthropomorphic to the noncorporeal, the immanent to the transcendent, the punitive to the merciful, the just to the forgiving, the God whose power has not yet been realized on earth or who has limited his power in order to provide for human free will to a God who is at all times omnipotent—provides opportunities for responding to specific challenges to one or another aspect of the belief system without giving up the belief in God.

Thus, someone who believes in an omnipotent and benevolent God, who then experiences oppression by the wicked, may revise his belief in God, in accordance with the tradition's flexibility, so that God is now understood to be of limited power, perhaps because he deliberately "contracted" his power to provide the gift of free will to humans. This gift, in order to be real, rather than a sham, has to allow for humans to choose to do evil, and, unfortunately, some do.

If the only acceptable conception of God in the tradition had been one of absolute and unconditional divine omnipotence and benevolence, at all times, the lack of flexibility might have resulted in the believer's giving up the belief in God in the face of oppression by the wicked. (There are, of course, other cognitive theological approaches to dealing with human evil in the face of belief in divine omnipotence and benevolence, which would allow the oppressed believer, or the believer disturbed by witnessing the oppression suffered by others, to persist in his belief in such a God. He may, for example, deny the reality of the "alleged evil" or affirm that the rewards for suffering will far outweigh the tribulations endured. His God thereby remains omnipotent and benevolent.)

Similarly, if the believer felt that the only legitimate understanding of the doctrine that God revealed the Torah to Moses at Sinai was that the Pentateuch that we have in our possession was literally dictated by God to Moses sometime in the thirteenth century BCE, then evidence that would cast serious doubt on this belief, *assuming it would be accepted as reliable and "admissible" to the erstwhile believer,* would be more prone to result in rejecting the belief of Torah as divine revelation than if the notion of divine revelation to Moses at Sinai was understood *metaphorically,* or as somehow continuous through time, a kind of cumulative, progressive revelation.

Tamar Ross, in her feminist critique of Orthodox Judaism, attempts to develop a theology of cumulative, progressive revelation, so that Orthodoxy can with theological integrity appropriate some of the insights and values of feminism that conflict with the Bible and with rabbinic teachings and normative Jewish law. She argues that such a notion of revelation remains "Orthodox" and, indeed, has precedents in certain important streams of traditional Jewish thought.[36] I seems to me, though, that Ross is evading rather than confronting the challenges to Orthodoxy not only from feminism but, more fundamentally, from biblical scholarship, and that this evasion is motivated by her overall love for halakhic tradition, and for many Orthodox values, and her fear of the collapse of halakhic authority were she to conclude that the whole notion of divine revelation of the Torah at Sinai is no longer tenable.

When a belief is rigid, and in a sense brittle, one result, either initially or permanently, is the development of strong mechanisms for denying the reliability and admissibility of counterevidence, if the belief is too important to the believer to give up. On the other hand, its rigidity makes it more vulnerable to challenges because there is little room for reinterpreting it, and the weight of the evidence or arguments against it may overcome the believer's initial resistance to them, if he is rational and values truth, or what appears to be closer to the truth.

Believers who attempt to defend or justify their beliefs will often resort to arguments that have two related qualities—they cannot be refuted, nor can they be confirmed. For example, haredi Jews who believe that the world is no older than 5,768 years, when faced with fossils whose age (as dated by scientific methods of dating that the believer is willing to accept as reliable) is ascertained to be millions of years old, argue that God, who is omnipotent, could and did create in the first week of creation (as described in Genesis chapter 1) those fossils with the chemical and other qualities that would be manifested in objects had they indeed been millions of years old, even though in reality these fossils are no older than 5,768 years. It is difficult or impossible to refute such a claim, while at the same time it is difficult or impossible to confirm it.

Although a philosopher might argue that because it is not subject to disconfirmation such a claim is useless in reasoned argumentation, the believer may be satisfied that the claim wards off challenges to the veracity of his literalist understanding of biblical chronology.

Most of us believe or affirm many things that we (or anyone) might not be able to confirm or disconfirm, such as that there *are* certain absolute moral truths, or that there *aren't* any, and we lead our lives in accordance with these beliefs, perhaps because we need to believe in some fundamental ideas if we are to function in a socially or psychologically normal way. Why then should the person who believes that "aged" fossils were embedded in the earth at the time of creation only a few thousand years ago be considered less rational than the "strong" atheist who believes that God doesn't exist, or someone who believes that the universe was created by a Big Bang billions of years ago—a belief that may be confirmable or disconfirmable to astrophysicists but not to anyone else, as was pointed out in chapter 3. Most people who "believe" in the Big Bang and in many other scientific theories are relying on the *authority* of scientists rather than on their actual arguments or evidence. The religious literalist relies on the *authority* of his rabbis.[37]

I am not claiming that the two cases are identical, but only that they are sufficiently, albeit superficially, similar, so that at the *psychological level* it is not difficult to understand the mental processes of the biblical literalist. Most of us function in life with beliefs and assumptions that may be logically false but psychologically "normal." We all have biases and prejudices and fears and hopes that aren't rational or logical. Most people aren't logicians or philosophers. People don't "believe" only those things which can be proven logically or with empirical evidence. Even logicians and philosophers don't usually do so in many realms of their personal experience that are not part of their professional activities. If a distinguished philosopher like Martin Heidegger could subscribe to the irrational and false beliefs of Nazism, why be surprised at a less sophisticated thinker who believes that a human being was God or that the world is less than six thousand years old?

There are several defense mechanisms, or strategies, which the believer is not necessarily aware that he is "using" as he responds to logical or empirical challenges to his beliefs.[38] One of these is *cognitive restructuring,* which includes *selective attention, selective interpretation,* and the *discrediting of contradictory information.*

SELECTIVE ATTENTION

In the case of *selective attention* the believer takes note only of facts or arguments that support his beliefs, while ignoring those that challenge them. For example, in the commentary of Hertz on the Pentateuch, or in Kelemen's *Permission to Receive,* archaeological evidence that supports the veracity of the biblical text is amply cited as evidence for the historical truth of biblical narratives, whereas the archaeological evidence that casts serious doubt on the historicity of biblical accounts is ignored. Some selective attenders will allow themselves to be exposed only to confirming evidence and will not expose themselves to suspected disconfirming evidence, to the extent that it is possible for them to control their exposure. Others will read widely, including disconfirming evidence, but will then "forget" it, or minimize its force or significance. Others will read it, understand its "dangerous" implications for faith, but will not include it in their commentaries or other writings because they feel that although they know how to respond to its challenge and maintain their beliefs, the audiences for whom they write cannot be relied upon to be so sophisticated in "protecting" their beliefs against the evidence. This has the effect of "selective attention" to evidence and arguments against the belief, even if the author of the self-censored book or commentary himself did not attend selectively to them.[39] The reader, whose only exposure to archaeology or modern biblical studies is mediated through paternalistic protectors of the faith, is not himself engaging in the psychological process of selective attention, because he trusts the author, such as Kelemen, and assumes that all of the relevant data have been studied and reviewed by him. The result, however, is similar to that of the selective attender, because in both cases only those facts that support the belief are known and assimilated, whereas those that do not are ignored.

Let us consider another example of selective attention. The person who is saved in a plane crash in which many others died, who interprets his survival as proof of God's benevolence, is ignoring the evidence for God's malevolence, given that the survivor is assuming that God determines the fate of individuals on airplanes. (This reaction is different from that of the survivor who thanks God for saving him but does not use his survival as proof of general divine benevolence.) Similarly, to see divine benevolence when there is ample rain for the crops to flourish, but to disregard the malevolence of natural catastrophes, is an instance of selective attention. In some instances of selective attention the believer may actually not take conscious notice of the counterevidence. In other instances he may take note of it but ignore its logical implications.

Let us consider one more example. The believer who believes that God is ethical, in accordance with the believer's own ethical standards, will often fail to note, or will note but fail to process, the implications of actions and laws that are ascribed to God in the sacred texts of his religious tradition that would be considered unethical by the believer. For example, I once believed in the divine status of the Bible and of its rabbinic interpretation. I had also internalized the democratic value that slavery is a moral evil. Yet for years I studied biblical and rabbinic texts that accepted and regulated the institution of slavery, without being particularly troubled by the obvious contradiction between my belief that God acts and legislates ethically, and the teachings of the tradition that God sanctioned, and at times, mandated, enslavement of some humans. I had developed a certain "moral numbness" that acted as a barrier to my taking full cognizance of and responding to the evidence that challenged my belief in God, my beliefs about God, and my beliefs about the divine nature of the Written and the Oral Law.

This is not to say that I, when still a believer, and many other believers, responded with selective attention consistently and uninterruptedly. There were times when my awareness of the tradition's acceptance of slavery did induce me to question my beliefs, but there were long periods of time when it did not. There were also other ways in which I responded to the ethical challenge of slavery to my beliefs. I paid very careful attention to the challenge, was deeply bothered by it, and tried actively to resolve it in a way that allowed me to maintain my core religious beliefs. For example, I argued to myself (and to others) that slavery was a boon to the slave because relative to other cultures the biblical and rabbinic laws of slavery were more humane. Or my original assumption that my standard of what is ethical is the correct one, to which God's actions and laws must conform, is a wrong assumption. Rather, whatever God does or commands is ipso facto ethical, or God knows what is best for his creatures, and sometimes if what God wants of me is unethical by conventional human standards, so be it, and God's will has greater authority than human ethical standards. Or perhaps I need to reassess my ethical values, and my evaluation of democracy and its condemnation of slavery. Or, I thought, slavery might have been moral in the biblical and rabbinic contexts, but because times have changed, God considers it unethical today. In all of these instances I, a believer, was trying to respond to the challenge rather than to deny or ignore it. These approaches are part of a long tradition of "apologetics" in religious thought and discourse, in which believers attempt to "justify the ways of God to men," or what is often happening psychologically in "apologetics," justifying the ways of God to the apologist himself.

Another example of selective attention is demonstrated in the personal communication to me by the Orthodox philosopher whom I quoted earlier and cite again now: "I share your view that many Orthodox people (or "intellectuals")—and I include myself—have not developed certain sorts of evidence-based reasons for holding on to their beliefs. Some of us don't even know much about biblical studies or archaeology; I regard my own knowledge as limited—it's not my field. I further share your view that there is a psychological story to find and tell in these instances."

I ask, what does it mean for a *modern* Orthodox person, especially, but not only, a scholar, rabbi, and teacher, to say that modern biblical scholarship is of no interest or only of tangential interest to him or her, given that his core religious commitments are based upon assumptions about the authorship and authority of the Torah? Would a teacher of the history of the American Revolution or of the intellectual and social origins of the Constitution of the United States in a high school or college be allowed to ignore the last one hundred and fifty years of historical scholarship on these subjects that are central to the American ethos and values? Is it fair to socialize children, in school or at home, to believe in TMS and all of the commitments that this belief entails, and to ignore the most significant developments in the understanding of the Torah and of Judaism in the last two hundred years while doing so? I think it is somewhat disingenuous for modern Orthodox rabbis and scholars to claim that biblical scholarship is not of particular interest to them. If it isn't, then that is a problem. If it is, then the problem is their failure to think through its implications and address them appropriately.[40]

One would expect that because their most fundamental, existential commitments, their way of life, their values, their orientation to history, to current events, to child rearing, and to the education of their children, are based upon assumptions and beliefs about the origin and authorship of the Bible, they would want to acquire as much reliable information about it as is possible. If, for example, one of their children—heaven forbid—were struck with a serious, life-threatening illness, would they not expend their greatest intellectual energies and resources on trying to understand the latest that medicine and science know about that illness and its possible cures? I think they would. Or if they were asked to invest their life savings in a business venture, would they not examine all aspects and angles of the venture before committing their resources? Would they not read up on the most current state of knowledge about the industry to which they are being asked to commit? Would not one expect then that they would do no less when the investment that they are continually making and that they are socializing their children into making, is, it would appear, even more vital to their lives and to the lives of their families than any possible business venture could be? And they cannot argue that the information is beyond their capacity to comprehend, or is too technical for them to master, or too inaccessible, because biblical scholarship is neither of the above for individuals with the level of intelligence and knowledge that they possess. So why does a distinguished, brilliant philosopher, and other bright Orthodox Jews choose to ignore biblical scholarship?

There are several possible explanations.

It is precisely because they have invested so much of their intellectual, emotional, social, and financial energy and resources into their belief system and religious way of life that they are afraid or reluctant to examine its foundations. It is because they sense that the pillars of all they believe and have invested in might be exposed to be pillars of sand. Better to be an intellectual ostrich with respect to their religious beliefs than to face the reality of the demise of all that is dear to them, which they imagine (rightly or wrongly) will be the consequence of honestly studying biblical scholarship.

The problem with this approach—the ostrich—is that the believer is transmitting to his children these same pillars of sand. This isn't fair to his children. Why burden them from birth until they reach intellectual maturity with a belief system and a lifestyle that may be based upon pillars of sand, and which will condition them with years of guilt if and when, upon maturity, they discover that what they had been taught to believe is true isn't really so? Why burden them with powerful emotional conditioning about the evil and sinfulness of certain actions (or failures to act) that aren't really so? Why must they feel that certain sexual desires or behaviors (e.g., masturbation, or eating pork, or writing on the Sabbath) are wrong, if the basis for these ideas is the false idea of the divinity of the Bible (and the rabbinic interpretations of it)?[41] Just because you were socialized into this belief system and lifestyle doesn't justify your imposing them on the next generation. Of course, many parents who have avoided confronting challenges to their belief in TMS, or who repress the truth of MSPM of which they might have once been aware, are acting out of a deep love for their religious tradition and its values and lifestyle. They consider it in the best interests of their children to be socialized into the system, notwithstanding some of the negative consequences that it can also bring about. From their perspective the net gain far outweighs the negative costs.

Another explanation for avoiding biblical scholarship and other threats to doctrine is that although on the surface it may appear that the parent holds deeply felt beliefs and a lifestyle he loves, the truth is that he might really like only the lifestyle, but the beliefs are essentially unimportant to him. Because they are unimportant—it really makes no difference whether the Torah was authored God or by humans—it is not worth investing time and energy in studying biblical scholarship. He will continue with his satisfying lifestyle in either case.

In fact, the parent might argue that even if he were to be fully convinced that the belief system is false, he is willing to teach it to his children as if it were true because of the way of life it produces, which he considers to be superior to other culturally available options. There is precedent for this in philosophical and religious thought, known as the doctrine of necessary beliefs, espoused by Plato and medieval theologians. For example, even though virtue and vice are their own intrinsic and sole reward and punishment, the masses need to believe in reward and punishment by the hand of God, either in this world or, after death, in Heaven and Hell. So the Bible, according to the medieval theologian, and the theologian himself, will propagate these teachings knowing full well that they are false when understood literally, which is how they will be taught to the masses, because it is in the best interest of the masses that they have the necessary sense of anticipated reward or dreaded punishment in order that they lead religiously proper lives.

The perceived and experienced value of an Orthodox lifestyle is one of several reasons why some Jews practice Orthodox religious rituals and recite traditional Orthodox prayers even after they give up their traditional religious beliefs that would seem to have been the basis for their performing the rituals and praying in the first place. Within Judaism, there are some who leave Orthodoxy and affiliate with Conservative, Reform, Reconstructionist, Renewal, non-denominational religious, or Humanistic Judaism, all of which include some of the traditional rituals and prayers but which consciously redefine or reformulate them so that they can be in intellectual accord with their non-Orthodox religious, or their nonreligious humanistic, Judaic ideology. However, there are a good number of Jews who are "Orthodox"

Jews as *sociologically* defined but who have grave doubts about, or who reject, the traditional Orthodox beliefs and doctrines. They are often very meticulous in their performance of the Orthodox rituals and prayers in their traditional forms and formulations. They are often referred to as (or define themselves as) ortho*prax* rather than Ortho*dox*. Their motives for such behavior, and the emotional, moral, and intellectual costs (and benefits) of such behavior, the implications of such a lifestyle on the socialization and education of their children in Judaism, the difference between their public and private religious behavior, and the degree to which they feel comfortable in acknowledging their *hereto* [from "heresy"]–*doxy* in the Orthodox synagogues, schools, and other institutions with which they affiliate, are of increasing interest in the world of Orthodox Judaism, being widely discussed on various blogs and other forums, if not openly in Orthodox schools and synagogues.

SELECTIVE INTERPRETATION

Events or facts can often be interpreted in several ways. The believer tends to accept the interpretation that confirms his belief or that neutralizes the threat that the event or fact poses to his belief. He will do this *even when the interpretation he accepts is much less plausible than the alternatives.* We saw this in fundamentalist Christian interpretations of the empty tomb of Jesus and the visions of Jesus seen by his followers as proof of his bodily resurrection. As we have said before, some Abrahamic creationists who believe that the universe was created in six days account for fossils, which according to scientific methods of dating are millions of years old, as having been created by God with chemical and physical characteristics that would appear to be so old but really are not. Why did God do this? Because God wanted these fossils to be a test of the commitment of believers to a literal and inerrant acceptance of Genesis 1. In 1993 when a fragment of a basalt stone that had been part of a stele was found at Tel Dan in northern Israel with the words "House of David" inscribed on it, fundamentalists cited this as evidence for the historicity of all of the Book of Samuel, rather than as possible evidence only for the historicity of a Davidic dynasty. Ancient Near Eastern texts with stories of a universal flood are interpreted by Jewish and Christian fundamentalists to prove that the global flood described in Genesis actually occurred (notwithstanding substantial geological evidence that there has never been a flood as described in Genesis in the less than 6,000 year time span since creation according to the creationists' dating), rather than that the Genesis story was based on a local flood, or was borrowed from or is a variant of earlier

Mesopotamian flood myths. Some Jewish and Christian fundamentalists have even acknowledged that from a purely human perspective, the evidence for the multiple-source theory of the composition of the Pentateuch is indeed overwhelming. But because they assume divine authorship, there is no problem in positing that God was able to be the single author of a text but make it appear as if it were authored and edited by many people. But why would he do that? Once again, to test our faith in the doctrine of divine authorship, or perhaps to encourage us to try to harmonize all of the apparent contradictions so that we will uncover profound, hidden meanings. Even though all of these interpretations are less plausible than those offered by science and scholarship, selective interpretation carries the day for the fundamentalists.

Rabbinic midrashic exegetes and traditional Jewish biblical commentators have been engaged in text harmonization for more than two thousand years. In trying to harmonize discrepancies and account for redundancies, they have uncovered or "invented" many fascinating lessons from the Bible and generated myriad legal, moral, and theological teachings of great wisdom and didactic value. However, the much more parsimonious explanation for the discrepancies and redundancies in the Bible is the multiple-source human composition theory rather than the thousands of traditional "exegeses of harmonization" of the divine word. Contemporary scriptural fundamentalists neglect the more plausible multiple-source human authorship interpretation.

DISCREDITING OF CONTRADICTORY INFORMATION

In chapter 3 I pointed out how Jewish fundamentalists either downplay or discredit information that challenges their belief in TMS. Moreover, they will often try to discredit the information by discrediting the source of the information. Haredi fundamentalists in particular will claim that critical biblical scholars are anti-Semites or heretics or evil or ignorant of traditional Jewish modes of dealing with the challenges posed by modern scholarship. There definitely have been some scholars who were one or another of these, and there probably still are some around. However, attacking the person who presents evidence or argument does not disprove them. Moreover, most contemporary critical Biblical scholars, of whom many are strongly identifying Jews, are not wicked, ignorant anti-Semites, but rather upright and, especially of the Jewish ones, quite learned in traditional Jewish biblical exegesis. I can't deny that by haredi standards they are heretics.

Selective Evaluation

Another defense mechanism is selective evaluation, whereby believers "see congruent events as more important than incongruent ones. For a believer the occasional report of a miraculous cure can never be out-weighed by reports of innumerable failed ones."[42] For the biblical fundamentalist, one archaeological find corroborating a biblical passage is worth more than ten that contradict it, and one biblical prophecy that was fulfilled is worth more than ten that were not. The belief system can also invoke other strategies that we have described earlier in order to support the selective evaluation. The reason why some prophecies weren't fulfilled was because the people whom the prophet said were going to be punished, repented and God therefore decided not to punish them. Or the people whom the prophet said would prosper didn't, because they subsequently sinned. The only prophecies that "count" when evaluating the truthfulness of the belief system are those that were fulfilled, whereas the others can be ignored because they can be explained away by other components of the belief system.

Hinde discusses several other belief maintenance mechanisms, among which are *selective interaction* and *social forces.*

In *selective interaction* "believers prefer to associate themselves with those who share their beliefs" and this tendency results in mutual reinforcement of the belief system when it is challenged. Among *social forces* are the existence in every society of individuals who benefit from the maintenance of the belief system; people's tendency to rely for "truth" on authorities of high status, such as scholars, pastors, priests, mullahs and ayatollahs; religious ceremonies, rites, and festivals that reinforce belief; and the social rewards of feeling oneself to be part of a group that shares your beliefs.

Why Do People Maintain and Protect Their Religious Beliefs?

Having just discussed *how* believers maintain and protect their belief systems, I now return to the question of *why* do they do so, which I have addressed in depth earlier. As I pointed out in the beginning of this chapter, and as we have seen earlier in the book, religion in general satisfies many human needs: social, emotional, psychological, and intellectual. This reinforces its hold on someone socialized from birth into it and attracts new converts to it. It can provide, for many people, meaning and purpose to life, hope and support in the face of adversity, transcendence of the finality of death, occasions for joy and festivity, alleviation of existential uncertainty and anxiety, a moral code, a strong sense of individual identity meshed with group identity and cohesion, and, particularly in scientifically ignorant societies, explanations of the mysteries of the universe and of life on earth.[43] Secular, science-based worldviews and cultures might offer more rationality but are less effective than religion in providing most of these benefits. Rituals, ceremonies, memories of childhood experiences, family attachments, and values are integrally connected with religious beliefs. When these practices, emotions, and values are very positive, there is a reluctance to give up the beliefs out of fear that doing so will undermine the positive benefits. There is also the anxiety about feeling guilty for betraying loved parents, friends, and teachers. Therefore, the believer harboring doubts will expend a tremendous amount of intellectual and emotional energy in defending the beliefs, even appealing to arguments that he would not find convincing in the absence of an emotional attachment.

Why Do People Give Up Their Beliefs?

Why do some believers defend rigid beliefs without ever conceding that they are false, whereas other believers eventually give up the rigid beliefs in the face of evidence and logic? Is there something about the personality structure of a person that accounts for the different reactions? Perhaps factors such as the individual's degree of tolerance of cognitive and emotional uncertainty or of the responsibility of making difficult life choices on his own play a role.

I have compiled the following, nonexhaustive, list of factors that contribute to loss of faith and of religious commitment.[44] It seems to me that there is usually a constellation of factors, including the *degree* to which one or more of these factors is applicable to a particular individual, that influences the direction that will be taken by the believer who is an incipient doubter.[45] Some of these are part of the general sociocultural process known as "secularization":

1. The believer experiences intellectual doubts about the rationality of the beliefs of the religion.
2. The believer finds another belief system that is more plausible and/or attractive.
3. The believer finds the requirements of the religion to be too demanding and so he abandons the religion.

4. The religion generates deep guilt in the believer. Rejection of the religion alleviates the sense of guilt.
5. The life experiences of the believer are inconsistent with the dogmas of the religion or with the person's feelings about God.
6. The believer comes to see his religion as incompatible with his emotional or moral sensitivities.
7. The religion stifles the creative impulses of the believer (e.g., with restrictions on artistic, musical, or literary expression), and he reacts to that by modifying or discarding his beliefs.
8. The repressed sexual impulses of the believer, which are controlled or inhibited by the religion, become so powerful that they lead the believer to reject his religious beliefs in order to find libidinal satisfaction.
9. The attempt of the religion and its authorities to control other needs or desires, such as food consumption, the nature of one's work, or one's leisure activities, causes the believer to reject the beliefs that justify the control.
10. The believer comes to see that religion is an obstacle to his or her social or economic advancement and therefore discards it.
11. The believer experienced a harsh upbringing focused around religious issues and has strong negative feelings toward one or both of his parents or other family members.[46]
12. The believer becomes disillusioned with his religious leaders and teachers.
13. The believer has bitter social experiences with the community of believers.
14. The believer develops feelings of spiritual emptiness and no longer experiences the presence of God in his life.
15. Substitutes are provided that serve the functions served by religion. This can, for example, be a nonfundamentalist version of the same religion or an entirely different ideology or worldview that serves purposes similar to those served by a fundamentalist or by a nonfundamentalist religion.[47]
16. The believer is persecuted by powerful authorities for his adherence to his beliefs.[48]
17. The believer is exposed to satire and mockery of his religious beliefs and his religious leaders and teachers.
18. Religious leaders venerated by the believer publicly declare that they no longer adhere to those beliefs.

The Return of the Creationists

I have focused on psychological descriptions of and explanations for the tenacity of unreasonable beliefs. However, we cannot rely exclusively on psychology to understand fundamentalism. It is useful to consider other "levels of explanation," such as the historical and cultural, especially when we are considering group behavior or social movements, and not just the behavior of the individual. Broad cultural forces eventually filter down to the individual and affect his religious beliefs, behaviors, and feelings—his religious psychology—but it is myopic to consider only the latter without understanding its historical-cultural context. George Marsden's analysis of the "creation science," antievolution fundamentalists, especially since the mid-twentieth century, is a fine example of a broad and deep historical-cultural approach.[49]

Marsden documents the fact that in the first few decades after the publication of Charles Darwin's *On The Origin of Species* in 1859, many Christian theologians and leading religious leaders, including conservative evangelicals, made their peace with evolution, and with an earth that was millions if not billions of years old, and did not consider this to be incompatible with Christian belief. Even Benjamin B. Warfield, a staunchly conservative proponent of the doctrine of biblical inerrancy, stated that evolution is compatible with Genesis, as long as "it is thoroughly understood in all quarters that 'evolution' cannot act as a substitute for creation, but at best can supply only a theory of the method of divine providence." One could believe in biblical inerrancy without being a biblical "literalist." As long as God remains in control of the general process of evolution and intervenes at critical junctures, such as the appearance of Homo sapiens and the implantation of the soul in Homo sapiens, there need not be a conflict between biological science and religious belief. Indeed, "by the 1970's most evangelical scientists teaching at Christian colleges accepted some form of theistic evolution or 'progressive creationism,' as they often preferred to call it."[50]

Marsden then poses the interesting historical question, "Why, even when such illustrious leaders of the early fundamentalist movement pointed out the viability of mediating positions, did opposition to all biological evolution become for so many a test of the faith?" (156) Why, he asks, has the creation-science movement been so influential in popularizing among many (though far from all) conservative Christians its polarizing claim that to believe in *theistic* evolution is to be the Devil's advocate? The movement has even succeeded in getting many state legislatures to adopt their extreme view that belief in God as creator is absolutely incompatible with affirming the reality of evolution. If you are for God, you are against evolution; if you are for evolution, you are against God. Why have creationists insisted on this black-and-white dichotomy, and why has it garnered so much support?

To answer these questions, Marsden points to several factors.

First, there has been a "convergence of two powerful traditions of biblical interpretation in America," millenarianism and Protestant scholasticism. Biblical millenarians assume that the "Bible . . . is susceptible to exact scientific analysis," and they apply "scientific" interpretations to the numbers in biblical prophecies, claiming that "some aspects of the future can be predicted with some exactitude." For these groups, it is important that the principle by which they interpret biblical prophecies should apply as well to reports of past events in the Bible. One group of these, the dispensationalists, use as a principle of biblical interpretation the "formula 'literal where possible.'" They do not go so far as to insist on a literalist interpretation of what are clearly poetic or figurative scriptural passages, such as "the mountains shall clap their hands." However, they maintain that in the absence of a very strong reason otherwise, the default option is to understand biblical passages that refer to (ostensibly) historical events literally, down to their precise details:

> It is not surprising, therefore, that such groups who derive some of their key doctrines from exact interpretations of prophecy should be most adamant in interpreting Genesis 1 as describing an exact order of creation in six twenty-four hour days. Fundamentalists, often with dispensationalist ties, have been among the most ardent supporters of the recent "creation-science" movement that insists on a young earth, and hence on an entirely antievolutionary view of creation. (158–159)

These millenarian views have been widely disseminated and been influential beyond the fundamentalist communities themselves.

There are, however, creation-scientists who are not millenarians. The tradition of Protestant scholasticism, which includes the principle of biblical inerrancy, dates back to the seventeenth century and was accepted by many nineteenth-century American Protestants. "The substance of the inerrancy view [is] that because the Bible is God's Word it must be accurate in matters of science and history as well as in doctrine." Although not all "inerrantists" denied evolution in toto, some did, because "the emphasis on scientific exactness of scriptural statements was conducive to views of those who insisted that Genesis 1 referred to literal twenty-four hour days" (160).

Another trend in both millennial and Protestant scholastic traditions has been a desire to establish a firm rational basis for Christian belief... especially in the eighteenth and the nineteenth centuries, defenders of Christianity assiduously collected evidences from natural sciences to confirm truths revealed in Scripture... Crucial to the creation-science movement is the desire to restore this harmony of science and Scripture which the twentieth-century intellectual climate seemingly had shattered... Fundamentalists and their allies regard the Bible as filled with scientific statements of the same precision as might be found in twentieth-century scientific journals. God, they assume, would not reveal himself any less accurately... (162–164)

If God, through the Bible, speaks with the accuracy of a scientist, then the Bible must be as unambiguous as scientists are in their writing. So, for example, we must understand the passage that is repeated several times in the opening chapter of Genesis, that plants and animals should produce "after their kind," to mean that the offspring of plants and animals can forever and only be plants and animals that are of the same species as their "parents" and ancestors. To claim that a particular species evolved over time into a new, different one is heretical—it contradicts the clear and transparent word of God. Creation-scientists are not willing to be flexible in their interpretation of "after their kind" to allow the phrase to subsume a new species that is similar to an ancestor species in many ways even though it is not identical to it.

Another factor in the resurgence and popularity of creation-science is that many people think that the fundamentalist readings of the Bible are most in accord with common sense. Things mean what they say. Engineers in particular seem to be attracted by this "commonsense realism" as applied to Scripture. The commonsense orientation as applied to nature also can support an antievolutionary position. More recently this is manifested in the "intelligent design" movement, which while not always explicitly denying evolution (although many "intelligent designers" are creationists in disguise), does deny the generally accepted scientific explanations for how evolution has been taking place. Surely, goes the commonsense orientation, the orderly laws of nature, the complexity and variety of life, and the sophisticated organs such as the eye or the brain could not have been the product of accident or randomness unguided by an intelligent designer. Supernaturalism, for many people, makes more sense than does complicated scientific explanations of the world, which require a significant amount of scientific and mathematical education in order to understand. It just makes a lot more sense to believe that God created everything in a few days, a time span to which we can readily relate, rather than that the universe has evolved over an almost incomprehensible billions of years, and humans over millions. The fact that many scientists find it difficult to understand the popular appeal of such a "commonsense" denial of evolution suggests that they are an intellectual elite not in tune with populist thinking, which is not antiscience but simplistic science. The creation-scientists believe that eventually science will confirm, rather than challenge, their understanding of Genesis and the rest of divine revelation.

In a 2005 survey people were asked to respond "true," "false," or "not sure" to the statement, "Human beings, as we know them, developed from earlier species of animals." Only 40 percent answered that it was true.[51] This reflects both the inadequacy of science education in the United States and the influence of creation-science attitudes beyond those active in the movement.

In an essay lamenting the scientific illiteracy of many American children Lawrence Kraus writes,

> The chairman of the Kansas school board, Dr. Steve Abrams, a veterinarian, is not merely a strict creationist. He has openly stated that he believes that God created the universe 6,500 years ago...A key concern should...be how someone whose religious views require a denial of essentially all modern scientific knowledge can be chairman of a state school board...the age of the earth, and the universe, is no more a matter of religious faith than is the question of whether or not the earth is flat. It is a matter of overwhelming scientific evidence. To maintain a belief in a 6,000-year-old earth requires a denial of essentially all the results of modern physics, chemistry, astronomy, biology and geology...[52]

Yet there seem to be many people in Kansas who agree with Mr. Abrams.

The next factor that strengthens the opponents of evolution is their argument, which many people find convincing, that the theory of evolution and its moral, ethical, and spiritual implications constitute a threat to civilization. Evolution becomes a battleground between Christianity, a force for good, and secularism, a force for evil. Because of the inroads of secularism, of which the theory of evolution is a central element, American (primarily North European Protestantism) civilization is in a state of decay and decadence. If human beings are just another species of animals that evolved from even more primitive species, and are not specially created by God in his divine image and endowed with a soul, then, the fundamentalists feel, it is difficult to argue for moral norms based upon the uniqueness of humans.[53] In several Southern states the evangelical opposition to evolution predates the organized creation-science fundamentalist movement in the Northern states. It gained strength after the Civil War and as a reaction to the defeat of the South. In one case, a conservative professor at a Presbyterian seminary who was a proponent of scriptural inerrancy admitted in 1884 that he accepted a very truncated version of theistic evolution. He felt that science must be harmonized with direct statements of Scripture, and in conceding that evolution had occurred, "held that, while God could have created the body (not the soul) of Adam 'mediately' by evolution from the dust of the ground, the body of Eve was created immediately from Adam's ribs." After debate and discussion in the Southern Presbyterian community, the professor was dismissed from his position in 1886, and the Presbyterian General Assembly declared that "'Adam and Eve were created, body and soul, by immediate acts of Almighty power'...and that any method of biblical interpretation that led to denial of [this] conclusion...would eventually 'lead to the denial of doctrines fundamental to the faith'" (171).

Why, asks Marsden, was there opposition to "even the most modest accommodation between creation and evolution?". He explains that several factors had converged. The first of these was the effect of the Civil War on the dynamics of white churches in the South and on Southern religious life. Although the victory of the North restored the Union, it did not lead to a reunion between Northern and Southern churches. In order to justify the continuation of the rupture, the Southern churches argued that the Northerners had "been infected by a liberal spirit," the proof of which was their critique of the institution of slavery, which, after all, had been a recognized institution in biblical times and even had some explicit biblical verses to justify it. The Northern churches, therefore, could not be trusted to be faithful to the Bible. Given the Northern churches' lack of true fidelity to the Bible (from the Southerners' perspective), their views on other biblical-related matters, such as evolution, were subject to suspicious scrutiny for liberal laxities of interpretation: "Such justifications of separation from the northern churches were an integral part of the southern glorification of the lost cause in the half-century after the War Between the States. Although Southerners had lost the war on the battlefield, they were determined to win the war of ideas. The effect of this determination was to preclude change in any area and to celebrate whatever had been dominant in the pre-bellum era." (172).

So although evolutionary ideas were rapidly gaining ground after the publication in 1859 of the *On the Origin of Species,* Southerners resisted change. For them the new theory of evolution was change, and change was decline rather than progress. Moreover, the Southerners had defended slavery on the grounds that the Bible clearly permitted it, and in some cases mandated it.

Northern Christian opponents of slavery read the Bible with a nonliteralistic hermeneutic and substituted a presumed underlying liberal biblical, anti-slavery ethos for the actual letter of the biblical text. "Committed to the letter of Scripture regarding slavery, southern conservatives were hardly in a position to play fast and loose with other passages that might be interpreted in the light of alleged modern progress" (173).

Marsden points out, "[A]ntievolution does not typically appear in the various lists of 'fundamentals' drawn up by fundamentalists in the years immediately after WWI" (174n51). However, in the 1920s, there were renewed fundamentalist battles against evolution, and antievolution was eventually elevated to a central fundamentalist doctrine. Marsden attributes this to the convergence of several forces that eventually emerged in the United States after World War I. Conservative Protestant premillenarians attributed modernist theological thinking to German theology and "kultur," which they claimed was imbued with evolutionary philosophies. And evolution, they said, maintains that "might is right," and it is what produced the "ideology [that] had led to disaster for that civilization, which had lost all sense of decency" (174).

The threat of evolution connected for fundamentalists their "defense of conservative readings of Scripture, their battles to combat modernist theology, and the entire destiny of America." They considered the abandonment of the infallible authority and absolute truth of the Bible, which the theory of evolution produces, a direct threat to civilization:

> The fundamentalists were pointing to a real phenomenon of major cultural significance. American young people, especially those who were attending colleges, were forsaking traditional faith in the Bible in droves ... Science courses, especially those that taught naturalistic evolution, were leading contributors to this revolution. In fact, nearly two-thirds of the nation's biologists professed not to believe in a personal God or in immortality for humans. The teaching of evolution was, then, a real contributor to a trend that many considered to have ominous implications for the future of civilization. (175–176)

Metaphors of warfare are common in the clashes between creationists and antisupernaturalist evolutionists, and both camps sometimes write as if the survival of society hinges on acceptance of their worldview. Creation-science, as aggressive, assertive, and combative as its books, tracts, websites, and political activism might be, is basically a defensive posture against contemporary secular, agnostic, or atheistic culture, which is pervasive in academia. Some Christians resent what they perceive to be the elevation of the principle of evolution to a kind of explanatory myth founded on a dogmatic naturalism and a moral relativism. This myth is used in the secular intellectual world not only to explain the origin of species, but to account for all of human culture. It has become for some a secular religion, a "cosmic myth—a worldview which purports to provide, for example, guidelines for ethics and a coherent account of reality" (180).

All of these historical, cultural, and ideological factors account for the renascence of creation-science among fundamentalist Protestant evangelicals and are expressed in the beliefs and defense of beliefs of individuals. As we have seen, some Jewish and Muslim fundamentalists, although not affected by these uniquely English and American factors, share anxiety about the authority of the Bible or of the Koran, a contempt for the alleged decadence of secular culture, and a fear of change. They have on their own, or more recently, through borrowing from Christian fundamentalists, hitched themselves to the antievolution, creation-science bandwagon.

CHAPTER SEVEN

On "Defundamentalizing" Fundamentalists

IN THE COURSE of this book I have discussed or alluded to some of the harmful consequences of scriptural fundamentalisms, which is one of the reasons for my writing the book in the first place. There are many harmful effects of traditional, conservative religion, whether fundamentalist or not that I have not touched upon.[1] For example, one of my correspondents noted the following:

> Religion is used to rationalize evil as in the cases of Protestantism in South Africa under apartheid, Catholicism in horrific human rights violations in South America, often tacitly supported by the Catholic Church, especially in Argentina...Traditional religious faith, with few exceptions, was a major reason why the Holocaust happened without Christians protesting it and why few people tried to rescue Jews. Traditional religious faith can foster apathy towards minorities at risk, as it did in WWII and as it still does today amongst some southern whites and conservative Republicans.[2]

In a sequel to this book I hope to examine in greater depth and breadth the social, psychological, political, and physical harm wrought by some scriptural fundamentalists and other dogmatic religious people. I will also discuss justifications for attempts to undermine their beliefs, and strategies and tactics for how individuals, organizations, and governments can and should attempt to do so. The various fundamentalist versions of each of the Abrahamic faiths harm *both their adherents and nonadherents* in their own unique way, and *to different degrees.* When combating them is called for—*which isn't always the case*—individualized tactics and strategies for doing so need to be used.

I have indicated that one purpose of this book is to persuade or encourage fundamentalists who might, by chance, read it to question and eventually give up their fundamentalist beliefs. Inasmuch as this book might be an instrument for undermining the religious faith of fundamentalists, in concluding the book I will briefly reflect upon the morality of such an enterprise.

When I assert that scriptural fundamentalisms often cause harm, I am in no way denying that they often also have many positive ethical, psychological, spiritual, and social consequences. In light of this, it pays to bear in mind the comment by Hinde in *Why Gods Persist,* who considers most traditional religions, especially when their beliefs and dogmas are understood literally, to be incompatible with modern knowledge:

> [A] purely destructive approach to religion is at present inappropriate . . . it would involve taking away what appears to be a source of comfort to many people without an adequate substitute. Such an approach assumes that belief in dogma is all there is to religion, and neglects the fact that moral principles have been purveyed by religious systems, within which they were part of a whole way of life . . . And that poses a question of critical importance for the next millennium: how can those products of a religious outlook that are valuable be preserved when the basic beliefs are rejected as literal portrayals of reality?[3]

In the course of writing this book some of my Orthodox Jewish friends, colleagues, and correspondents have argued that it is unethical for me to write it because to weaken or destroy faith in the divine revelation of the Torah would have undesirable negative consequences for Judaism and the Jewish people. Similarly, defenders of traditional Christian and Muslim faith believe that the contributions of Christianity and Islam to the welfare of their adherents are so great that criticism that will weaken religious commitment is immoral.

What are some of the ethical issues that arise when someone challenges beliefs that are existentially significant for a believer or a community of believers? What factors and possible consequences should be taken into consideration when one critiques a religious belief system? Is it indeed unethical to try to convince fundamentalist believers that their beliefs are based upon false assumptions?

When the harmful consequences of beliefs are clearly greater than their positive ones, I believe that it is ethical to try to undermine them, and it might be unethical not to try to do so. Of course, what is positive and what is negative is subject to debate, and the believer will usually differ from the critic in his assessment. I am writing from my subjective perspective of positive and negative, well aware that many will disagree with me. It would require another book to defend my moral and ethical judgments. For me, beliefs that express or generate suppression of women's rights, racial prejudice, homophobia, self-righteous arrogance, coercion of the believer's views on nonbelievers, antidemocratic behavior, injustice, repression of the intellect, hatred, violence, and, worst of all, the killing of innocents, are negative. Not all scriptural fundamentalist beliefs do all of the above, but they all do some of the above.

However, what about a situation in which the positive consequences of the belief system for the believer outweigh its negative consequences for both the believer and for others (assuming these can be measured comparatively in some way)? For example, the believer's religious beliefs provide him with existential meaning and purpose, happiness, close family relationships, friendships, communal bonds, ethical and moral values (usually in his relationship with fellow believers, but not necessarily toward nonbelievers), and other positive outcomes. The negative consequences may be *mild* forms of some of the above-listed ones—for example, disdain for, but not hatred of, nonbelievers; coercion expressed only via democratic processes by influencing the passage of laws that reflect the values the believers derive from their beliefs; and no use of violence. In such a case, too, I think the nonbeliever has the moral right to try to undermine the belief system. Why should the happiness of the believer and the benefits he derives from his beliefs be given priority over the rights and interests of the nonbeliever? Indeed, many believers regularly try to undermine the belief systems of people who are not religious, or who might even be religious but who are not scriptural fundamentalists. This is what missionizing and outreach are about. If the religious fundamentalist can try to dissuade the nonfundamentalist from his worldview, why shouldn't the nonfundamentalist be allowed to try to dissuade the fundamentalist from his?

However, when the scriptural fundamentalists live in an isolated enclave and do not seek to influence nonfundamentalists, as is the case, for example, with some ultra-Orthodox Jewish Hasidic sects, Christian snake handlers, and some Muslim communities, and their interaction with the broader society is minimal, and hence has little negative impact on it, the claim that it is unethical to try to undermine their beliefs is stronger.

Some people, however, claim that they have an ethical right, and even an imperative, to challenge and try to undermine the beliefs of even these isolated fundamentalists, because the fundamentalists are harming the members of their own group and especially the children whom they are socializing into their belief system and religious lifestyle. An extreme formulation of this claim is Richard Dawkins' assertion that religious education and training is a form of child abuse.[4] From these aggressive critics' perspective, the beliefs— and the religion, culture, and society in which they are embedded—need to be vigorously combated. Even though the members of the religious group, such as women, who are presumed by the critics to be victims of the group's beliefs, may have internalized its values and even consider themselves to be privileged to be members of the group, and accept the roles it accords them, the critics claim to know better than the "victims" themselves what is in their best interest. Many, probably most, Hasidic, Christian fundamentalist, Mormon, and Muslim women do not view themselves as oppressed. They have their own hierarchy of values, in which, for example, gender role differentiation, modest dress, "family values," strict constraints on sexual behavior, and limitations on abortion are positive. The feminist critics may preach women's sexual freedom, abortion on demand, and gender equality. But as long as the enclaved group doesn't try to impose its views on nongroup members, isn't it hubris for the critics to assume that their values are somehow superior?[5] This is a condescending attitude and presumes that the women in the enclaved group lack the intelligence or the agency to decide what is best for themselves. Why try to "raise the consciousness" of women who are overall happy in their faith and content in their lifestyle?

The situation is different with respect to determining what is in the best interests of the children of the enclaved fundamentalist group. On the one hand, one can claim that parents have the right to decide what is best for their children, and hence no one should interfere with how they socialize and educate them. Infants and young children lack sufficient knowledge and agency to decide for themselves as to what they believe and how to live, and in our society parents are indeed given the legal right to make these choices for them, and this right should extend to enclaved fundamentalists.

On the other hand, however, when the general society considers parental behavior or parental neglect to be harmful to the child or, sometimes, just not in the child's best interest, it imposes its views and restricts or prohibits the parents from acting as they please. Thus we have laws requiring a minimum level of education and health care, which if the parents cannot, or refuse to, provide, allows government agencies to remove the child from parental control. Some religious groups, such as Jehovah's Witnesses, object to certain accepted medical procedures, for example, blood transfusions. In cases in which, in a life-threatening situation, a parent refuses to consent to their child's receiving a transfusion, the state will override parental authority. It goes without saying that in our society when the parent abuses his or her child, the action is criminal and punishable—which is not the case in all societies.

Critics of fundamentalism might have greater moral weight for their attempts to undermine religious beliefs when they can plausibly argue that these beliefs result in harm to children, which they wish to prevent. I am not referring to actual physical harm, which is illegal and the responsibility of the legal system to prevent. I am talking about what the critic perceives to be intellectual and moral harm to the children of the fundamentalist. The critic argues that raising a child to be a fundamentalist deprives the child of access to knowledge, values, and skills, which from the critic's point of view are desirable, and necessary for a healthy life. He argues that fundamentalism engenders irrational and psychologically harmful fears and anxieties. The critic feels that it his ethical right, and maybe even his duty, to try to undermine the belief system of the parents in order to protect the present and future children of the fundamentalists from the negative consequences of the fundamentalist belief system, as long as he does not engage in illegal behavior to accomplish this goal. The fact that the parents differ from the critic in their assessment of their fundamentalist beliefs and their consequences is not sufficient grounds to make it unethical for the critic to try to undermine those beliefs, when the critic is acting out of what he perceives to be in the best interest of the children.

Another factor to take into consideration when critiquing a religious belief system is whether or not a preferable alternative is offered in lieu of the one being undermined.[6] One could claim that this is irrelevant—the issue is truth and not a better way of life.[7] However, I think the case for undermining a belief system will be stronger if there is a desirable substitute available in its stead. Many religious fundamentalists could reasonably argue that despite any flaws or faults of their belief system and way of life based on it, the alternative offered by majority American culture and society is considerably more flawed and harmful. Many an ultra-Orthodox Jew, for example, spends inordinate amounts of time and intellectual and emotional resources studying texts that deal with laws and rituals that have no practical application for him today, for example, how to offer sacrifices in a Temple that does not exist. Similarly he invests—sometimes to the point of obsessiveness—time, energy, and money on the scrupulous performance of rituals, which to a critic is inane, if not bordering on the insane. The ultra-Orthodox Jew has an elaborate theology that accords profound spiritual meaning to these religious studies and ritual preoccupations and performances, and can dismiss the critic's critiques by arguing that the critic simply doesn't appreciate the spirituality and other benefits that they produce. But even without this argument, the devout Jew (and the same goes for the Christian, Muslim, and Mormon) can argue that much of general American culture is vapid, inane, and immoral. It is replete with gun violence, substance abuse, sexual promiscuity, crass and vulgar materialism and consumerism, greed and selfishness, and political corruption. How many millions of hours do Americans spend watching idiotic TV shows, browsing pornographic Internet sites, following baseball, football, basketball, hockey, horseracing and NASCAR races, and guzzling six-packs or more of beer while doing so? Why are these activities preferable to studying arcane Talmudic texts, expending hours on rituals and prayers, and spending money on strictly kosher food or on purchasing an expensive ritual object, such as a beautiful citron for the festival of Tabernacles? How many American women are preoccupied with the cult of beauty and the illusory quest for eternal youth, expending time, energy, and money on exploring, purchasing, and applying numerous colors, hues, and shades of hair dye, nail polish, lipstick, mascara, and eye shadow, and seeking "salvation" from aging and attention from men, in the promise of wrinkle-hiding creams and cosmetic surgery? How many women feverishly and frenziedly monitor and buy the latest fashions in clothing, so many of which, if not actually promiscuous, border on promiscuity? Why are these activities and values preferable to the religious individual's acceptance of aging as natural, of beauty as skin-deep, of modesty and simplicity in dress as virtuous, and of channeling one's time and energy into doing good rather than to looking good?[8] Why, critic, would you want to tear me and my children from our fundamentalist religious beliefs, lifestyle, and values if all you can offer instead is the morally corrupt and insipid popular American culture?

The critic might answer on three fronts. First, don't underestimate your faults that I have pointed out to you. Second, you can keep most of the benefits of religion without being an irrational fundamentalist. Third, America offers high culture and values and not only the low. I seek to undermine not religion per se but your particular fundamentalist version of it. And the alternative I offer is democracy, rationality, freedom of thought and expression, the rich cultural and intellectual repository of Western civilization, and the opportunity to contribute to the alleviation of human suffering by devoting your energies to more productive pursuits than the preoccupations of your fundamentalist religion.

Biblical or Koranic fundamentalists often argue for the moral/ethical superiority of biblical or Koranic values over other value systems.[9] If they are evaluating biblical or Koranic norms according to criteria of ethics/morality that are independent of the biblical or Koranic texts themselves, then I would agree that in many instances biblical or Koranic morality was and still is quite advanced even according to many contemporary (twenty-first century) standards and norms. However, according to these same twenty-first-century criteria, there are also many morally and ethically offensive norms and values in the Bible and the Koran, such as commands to annihilate groups or nations, including women and children; acceptance of slavery; lack of equality between men and women in certain areas of law and social status; collective punishment; capital punishment for male anal sex; and more. If, in response, the fundamentalists assert, as they often do, that the Bible or the Koran is divine in origin and therefore cannot be judged by human standards of ethics/morality, they are begging the question of which system is more ethical, and there is no room for discussion with them, because for them whatever God commands is ipso facto superior to any humanly devised ethical/moral system.

Another factor relevant to the ethics of challenging fundamentalist religious beliefs is the *occasion* and the *forum* for raising questions about the beliefs. One might question the ethics of clandestinely planting "heretical" tracts in the schools, churches, mosques, and synagogues of believers, the way an activist anti-haredi group in Israel used to stealthily distribute such tracts in yeshivot (rabbinical seminaries). It is quite another thing to critically analyze fundamentalist religion in an academic setting, one of whose missions is to question received ideas and values and cultivate critical thinking. A scriptural fundamentalist who attends a public school or a university has no right to expect that his religious views will be "respected," in the sense that they will not be subject to criticism in courses in which such criticism is relevant. This would include most of the humanities, social sciences, and life sciences, in which many ideas and values will be expressed and facts and theories will be taught that will collide with scriptural fundamentalisms. If, for example, he has chosen to take a course in social psychology and the instructor includes discussion of the psychology of religion, which might undermine the grounds of his religious beliefs and commitments, so be it. To the extent that the school sets forth in advance core requirements, which might, for example, include a course in which scholarly approaches to the study of classic religious Scriptures such as the Bible and the Koran are invoked, the religious student cannot object that his religious sensibilities or feelings are hurt because the professor "demeans" the sanctity of these texts from the perspective of the believer.[10]

Finally, I see no ethical problem in critiquing the beliefs of scriptural fundamentalists by writing *academic* books, or publishing articles in journals that are acquired, read, or accessed by the free choice of whoever wishes to do so. Fundamentalists use the same methods to promulgate their views and to critique nonfundamentalists and skeptics. If fundamentalists are not interested in how they, their beliefs, and their views are being analyzed by critics, they can ignore this material. I hope, however, that they will not.

A more complicated question, which I will discuss in the sequel to this book, is when and how the *popular mass media*—radio, television, the plethora of Internet sites and portals, and print journalism—should broadcast and publish stories, essays, and documentaries that are critical of fundamentalists and that seek to undermine their beliefs by rational, scholarly scrutiny of them, or, more offensively, to broadcast and publish music, art, cartoons, satire, humor, and mockery that expose their foolishness, hypocricy, and harmfulness.

I believe that in the long run the engagement of scriptural fundamentalists and their critics, like me, in honest, nonviolent debates about religious beliefs, attitudes, and behaviors will enhance understanding, morality, and the positive contributions that religions can make to humanity.

Chapter 1

1. See Jay Harris's (1994) insightful critique of the imprecise use of the term *fundamentalism* and especially his wariness about using it to refer to or describe traditional, or Orthodox Judaism. Notwithstanding his reservations, I designate Orthodox Jews as "biblical or scriptural fundamentalists" because of how I have defined the sense in which I am using the term.

See also Samuel Heilman's (1995) illuminating comparison of the Orthodox Jewish bes medrash and the Muslim (especially Shia) madrasa. Notwithstanding several caveats about using the term *fundamentalist* to apply to haredi Jews and contemporary devout Muslims, he does use it in the sense in which I am using it. He writes, "Indeed, as Bernard Lewis has pointed out, 'among Muslim theologians there is as yet no . . . liberal or modernist approach to the Qu'ran, and all Muslims, in their attitude to the text of the Qu'ran, are in principle at least fundamentalists' (citing Lewis, 1988, 118n3). Much the same could be said about yeshiva students. Although some variations in approach to the texts studied exist, they by and large support a view of the inerrancy of the holy books and their rabbinic commentaries" (81).

With regard to using the term *fundamentalist* to refer to *modern* Orthodox Jews' attitudes toward the Hebrew Bible, Jonathan Sacks, Chief Rabbi of the United Kingdom, who is as "modern Orthodox" a Jew as one can find, states his belief "that the Five Books of Moses are the unmediated word of God . . . In this sense, therefore, Orthodoxy *is* fundamentalist" (Sacks, 1989). See chapter 3 of this book, pp. 90–92.

Early twentieth-century Protestant biblical inerrantists, of course, are the source for the term Christian *fundamentalism,* inerrancy being one of the fundamentals of Christian faith as they understood it.

Heilman appropriately distinguishes between "traditional" religion and "fundamentalist" religion. For example, "Often the key element that turns an Orthodox attachment to tradition into a form of fundamentalism is the context in which it occurs. To be insistently traditional when others all around are not is to transform that tradition into something more than a simple handing on of the old ways to another generation" (1995, 71).

With respect to the belief in scriptural inerrancy, Orthodox Jews, Protestant "fundamentalists," and devout Muslims are actually being "traditionalist," in that they are maintaining and transmitting beliefs about their sacred scriptures that did not arise as a response to modernity, but go back many centuries before "modernity." Their "response to modernity" is in their refusal to change their traditional beliefs in light of new knowledge about the origins and authorship of their scriptures.

2. Nehemia Polen.

3. However much this might explain the motive, or at least one powerful motive, for his "crusade" against the haredi community, it does not necessarily affect the merits of his criticism of that community's beliefs or behaviors.

4. Although these are motives of mine, whether or not I was fully aware of them throughout, I believe that they should not affect an assessment of the points I make, which should be judged on their own merits, irrespective of what my motives for bringing them to public awareness might be.

5. Now that I have expanded my paper that originally dealt only with Orthodox Jews to include Christian and Muslim fundamentalists, this book can serve a similar function for members of Christian and Muslim fundamentalist communities who are unhappy with their lot.

6. Hume, 1959; 1986.

7. Quoted by James, 1978/1902, 183.

8. As I will point out later, there are many halakhically committed Jews who do not believe that their decision to maintain an orthodox way of life is contingent upon accepting all of the tenets of orthodox theology. For one articulate formulation of this position see James Kugel's response to a questioner who feels that if the Torah is not divine he would not be able to take the halakhic system seriously, at http://www .jameskugel.com, a section of which is in endnote 33 on page 258. See there Baruch Schwartz's comments as well.

9. Mintz, 1987, 4.

10. My journey from faith to doubt to agnosticism, while remaining "orthoprax" to a significant degree, also affected my relationships with my wife and children in many ways, but I defer a discussion of this to another occasion.

11. *Complete ArtScroll Siddur (Sefard)*, 1985, 636.

12. *JPS Hebrew-English Tanakh*, 1999, Ps. 42:2–3, 42:6, 42:12.

13. I discuss some of the rationales for orthopraxy (in contrast to orthodoxy), and attitudes of traditional and Orthodox Judaism to orthopraxy, in my unpublished paper "Orthopraxy and Spirituality," which will be posted on my blog associated with this book.

14. Bernard Susser, a professor of religion and political science at Bar-Ilan University, offers his interesting personal reflection on the experience and consequences of making a break from Orthodox Jewish tradition.

Certainly my father and grandfather would count my break with religious Judaism as a mutiny against the historical trust I should have accepted. They would, no doubt, point to the extensive Yeshiva education I had received, to the years when Talmudic study was my central vocation, to the deep awe at Jewish learning that persists even now. At one point in young adulthood, there was not very much that separated me from being ordained into the Rabbinate. This then was no ordinary chain-breaking . . . I needed to fight myself loose of ideas and practices that informed my identity down to its very roots. This was a conscious insurrection, treason aforethought.

I count the more than ten years it took for the transformation to take place neither as a heady liberation from obscurantism nor as a tragic loss of faith in which tales of "a faith lost" are usually told. There was nothing exhilarating about it because forsaking the world of belief, of cohesive community, and of commanding moral compulsions was often a wrenching personal ordeal that I cannot, even now, remember without wincing. Neither is the "tragic loss of faith" genre appropriate because in place of one faith another commitment opened before me: dedication to the world of academia . . .

Whatever the idiosyncratic mix of biographical, intellectual, and social factors that went into my change of life-course, they did not take place overnight . . . These difficult years matured into the recognition that one form of Jewish life—the traditional Orthodox—had become impossible for me. Years of cultural migration ensued. And they posed the question with which I have been wrestling ever since: Having broken the chain is there any way of forging new kinds of Jewish links that can take the place of the Orthodox Judaism I abandoned? Can Jewishness be reconstructed to make it be more than ethnic nostalgia? Can it be suffused with life-giving meaning, even if it is not the meaning that moved my father and grandfather? Does the historical insurrection of modernity necessarily entail the slow extinction of Jewish civilization? (Susser and Liebman, 1999, 5–6)

For a personal account of loss of faith by an evangelical, fundamentalist Christian, see Barker, 1992, 13–34; see also Babinski, 2003. For Muslims, see, for example, http://www.apostatesofislam.com/testimonials.htm (retrieved September 23, 2007).

Chapter 2

1. Paul Helm (1999, 3–14) provides a useful summary of the key concepts and questions in the faith-reason relationship in his Introduction to the reader he edited.

2. See, for example, Rosenberg, 1984, 273–307, for various meanings of *emunah* ("belief," "faith") in medieval Jewish philosophy.

3. Helm, 1999, 6.

4. Husik, 1916, 28, 35.

5. *Encyclopedia Judaica,* 14:550.

6. For an interesting analysis of the evolutionary relationship between emotion and reason, and how it manifests itself in politics (but is relevant to most spheres of life), see the chapter "The Evolution of the Passionate Brain" in Westen (2007).

7. Peterson et al., 2001, 70–71.

8. Ibid., 76.

9. Numbers 16; John 20:24–29; e.g., Koran Sura 25.

10. See Davis, 1989.

11. J. Bowen, personal communication.

12. Hick, 1982.

13. See, for example, Hinde, 1999.

14. See, for example, Boyer, 2001; Wilson, 2002.

15. There are, however, a good number of contemporary philosophers who either consider their faith commitments to be compatible with their philosophical commitments or even to be reinforced by their philosophical commitments. See, for example, the personal testimonies of religious philosophers in Morris, 1994.

16. Many skeptics of religious claims, however, do deny, a priori, the possibility of supernatural miracles.

17. Peterson et al., 2003, 272–273, based on Plantinga, 2000.

18. The morality of forgiveness can be dubious in certain situations. See my book (Schimmel, 2002).

19. See, for example, my book (Schimmel, 1997).

20. Jesus' miracles are not the only grounds for why he was considered to be a reliable spokesperson for God's will. See Sanders, 1996, chap. 10, "Miracles."

21. See Norowitz, 2003, for a detailed refutation of the Kuzari argument and variations of it.

Modern technology, such as the Internet, can and does generate and distribute around the world in a few seconds false stories that are believed by millions within days, hours, or even minutes. Millions of Muslims believe that Jews, or the U.S. government, or both in collusion, conspired to bring down the two World Trade Center towers on September 11, 2001. In ancient times, it might have taken a few centuries for legends to originate, elaborate, spread, and be believed by many, given the slowness and limited range of communications.

22. See Kent, 1999, for one plausible psychological explanation for how the resurrection "myth" developed, and Ehrman's debate with Craig in chapter 4.

Chapter 3

1. Friedman, 2003, 7–31.

2. Modern Orthodox Jews will also benefit from James Kugel's *How to Read the Bible* (2007), in which he analyzes the Hebrew Scriptures from both modern critical scholarly perspectives and early pre-rabbinic and rabbinic ones. In the final chapter of this work, Kugel, a traditionally observant Jew and one of the most distinguished contemporary scholars of Bible and of the history of biblical interpretation, argues that modern biblical scholarship is not inherently incompatible with religious faith and halakhic commitment, although it *is* incompatible with traditional rabbinic and medieval Jewish assumptions about who authored the Pentateuch (and the rest of the Hebrew Bible) and how it came to be written in its present form. Kugel's book provides numerous examples of the plausibility of the MSPM theory and the implausibility of the TMS theory in explaining and interpreting the original sense of Pentateuchal texts in their ancient Near Eastern context. He incorporates internal biblical analyses, archaeology, Hebrew and Semitic linguistics, ancient near eastern history, culture and literature, and the social sciences. The combination of Friedman, Kugel, and Michael Coogan's excellent *The Old Testament: A Historical and Literary Introduction to the Hebrew Scriptures* (2006) provide an accessible summary of the history, methods, assumptions and findings of contemporary Biblical scholarship. Anyone who is struggling with belief about the divine authorship of

the Torah and its revelation to Moses at Sinai will find in these books (and their bibliographies) a wealth of information and concepts that should enable them confidently to conclude that the MSPM theory has been demonstrated to be true beyond a reasonable doubt—even if not beyond *unreasonable* doubt.

3. The Orthodox doctrine of TMS is often supported by the rabbinic statement that the "Torah is from Heaven" and variants of it. However, this expression did not necessarily mean to all rabbinic sages (and even to some medieval ones) what Orthodoxy has interpreted it to mean—that the Pentateuch in its entirety, or almost in its entirety, was dictated to Moses by God at Mt. Sinai. See Heschel, 2005, 368–386, and Shapiro, 2004, 90–121.

4. Lukes, 1974, 194.

5. Snow and Machalek, in their analysis of how members of a cult with unconventional beliefs respond to events that would seem to disconfirm them, point out the following:

Upon encountering an unconventional belief system, people are often heard to exclaim: "How could anyone in his right mind believe such nonsense?"

... [B]elief systems may feature validation logics that help insure their persistence ... [E]vidence discrepant with belief does not necessarily create cognitive dissonance.

... [In] many non-scientific belief systems the decision as to whether an event confirms or falsifies belief is often not made until after the event has occurred. In many cases, this allows the believer great interpretive discretion. Furthermore, as taught by sociologists of knowledge, one's social position is a powerful determinant of meanings that are ascribed to events. Simply put, "insiders" to a religious group may believe that the suffering of children is evidence of the visitation of God's wrath on the sins of their parents, while "outsiders" may interpret the same event as compelling evidence against the very existence of God.

Perhaps another reason for social scientists' presuming the fragility of unconventional beliefs is their tendency to be more concerned with accounting for belief rather than for disbelief ... there is sound theoretical reasoning on which to assume that people are typically inclined toward belief than toward disbelief ... It is thus possible that social scientists have projected the assumptions of the "scientific attitude" onto those whose unconventional beliefs they would explain. As such, they regard as curious the persistence of belief in the face of what may be disconfirming evidence only to them. If so, ... then perhaps social scientists should find less curious the persistence of unconventional beliefs and begin to examine instead the question of how does doubt emerge in spite of the "natural attitude" to believe. (1982, 21(1), 23–25)

6. See Clark, 1996; Heilman, 2006; Heilman and Cohen, 1989, especially 18–37; Liebman, 1974; Liebman, 1998; Waxman, 1993.

7. I do discuss *haredi,* or ultra-Orthodox belief in TMS, in various places in this book where appropriate.

8. One can classify subgroups of "Orthodox," not only in terms of "ultra-Orthodox haredi" and "modern Orthodox, Torah U'Madda," but into subgroups based upon a number of criteria, for example, Israeli—Diaspora; *ffb* ("frum from birth," i.e., raised

Orthodox from childhood)—*baalei teshuva* (Jews raised in nonobservant homes who become observant, usually following Orthodox practice and belief); Ashkenazi-Sephardi; Mitnagdic-Hasidic. Jonathan Sacks (1989, 8), in discussing the various uses of *fundamentalism,* notes that " . . . when the word is used in a Jewish context it is sometimes taken to refer to all Orthodox Jews, on the ground that Orthodoxy involves a belief that the Torah is the word of God and not—even partially—the work of man. Such a belief, Conservative and liberal theologians argue, is incompatible with modern historical scholarship and therefore fundamentalist. At other times it is used to refer to those who understand the Torah literally; or to those who argue that all halakhic change is impermissible; or to those who invest the words of great Torah sages with absolute authority; or to those who see no value in secular culture—four very different sub-groups within Orthodoxy." See also the Wikipedia online entry for "Modern Orthodox Judaism."

9. Carmy, 1996, 3, 26, 27. In an online discussion about whether Orthodox Judaism is characterized by "intellectual honesty," the anonymous blogmaster of godolhador .blogspot.blog (May 2006) commented on this excerpt as follows:

Rabbi Carmy's approach is a frequently used one, but is quite disingenuous. In his approach, the truth of revelation at Sinai is "proved" or upheld through various means, via appeals to personal experience, the Kuzari proof, the miraculous history of the Jewish people and other similar methods. Then, once the truth of the Torah has been proved, they proceed to disregard or discount all other evidence to the contrary.

While all these "proofs" for the truth of Torah certainly have merit (some more than others), this approach commits a serious methodological mistake. By arguing for the truth of revelation through the use of evidence and reason, they are implicitly declaring that evidence and reason are acceptable methods to verify the truth of belief claims. However, rather than considering the entire gamut of evidence both for and against these claims, they instead focus on one small subset of all the available evidence, claim that the truth of revelation has been proved, and then declare that all other evidence to the contrary in other areas is no longer admissible, or even worse, forbidden to even be contemplated, because the truth of revelation has already been shown. This is not an intellectually honest approach.

Certainly the "truth" of revelation can be upheld through an appeal to faith, but faith is not intellectual honesty, it is faith. What Rabbi Carmy is really saying is that he believes in the truth of Torah through Faith, and then this dictates what he is able to believe in other areas. This approach is not an intellectually honest approach, and while it may not actually be intellectually dishonest, it certainly is intellectually dishonest for Rabbi Carmy to portray it as anything more than faith.

10. Bernstein, 1991–1992, 24–25.

11. Shatz, 1991–1992, 105.

12. Kaplan and Berger, 1990, 38–39.

13. David Berger, personal communication.

14. Maimonides (1963), interestingly, states in his introduction to the first part of the *Guide* (pp. 5–6) that he is writing it for the individual who, having begun to question

fundamentals of the faith, needs guidance to help him deal with his doubts that arose from the exercise of his reason, because to suppress them is emotionally troubling, ineffective, and undesirable.

15. Berger, 1999, 87.

16. Berkovits, 1966, 78.

17. Breuer, 1996, 170–171.

18. Breuer provides his own hermeneutic and specific exegeses in order to resolve apparent contradictions and inconsistencies in the Pentateuch. These explanations are often forced and unconvincing.

19. E. Abrahamson; A. Rubin, "Mada," Discussion Group for Jewish Scientists, mada@jer1.co.il, Oct. 14, 1996.

20. Leiman, 1996, 186.

21. Deconchy, 1984, 428–429. See also Peter Berger's (1969, 45–51) summary of what the sociology of knowledge says about beliefs and plausibility structures.

22. Barry Levy (1992), repeatedly refers to the role of fear in his explanation of Orthodoxy's refusal to engage the world of academic biblical scholarship. See, for example, pp. 167, 185, 187, and 188. He notes that there is a real and constant fear that if Orthodoxy embraces biblical scholarship, many Jews will become less Orthodox, as reflected in weaker commitment, observance or religiosity.

23. Leiman, 1996, 181–182.

24. Levy, 1992, 179–180.

25. "The State of Jewish Belief," 1966, 73–160, at 73.

26. Fox, 1966, 89.

27. In chapter 1, where I recounted my own journey from faith to doubt, I quoted the section from Mintz that follows, as well as the next quote, from the French philosopher Jouffroy, cited by William James, both of which described so well aspects of my personal experience. I am including them again here because of their relevance to the general theme I am now discussing.

28. Mintz, 1987, 4.

29. Cited in James, 1978/1902, 183.

30. Jacobs, 1964; 1990.

31. Levenson, 1993, 62–66.

32. Baruch Schwartz, in a personal communication, pointed out that "the statement 'the Orthodox community's lifestyle, which is structured around halakha, is built upon the doctrine of TMS,' is not a fact, only a perception . . . the halachic lifestyle derives primarily from the belief that the Oral law has some sort of divine sanction, and from a choice to devote one's life to serving God. Socially and anthropologically, especially in traditional circles, the halachic lifestyle derives from a loyalty to community and family and tradition." He then raises some interesting questions. Because "the idea that halachah stands or falls on TMS is not self-evident . . . the question becomes: why have Orthodox educators persistently presented it as though it were? Why has this perception been perpetuated? Is it believed to be a fact? Or is it believed to be the only way to get people to remain loyal to halachah? Or maybe there is something else about TMS that makes people reluctant to admit that it is dispensable?"

I think that most Orthodox rabbis believe it to be a fact that over time an erosion of belief in TMS will lead to an erosion in halakhic observance. They also believe that halakhic observance based upon non-Orthodox theological principles, or on no theological principle at all (orthopraxy), though preferable to nonobservance, is spiritually inferior to observance based upon belief in TMS and the simultaneously revealed Oral Law.

33. Kugel, 2007, chap. 36.

34. Heschel, 2005.

35. The very contention that the Pentateuch is TMS suggests for some Orthodox Jews, including some modern Orthodox ones, that it alone is the source of ethical and moral values. They believe that ethics and morality are defined by God and we need God to inform us of his rules, which he has done exclusively in the laws of the Pentateuch and their "authorized" detailed rabbinic interpretation. Someone who doesn't accept belief in TMS and rabbinic authority, though he may behave in some moral and ethical ways, is still doing so in an imperfect way.

Similarly, many haredi and some modern Orthodox maintain that true, legitimate spiritual fulfillment cannot be found outside of Orthodoxy. The fact that the modern Orthodox live amidst, and interact positively with, the non-Orthodox Jewish community, and participate with it in some religious activities, or that they interact positively with the non-Jewish world, religious and secular, does not mean that they necessarily consider the non-Orthodox and the non-Jewish world to be capable of providing authentic, maximal spiritual realization and fulfillment, especially for Jews.

36. Jews who had lived for centuries in Spain until 1492 and then primarily in the Middle East and North Africa, before immigrating more recently to Israel, the United States, and other countries.

37. Feierberg, 1899/1973, 125–126.

38. Levy, 1992, 180. See also Heilman and Cohen, 1989, 95–111, and 159–160, for a discussion of the phenomenon of Orthodox compartmentalization with respect to belief and halakhic practice, and with respect to traditional beliefs and scientific knowledge.

39. Lilienblum, 1876/1970, 114.

40. See Dov Greenspan's experience with Aish HaTorah's Discovery Seminar and allegedly encrypted biblical codes on p. 81.

41. Lamm, 1966, 110.

42. Levenson, 1993, 43.

43. This critique was made by Eli Clark in a personal communication.

44. See note 49 below.

45. See Ferziger, 2005.

46. Sternberg, 1997a, 86–87. See Dennett, 2006, 217–222, where he discusses the difference between relying on theologians and other religious experts as a basis for believing religious propositions and relying on scientists as a basis for believing scientific propositions.

47. The modern Orthodox also often need to resort to contorted logic in trying to rationalize difficult *moral* questions posed by biblical law and narrative.

48. See my article (Schimmel, 2004). See also Mittleman, 2003, on the "dangers" of the university to Orthodox students.

49. Modern Orthodox Jews (and even nonmodern Orthodox Jews) do not call nowadays for the actual punishment of those who violate Jewish law, for several reasons, practical and theoretical. Practically speaking, they are not for the most part in positions of authority to impose such punishment. In addition, they have developed several jus-

tifications for the view that, unlike in earlier centuries, most contemporary violators do not deserve to be punished even though they are sinners. See Ferziger, 2005.

50. Samuel Heilman, H-JUDAIC Discussion Group, Jan. 15, 1997.

51. A. Fiorino, "Mada" Discussion Group for Jewish Scientists, mada@jer1.co.il, Mar. 30, 1997.

52. Robinson, 2006, 79.

53. Yeshiva University is the flagship institution of modern Orthodoxy, although there are numerous modern Orthodox college students at colleges and universities throughout the United States.

54. Selya, 2006, 197, based on Nussbaum, 2002, 38–43.

55. This approach is not unique to Orthodox Jews but is shared by some Jewish theologians from the Conservative and Reform denominations insofar as they are theists who believe in divine providence. Like the Orthodox they are uncomfortable with a strictly materialist view of the world which seeks to account for all of reality and human experience without positing the existence of any transcendent, divine Being. Even though these rabbis have no problem with Genesis 1 per se, because they can consider it to be a humanly authored creation myth, the Bible and pre-modern post-biblical Judaism are based on the assumption that God acts in history, cares about human beings whom he has created for a purpose, and has endowed the people Israel with a mission to achieve for mankind. (See Swetlitz, 2006, 47–70).

56. Aviezer, 2007, 24. Actually, however, the Torah does not make any 'predictions' that relate to creation—it describes, asserts, and imagines how creation, or at least the perceived order in the world, came about in the past.

57. There is a rabbinic midrash which states that everything that exists, even a single spider, has been created to serve some divine purpose. This is not the same as saying that the world was created for the sake of creating the spider, but it shares the idea that everything that exists was brought into existence by a divine plan.

58. Cherry, 2006, 170.

59. Ibid., and Cherry's citation, for example, of Falk (1994).

60. Feinstein, 1982, 323. See also Robinson, 2006, 75–78, on the position of the Orthodox 'rejectionists' of evolution.

61. As we shall see in chapter 5, some Muslim scientists make the same specious claims about the Koran.

62. See Cherry, 2006, 169–172, on Aviezer.

63. Ibid., 177. See Cherry's excellent chapter for his detailed critique of Aviezer, Schroeder, and other Orthodox scientists' attempts at the reconciliation of Torah with science.

64. Ibid., 186; Robinson, 2006, 87–88.

65. Selya, 2006, 207.

66. Ibid., 203.

67. What follows is based upon an unpublished paper I presented at the American Academy of Religion, (Schimmel, 2002). See also Shatz, 2006.

68. Brown et al., 1998.

69. Rabbi Richard Israel, personal communication.

70. My translation of Statman.

71. Sagi, 1997, 432.

72. David Weiss HaLivni, 2001, also develops a novel and unconvincing theory about the divine origin but inaccurate transmission of the Torah.

73. See p. 44 on the RCA.

74. Nosson Scherman, 1993, xix–xx. Subsequent Scherman citations are also from this source. For a detailed scholarly discussion of the numerous attested variations in the text of the Pentateuch, and the origin and development of false claims to the contrary, see Mark Perakh (online) and the Hebrew article by Menahem Cohen, 1979.

75. See, for example, the article by Berel Wein, on the Aish HaTorah website, who asserts that most scholarly emendations of the text of the Bible are "shenanigans" that by now "have been consigned to the ash heap of history."

76. J. J. Schacter (1998–1999) vociferously and convincingly critiques the refusal of the right-wing Orthodox to face the truths of history. Yet, I wonder how Schacter, a leading proponent and representative of modern, centrist, Orthodox Judaism, would respond to the comment made by Jon Levenson (2000) in his letter to the *Torah U-Maddah Journal* praising Schacter for his "learned and courageous piece":

> The issue that Rabbi Schacter raises in this masterful article is not only historiographical but also theological, since it involves the nettlesome issue of how traditional believers can reckon with the findings of historical scholarship that is so intellectually honest that it challenges our religiously based preconceptions. Or, to ask the question from the opposite direction, how can the truths uncovered by research enter the bloodstream of a community of faith in a way that does not compromise either?
>
> As difficult as this issue is to face and resolve, it is more costly not to face it. For the stance of fideism that the latter course inevitably reinforces progressively weakens the capacity of the tradition to answer critiques from the larger culture and requires a degree of intellectual isolation that is impossible for most Jews to attain. Ironically, the insistence on that stance of isolation is itself, at the least, a narrowing of the very tradition it aims to conserve and requires the dubious notion that emet [truth] and emunah [faith] can be at odds. (276)

Levenson, who is among the most distinguished of contemporary biblical scholars, is alluding to, perhaps among other areas, his own area of biblical scholarship and biblical theology, which modern Orthodoxy, of which Rabbi Schacter is a prominent leader, as well as right-wing Orthodoxy, has still failed or refused to assimilate into its theology of Judaism.

77. Schacter, 1998–1999, 217–218.

78. Dov Greenspan, personal communication.

79. Shapiro, 2004, chap. 7, pp. 91–121.

80. Tirosh-Samuelson, 2003, 447.

81. See my discussion of different meanings of and attitudes toward *truth* in chap. 6.

82. Nahmanides believed that these esoteric teachings were transmitted by God to Moses and from him to a select few in every generation, and their profundities can only be grasped by an elite who have been initiated into Jewish mysticism.

83. Citations from Nahmanides are from the translation by Chavel, 1972, 65.

84. For more than two decades, Barry Levy has been critiquing contemporary Orthodoxy from within. One of his main contentions is that historically, traditional Ju-

daism has been much more diverse and open in its approaches to understanding and interpreting the Bible than what is considered legitimate today in most of the Orthodox community. See the bibliography for several of his articles.

85. Compare the similar experiences described by Chaim Potok in his novel *In the Beginning,* chap. 6, in which he describes his reaction upon almost "accidentally" encountering the traditional Hertz Commentary on the Pentateuch, which mentions and dismisses the documentary hypothesis, and his subsequent study of modern biblical scholarship and grappling with its implications for his Orthodox beliefs.

86. Sacks, 1989, 8–12.

87. For an analysis of Protestant fundamentalism's approaches to the Bible, see chap. 4. Although it is true that rabbinic and Orthodox Judaism do not read the Bible as literalists, they do read it as "inerrant" because being revealed by God, it can contain no errors. Because, however, there is considerable latitude for biblical interpretation in Orthodox Judaism, some of the problems generated by the claim of biblical "inerrancy" can be mitigated by creative interpretation. See, for example, Halbertal, 1999, on how rabbis of the Talmudic period used midrashic modes of interpretation to circumvent problems of a moral or ethical nature that a literal reading of the Bible generated for them. Many books have been written by Orthodox Jewish scientists to demonstrate how the first few chapters of Genesis are compatible with modern scientific accounts of the origins of the universe, mankind, languages, and so forth. (See, e.g., Schroeder, 1991; Schatz, 1973.) This methodology is one used extensively in the highly influential and sophisticated Orthodox, "apologetical" commentary of Rabbi J. H. Hertz to the Pentateuch (1937). Although many of the midrashic interpretations of biblical texts are in themselves of considerable religious and ethical value, contemporary readers of the Bible who do not a priori assume that rabbinic interpretations are authoritative and reflect the original intent of the Bible will more often than not find them far from convincing as explanations of what the Bible intends to convey in a law or narrative.

88. With respect to the persuasiveness, or lack thereof, of arguments in defense of Orthodox belief offered by Sacks, and other modern Orthodox scholars, such as J. J. Schacter, a graduate of Cambridge University (who prefers to remain anonymous) who was studying for an advanced degree in philosophy in London wrote the following to me:

> There's a series of private talks being given here under the auspices of Jews College/London School of Jewish Studies consisting of Modern Orthodox speakers. Last time we had Jacob Schacter and this time the Chief Rabbi, Jonathan Sacks. It's interesting that all the younger generation (most of whom have a reasonably wide education) are completely unimpressed by the positions and arguments being portrayed, but the older lot seem quite content with the level. It looks like our parents were happy saying "I think this far and no further" whereas my generation wants to think all the way.

89. In this book I often use the adjectives *unreasonable* and *implausible* interchangeably, although *unreasonable* has a somewhat stronger negative connotation than *implausible*. Someone who affirms a very implausible belief or theory (implausible because there is strong evidence or logical argument against it) can be called *unreasonable* for doing so. As I indicated earlier in this chapter, ideally, it would be useful to have some kind of objective, or at least semi-objective, scale for assessing the degree of plausibility or

implausibility of beliefs or assertions—as is indeed done with respect to beliefs or assertions in certain areas of psychology, philosophy, laws of evidence, and many academic disciplines. I haven't established such a scale for assessing the plausibility of believing in TMS versus MSPM (multiple source post-mosaic), even though I assume that these are meant to be statements about events or authorship whose degree of plausibility can be reasonably assessed. Proponents of MSPM are always assessing, even if only implicitly, the plausibility of competing explanations for the source of a Pentateuchal verse.

90. With respect to this claim, Barry Mesch, a historian of Jewish philosophy, wrote to me very thoughtfully as follows:

> The question one asks of adherents of a religious tradition which poses a conflict between the literal meaning of the sacred text(s) and the overall rationality of a system of beliefs also held by the believer can be understood as asking, "you live in your normal working life in a universe of discourse which views science, scientific evidence and rational discussion as the preferred way to reach conclusions about any questions about the nature of reality which may arise. It seems that when you come to religion and the Bible that you leave that universe of discourse and enter one which has a different set of rules. If one believes that the text of the Bible claims that God created the universe 5757 years ago or that God split the Red Sea, Joshua made the sun stand still, etc., where does the rationale for belief in these things come from? Clearly belief in these events would not stand up to the rational and scientific rigor which you would require for testing beliefs in every area outside of religion. Would one want to claim that these are in fact two ways of looking at the world—if so, how does one human being live in both worlds at the same time and how does one justify it?
>
> If the discourse about God and religion is different from that of science— what are the ways that it is different? Some philosophers have claimed that religious language is fundamentally different from scientific language in that it really makes no claim about reality (even though it looks like it does). In fact it is only stating a view that I hold and an attitude I have about the world (A. J. Ayer, *Language, Truth, and Logic*) but not a descriptive ontological claim. What constitutes evidence for the religious point of view? Is it subject to the same scientific analysis and judgment that would be required in the scientific universe of discourse? Falsifiability has been offered as a criterion for the scientific character of a proposition. It has been suggested that propositions found in religious discourse do not partake of this characteristic. Statements like God exists or even God created the universe really mean "There is a force which I believe in which is watching over me and which infuses the world with meaning, and my whole life reflects my belief that the world has meaning and my actions are not for naught." There is thus no way to present evidence that such a belief is false since it is based on my attitude towards the world.

91. Wasserman, *Kovetz Ma'amarim,* from http://www.shemayisrael.co.il/2001/elchonon.htm.

92. See Sternberg, 1997.

93. In all honesty I must admit that I feel a similar way, for example, about claims made by people in support of parapsychology, clairvoyance, and certain types of "alter-

native medicine," as well as claims in support of "hidden biblical codes." For the most part I do not bother to read the writings of people advocating the reality of these phenomena (except if I want to study the reason why people believe in them, rather than whether or not the claims are actually true), and dismiss them as nonsense, self-deception, or calculated deception. Some people consider me narrow-minded because I am reluctant to read about or consider the possibility that non-Western modes of medicine and healing might be more insightful into human physiological and psychological functioning, and their interrelationships, and more effective in "healing," than are "scientifically" based theories and practices. Am I any different from the respondent to my questions about belief in TMS who will ignore the arguments and evidence put forth by nonbelievers? I intuitively feel that I am more justified in ignoring such "evidence" than are believers in TMS who ignore biblical and other scholarship, but perhaps I am not.

Chapter 4

1. Grudem, 1999.

2. See Barr, 1977, 190–207, for a discussion of the implications of dispensationalism for fundamentalist premillenarian eschatology; and Boone 1989, 40–46, for its relationship to fundamentalist readings of apocalyptic biblical texts, such as the *Book of Revelation,* which are read not necessarily literally but "literalistically" and reach absurd heights (or depths).

3. Scofield, 1967, 3.

4. The Muslim concept of *abrogation* as an exegetical method for resolving contradictions in the Qur'an, as discussed in chapter 5, has some affinity with the exegetical use of dispensationalism by Christian fundamentalists.

5. Barr, 1977, 194–195.

6. See Boone, 1989, for an application of contemporary theories of literary analysis and principles of interpretation to fundamentalist readings and interpretations of the Bible, and the use of the "discourse of inerrancy" on the part of fundamentalist preachers, teachers, and theologians, to establish authority over the lives of believers. They do so ostensibly on the basis of the dictum that "the Bible says such and such," which must be true and must be obeyed, whereas the real source of the authority is the Bible *as interpreted by these leaders* who consciously or unconsciously obscure or camouflage the role that they play in wielding authority.

7. Cited in Barr, 1977, 243. See 243–245 for his analysis of the reasons for this approach to the story.

8. The commentator is Hugh Blair in *The New Bible Commentary Revised,* 1970.

9. Barr, 1977, 9. Barr wrote write another book, *Beyond Fundamentalism* (1984), with a more practical and pastoral goal of assisting individuals to resist or reject fundamentalism while embracing a nonfundamentalist Christianity.

10. In chapter 6, based on Marsden's (1991) analysis, I discuss the reasons for the rise and influence of "creation science" among some fundamentalists in the mid-twentieth century, even though many fundamentalists and evangelicals had already come to terms with a notion of "theistic evolution" shortly after the publication of Darwin's *On the Origin of Species* in 1859.

11. Barr, 1977, 46; see 40–89 and 235–259 for numerous examples and a harshly critical analysis of fundamentalist approaches to and interpretations of the Bible.

12. There are numerous websites and blogs devoted to pointing out the flaws and faults of Christian fundamentalism, which provide articles and essays (some sophisticated, others not so), testimonies from former fundamentalists, and links to related websites. See, for example, http://www.fundamentalists-anonymous.org and http://www.losingmyreligion.com.

13. For example, consigning, in their imaginations and preaching, most of mankind, past and present, to eternal damnation in the torture chambers of Hell.

14. Grudem, 1999, 33–39.

15. See Barr, 1977, 286–299, for a detailed analysis of "verbal inspiration" and the tangle of logical, textual, and theological problems it raises.

16. Some translations render the Greek "every scripture inspired by God," which differs significantly in its meaning from "all scripture is inspired by God," with the latter being the reading the fundamentalist needs in order to make his claim about the entire Bible.

17. Which itself need not necessarily be understood as "verbal inspiration" in the fundamentalists' sense, but that is how Grudem chooses to understand it. See Barr, 1977, mentioned above on "verbal inspiration."

18. Some philosophers argue that most, or even all, of our knowledge and assertions about "objective reality" are ultimately based on subjective experience, even the hard facts and most robust theories of chemists and physicists. Sensory experience, perception, and cognition are all aspects of our consciousness. Even the empirical and experimental verification of our scientifically based predictions are ultimately "subjective" in the sense that we only experience "reality out there" through our bodily organs and the consciousness that they generate. For example, the recordings of the scientific instruments that measure "reality" are something we *experience* in our consciousness. However, unlike subjective religious experiences, of which there are many different ones, making mutually exclusive claims about the ostensible divine "reality" to which they point or from which they derive, the subjective experiences of scientists, when they are engaged in scientific experimentation, measurement, and discourse are almost universally shared by fellow scientists. Scientists, and those who understand scientific methods, concepts, and theories (and all whose skills are derived from science), can predict and control the course of numerous (but far from all) natural events with a high degree of reliability and replicability, notwithstanding the subjectivity of their experience in arriving at their scientific conclusions. This makes it pragmatic for us to rely on them in leading and structuring our lives much more so than to rely on mutually exclusive religion-based assertions about reality (although to the extent that religions over thousands of years have accumulated wisdom and insight about human nature, they provide a useful and pragmatic source of guidance for human affairs).

19. These are as follows: not to murder, not to steal, not to commit adultery, not to commit idolatry, not to commit blasphemy, not to eat flesh from an animal that is still alive, and to establish courts of justice to enforce a just society. There are differences of opinion in medieval Jewish thought as to the status of a non-Jew who accepts and lives by these seven laws because he arrives at them solely by the exercise of reason rather than because he accepts that they were commanded by God in the Torah. One view would accord the former as well as the latter a "share in the world to come." A second view requires that all people accept these laws because they are commanded in the Torah, and

only then do they "earn" or become entitled to a share in the world to come. See Novak, 1983, on the seven Noahide laws.

20. See, for example, Luke chap. 24 and John chaps. 20 and 21.

21. See Kent, 1999, *The Psychological Origins of the Resurrection Myth*. Kent is a Unitarian minister. The blurb on the jacket, by Antony Flew, describes this book as "by far the most plausible of so far available hypotheses to explain the origin of the Christian Church." It is, however, only one of several possible psychological explanations for the New Testament accounts of the resurrection and sightings of Jesus, and the belief in Jesus' resurrection. See, for example, Ehrman's suggested explanation referred to in note 39.

22. The Discovery Institute is a leading force in the intelligent design movement and in attempts to have intelligent design theory taught in public school biology classes. Craig's publications pertain to other areas of interest to the Institute.

23. See, for example, Flew's interview with Gary R. Habermas at http://theroadtoem maus.org/RdLb/21PbAr/Apl/FlewTheist.htm (accessed September 26, 2007).

24. See Flew in Wallace, 2003. This volume includes analyses of the original debate by nine philosophers, as well as replies to them by Craig and Flew; see also Craig and Ehrman, 2006.

See also Robert Price's trenchant and sarcastic critiques of Craig and his fundamentalist evangelical colleagues from psychological, logical, and critical biblical/historical perspectives, in his books and articles, many of which are available at http://www.infidels.org (e.g., http://www.infidels.org/library/modern/robert_price/beyond_born_again/chap1.htmlat).

25. These are readily available in the sources noted above.

26. Wallace, 2003, 23.

27. See, for example, Levenson, 2006.

28. Kent, 1999, 115.

29. In a few biblical stories dead individuals were brought back to life, but the historical credibility of these narratives is dubious.

30. Wallace, 2003, 210–211.

31. Even in the "hard" sciences, we don't prove the "laws of nature" unequivocally but demonstrate only that based upon the facts in hand and the theories that organize and explain them, we can coherently account for all of the data, or predict that we will discover something and then do, or predict future events, which then occur. Any explanation for a phenomenon that is based upon induction is never "proven" to be true in an absolute sense because we might discover some phenomenon or event tomorrow that will be incompatible with our theory today. However, in the "hard" sciences the standards of "proof" and of "disproof" are significantly more rigorous in several ways than they are in the humanities and social sciences; hence scientific theories about nature have proven to be more reliable and stable than nonscientific ones.

32. What does it mean to personally experience the resurrection of Jesus? Did Craig see, hear, or touch Jesus? Perhaps he is not saying that he believes in the resurrected Jesus on the basis of experiencing the resurrected Jesus in the way described by the disciples in the New Testament but that his religious experiences, refracted through his belief in a resurrected Jesus (and its theological implications for him), reinforced his belief that Jesus was resurrected.

33. Craig and Ehrman, 2006. This and subsequent passages cited in my discussion of the Craig and Ehrman debate are taken from the online version of their debate transcript; thus, no page numbers are available.

34. If a belief is unreasonable (the determination of which depends on factors such as the individual's socialization and his cultural and intellectual setting) in the first place, then the motives for believing it have less to do with the force of reason than with other factors, such as social or emotional ones. If so, it is not hard to understand why "unreasonable" beliefs are tenacious, even more so than are reasonable ones, which are responsive to reasoned critiques of them.

35. An interesting question that needs further exploration is whether those who created such stories actually believed that they were historically true, or believed only that the story conveys a "true" religious message and the "historicity" of the "facts" reported in the story is not important, or knew that they were fabricating stories but believed that this was permissible if it served a desirable and noble objective, in this case converting others to faith in Jesus. Perhaps these distinctions in motivation and self-awareness and other possible psychological processes which transpired when the ancients created stories about divine beings, heroes, and saints, were not as clear and demarcated in the consciousness of first-century individuals as they might be to us.

36. Or at most only the few individuals about whom it is said in the Bible that they were resurrected.

37. One person commented on the debate between Craig on the one hand, and Flew and Ehrman on the other, as follows:

> One thing that strikes me as odd in this whole discussion is that no one mentions that Jesus is, according to Christian belief, God. If one accepts this idea, the fact that no one else has been raised from the dead is fairly irrelevant. Also, it is clear from the New Testament texts that the post-Resurrection body had some unique characteristics. No one recognizes the risen Christ at first sight, no matter how well they knew him before, and he apparently has the ability to walk through walls. I'm not putting forth an argument for the credibility of these beliefs, just wondering why anyone would care in this context that there is no precedent for such a resurrection.

I think that even if Craig believes that Jesus was not only resurrected but is himself God, because he is trying to convince people who do not share his beliefs, he has to build his case for the historicity of Jesus' resurrection on the kinds of evidence and argumentation that would appeal to them, which is what he indeed tries to do. He can't simply state that Jesus is God and therefore the fact that there is no precedent for resurrection is irrelevant to maintaining that Jesus was resurrected. Because Flew and Ehrman do not believe that Jesus is God, for them the argument that the resurrection is improbable depends in part on the fact that no one else has ever been raised from the dead.

38. In the course of his "proof," Craig also cited several New Testament scholars to support the three historical facts on which he based his argument. On this Ehrman (Craig and Ehrman, 2006) commented, "I should note that the majority of historians do not agree with Bill's conclusion . . . Having said that, I'm surprised by some of [the] so-called authorities that Bill cites, for the reality is that the majority of critical scholars studying the historical Jesus today disagree with his conclusion that a historian can show that the

body of Jesus emerged physically from the tomb. Bill might find that surprising, but that would be because of the context he works in—a conservative, evangelical seminary. In that environment, what he's propounding is what everyone believes."

On the selective and disingenuous use of scholarship by fundamentalists to support their own views, see Barr, 1977, 307–308. With respect to the style and presentation of much conservative polemical literature, he points out that the fundamentalist polemicist will often approvingly cite the view of nonfundamentalist, or nonreligious, scholars on a specific point or issue, but without indicating that these scholars repudiate the very position that the fundamentalist is upholding. This can, and often does, mislead the innocent lay reader, leading him to suppose that modern biblical scholarship on the whole accepts the fundamentalist doctrines. Honesty would require that after such citations, an annotation would be added: "The scholar just quoted would, of course, totally repudiate the whole conservative position advocated in this book." Kelemen, a Jewish biblical fundamentalist, in his *Permission to Receive,* and Hertz, as well, in his *Commentary on the Pentateuch,* use a similar technique. The *Artscroll* Jewish biblical fundamentalists, however, do not deign to quote, even in support of their views, a heretical biblical scholar, in their commentary on the *Chumash (Pentateuch)* and other volumes. First of all, those works are impure. Second of all, there is the danger that if their existence is acknowledged or their wisdom accessed, the innocent Jewish reader might actually decide to look at one of those heretical works and might, Heaven forbid, be influenced by it.

39. Ehrman then gives his own very detailed and quite plausible naturalistic explanation for the origin of the resurrection stories and for the experiences reported by Jesus' followers. If Craig-like Christian fundamentalists, or more realistically, those tending toward but not yet convinced of a fundamentalist reading of the New Testament, would seriously reflect upon Ehrman's, Kent's, and other nonmiraculous and nonliteral interpretations of the New Testament, they might reassess and reject the fundamentalist approach.

40. See Robert P. Prices's,1997 critique of fundamentalist Christians such as Craig.

41. See Barr, 1977, 317–328, who suggests a few psychological processes that might explain aspects of fundamentalism and fundamentalists while deliberately refraining from overemphasizing such an approach to understanding the phenomenon.

42. This section makes extensive use of chap. 5, "Fundamentalism among Religious Serpent-Handling Sects," from Hood, Hill, and Williamson, 2005.

43. James, *Varieties,* 1978 [1902], chap. 2.

44. The fact of the matter, however, is that no one ever relies "only on the text" because every text assumes some interpretation of it. Much, if not all, of those interpretations come from outside the text, even though the fundamentalist will either not realize this or, if he does, be loathe to admit it.

45. I think that Hood et al.'s (2005) concept of "intratextuality," though useful as a descriptive one, doesn't by itself provide sufficient explanatory power for understanding "the psychology of fundamentalism," the title of their book. Why do fundamentalists relate to the Bible "intratextually" in the first place? Is there any significant psychological difference between the commitment to "intratextuality" of someone who was raised as a fundamentalist and someone who became one voluntarily as an adult? What sustains the commitment to an "intratextual" approach to the Bible? Under what conditions will an "intratextualist" free himself from "intratextual" bondage to the text? Although Hood

et al. relate "intratextuality" to the human need for a meaning system and to a few other psychological concepts, and acknowledge that the "intratextuality" model is descriptive rather than explanatory, they give it more prominence than it deserves and neglect other psychological aspects of religious fundamentalism.

46. Collins, 1947, 1–2, quoted in Hood et al., 2005,117.

47. See Hood et al., ibid., 123, in which one minister tells a troubled inquirer that the serpent referred to in Mark 16 is a spiritual serpent, not a physical one. The serpent in the Garden of Eden, and elsewhere in the Bible, is understood to be either an actual evil being, an opponent of Yahweh, or a symbol of evil. Mark could mean that true believers in Jesus are those who struggle with evil and overcome it, and that overcoming evil is a sign that one is a true believer.

48. *Sand Mountain Homecoming Video,* 1998, quoted by Hood et al., 2005, 121. The reference to colleges is presumably to non-Pentecostal, fundamentalist Bible colleges with their focus on Bible study rather than on spiritual discernment by way of subjective religious experience.

49. I assume that there have been *some* serpent handlers who eventually came to the conclusion that the truth they once knew was not really true, but that probably has less to do with persuasion by way of argument and debate than with other factors. See http:// www.fundamentalists-anonymous.org/ for testimonies from many and varied former fundamentalists as to how they "recovered" from their fundamentalism. See the discussion of psychological and social explanations for fundamentalism in chapter 6 of this book. How fundamentalist beliefs can be undermined will be analyzed in depth in a sequel to this book.

50. Williamson, 1999, quoted in Hood et al., 2005.

51. The verse is most probably affirming that the serpent, or sea monster, well known in ancient Near Eastern and Israelite mythology as a powerful quasi-divine being, was himself created by God and hence is subservient to him.

52. The murderer might escape human justice but cannot escape divine justice. See a similar story in *Babylonian Talmud, Tractate Sanhedrin,* 1935, 37b.

53. Similarly, rabbinic midrash makers read many of their norms, values, and beliefs into biblical texts that modern biblical scholars do not see there. See Kugel, 2007.

54. Of course some, maybe most, Catholics and other Christians who practice the sacrament of the Eucharist do not believe that this "actually happens" in a material sense. But many have in the past, and many still do.

55. Hood et al., 2005, 131.

Chapter 5

1. More recently Ibn Warraq and other Muslim critics of Islam have gone public. In 2007 he was among the organizers of an important conference, the Secular Islam Summit.

2. Ibn Warraq, 2003 [1995], xiii, xiv.

3. See Hood et al., 2005, 155–182, for a discussion of the Islamic rationale for the fatwa against Rushdie, analyzed within the framework of their "intratextuality" versus "intertextuality" psychological explanation of fundamentalism. See a range of knowledgeable Muslim opinions and analyses with respect to how to deal with apostasy and blasphemy at http://www.islamonline.net/English/contemporary/2006/04/article01 .shtml.

Although modern Western democracies do not prohibit blasphemy or apostasy with respect to religious beliefs and behaviors (albeit with some anachronistic vestiges of blasphemy laws still on the books in some countries), they do have laws that prohibit certain kinds of speech, even when they pose no immediate danger to anyone. For example, in some countries or sections thereof, it is prohibited to advocate, by word or print, child pornography, holocaust denial, racism, or other "isms," even when by doing so there is no obvious immediate and direct threat to the life, limb, or property of anyone. Is this not analogous to religious prohibitions on blasphemy or public espousal of apostasy? (See Hood et al., 2005, 176–179.) However, none of these Western laws mandate a death penalty for their violation. In fact, most Western democracies (excluding among others, the United States) have outlawed capital punishment.

4. Heresy is much more sinful than licentiousness, alcohol, or gambling. After all, many members of the Saudi royal family are devout Wahhabists when it comes to "beliefs," even as they indulge in these "degenerate" and "corrupt" pleasures of the West as soon as they land in London, Paris, New York, or Las Vegas.

5. Lester, 1999.

6. See the multivolume *Encyclopaedia of the Qur'an*, 1999–2006, for a compendium of scholarship on the Koran and its history, and, specifically, Bowering's (1999) article "Chronology and the Qur'an" in it, in which he writes, "Finally, it may be necessary for scholarly research to espouse more unequivocally the view that Muhammad was not the mere mouthpiece of the Qur'an's proclamation but, as its actual historical human author, plays a major role in its collection and compilation" (335). The *Encyclopaedia* is a significant advance in applying the methods of modern scholarship to the study of the Koran, although overall it is somewhat timid in directly challenging traditional beliefs about its authorship.

7. R. Stephen Humphreys, cited by Lester, 1999.

8. "The elements of the biblical tradition included in the Qur'an echo themes found in the apocryphal and midrashic writings of Judaism and Christianity . . ." Bowering, 1999, 315.

9. Certain Muslim states, such as Saudi Arabia and Iran, and Islamic terrorist groups, such as Hamas in Palestine and Hezbollah in Lebanon, react to the existence and flourishing of the Jewish State of Israel, in the "Arab-Muslim" Middle East, and the displacement of many Arabs in 1948–1949 during the Israeli-Arab war with shame, envy, hatred, and religious arrogance. This displacement was primarily, though not exclusively, a result of Arab aggression, intransigence, and hatred of Jews in pre-1948 Palestine, and afterward, in the State of Israel, which of course the Arabs deny. They have exacerbated the historical Muslim derogation of Jews as low-status *dhimmis* into a virulent form of religiously motivated Islamic anti-Semitism approaching the level of Nazism. Can they acknowledge Islam's dependency on Judaism?

10. Jews who identify with the teachings of Rabbinic Judaism consider the Hebrew Bible to be holy, but not the New Testament or the Koran. Christians consider the Hebrew Bible to be holy, but superseded by the teachings of Jesus and Paul as recorded in the New Testament. They do not consider the Koran to be holy. Traditional Muslims consider only the Koran to be intrinsically holy, whereas the Hebrew Bible and the New Testament record some authentic revelations but are not holy. These views impact the way in which each tradition relates in word and behavior to the sacred texts of the other. The

modern, Western notion that one should be respectful of multiple religious traditions—
and sensitive to the religious feelings of those who do not share one's own beliefs—is
modern. In other words, the premodern world of religious polemic and behavioral norms,
for the most part, shows contempt for the scriptures and beliefs of the "other."

It is quite true, that there are many devout Muslims who sincerely preach and
practice tolerance and respect for the "other" and consider this attitude to be what is
taught and required by the Koran and Islam, and they can cite many texts to this effect.
See, for example, http://www.islamonline.net/servlet/Satellite?pagename=IslamOnline-
English-Ask_Scholar/FatwaE/FatwaE&cid=1119503544482. My criticism is not of
them, but of Muslims who do not show such respect for non-Muslims and their sacred
texts, be they Jews, Christians, Hindus, Buddhists, Baha'is, or secular humanists (who
have a "sacred" civil canon in the core texts of their political philosophy).

11. Wansbrough, 1977.

12. The scholarly study of the specifics of the natural cultural and literary processes
by which the Koran emerged is still subject to much contention and debate in the
academic community, but, as with modern critical biblical scholarship (Hebrew Bible
and New Testament), steady progress in evidence and understanding is being made.

13. This same tactic is used by fundamentalist Jewish and Christian fulminators
against modern biblical scholarship and threats from science.

14. The same, of course, applies to Muslim critiques of Judaism, Christianity, and
"Western values," mutatis mutandis. From the Muslim perspective, Judaism and
Christianity are inferior to Islam, and Muslim societies at various historical periods either
dominated Jews and Christians in their midst or perceived Judaism and Christianity as
threats to the real or desired hegemony of Islam. See Buruma and Margalit, 2004.

15. As we have seen earlier, however, many traditionalists of all religions base their
beliefs on "faith" even if the faith-based beliefs are contradicted by "reason" or science.
For them, faith trumps reason as a basis for religious commitments, for interpreting
history and reality, and in the extreme, for the ways in which the world is perceived and
experienced.

16. Manzoor, 1987.

17. Leo Strauss made a similar point about the a priori denial on the part of secular
scholars, of the possibility of divine revelation, with respect to biblical and Judaic claims
that the Torah was divinely revealed. See p. 92, for Jonathan Sacks's reference to this; and
Samuelson, 2002.

18. Akyol, 2005.

19. The most reliable estimates of the Muslim population of the United States (e.g.,
that of the Pew Research Center, 2007, *Muslim Americans*) put it at approximately 2.5
million individuals (although several Muslim organizations tendentiously cite higher
numbers), which is less than 1 percent of the U.S. population. Although the Muslim
population is growing at a high rate, it still constitutes a tiny percentage of the total U.S.
population. Is it not, then, paranoia to be worried about Muslim influence and power in
the United States? I don't believe that radical Muslims and radical Muslim groups in the
United States *at present* constitute a serious political danger. However, let us recall that
many totalitarian and fascist ideologies began with a small number of adherents and
eventually grew to the point of dominating the societies in which they had established
themselves. Moreover, such groups can affect politics insidiously, especially if they ac-

quire wealth to influence the political arena. They could use their wealth in legal ways to support politicians and political positions that are antidemocratic. It is critical to nip such groups in the bud and expose their views to public scrutiny and public critique, rather than to ignore them. We should also keep in mind that according to the Pew survey some 28 percent of U.S. Muslims support suicide bombings, with a higher percentage in younger age groups. You don't need too many terrorist suicide (or more accurately, homicide) bombers to sow destruction and instability in our society.

20. Goodstein, 2006.

21. Some evolutionary psychologists might not have a problem coming up with such a justification for gender differences in the law of adultery, based upon genetic differences in the sexual needs and desires of men and women and the functions served by mating and marriage. Some anthropologists might also suggest good reasons for the fact that many cultures outlaw polyandry but permit polygyny (including biblical and rabbinic culture/law), and the gender differences in the law of adultery in these societies probably logically derive from the fact that a man is permitted to have more than one wife whereas a woman is prohibited from having more than one husband.

22. In a sobering remark, an editor at Oxford University Press wrote the following to me:

> You can advocate honest critiques of religion in the schools, but in practice it can't be done. OUP published a world religions text that was adopted by the California school system and it has been the subject of endless protest, petitions, and litigation because some Hindus don't like the way in which Hinduism is described, or rather they don't approve of non-Hindus writing about it. Also, the Sikhs objected to the portrait of Guru Nanak we chose to illustrate it with and we agreed to replace it with something more "devotional." This has been going on for at least three years now. California was very nearly prevented from adopting the text at all.

This is all the more reason for academics to double their efforts in challenging such attempts at stifling the teaching of religion(s) from a scholarly perspective, at least in public schools.

23. Does democracy advocate or promise a compassionate society? Perhaps not explicitly. However, the religious and other ideological freedoms, which democracy protects, provide space for religious and other worldviews to advocate for and contribute to making our civil society not only just, but compassionate as well. Islam has within it many values and teachings that promote compassion, as well as justice, and can play a significant role in enhancing these in both the private and the public domain. See my article "Developing an Internet-Based Trialogue on Peace and Reconciliation in Judaic, Christian, and Islamic Thought" (Schimmel, 2006).

24. With the globalization of communications through the Internet and other technological advances, many Muslims who live in closed and authoritarian societies will also be able to access critical debates about Islam and the fruits of contemporary scholarship. We should be doing what we can to facilitate and promote this access. Creative and conventional ways to do so will be discussed in a sequel to this book.

25. For a brief discussion of Muslim attitudes toward women and wife beating and diverse interpretations of the relevant Koranic verses by different commentators, see Cook, 2000, 37–40; 104–105.

26. Fundamentalist Jews and Christians exposed to the challenges of modernity to their beliefs respond in similar ways. First there is resistance to exposure through either self-isolation or active suppression and censorship of threatening works and ideas. When that is not effective, and the challenging ideas are encountered, one or another of the three responses usually occurs. It is difficult to predict which exposed believer will retrench with even greater dogmatism and fanaticism, which will jettison the faith, and which will opt for reinterpretation and integration, and it is important that research be conducted to try to ascertain this. See chapter 6 of this book.

27. In summarizing and paraphrasing Ibn Warraq's points, I add to or explicate them.

28. Ibn Warraq, 2003 [1995], 111, quoting Noldeke.

29. The same can be said of Judaism and Christianity.

30. Cook, 2000, 47.

31. Goldziher, 1981 [1910], 63–64.

32. Cook, 2000, 47.

33. Ibn Warraq himself, following the view of David Hume, maintains that polytheism is actually more plausible than monotheism.

34. Ibn Warraq, 2003, 119. As we have already seen, these attitudes are characteristic of fundamentalist Christianity as well.

35. Some Muslim interpreters of the Koran explain that these descriptions of the punishments of nonbelievers and sinners are metaphors that are not to be understood literally. For example, Ali (2002) interprets Sura 14: 49–50, "And thou wilt see the Sinners that day bound together in fetters; their garments of liquid pitch, and their faces covered with Fire, that God may requite each soul according to its deserts..." to mean "[T]he fetters will be their evil actions, thoughts, and motives, which they cannot shake off as they could have shaken them off by repentance and amendment while there was yet time and opportunity to do so... the metaphor of fetters is now changed to that of pitch, which darkens and sets on fire the soul of man" (633). However, many Muslims, both scholars and surely nonscholars, understand these verses literally and believe that the God whom they venerate and worship is a harsh, punitive, torturer of nonbelievers. He is meting out justice to them—they are getting what they deserve. Of course, this Muslim conception of a punitive, sadistic God is not exclusive to Islam; other religions have similar notions about how their gods or God will deal with sinners and nonbelievers. It seems that many people find it satisfying to project their hatreds and vengeful and sadistic impulses on to their deities. It wouldn't be so bad if these projections made the people themselves less sadistic in their own behaviors, and maybe sometimes that is the psychological impact of these imaginations of punishments to come on our enemies. We can leave it to God or to Allah to exact punishment in due time, so we do not have to act out our own hostile impulses. Unfortunately, however, as I suggest in the text, sometimes sacred scriptures can model, inspire, and justify the very brutal attitudes and behaviors that are ascribed to God at some future eschatological era of judgment, in the here and now of human interactions.

36. Later Muslim traditions do attribute numerous miracles to Muhammad.

37. This is a commonly used method of resolving apparent contradictions in laws that appear in a single code. It was highly developed in Talmudic literature as one of several means of resolving contradictions between biblical laws. Muslim Koranic com-

mentators use the same approach. Sometimes it results in a plausible harmonization of contradictory texts, but often it is far-fetched. Moreover, it requires many more explanations—each contradiction requiring a "local" harmonization—than the more parsimonious explanation for the contradictions, namely, that the Torah and the Koran are composite compositions. The "editors" (or perhaps a less formal process of textual accrual and consolidation), for religious or other reasons, did not feel it proper or necessary to eliminate the contradictions by "smoothing out" the various texts that were being combined into a single work. The harmonization by contextualization approach is also used to reconcile contradictions in biblical and Koranic narratives. This is done in rabbinic midrash and Toraitic commentary and in Islamic Hadith and Koranic commentary.

38. See also "Harun Yahya: An Invitation to the Truth," at http://www.harunyahya.com/index.php.

39. See Goldziher, 1981 [1910], 92–93.

40. See Edis, 2007, for the difficulty that classical Islam has in harmonizing science with Islam.

41. See the section on faith and reason, and the interview with Dr. Bruno Guiderdoni, at http://www.islamonline.net/English/Science/FaithSciences/Scientificmiraclesin Quran/2006/06/01.shtml.

42. Ibrahim, 1997, 4.

43. *Aloqah* has been variously translated as "a clinging form," "a blood clot," "a leech," and "a suspended thing."

44. Also translated as "a chewed substance."

45. Haleem, 2004, 214.

46. A similar argument in defense of the belief in resurrection is found in much earlier Jewish sources. See *Babylonian Talmud, Tractate Sanhedrin,* 90b-91a, where a heretic asks, how can a clod of earth, which the human body reverts to after death, become alive? The response is that if God can create life from a liquid, in other words, semen, surely he can create it from clay, because a potter who makes vessels from water is more skilled than a potter who makes them from clay.

47. Musallam, 1983, 54. See also Needham, 1959, 82, who concludes that what the Koran has to say about embryology is but an echo of Greek and Indian science and teachings.

48. Haleem, 2004, translated it as "lump of flesh."

49. Citing Keith L. Moore and T. V. N. Persaud, 1993, 8.

50. Ibrahim, 1997, 8–9, quoting Professor Keith Moore from videotaped remarks at a conference in Saudi Arabia. For the full description of the alleged correspondence between the Koranic description of the stages of embryonic development and modern embryological knowledge, see pages 6–11, and the Web site referred to there, http://www.islam-guide.com/truth. The website expands upon the themes of the printed Guide.

51. See "Proving the Qur'an Is the Word of God," at http://www.islamonline.net/servlet/Satellite?pagename=IslamOnline-English-AAbout_Islam/AskAboutIslamE/Ask AboutIslamE&cid=1123996016306.

52. The ideological/intellectual struggle against fundamentalist Islam needs to be waged on several fronts, and use of the electronic mass media and the Internet is more effective than books published by an academic press. However, there might be a few

Muslims who read this book, and other books that question the fundamentals of their fundamentalism, who perhaps will be influenced by what I and others write, and reconsider their beliefs and derivative behaviors, and those of the fundamentalist community with which they identify.

53. See Gold, 2004. It was disturbing to read that in 2006 there were more students from Saudi Arabia admitted to the United States to study in our universities than were here in 2001, the year in which a group of Saudi terrorists (some of whom were students) murdered almost three thousand innocent people on 9/11. The arguments in defense of admitting Saudi students are that the government of Saudi Arabia is itself a victim of Islamic terror and our partner in combating it; that the best way to increase appreciation of American values on the part of Saudis is by exposing them to our values by having them study at our educational institutions; that the Saudis are loyal friends of the United States; and that we, or at least our European and Japanese friends, need Saudi oil.

However, the terror that the Saudis have experienced is in part a boomerang result of their preaching Wahhabi antipathy toward the West, and hence toward the Saudi government itself, which cooperates with the West on business and military ventures. I doubt that this justifies referring to them as loyal friends. A more apt description would be that the United States and Saudi Arabia have certain mutual business and strategic interests that some people in both governments feel overrides the fundamental chasm between our values and theirs. As far as exposure to American values such as religious freedom, gender equality, cultural pluralism, and tolerance of non-Muslims, perhaps some Saudi students might adopt a more positive attitude toward us that will attenuate somewhat the antipathy toward the West in which they have been nurtured in their Muslim educations back home. Perhaps it might be a worthwhile idea for us to consider in our policy of granting visas to foreign students that those who come from countries such as Saudi Arabia, which are nondemocratic, should be required to take a course prior to their being granted a visa, via distance education, on the fundamental political, civic, and social values of the American ethos and on the nature of American democracy, or that they be required to take such a course within the first year of their studies in the United States. Such a course should not be an exercise in propaganda, but a serious, academically sound course, which will, in its very essence, demonstrate the freedom we have to choose and to criticize our government, and reasons why we take pride in the principles of our Constitution, even though we do not always live up to its ideals. The logistics of who would offer such a course as a prerequisite to the right to study here would need to be worked out between the Department of State and various universities or colleges.

54. I do not worry that a fundamentalist Muslim embryologist or obstetrician who was trained in and practices Western medicine will discard what he has learned and instead provide care for a developing embryo based upon presumed Koranic medical knowledge. Neither Ibrahim nor Professor Moore are advocating this—they are not rejecting modern medicine but are rather saying that Muhammad was informed by God of that which modern medicine has only recently learned. There are, of course, some Muslims who would reject modern medicine in favor of traditional medicine if they believed the traditional modes of healing were derived from the divine wisdom of the Koran and the Hadith. After all, even a Harvard Medical School education can't compete with Allah and Muhammad. Such Muslims might be dangerous to themselves and to their families, but they would not be licensed to practice medicine in the United States.

55. El Fadl, 2001/2002.

56. Ibid. See also El Fadl (2003a; 2003b), which include his article, the responses to his article, and his reply to the respondents. With respect to the moral responsibility of the interpreter of a sacred text, El Fadl (2001/2002) writes the following:

> Ultimately, the Qur'an, or any text, speaks through its reader. This ability of human beings to interpret texts is both a blessing and a burden. It is a blessing because it provides us with the flexibility to adapt texts to changing circumstances. It is a burden because the reader must take responsibility for the normative values he or she brings to the text. Any text, including those that are Islamic, provides possibilities for meaning, not inevitabilities. And those possibilities are exploited, developed and ultimately determined by the reader's efforts—good faith efforts, we hope—at making sense of the text's complexities. Consequently, the meaning of the text is often only as moral as its reader. If the reader is intolerant, hateful, or oppressive, so will be the interpretation of the text.
>
> It would be disingenuous to deny that the Qur'an and other Islamic sources offer possibilities of intolerant interpretation. Clearly these possibilities are exploited by the contemporary puritans and supremacists. But the text does not command such intolerant readings. Historically, Islamic civilization has displayed a remarkable ability to recognize possibilities of tolerance, and to act upon these possibilities. Islamic civilization produced a moral and humanistic tradition that preserved Greek philosophy, and generated much science, art, and socially benevolent thought. Unfortunately, however, the modern puritans are dissipating and wasting this inspiring moral tradition. They are increasingly shutting off the possibilities for a tolerant interpretation of the Islamic tradition.

57. El Fadl, 2003b.

58. El Fadl's reading and interpretation of the classical Islamic sources has been challenged by religious Muslims, secularized Muslims, and non-Muslims as not accurately reflecting the views of those sources.

59. As I have already pointed out, the same approach, of course, applies to those fundamentalist Christians who would impose their biblically based beliefs and norms on nonbelievers. It would be desirable or even necessary to undermine their core beliefs that the Bible is inerrant divine revelation and universally authoritative. In the United States, ultra-Orthodox fundamentalist Jews, a miniscule percentage of the population, have minimal influence outside of their relatively self-contained communities and for the most part do not try to impose their views on those outside of their own communities.

60. Would the proof be affected by the brand or type of gum chewed—for example, regular or bubble gum? Where is the tail on a chewed piece of gum that corresponds to the tail of an embryo? Where are the similarities in a chewed piece of gum to the emerging organs in the embryo? I can imagine a satire "documenting" this demonstration and proof for the divine origin of the Koran. Unfortunately, the satirists might be endangering their lives because although it is permitted and even meritorious, according to the teachings of *some* fundamentalist Muslims, to mock, condemn, attack, and kill Christians, Jews, Hindus, Buddhists, and infidels, it is, in their view, blasphemy for a Muslim or a non-Muslim to mock Islam or show disrespect to the

Koran or to Mohammed, a sin punishable by death by lynching or other forms of murder. Critics of Islam in the United States and in Canada, such as Asra Q. Nomani, Wafa Sultan, and Irshad Manji, have received death threats.

61. Ali, 2002; Haleem, 2004.

62. Hippocratic Writings, 1983, 317. See "Scientific Errors and the Myth of Embryology in the Koran," at http://www.bible.ca/islam/islam-myths-embryology.htm, for Christian attempts to discredit the Koran and Islam, one approach of which is to point out the errors in Koranic scientific or medical statements. Although I do not share the motives of such Christian critiques, they often provide useful information in refutation of, and arguments against, the claims and beliefs of Islam. Similarly, there are numerous Muslims who devote time, energy, and resources to discredit Christianity. As someone who believes in neither Islam nor Christianity (nor fundamentalist Judaism), I can benefit from the efforts of these antagonists against each other without sharing their motives, which is to validate their own religious beliefs.

63. Ibrahim, 1997, 11–13.

64. Dr. Alfred Kroner, as cited in Ibrahim, 1997, 14, 16.

65. We find a similar strategy among Jewish and Christian scientists who are fundamentalists, who will try to squeeze scientific facts or theories into nonscientific texts, such as Genesis 1.

66. Mormonism, too, whether understood to be a sect of Christianity or a separate religion, is replete with irrational claims and beliefs. The fact that it is a fast-growing religion tells us nothing about its "truth value" but much about the emotional and meaning functions served by religions, and the fragility of reason.

67. In his paper comparing the haredi educational institution known as the "yeshiva" or "bes medrash" with the Muslim educational institution known as the "madrasa"—"medrash" and "madrasa" share a common Semitic root—Heilman (1995) analyzes the ideological, theological, and pedagogic similarities between the two.

68. Rabbi Aharon Feldman, Rosh Yeshiva of Ner Israel Talmudical Academy in Baltimore, one of the leading institutions of "right-wing" Orthodox Judaism in America. See Yehuda Gellman, "A Response to Rabbi Aharon Feldman's 'The Slifkin Affair: Issues and Perspectives,'" at http://www.zootorah.com/controversy/Gellman%20Response.doc.

69. Ibid.

70. Ibid.

71. Ben-Zvi (pseudonym), "A Response to Rabbi Aharon Feldman's Article, 'The Slifkin Affair: Issues and Perspectives,'" p. 23, http://www.zootorah.com/controversy/Feldman,%20Rav%20Aharon,%20Second%20Version%20Response.rtf (retrieved September 30, 2007).

72. Haleem, 2004.

73. Ibrahim, 1997, 32–33.

74. "Reading Islam: Muhammad and the Message," at http://www.islamonline.net/servlet/Satellite?pagename=IslamOnline-English-AAbout_Islam/AskAboutIslamE/AskAboutIslamE&cid=1123996016306).

75. Ali, 2002, 1763n 6213. On the other hand, Abdel Haleem, who translates the verse as, "We shall drag him by his forehead—his lying, sinful forehead," explains that the dragging will take place in Hell, and justifies his preference for "forehead" rather than "forelock" by noting that it is the sinner's head that is sinful, not his forelock. Although

Haleem might not appreciate poetic license to the extent that Ali does, he doesn't get into the inner anatomy of the brain as does Ibrahim.

Chapter 6

1. Boyer, 2001, 277–279.
2. Ibid., 4–33.
3. In the case of Jesus' first disciples, although they hadn't been socialized from infancy to belief in Jesus as a Messiah, they had been socialized as Jews from infancy to believe in and expect a messiah, and Jesus was initially incorporated into the traditional Pharisaic belief system to which they were deeply committed. Rather than give up the whole system when he was crucified, they reinterpreted it. Many of the first disciples continued to practice Judaism after the crucifixion and to simultaneously believe in the resurrection and the imminent return of Jesus.
4. Festinger et al., 1956.
5. Naturally, there are many instances of Orthodox families, schools, and communities in which Orthodoxy is not functioning as it ideally claims it is or should be. See, for example, Davidman, 2007; Margolese, 2005; Winston, 2005. There are now many blogs, often anonymous, that discuss disillusionment with Orthodox Judaism and a proliferation of books and articles on this subject being published in the United States and in Israel, in Hebrew.
6. See Sachs, 2006, for some descriptions and statistics of contemporary human suffering. Add to poverty the wars throughout the globe, in which innocents are tortured and slaughtered by the hundreds of thousands. For the responses of Holocaust survivors to the teachings and doctrines of traditional, Orthodox Judaism, see, for example, Brenner, 1990. See also Katz, 2007, for the impact of the holocaust on Jewish theology.
7. Evans-Pritchard, 1937, 329–330; 338–339.
8. Some recent studies (challenged by others) claim that there is empirical evidence that prayer by one person on behalf of another, even when the latter is unaware that the former has prayed for him, can be efficacious. For the most part, however, religious people do not look for scientific studies to corroborate their belief in the efficacy of prayer but justify their praying by appealing to other reasons or explanations for it, or to anecdotal evidence of its efficacy. For example, "As [General George S. Patton's] armored columns rolled into Belgium in December 1944, rain and snow slowed the advance and gave the enemy cover. Patton ordered his chaplain to write a prayer for good weather. The skies cleared for eight straight days; American air power decimated the Nazis. Patton gave his chaplain a Bronze Star." *Newsweek,* May 7, 2007, p. 36.
9. Horton, 1970, 162.
10. See Dennett, 2006, 227–228. One critic of Dennett pointed out that "Dennett misunderstands the doctrine of transubstantiation. It is based on Aristotelean physics. The 'substance' of the bread and wine is changed into the 'substance' of the body and blood of Christ but the 'accidents' of bread and wine are preserved. There can be no possibility of detecting any 'outward signs' of the blood—no question of the presence of 'hemoglobin.'" She rightly concludes, "Not that this makes the doctrine more plausible, but one should understand what one is ridiculing. (I'm not suggesting that the average Catholic understands this either.)"

Although Dennett should have known better, the point that he is making, that the affirmation that one believes in a doctrine is more important for many people than their actually understanding of and belief in the content of the doctrine per se, is applicable, at least for those Catholics who are not familiar with the rather complex and subtle metaphysical and theological nuances of the doctrine of transubstantiation. Moreover, the doctrine of transubstantiation as understood by the most sophisticated of Catholic theologians cannot be confirmed or disconfirmed empirically, but must be accepted on faith:

> The principal aim of speculative theology with regard to the Eucharist, should be to discuss philosophically, and seek a logical solution of, three apparent contradictions, namely:
>
> (a) the continued existence of . . . the outward appearances of bread and wine, without their natural underlying subject (accidentia sine subjecto);
>
> (b) the spatially uncircumscribed, spiritual mode of existence of Christ's Eucharistic Body (existentia corporis ad modum spiritus);
>
> (c) the simultaneous existence of Christ in heaven and in many places on earth (multilocatio)." (The Catholic Encyclopedia, 1913, http://www.newadvent.org/cathen/05573a.htm#3 [retrieved September 18, 2007])

Resolving apparent logical contradictions in a doctrine does not, however, mean that it can be empirically tested.

11. See Babylonian Talmud, Tractate Sanhedrin, 37b.

12. Paul Helm, in Faith and Reason, 293, summarizing the views of the logical positivist A. J. Ayer, as argued in Ayer's book Language, Truth, and Logic..

13. J. H. M. Beattie, 1970, 264–265, notes that many traditional African cultures are aware of alternative beliefs to their own. It is more accurate to speak of degrees of closedness or openness to alternatives than of a dichotomy of "closed" and "open."

14. Evans-Pritchard, Witchcraft, quoted by Horton, 1970, 194.

15. Horton, 1970, 163.

16. Evans-Pritchard, 1937, 338.

17. The Tower of Babel story is an account of the origin of different but related Semitic languages which, of course, is not how modern linguists account for the phenomenon. See Kugel, 2007, 86.

18. Horton, 1970, 163–164.

19. David Shatz, personal communication.

20. Shatz clarified for me his view on pragmatism and truth in further communications between us:

> You assume a dichotomy between pragmatically motivated belief and truth, and imply that my approach neglects truth in the name of pragmatic benefits. This I think misstates the point of my pragmatic approach. The point is that as seen in the case of common sense beliefs our criteria of truth include pragmatic considerations . . . truth is not always based on evidence. The American pragmatists were I think very clear on this point: the criteria for truth are pragmatic, and indeed truth is defined in pragmatic terms.

21. See citation from Fox on page 53.

22. Shatz, in Morris, 1994, 273.

23. See M. Berger, 1998, for a philosophical analysis of traditional claims for rabbinic authority.

24. It would not be difficult to write a paper on the tenacity of this unreasonable belief as well, in the light of modern scholarly studies of the development of rabbinic literature and rabbinic beliefs.

25. See my article, Schimmel, 2004. On violence and warfare in the Bible, see Niditch, 1995.

26. The recently established modern Orthodox Rabbinical School Yeshivat Chovevei Torah is more open to a direct engagement with contemporary challenges to Orthodox doctrines, but still retains its basic commitment to them. The Union for Traditional Judaism, an offshoot of the Conservative movement, straddles the fence with respect to biblical scholarship, as can be seen in these two mutually exclusive principles it adopts:

The Jewish tradition teaches that:

... God revealed Torah to Israel (torah min hashamayim[Torah from Heaven]), and Torah—both written and oral—as transmitted and interpreted by our sages, from Sinai down through the generations, authoritatively expresses the will of God for the Jewish People.

Free and Open Inquiry with Intellectual Honesty—(Yosher Da'at). It is a sacred imperative to apply our God-given intellect and abilities to any and all fields of human endeavor in order to better understand and appreciate our universe. Our quest for all forms of knowledge, when carried out with a sense of awe at the wisdom of God's creation, is a religious act. Since the universe and Torah issue from the same Source, they must each be understood in light of the other. We must therefore strive to deepen our understanding of Torah in the context of God's creation. Thus we utilize all available methods and all potentially relevant disciplines in interpreting the sacred texts of our tradition. Intellectual honesty requires that we seriously consider new discoveries in any field of knowledge in our search for new meanings (hiddushim) in Torah; but intellectual honesty also requires that we recognize the fallibility of our human perceptions and the limitations of our methodologies. This recognition keeps us from drawing conclusions which contradict any of the ... beliefs stated above. (http://www.utj.org/principles.html)

Are "free and open inquiry with intellectual honesty" compatible with the commitment not to contradict the belief in Torah min Hashamayim as defined above? I don't think so.

27. See, for example, Rosenak, 2003 and 1983, on indoctrination and on teaching Bible in Jewish education. See also Philip Roth's short story "The Conversion of the Jews" in *Goodbye Columbus,* and Shalom Auslander's *Beware of God.*

28. Israel Chait, "Torah from Sinai," http://www.ybt.org/essays/rchait/torahsinai.html (retrieved October 2, 2007).

29. I am indebted to Dr. Theo Dagi for his substantial contribution to this discussion of attitudes toward truth. Dagi, after reading an early draft of a section of this book, which dealt with Orthodox Judaism and its attitudes toward truth and "truth seeking," expanded on this theme in a personal communication, with a detailed classification of

different attitudes toward truth, some of which I had explicitly or implicitly addressed. I have found Dagi's classification very useful and have modified and elaborated upon it here. It is applicable to many aspects of Christian and Muslim fundamentalists' attitudes to truth as well.

30. Theo Dagi's original list, upon which I expand, is set off from the main text as display type in italics.

31. Boyer, 2001, 320–322.

32. Theo Dagi.

33. Baruch Schwartz writes the following:

The halakhic lifestyle derives primarily from the belief that the Oral Law has some sort of divine sanction, and from a choice to devote one's life to serving God. Socially and anthropologically, especially in traditional circles, the halakhic lifestyle derives from a loyalty to community and family tradition . . . *Dispelling* the notion that faith and practice are adversely affected by discarding belief in TMS *ought to be* an attractive option and indeed a desideratum for enlightened orthodoxy. Confronted by the evidence for MSPM, orthodox thinkers *ought to* rush to explain why commitment to halakhah is not affected by it. Instead, attempts to do this are resisted, and instead energies are exerted on "disproving" or at least disallowing MSPM . . . [R]ejecting TMS doesn't necessarily imply a rejection of the *content* of the Torah . . . [I]t is important to distinguish between abandoning the belief in TMS and abandoning the belief that the Torah is some form of record of revelation and that its content is divinely inspired.(personal communication)

In response to a questioner who fears that accepting modern biblical scholarship undermines serious commitment to the halakhic system, James Kugel writes as follows:

. . . it is simply not true that the whole system of halakhah depends on the words of the Torah. Those words were the starting-point, but what has truly proven determinative in them . . . was the general direction that those words point in and embody, and whose trajectory was then carried forward through the Mishnah and Gemara and all later writings. That "general direction" is the basic idea that Israel's connection to God is to be articulated through avodat H' [worship of/ service to God]. This is the whole substance of the Sinai revelation . . . What would happen if someone could demonstrate definitively that God had truly given only one commandment to Moshe at Mount Sinai, the one in Deuteronomy that says: "You shall serve the Lord your God with your whole heart and soul." Then He said to Moshe: "Okay, you and the zeqenim [the "elders"] and their later successors can work out the details." . . . Of course I do believe in nevu'ah, in divine revelation, and I don't think that Israel got only that one commandment from God. Theoretically, however, I think it would be enough if that were all, since that would provide the firm basis for everything that followed—Moshe's, or Rabbi Akiva's, elaboration of how this primal divine commandment is to be carried out . . . This is the whole idea of Judaism. If you want to come close to God, the only way is to become His employee . . . I think that modern scholarship does not, because it cannot, undermine the essence of Judaism or what Jews actually do in their lives; it cannot, as you suggest, cause the system to collapse. (Kugel, 2007, Web site)

34. Theo Dagi. See note 29.

35. See Hinde, 1999, especially chap. 17, pp. 207–232.

36. Ross, 2004a; 2004b.

37. See quote from Sternberg on p. 63–64.

38. These defensive strategies are not unique to the defense of religious beliefs, but are employed in defense of any challenges to what Hinde calls the self-system.

39. The author may, however, be guilty of deception, although he believes that his "ends" of protecting the "vulnerable" faithful flock justifies the "means" of censorship. I don't think that Kelemen or the authors of the *ArtScroll* commentaries on the Bible are being maliciously deceptive, but just paternalistically, or self-righteously, or arrogantly deceptive.

40. See Baruch Schwartz's comment in note 33.

41. I personally do not find the views of Heschel, Jacobs, Kugel, Schwartz, and Ross about the divinity of either the Torah, or parts thereof, or of the rabbinic interpretations and elaborations of it to be convincing.

42. Hinde, 1999, 214.

43. Some of these functions served by religion can, of course, have very negative consequences, for believers and for others. Indeed, some argue that overall, religion has been, and still is, more detrimental to human welfare than advantageous to it. For example, in recent decades Islamic radicalism and its manifestations in terrorism have brought (and threaten to bring even more) pain, suffering, and oppression to millions of people. However, it is not useful to try to assess the effects of "religion" in general, because there are so many varieties of religion (including Islam), and of religious people, and of sociocultural contexts in which religion is practiced. One needs to look at very specific manifestations of a religion and assess its particular impact on human welfare in its particular historical or contemporary setting. For a very negative view of the Abrahamic religions, see, for example, Sam Harris, 2005, and Richard Dawkins, 2006.

My own view is that some versions of the Abrahamic religions have made, do make, and can continue to make significant positive contributions to human welfare. Their negative features, however, of which, unfortunately there are many, have to be exposed and vigorously combated. For their positive contributions, and the potential for such, see, for example, my books *The Seven Deadly Sins* and *Wounds Not Healed by Time.* See also David Sloan Wilson's *Darwin's Cathedral.* Wilson argues that religions have evolved and thrived because, overall, they provide many positive benefits to humans. They have contributed to group survival and to the development of adaptive moral and ethical systems.

44. See Spilka et al., 2003, 129–143; Altemeyer and Hunsberger, 1997; Bar Lev and Shaffir, 1997; Bromley, 1988.

45. In a sequel to this book I will discuss how these factors can be developed into tactics and strategies to undermine dangerous religious beliefs—to "defundamentalize fundamentalists." The first and most respectful approach to "defundamentalizing fundamentalists" is to try to understand the logic and rationale of their beliefs, and respectfully engage them with reason in order to persuade them that their beliefs are false or wrong. Such a project would also require examination of personality traits that might

be correlated with cognitive and/or emotive rigidity, and how such rigidity might be attenuated.

46. See Rabbi Benzion Sorotzkin, "The Role of Parents in the Current Crisis of Rebellious Adolescents," http://www.rabbihorowitz.com/PYes/ArticleDetails.cfm?Book_ ID=872&ThisGroup_ID=261; Margolese, 2005; Bar-Lev and Shaffir, 1997.

47. The advantage of retaining a nonfundamentalist religion, or even a fundamentalist but nonviolent version of the same religion, is that it retains many of the values and institutional structures of the society. It is less disruptive emotionally and socially than jettisoning a religion entirely.

48. Can this work, or does it not usually backfire and in fact increase religious zeal? Coercion might prevent overt religious behaviors (and even that doesn't always work because some religious fundamentalists seek martyrdom), but it is harder to suppress or eliminate thoughts merely by external coercion.

49. Marsden, 1991, 153–181. Some of the elements of Marsden's analysis are incorporated in my earlier chapter on Christian fundamentalism. Here I provide a more expanded summary of Marsden's analysis of the historical-cultural context of one specific manifestation of that phenomenon, "creation-science."

There are "creation-scientists" in fundamentalist Judaism and Islam. There are also fundamentalist Jews (and Muslims) who are "theistic evolutionists," such as Hertz in his commentary on the Pentateuch, Rabbi Abraham Issac Kook, and most modern Orthodox Jews. See the methodologically and conceptually flawed, but interesting, article by Nussbaum in *Skeptic Magazine* about modern Orthodox college students who deny evolution (http://www.skeptic.com/the_magazine/featured_articles/v12n03_Orthodox_ judaism_and_evolution.html). Some haredi (ultra-Orthodox) Jews also have made their peace with a theistic notion of evolution.

50. Marsden, 1991, 156; 156n7.

51. Miller et. al, 2006, 765–766.

52. Kraus, 2006.

53. Interestingly, some evangelical scientists have suggested that the traditional Christian understanding of the nature and functions of the "soul" need to be drastically revised in light of contemporary scientific understandings of neurology and its relationship to consciousness. See Brown et al., 1998. The Orthodox Jewish philosopher David Shatz, 2006, has similarly called upon Orthodox Jews to seriously reevaluate their notions and theologies of the soul and free will. Upon reading Shatz's courageous chapter, I commented to him that I would like to see him call upon Orthodoxy to address modern biblical scholarship as well with intellectual honesty and integrity, if and when he were to eventually accept MSPM instead of TMS.

Chapter 7

1. For Christian fundamentalism, see, for example, Chris Hedges' discussion of an extreme subgroup of Christian fundamentalists, the "dominionists," in his *American Fascists,* 2006. See also Stern, 2003. For a cataloging of Muslim suicide bombings, and Islamic justification of them, see Charny, 2007. For messianic Jewish fundamentalism in Israel and its impact on "messianic" politics and on social policy, see Ravitzky, 1996, and Silberstein, 1993.

2. The correspondent requested anonymity. I would add to his examples that the Catholic Church's opposition to birth control has been responsible for untold human misery in those countries with substantial Catholic populations who cannot emerge from abject poverty because of their high birthrate. Were the Church to permit, or, better yet, promote birth control methods, and assist in distributing birth control pills and other medicines and devices to their impoverished followers, it would have a significant impact on the amelioration of poverty. I find it difficult to understand how the Church that preaches (and often practices, with its extensive social and relief services) concern for the poor and vulnerable of society cannot, with its many brilliant theologians and moral philosophers, find a way to reinterpret its sacred texts so as to permit or even espouse birth control for the poor, who want to have fewer children but cannot realistically be expected to abstain from sex. Many Catholic dogmas and doctrines have been subject to adaptive reinterpretation. The Church, for example, now accepts Copernican/Galilean heliocentrism and some form of neo-Darwinian evolution, even though these were for many years considered to be heresies. Were there a will, there would be a way. The "will" will eventually come, but consider all of the misery that could have and can be avoided if the Church would act now.

3. Hinde, 1999, 233.

4. Dawkins, 2006.

5. See Peter Berkowitz's (2004) review of Jan Feldman's book *Lubavitchers as Citizens: A Paradox of Liberal Democracy.*

6. Several correspondents of mine asked me if I was at all concerned that if as a result of my writings many Jews not only rejected the Orthodox belief in the revelation of the Pentateuch to Moses at Sinai, but belief in *any* revelation, because revelation, according to my criteria, cannot be corroborated by empirical evidence, and a case can be made that belief in it might be considered irrational. Wouldn't this be extremely detrimental to Jewish continuity?

I am not sure that loss of belief in TMS or in other traditional beliefs or in revelation in general would over the long run *inevitably* have net negative social consequences. Have Jewish "heretics" who lost their belief in revelation but who went on to contribute to Jewish thought and society been detrimental to Jewish continuity? It seems to me, for example, that Ahad Ha'Am, Haim Nahman Bialik, Mordechai Kaplan, and numerous other "heretics" have contributed significantly to Jewish continuity. There are many Jews who define themselves as non-religious who are contributing to the vitality of Jewish life, culture, and values in the United States, Israel, and elsewhere. I don't think that contemporary "secular" or "cultural Judaism" demonstrates the same degree of passion and power that are so important for cultural continuity, as do some fundamentalist versions of Judaism, but there have been times and places in the nineteenth and twentieth centuries when it did. Whether it will be able to contribute significantly to Jewish continuity in the twenty-first century remains to be seen.

7. If someone felt that religious belief was more conducive to moral behavior than was atheism, but was convinced that atheism was more rationally defensible than religious belief, how should he educate his children? Should he teach them to believe in God and other religious beliefs that he himself either doesn't believe or seriously doubts, so that they will be more moral, or should he be intellectually honest with his children about his skepticism, agnosticism, or atheism and try to find other supports for a moral

system and for moral behavior, even though they would, from his perspective, be weaker than a moral code based upon religious belief? I have no simple answer to this question. It would depend on the ages of his children, their own intellectual curiosity and concerns about truth, and the strength of the nonreligious support for the moral code.

8. I am not suggesting that religious people do or should dress shoddily or ignore their physical appearance. But religious values, in principle and in practice, provide a critique of and an antidote to the extreme materialism, consumerism, and promiscuity that characterize much of secular American culture and society. I am also aware that notwithstanding their professed beliefs, there are many religious people who are influenced by the secular American culture and who engage in the activities that I have attributed to it.

9. See, for example, Kelemen, 1996, 125–183.

10. See Statman, 2000.

BIBLIOGRAPHY

Akyol, Mustafa. "In Defense of Mary the Virgin." Available at http://www.islamonline
.net/english/Contemporary/2005/01/Article04.shtml (accessed Feb. 24, 2008).
Ali, Abdulla Yussuf, trans. *The Qur'an: Text, Translation, and Commentary.* 4th U.S. ed.
Elmhurst, NY: Tahrike Tarsile Qur'an, Inc., 2002.
Al-Khateeb, Motaz. "Are Science and Islam Compatible? An Interview with Bruno
Guiderdoni." Available at http://www.islamonline.net/English/Science/Faith
Sciences/ScientificmiraclesinQuran/2006/06/01.shtml (accessed Feb. 24, 2008).
Altemeyer, Bob, and Bruce Hunsberger. *Amazing Conversions: Why Some Turn to Faith and
Others Abandon Religion.* Amherst, NY: Prometheus Books, 1997.
Auslander, Shalom. *Beware of God.* New York: Simon and Shuster, 2005.
Aviezer, Nathan. "Knowledge in the Realm of Science and Knowledge in the Realm of
Religion: Are They Different?" *Jewish Action,* 68, no. 2 (Winter 2007), 21–25.
Babinski, Edward, ed. *Leaving the Fold: Testimonies of Former Fundamentalists.* Amherst,
NY: Prometheus Books, 2003.
Babylonian Talmud, Tractate Sanhedrin, vols. 1 and 2. Translated by Isadore Epstein.
London: Soncino Press, 1935.
Barker, Dan. *Losing Faith in Faith: From Preacher to Atheist.* Madison: Freedom from
Religion Foundation, 1992.
Bar-Lev, Mordechai, and William Shaffir, eds. *Leaving Religion and Religious Life.*
Religion and the Social Order 7. Greenwich, CT: JAI Press, 1997.
Barr, James. *Beyond Fundamentalism.* Philadelphia: Westminster John Knox Press, 1984.
Barr, James. *Fundamentalism.* Philadelphia: The Westminster Press, 1977.
Bayme, Steven. Letter to the Editor. *Tradition: A Journal of Orthodox Jewish Thought* 20
no. 4 (1982): 370–371.
Beattie, J. H. M. "On Understanding Ritual." In *Rationality,* edited by Bryan R.
Wilson, 240–268. Oxford: Basil Blackwell, 1970.
Berger, David. Review of *Must a Jew Believe Anything?* by M. Kellner. *Tradition* 33, no. 4
(Summer 1999): 81–89.
Berger, Michael. *Rabbinic Authority.* New York: Oxford University Press, 1998.

Berger, Peter. *The Sacred Canopy: Elements of a Sociological Theory of Religion.* New York: Doubelday/Anchor, 1969.

Berkovits, Eliezer. "The State of Jewish Belief: A Symposium." *Commentary* 42, no. 2 (1966), 78–80.

Berkowitz, Peter. Review of *Lubavitchers as Citizens: A Paradox of Liberal Democracy,* by Jan Feldman. *Policy Review,* August/September 2004, Hoover Institution–Stanford University. Available at http://www.hoover.org/publications/policyreview/4930706 .html (accessed Feb. 24, 2008).

Bernstein, Moshe. "The Orthodox Jewish Scholar and Jewish Scholarship: Duties and Dilemmas." *The Torah U'Madda Journal* 3 (1991–1992): 8–36.

Boone, Kathleen C. *The Bible Tells Them So: The Discourse of Protestant Fundamentalism.* Albany: SUNY Press, 1989.

Bowering, Gerhard. "Chronology and the Qur'an." In *Encyclopaedia of the Qur'an,* vol. 1, edited by Jane Dammen McAuliffe, 316–335. Boston: Brill Academic Publishers, 1999.

Boyer, Pascal. *Religion Explained: The Evolutionary Origins of Religious Thought.* New York: Basic Books, 2001.

Brenner, Robert. *The Faith and Doubt of Holocaust Survivors.* New York: Free Press, 1990.

Breuer, Mordechai. "The Study of Bible and the Primacy of the Fear of Heaven." In *Modern Scholarship in Torah Study,* edited by Shalom Carmy, 159–180. New York: Jason Aronson.

Bromley, D. G. "Religious Disaffiliation: A Neglected Social Process." In *Falling from the Faith: Causes and Consequences of Religious Apostasy,* edited by D. G. Bromley, 9–25. Newbury Park, CA: Sage, 1988.

Brown, Warren S., Nancey Murphy, and H. Newton Malony, eds. *Whatever Happened to the Soul? Scientific and Theological Portraits of Human Nature.* Minneapolis: Fortress Press, 1998.

Buruma, Ian, and Avishai Margalit. *Occidentalism: The West in the Eyes of Its Enemies.* New York: Penguin Press, 2004.

Cantor, Geoffrey, and Marc Swetlitz, eds. *Jewish Tradition and the Challenge of Darwinism.* Chicago: University of Chicago Press, 2006.

Carmy, Shalom. "A Room with a View, but a Room of Our Own." In *Modern Scholarship in Torah Study,* edited by Shalom Carmy, 1–38. New York: Jason Aronson, 1996.

Chait, Israel. "Torah from Sinai." Available at http://www.ybt.org/essays/rchait/ torahsinai.html (accessed Oct. 2, 2007).

Charny, I. W. *Fighting Suicide Bombing: A Worldwide Campaign for Life.* Westport, CT: Praeger Security International, 2007.

Chavel, Charles, trans. *Ramban (Nachmanides) Commentary on the Torah: Genesis.* New York: Shilo Publishing, 2005 [1972].

Cherry, Shai. "Crisis Management via Biblical Interpretation: Fundamentalism, Modern Orthodoxy, and Genesis." In *Jewish Tradition and the Challenge of Darwinism,* edited by Geoffrey Cantor and Marc Swetlitz, 166–187. Chicago: University of Chicago Press, 2006.

Clark, Eli D. "Orthodoxy Lurches to the Right." *Moment Magazine* 21, no. 3 (June 1996): 28–35; 58–59.

Cohen, Menahem. "The Idea of the Sanctity of the Letters [of the traditional version of the Torah] and Textual Criticism." In *HaMikra VeAnahnu* [The Bible and Us], edited by Uriel Simon, 42–69. Tel Aviv: Dvir, 1979.

Collins, J. B. *Tennessee Snake Handlers*. Chattanooga, TN: Chattanooga News-Free Press, 1947.

Coogan, Michael D. *The Old Testament: A Historical and Literary Introduction to the Hebrew Scriptures*. New York: Oxford University Press, 2006.

Cook, Michael. *The Koran: A Very Short Introduction*. Oxford: Oxford University Press, 2000.

Craig, William Lane, and Bart D. Ehrman. *Is There Historical Evidence for the Resurrection of Jesus?: A Debate between William Lane Craig and Bart D. Ehrman*. College of the Holy Cross, March 28, 2006. Transcript available at http://www.holycross.edu/departments/crec/website/resurrection-debate-transcript.pdf (accessed Feb. 24, 2008).

Darwin, Charles. *On The Origin of Species,* Cambridge, MA: Harvard University Press, 1966 [1859].

Davidman, Lynn. "Characters in Search of a Script: The Exit Narratives of Formerly Ultra-Orthodox Jews." *Journal for the Scientific Study of Religion* 46, no. 2 (June 2007): 201–216.

Davis, Caroline Franks. *The Evidential Force of Religious Experience*. New York: Oxford University Press, 1989.

Dawkins, Richard. *The God Delusion*. Boston: Houghton Mifflin, 2006

Deconchy, Jean-Pierre. "Rationality and Social Control in Orthodox Systems." In *The Social Dimension: European Developments in Social Psychology,* vol. 2, edited by Henri Tajfel, 425–445. Cambridge: Cambridge University Press, 1984.

Dennett, Daniel. *Breaking the Spell: Religion as a Natural Phenomenon*. New York: Viking, 2006.

Edis, Taner. *An Illusion of Harmony: Science and Religion in Islam*. Amherst, NY: Prometheus Books, 2007.

El Fadl, Khaled Abou. "Islam and the Challenge of Democracy: Can Individual Rights and Popular Sovereignty Take Root in Faith?" *Boston Review: A Political and Literary Forum* (April/May 2003). Available at http://bostonreview.net/BR28.2/contents.html (accessed Feb. 24, 2008).

El Fadl, Khaled Abou. "Khaled Abou El Fadl Replies." *Boston Review: A Political and Literary Forum* (April/May 2003). Available at http://bostonreview.net/BR28.2/abouRE.html (accessed Feb. 24, 2008).

El Fadl, Khaled Abou. "The Place of Tolerance in Islam: On Reading the Qur'an—and Misreading It." *Boston Review: A Political and Literary Forum* (December 2001/January 2002). Available at http://bostonreview.net/BR26.6/elfadl.html (accessed Feb. 24, 2008).

Encyclopedia Judaica. Jerusalem: Keter Publishing Company, 1971.

Encyclopaedia of the Qur'an, vols. 1–6. Edited by Jane Dammen McAuliffe. Boston: Brill Academic Publishers, 1999–2006.

Evans-Pritchard, E. E. *Witchcraft, Oracles and Magic among the Azande*. Oxford: Clarendon Press, 1937.

Feierberg, M. Z. *Whither?* Trans. by Hillel Halkin. Philadelphia: Jewish Publication Society of America, 1973 [1899].

Feinstein, Moshe. *Igrot Moshe. Yoreh De'ah,* v. 3, responsum 73. New York: Noble Press, 5742 [1982], 323.

Ferziger, Adam S. *Exclusion and Hierarchy: Orthodoxy, Nonobservance, and the Emergence of Modern Jewish Identity.* Philadelphia: University of Pennsylvania Press, 2005.

Festinger, Leon, Henry W. Riecken, and Stanley Schachter. *When Prophecy Fails: A Social and Psychological Study of a Modern Group that Predicted the Destruction of the World.* New York: Harper and Row, 1956.

Flew, Anthony. Interview with Gary R. Habermas. Available at http://theroadtoemmaus.org/RdLb/21PbAr/Apl/FlewTheist.htm (accessed Feb. 24, 2008).

Fox, Marvin. "The State of Jewish Belief: A Symposium." *Commentary* 42, no. 2 (1966): 89–92.

Freud, Sigmund. *Moses and Monotheism.* New York: Vintage Books, 1955 [1939].

Friedman, Richard Elliott. *The Bible with Sources Revealed.* San Francisco: Harper SanFrancisco, 2003.

Gellman, Yehuda. "A Response to Rabbi Aharon Feldman's 'The Slifkin Affair: Issues and Perspectives.'" Available at http://www.zootorah.com/controversy/Gellman%20Response.doc (accessed Feb. 24, 2008).

Gold, Dore. *Hatred's Kingdom: How Saudi Arabia Supports the New Global Terrorism.* Washington, DC: Regnery Publishing, 2004.

Goldziher, Ignaz. *Introduction to Islamic Theology and Law.* Princeton, NJ: Princeton University Press, 1981 [1910].

Goodstein, Laurie. "American Muslim Clerics Seek a Modern Middle Ground." *New York Times* (online), June 16, 2006.

Grudem, Wayne A. *Bible Doctrine: The Essential Teachings of the Christian Faith.* Grand Rapids, MI: Zondervan Publishing, 1999.

Halbertal, Moshe. *Mahapeykhot Parshaniyot Behithavutan* [Interpretative Revolutions in the Making: Values as Interpretative Considerations in Midrashei Halakhah]. Jerusalem: Magnes Press, 1999.

Haleem, M. A. S. Abdel, trans. *Qu'ran: A New Translation.* Oxford: Oxford University Press, 2004.

Halevi, Judah. *Kuzari: An Argument for the Faith of Israel.* New York: Schocken, 1987.

HaLivni, David Weiss. *Revelation Restored: Divine Writ and Critical Responses.* London: SCM Press, 2001.

Harris, Jay. "'Fundamentalism': Objections from a Modern Jewish Historian." In *Fundamentalism and Gender,* edited by John Stratton Hawley, 137–173. New York: Oxford University Press, 1994.

Harris, Sam. *The End of Faith: Religion, Terror, and the Future of Reason.* New York: W. W. Norton, 2005.

Hedges, Chris. *American Fascists: The Christian Right and the War on America.* New York: Free Press, 2006.

Heilman, Samuel. *Sliding to the Right: The Contest for the Future of American Jewish Orthodoxy.* Berkeley: University of California Press, 2006.

———. "The Vision from the Madrasa and Bes Medrash: Some Parallels between Islam and Judaism." In *Fundamentalisms Comprehended,* edited by Martin E. Marty and R. Scott Appleby, chap. 2. Chicago: University of Chicago Press, 1995.

————, and Steven Cohen. *Cosmopolitans and Parochials: Modern Orthodox Jews in America*. Chicago: University of Chicago Press, 1989.

Helm, Paul. *Faith and Reason*. New York: Oxford University Press, 1999.

Hertz, J. H. *Pentateuch and Haftorahs*. 2nd ed. London: Soncino Press, 1960 [1937].

Heschel, Abraham Joshua. *Heavenly Torah as Refracted through the Generations*. Edited and translated from the Hebrew with commentary by Gordon Tucker with Leonard Levin. New York: Continuum, 2005.

Hick, John. *God Has Many Names*. Philadelphia: Westminster Press, 1982.

Hinde, Robert. *Why Gods Persist: A Scientific Approach to Religion*. London: Routledge, 1999.

Hippocrates. *Hippocratic Writings*. Edited by G. E. R. Lloyd; translated by J. Chadwick. New York: Penguin Classics, 1984.

Hood, Ralph, Jr., Peter C. Hill, and W. Paul Williamson. *The Psychology of Religious Fundamentalism*. New York: Guilford Press, 2005.

Horton, Robin. "African Traditional Thought and Western Science." In *Rationality*, edited by Bryan R. Wilson, 131–171. Oxford: Basil Blackwell, 1970.

Hume, David. *Dialogues Concerning Natural Religion*. Edited with an introduction by Henry D. Aiken. New York: Hafner Publishing Company, 1959.

————. *Of Miracles*. LaSalle, IL: Open Court Publishing Company, 1985.

Husik, Isaac. *A History of Medieval Jewish Philosophy*. New York: Atheneum, 1960 [1916].

Ibn Warraq. *Why I Am Not a Muslim*. Amherst, NY: Prometheus Books, 2003 [1995]

Ibrahim, A. *A Brief Illustrated Guide to Understanding Islam*. 2nd ed. Houston: Dar-ussalam, 1997.

Intellectual Honesty and Orthodoxy. "Not the Godol Hador," May 11, 2006. Available at http://godolhador.blogspot.com/search?q=carmy (accessed 2/24/08).

Jacobs, Louis. *God, Torah, Israel: Traditionalism without Fundamentalism*. Cincinnati: Hebrew Union College Press, 1990.

Jacobs, Louis. *Principles of the Jewish Faith: An Analytical Study*. New York: Basic Books, 1964.

James, William. *The Varieties of Religious Experience*. Garden City, NY: Image Books/Doubleday, 1978 [1902].

Jewish Publication Society Hebrew-English Tanakh. Philadelphia: Jewish Publication Society of America, 1999.

Kaplan, Lawrence, and David Berger. "On Freedom of Inquiry in the Rambam and Today." *The Torah U'Madda Journal* 1 (1990): 37–50.

Katz, Steven T. The Issue of Confirmation and Disconfirmation in Jewish Thought after the Holocaust. In *The Impact of the Holocaust on Jewish Theology*, edited by Steven T. Katz. New York: New York University Press, 2007.

Kelemen, Lawrence. *Permission to Believe: Four Rational Approaches to God's Existence*. Jerusalem: Targum Press, 1991.

Kelemen, Lawrence. *Permission to Receive: Four Rational Approaches to the Torah's Divine Origin*. Southfield, MI: Targum Press 1996.

Kent, Jack. *The Psychological Origins of the Resurrection Myth*. London: Open Gate Press, 1999.

Kraus, Lawrence M. "How to Make Sure Children Are Scientifically Illiterate." *New York Times* (online), August 15, 2006. Available at http://www.nytimes.com/2006/08/15/

science/sciencespecial2/15essa.html?scp=1&sq=illiterate&st=nyt (accessed Feb. 24, 2008).

Kugel, James L. *The God of Old: Inside the Lost World of the Bible.* New York: Free Press, 2003.

———. *How to Read the Bible: A Guide to Scripture, Then and Now.* New York: Free Press, 2007. See also http://www.jameskugel.com.

———. *In Potiphar's House: The Interpretive Life of Biblical Texts.* 2nd ed. Cambridge, MA: Harvard University Press, 1994.

Lamm, Norman "The State of Jewish Belief: A Symposium." *Commentary* 42, no. 2 (1966), 110.

Leibowitz, Yeshayahu. Citations in Avi Sagi, "Contending with Modernity: Scripture in the Thought of Yeshayahu Leibowitz and Joseph Soloveitchik." *Journal of Religion* 77, no. 3 (July 1997): 421–441.

———. *Judaism, Human Values and the Jewish State,* translated and edited by Eliezer Goldman. Cambridge, MA: Harvard University Press, 1992.

Leiman, Shnayer (Sid). Response to Rabbi Breuer. In *Modern Scholarship in Torah Study,* edited by Shalom Carmy, 181–187. New York: Jason Aronson, 1996.

Lester, Toby. "What Is the Koran?" *Atlantic Monthly,* January 1999. Available at http://www.theatlantic.com/doc/199901/koran (accessed Feb. 24, 2008).

Levenson, Jon. "The Eighth Principle of Judaism and the Literary Simultaneity of Scripture." In *The Hebrew Bible, The Old Testament and Historical Criticism,* chap. 3. Louisville, KY: Westminster/John Knox Press, 1993.

———. Letter to the Editor. *The Torah U-Madda Journal* 9 (2000): 276.

———. *Resurrection and the Restoration of Israel: The Ultimate Victory of the God of Life.* New Haven, CT: Yale University Press, 2006.

Levy, Barry. "Judge Not a Book by Its Cover." *Tradition* 19 (1981): 89–95.

———. Letter to the Editor. *Tradition: A Journal of Orthodox Jewish Thought* 20 no. 4 (1982): 371–375.

———. "Our Torah, Your Torah and Their Torah: An Evaluation of the ArtScroll Phenomenon." In *Truth and Compassion: Essays on Judaism and Religion in Memory of Rabbi Dr. Solomon Frank,* edited by H. Joseph et al., 137–190. Waterloo, Ontario: Wilfred Laurier University Press, 1983.

———. "On the Periphery: North American Orthodox Judaism and Contemporary Biblical Scholarship." In *Students of the Covenant: Jewish Bible Scholarship in America,* edited by D. Sperling, 159–204. Atlanta: Scholars Press, 1992.

———. "The State and Directions of Orthodox Bible Study." *Modern Scholarship in Torah Study,* edited by Shalom Carmy, 39–80. New York: Jason Aronson, 1996.

———. "Text and Context: Torah and Historical Truth." *Edah Journal* 2 (2002): 1. Available at http://www.edah.org (accessed 2/24/08).

Lewis, Bernard. *The Political Language of Islam.* Chicago: University of Chicago Press, 1988.

Liebman, Charles S. "Modern Orthodoxy in Israel." *Judaism* 47 no. 4 (Fall 1998): 405–410.

———. "Orthodoxy in American Jewish Life." In *The Jewish Community in America,* edited with an introduction and notes by Marshall Sklare, 131–174. New York: Behrman House, 1974.

Lilienblum, Moshe Leib. *Hatot Neurim* [Sins of My Youth]. Sifriyat Dorot. Tel Aviv: Mosad Bialik, 1970 [1876].

Lukes, Steven. Some problems about rationality. In *Rationality,* edited by Bryan R. F. Wilson, 194–213. Oxford: Basil Blackwell, 1974.

Maimonides, Moses. *The Guide of the Perplexed,* translated by M. Pines. Chicago: University of Chicago Press, 1963.

Manzoor, P. "Method against Truth: Orientalism and Qur'anic Studies." Available at http://www.algonet.se/~pmanzoor/Method-Truth.htm (accessed Feb. 24, 2008).

Margolese, Faranak. *Off the Derech: Why Observant Jews Leave Judaism; How to Respond to the Challenge.* New York: Devora Publishing, 2005.

Marsden, George M. *Understanding Fundamentalism and Evangelicalism.* Grand Rapids, MI: Wm. B. Eerdmans, 1991.

Miller, Jon. D., Eugenie C. Scott, and Shinji Okamoto. "Public Acceptance of Evolution." *Science* 313, no. 5788 (Aug. 11, 2006): 765–766.

Mintz, Alan. *"Banished from Their Father's Table": Loss of Faith in Hebrew Autobiography.* Bloomington: Indiana University Press, 1987.

Mittleman, Alan. "Fretful Orthodoxy." *First Things,* October 2003. Available at http://www.firstthings.com/article.php3?id_article=530 (accessed Feb. 24, 2008).

Moore, Keith L., and T. V. N. Persaud. *The Developing Human: Clinically Oriented Embryology.* 5th ed. Philadelphia: W. B. Saunders, 1993.

Morris, Thomas V., ed. *God and the Philosophers: The Reconciliation of Faith and Reason.* New York: Oxford University Press, 1994.

Musallam, Basim. *Sex and Society in Islam.* Cambridge, UK: Cambridge University Press, 1983.

Needham, J. *A History of Embryology.* 2nd ed. Cambridge, UK: Cambridge University Press, 1959.

The New Bible Commentary Revised. Edited by D. Guthrie and others. Grand Rapids, MI: Wm. B. Eerdmans, 1970.

Niditch, Susan. *War in the Hebrew Bible: A Study in the Ethics of Violence.* New York: Oxford University Press, 1995.

Norowitz, Avi. "Critique of the Kuzari Argument." Available at http://www.talkreason.org/articles/kuzariflaws.cfm#myth (last updated Jan. 2003; accessed Feb. 24, 2008).

Novak, David. *The Image of the Non-Jew in Judaism: An Historical and Constructive Study of the Noahide Laws.* Toronto Studies in Theology. New York: Edwin Mellen Press, 1983.

Nussbaum, Alexander. "Creationism and Geocentrism among Orthodox Jewish Scientists." *National Center for Science Education Reports* 22, no. 1–2 (Jan.–Apr., 2002), 38–43.

———. "Orthodox Jews and Science: An Empirical Study of Their Attitudes toward Evolution, the Fossil Record, and Modern Geology." *Skeptic Magazine* 12, no. 3. Available at http://www.skeptic.com/the_magazine/featured_articles/v12n03_orthodox_judaism_and_evolution.html (accessed Feb. 24, 2008).

Perakh, Mark. "The Rise and Fall of the Bible Code." Available at http://www.talkreason.com/articles/Codpaper1.cfm (accessed Feb. 24, 2008).

Peterson, Michael, William Hasker, Bruce Reichenbach, and David Basinger. *Reason and Religious Belief.* 3rd ed. New York: Oxford University Press, 2003.

Peterson, Michael, William Hasker, Bruce Reichenbach, and David Basinger, eds. *Philosophy of Religion: Selected Readings.* 2nd ed. New York: Oxford University Press, 2001.

Plantinga, Alvin. "Pluralism: A Defense of Religious Exclusivism." In *The Philosophical Challenge of Religious Diversity,* edited by Philip L. Quinn and Kevin Meeker, 172–192. New York: Oxford University Press, 2000.

Potok, Chaim. *In the Beginning.* Greenwich, CT: Fawcett, 1975.

Price, Robert. "Beyond Born Again." Available at http://www.infidels.org/library/modern/robert_price/beyond_born_again/chap1.html (accessed Feb. 24, 2008).

Price, Robert P. "By This Time He Stinketh: The Attempts of William Lane Craig to Exhume Jesus" (1997). Available at http://www.infidels.org/library/modern/robert_price/stinketh.html (accessed Feb. 24, 2008).

Rabbinical Council of America (RCA). Mission Statement. Available at http://www.rabbis.org/ (accessed Feb. 24, 2008).

Ravitzky, Aviezer. *Messianism, Zionism, and Jewish Religious Radicalism,* translated by Michael Swirsky and Jonathan Chipman. Chicago Studies in the History of Judaism. Chicago: University of Chicago Press, 1996.

Robinson, Ira. "Practically I Am a Fundamentalist": Twentieth-Century Orthodox Jews Contend with Evolution and Its Implications." In *Jewish Tradition and the Challenge of Darwinism,* 71–88, edited by Geoffrey Cantor and Marc Swetlitz. Chicago: University of Chicago Press, 2006.

Rosenak, Michael. "Jewish Religious Education and Indoctrination." In *Studies in Jewish Education,* vol. 1, edited by Barry Chazan, 117–138. Jerusalem: Magnes Press, 1983.

———. *Tzarikh Iyyun* [On Second Thought: Tradition and Modernity in Jewish Contemporary Education]. Jerusalem: Magnes Press, 2003.

Rosenberg, Shalom. "Biblical Research in Recent Orthodox Thought." [In Hebrew.] In *The Bible and Us,* edited by Uriel Simon. Tel Aviv: Dvir, 1979.

———. "The Concept of 'Emunah' in Post-Maimonidean Jewish Philosophy." In *Studies in Medieval Jewish History and Literature,* vol. 2, edited by Isadore Twersky, 273–307. Cambridge, MA: Harvard University Press, 1984.

Ross, Tamar. *Expanding the Palace of Torah: Orthodoxy and Feminism.* Waltham, MA: Brandeis University Press, 2004.

Ross, Tamar. "Response to Y. Finkelman's Review Essay of *Expanding the Palace of Torah.*" *Edah Journal* 4, no. 2 (2004b). Available at http://www.edah.org/backend/JournalArticle/4_2_Finkelman.pdf (accessed Feb. 24, 2008).

Roth, Phillip. "The Conversion of the Jews." In *Goodbye Columbus and Five Short Stories.* Boston: Houghton Mifflin, 1959.

Sachs, Jeffrey D. *The End of Poverty: Economic Possibilities for Our Time.* New York: Penguin, 2006.

Sacks, Jonathan. "Fundamentalism Reconsidered." *L'eylah,* no. 28 (September, 1989), 8–12.

Sagi, Avi. "Contending with Modernity: Scripture in the Thought of Yeshayahu Leibowitz and Joseph Soloveitchik." *Journal of Religion* 77, no. 3 (July 1997): 421–441.

———, and Dani Statman. *Religion and Morality.* Amsterdam: Rodopi, 1995.

Samuelson, Norbert. *Revelation and the God of Israel.* Cambridge: Cambridge University Press, 2002.

Sanders, E. P. *The Historical Figure of Jesus.* London: Penguin, 1993.

Sand Mountain Homecoming Video, June 21, 1998. Hood-Williamson Research Archives on the Serpent Handlers of Southern Appalachia. Chattanooga, TN: Lupton Library, University of Tennessee at Chattanooga.

Schacter, J. J. "Facing the Truths of History." *The Torah U-Madda Journal* 8 (1998–1999): 200–276.

Schatz, Elihu. *Proof of Accuracy of the Bible.* Middle Village, NY: Jonathan David, 1973.

Scherman, Nosson. "Introduction to the Torah." In *Chumash: The Stone Edition,* xix–xxv. Artscroll Series. New York: Mesorah Publications, 1993.

———, trans. *Complete ArtScroll Siddur (Sefard).* New York: Mesorah Publications, 1985.

Schimmel, Solomon. "Developing an Internet-Based Trialogue on Peace and Reconciliation in Judaic, Christian, and Islamic Thought." *Journal of Interdisciplinary Study of Monotheistic Religions,* special issue 1 (2006): 40–60.

———. "Human Nature in Judaism and in Evolutionary and Neuro-Psychology: Implications for Traditional Ethics and Morality." Paper presented at the Annual Meeting of the American Academy of Religion, Toronto, November, 2002.

———. "Job and the Psychology of Suffering and Doubt." *Journal of Psychology and Judaism* 11, no. 4 (1987): 239–249.

———. "Moral and Intellectual Challenges in Teaching Bible." In *In Search of a Jewish Paideia: Directions in the Philosophy of Jewish Education,* edited by Jonathan Cohen. Studies in Jewish Education, vol. 10. Jerusalem: Magnes Press, 2004, 65–86.

———. *The Seven Deadly Sins: Jewish, Christian, and Classical Reflections on Human Psychology.* New York: Oxford University Press, 1997.

———. *Wounds Not Healed by Time: The Power of Repentance and Forgiveness.* New York: Oxford University Press, 2002.

Schroeder, Gerald. *Genesis and the Big Bang: The Discovery of Harmony between Modern Science and the Bible.* New York: Bantam Books, 1990.

Scofield, Cyrus I., ed. *The New Scofield Reference Bible.* New York: Oxford University Press, 1967.

———. *The Scofield Reference Bible.* New York: Oxford University Press, 1907.

Selya, Rena. "Torah and Madda? Evolution in the Jewish Educational Context". In *Jewish Tradition and the Challenge of Darwinism,* edited by Geoffrey Cantor and Marc Swetlitz, 188–207. Chicago: University of Chicago Press, 2006.

Shapiro, Marc B. *The Limits of Orthodox Theology: Maimonides' Thirteen Principles Reappraised.* Oxford: Littman Library of Jewish Civilization, 2004.

Shatz, David. "Is Matter All that Matters? Judaism, Free Will, and the Genetic and Neuroscientific Revolutions." In *Judaism, Science, and Moral Responsibility,* edited by Yitzhak Berger and David Shatz, 54–103. Lanham, MD: Rowman and Littlefield Publishers, 2006.

———. "The Overexamined Life Is Not Worth Living." In *God and the Philosophers: The Reconciliation of Faith and Reason,* edited by Thomas V. Morris. New York: Oxford University Press, 1994, 263–285.

———. "Practical Endeavor and the Torah u-Madda Debate." *The Torah U'Madda Journal* 3 (1991–1992): 98–149.

Silberstein, Lawrence J., ed. *Jewish Fundamentalism in Comparative Perspective: Religion, Ideology, and the Crisis of Modernity.* New York: New York University Press, 1993.

Snow, David, and Richard Machalek. "On the Presumed Fragility of Unconventional Beliefs." *Journal for the Scientific Study of Religion* 21, no. 1 (1982): 15–26.

Soloveitchik, Hayim. "Rupture and Reconstruction: The Transformation of Contemporary Orthodoxy." *Tradition* 28, no. 4 (1994): 64–130.

Sorotzkin, Rabbi Benzion. "The Role of Parents in the Current Crisis of Rebellious Adolescents." Available at http://www.rabbihorowitz.com/PYes/ArticleDetails.cfm?Book_ID=872&ThisGroup_ID=261 (accessed Feb. 24, 2008).

Spilka, Bernard, Ralph W. Hood, Jr., Bruce Hunsberger, and Richard Gorsuch. *The Psychology of Religion: An Empirical Approach.* 3rd ed. New York: Guilford Press, 2003.

Spinoza, (Baruch) Benedictus de. *Tractatus Theologico-Politicus: A Critical Inquiry into the History, Purpose, and Authenticity of Hebrew Scriptures,* translated by Samuel Shirley. New York: E. J. Brill, 1989.

"The State of Jewish Belief: A Symposium." *Commentary* 42, no. 2 (1966): 71–160.

Statman, Dani. "Hurting Religious Feelings." *Democratic Culture* 3 (2000): 199–214.

———. "Kiyyum Mitzvot Beolam Shenitroken Mimashmaut Datit" [The Observance of Commandments in a World that Has Been Emptied of Religious Meaning]. *Daat: A Journal of Jewish Philosophy and Kabbalah* 41 (1998): 31–45.

Stern, Jessica. *Terror in the Name of God: Why Religious Militants Kill.* New York: CCC-Harper Collins, 2003.

Sternberg, Shlomo. "A Review of *Guide to Masechet Chulin and Masechet Bechorot* by Rabbi I. M. Levinger." *BDD (Bekhol DeraKhekha Daehu)* 4 (Winter, 1997a): 81–201.

———. "Snake Oil for Sale." *Bible Review* 13, no. 4 (1997b): 24–25.

Strauss, Leo. *Philosophy and Law: Essays toward the Understanding of Maimonides and His Predecessors.* Philadelphia: Jewish Publication Society, 1987.

Susser, Bernard, and Charles S. Liebman. *Choosing Survival: Strategies for a Jewish Future.* New York: Oxford University Press, 1999.

Swetlitz, Marc. "Responses to Evolution by Reform, Conservative, and Reconstructionist Rabbis in Twentieth-Century America." In *Jewish Tradition and the Challenge of Darwinism,* edited by Geoffrey Cantor and Marc Swetlitz, 47–70. Chicago: University of Chicago Press, 2006.

Tirosh-Samuelson, Hava. *Happiness in Premodern Judaism: Virtue, Knowledge, and Well-Being.* Cincinnati: Hebrew Union College Press, 2003.

Union for Traditional Judaism. "Principles." Available at http://www.utj.org/principles.html (accessed Feb. 24, 2008).

Wallace, Stan W., ed. *Does God Exist? The Craig-Flew Debate.* Hants, UK: Ashgate Publishing, 2003.

Wansbrough, John. *Quranic Studies: Sources and Methods of Scriptural Interpretation.* Amherst, NY:Prometheus Books, 2004 [1977].

Wasserman, Rabbi Elchonon. "Kovetz Ma'amarim." Available at http://www.shemayisrael.co.il/2001/elchonon.htm (accessed Feb. 24, 2008).

Waxman, Chaim I. "Dilemmas of Modern Orthodoxy: Sociological and Philosophical." *Judaism* 42, no. 1 (1993): 59–70.

Wein, Berel. "Intellectual Honesty." Available at http://www.aish.com/jewishissues/jewishsociety/Intellectual_Honesty.asp (accessed Feb. 24, 2008).

Weiss HaLivni, David. *Revelation Restored: Divine Writ and Critical Responses.* London: SCM Press, 2001.

Westen, Drew. *The Political Brain: The Role of Emotion in Deciding the Fate of the Nation.* New York: Public Affairs Press, 2007.

Williamson, W. P. "The experience of religious serpent handling: A phenomenological study." *Dissertation Abstracts International* 62 (1999): 1136B.

Wilson, David Sloan. *Darwin's Cathedral: Evolution, Religion, and the Nature of Society.* Chicago: University of Chicago Press, 2002.

Winston, Hella. *The Unchosen: The Hidden Lives of Hasidic Rebels.* Boston: Beacon Press, 2005.

Web Sites

Apostasy and the Freedom of Religion. http://www.islamonline.net/English/contemporary/2006/04/article01.shtml

A Brief Illustrated Guide to Understanding Islam. http://www.islam-guide.com/truth

Darwinist-watch.com. http://www.darwinism-watch.com/index.php

Edah Journal (renamed *Meorot Journal*). http://www.edah.org/backend/coldfusion/display_main.cfm

Fundamentalists Anonymous Resources. http://www.fundamentalists-anonymous.org/

Harun Yahya: An Invitation to the Truth. http://www.harunyahya.com/index.php

Koran: The Myth of Embryology! http://www.bible.ca/islam/islam-myths-embryology.htm

Intellectual Honesty and Orthodoxy. "Not the Godol Hador." http://godolhador.blogspot.com/search?q=carmy

Losing my Religion.com. http://www.losingmyreligion.com

Method against Truth. http://www.algonet.se/~pmanzoor/Method-Truth.htm

Modern Orthodox Judaism. http:// en.wikipedia.org/wiki/Modern_Orthodox_Judaism

Skeptic Magazine. http://www.shttp://www.skeptic.com/the_magazine/featured_articles/v12n03_orthodox_judaism_and_evolution.html

Spirit of Tolerance in Islam. http://www.islamonline.net/servlet/Satellite?pagename=IslamOnline-English-Ask_Scholar/FatwaE/FatwaE&cid=1119503544482

The Torah/Science Controversy. http://www.zootorah.com/controversy

Why We Left Islam. http://www.apostatesofislam.com/testimonials.htm

YCT Rabbinical School (Yeshivat Chovevei Torah). http://www.yctorah.org

INDEX

divine planner arguments, 69–71, 237*n*55, *n*57

divine revelation. *See* revelation

documentary hypothesis, 47–48, 52, 89–90, 239*n*85

doubt, research potential, 233*n*5

Ecclesiastes, 11, 129

Edah, 44–45

education
evolution-creation story conflicts, 71, 72–73
heretics lack of, assumption, 95
impact of TMS affirmation, 64–65, 80, 89–90, 189–190

Ehrman, Bart, 116, 118–122, 244*n*38, 245*n*39

embryology-based proof for divine authorship of Koran, 152–153, 156–157

emotional motives, TMS adherence, 43–44, 50–52

Encyclopaedia of the Qur'an, 247*n*6

Epstein, Barukh HaLevi, 80

error assumption, in reasoning, 20–21

Esther, Book of, 87

Eucharist, 132, 178–179, 246*n*54, 255*n*8, *n*10

Evans-Pritchard, E. E., 175–177, 183

evidence challenge questions, TMS affirmation, 93–97

evidentialism, 187–190

evil impulses accusation, 95–96

evil rationalization, 221, 261*n*2

evolution
and Christian fundamentalism, 107–108
creation science movement, 214–220, 260*n*49
fossil planting by God argument, 49
fundamentalisms' commonalities, 150–151
Muslim fundamentalism, 150–151
and Orthodox Judaism, 68–73, 84–87

exclusivity arguments, 28, 29–31, 33, 247*n*10, 254*n*62

existential meaning
and certainty, 91
in exclusivity argument, 33
religion benefit argument, 169, 211–212
as TMS adherence motive, 53–54, 56

Exodus, 34–36, 132

Explaining Religion (Boyer), 122

Fadl, El, 155–156, 253*n*56

faith
meanings of, 17–18
and *mitzvot* observance, 76
motives of skeptics when analyzing, 26–27
personal experience argument, 24–26
and reason, 21–23, 66–67, 234*n*9
and revelation, 90–91

family
and author's loss of faith, 6–7, 9, 10–11
loss fears, 56–58

fear incentives
Koran adherence, 136–139
TMS adherence, 50, 51–59, 235*n*22

Feierberg, M. Z., 57

Feinstein, Moses, 71

Feldman, Aharon, 254*n*68

Festinger, Leon, 171–175

ffb (frum from birth), defined, 233*n*8

Flew, Anthony, 116, 117, 243*n*21

flood stories, 209–210

forehead-based proof for divine authorship of Koran, 163–164, 254*n*75

fossils, divine planting hypothesis, 49, 73, 203

Fox, Marvin, 53, 188

free will
Koran, 146, 149
and neuropsychology, 73–75, 260*n*53

Friedman, Richard Elliott, 40

"Fundamentalism Reconsidered" (Sacks), 90–91

Gabriel, angel, in Koran, 135

gender distinctions, adultery, 142, 249*n*21

Genesis, 68–73, 85–86, 107, 151, 216

Genies (jinn), Koran, 144–145

geology-based proof for divine authorship of Koran, 157

giving up beliefs. *See* loss of belief

God
description problem, 21, 182–183
as divine planner, 69, 237*n*55
faith's role in belief in, 17–18
Koran portrayals, 146–147, 250*n*35
in prayer outcome explanation, 177–178

God (*continued*)

 reason's role in belief in, 20, 22–23

 in resurrection argument, 115, 116–117, 120–121, 244*n*37

 in acceptance of slavery, 205–206

 in snake-handling sect beliefs, 127–128, 129–132

Goldman, Eliezer, 76–77, 78

Gould, Stephen, 69–70

Grudem, Wayne, 101, 103, 108–109, 111–112

The Guide of the Perplexed (Maimonides), 21, 234*n*14

halakha observance

 author's, 7, 12

 and TMS adherence, 55, 76–78, 235*n*32, 258*n*33

Haleem, Abdel, 254*n*75

HaLevi, Yehuda, 35

Hardy, Thomas, 8

haredi Orthodox Jews

 authority figure power, 51

 categorized, 43–45

Harris, Jay, 229*n*1

hedge, in Ecclesiastes, 129

Heilman, Samuel, 229*n*1

Hell

 in the Bible, 106

 in the Koran, 146, 250*n*35

 in theology, 208

Hensley, George Went, 123, 124–125

heresy, in club invitation comparison, 185–187

heresy fears, in scholarship opposition

 and biblical inerrancy doctrine, 183

 Islamic fundamentalism, 136, 247*n*4, 253*n*60

 Orthodox Judaism, 47–48, 51–52, 63–64, 235*n*32

Hertz, J. H., 244*n*38

Hinde, Robert A., 42, 201, 222

Hinduism, 249*n*22

Hood, Ralph, 124, 127, 128–129

hostility claim as reason for critical Koranic scholarship, 139–140

how question, 3

How to Read the Bible (Kugel), 232*n*2

humility, 21, 23, 87, 91

Husik, Isaac, 20

Ibn Warraq, 135–136, 143–148

Ibrahim, A., 154, 157, 163, 252*n*54

identity

 and belief persistence, 183, 207–208

 and loss of faith, 9, 12–15, 230*n*14

Ijaz al Koran, 160–161

image of God concept and neuropsychology, 73–75

immorality fears, 56, 61, 236*n*35, 261*n*7, 356

inerrancy beliefs. *See* biblical inerrancy doctrine

inferential systems, acquisition of religious beliefs, 168–169

inimitability of Koran (Ijaz al Koran), 160–162

intellect. *See* reason

intellectual consequences, TMS affirmation, 64–66, 80–88, 189–190, 206–207, 257*n*26

intelligent design theory, 216, 243*n*22

interpretation approach, biblical inerrancy doctrine, 103–104, 241*n*6

interpretation tradition, Torah, 4–5, 77–78, 88–89, 92, 189–190, 239*n*87

In the Beginning (Potok), 239*n*85

intolerance theme, Muslim fundamentalists, 154–155

intratexuality, 124, 132–133, 245*n*45

irrational beliefs, defined, 40, 185

 See also specific topics, e.g., biblical inerrancy doctrine; Koran; Torah to Moses at Sinai

Islam

 fundamentalism's threat, 141–143, 154–156, 248*n*19, 252*n*53

 fundamentalist nature, 114, 229*n*1

 and Judaism, 137, 138–139, 247*nn*9–10

 origins, 135

Israel, 247*n*9

Jacob, 86

James, William, 98, 124, 188, 195

Job, 23, 128, 246*n*51

job loss fears, 58–59

Joshua, 105

Jouffroy (philosopher), 9, 54

Joyce, James, 8

Judaism and the Koran, 137, 138–139, 247*n*10

Jude the Obscure (Hardy), 8

in miracles defense, 151–152

as plausibility examination tool, 41–42, 187–190

and revelation, 21–22, 23–26, 34–37, 48, 108

See also Torah to Moses at Sinai (TMS)

rebbe, power of, 51

rebellion motive, 6–7

religion courses, 143, 249*n*22

religious beliefs, generally

challenge arguments, 27–34

and evidence importance, 94, 240*n*90

faith's role, 17–18

functions of, 211–212, 259*n*43

and *mitzvot* observance, 76–78

motives of skeptics, 26–27, 106

personal experience argument, 24–26, 42–43

reason's role, 18–23, 244*n*34

resurrection belief, 101, 115–123, 244*nn*37–38, 245*n*39, 251*n*46

revelation

challenge arguments, 23–24, 28–31

and faith, 90–91

Koran, 147

and *mitzvot* observance, 76–78

reason's uses, 23–26, 34–37, 108, 234*n*9

as supplement to reason, 21–22, 48, 66–67

validity question for skeptics, 23–24

right-wing orthodoxy. *See* haredi Orthodox Jews

risk-aversion motive, TMS adherence, 50–52

Ross, Tamar, 202

Rushdie, Salman, 136

Saadia Gaon, 20

Sabbath violation penalty, Torah, 5

Sacks, Jonathan, 90–92, 229*n*1

sacrilege fear, TMS adherence, 55

See also heresy fears

Sagi, Avi, 78

Satanic Verses (Rushdie), 136

Saudi Arabia, 154, 252*n*53

Schacter, J. J., 238*n*76

Scherman, Nosson, 81–83, 84–87

scholarship resistance, overview, 250*n*26

See also specific topics, e.g., democracy and Islamic fundamentalism; intellectual

consequences; science and Orthodox Judaism

Schroeder, Gerald, 71–72

Schwartz, Baruch, 235*n*32, 258*n*33

science-Orthodox Judaism conflicts, resolution approaches, 67–75, 78

See also evolution

scientific knowledge proofs for divine authorship of Koran, 152–154, 156–160, 163–164, 254*n*75

Scofield Reference Bible, 104

scriptural fundamentalists, definitions, 4–5, 229*n*1

See also specific topics, e.g., biblical inerrancy doctrine; Koran; Torah to Moses at Sinai

secondary elaboration, defined, 178

secularization process, 212–213

See also loss of belief

Sefer ha-Mitzvot (Maimonides), 46–47

selective activities, in cognitive restructuring

attention, 204–209

interpretation, 209–210

restructuring, 211

selective interaction, as defense mechanism, 211

Selya, Rena, 72–73

Sephardim, Jews, 57, 236*n*36

serpent-handling sects, 101, 123–133, 246*n*47

Shakir, Zaid, 141

Shapiro, Marc, 83

Shatz, David, 256*n*20, 260*n*53

shirey neshama, emotional responses, 11–12

sin

snake-handling sect beliefs, 130

as suffering explanation, 170

slavery

and evolution opposition, 218–219

in selective attention argument, 205–206

Slifkin, Nosson, 159

snake-handling sects, 101, 123–133, 246*n*47

Snow, David, 233*n*5

socialization process, religious beliefs, 168–169, 224–225, 261*n*7

social motives, TMS adherence, 43–44, 50–59

social position, and belief persistence, 233*n*5

solidarity claim, 169–170